SEA OF THUNDER

EVAN THOMAS

Four Commanders and the Last Great Naval Campaign 1941–1945

SIMON & SCHUSTER   *New York   London   Toronto   Sydney*

SIMON & SCHUSTER
Rockefeller Center
1230 Avenue of the Americas
New York, NY 10020

SIMON & SCHUSTER and colophon are registered trademarks
of Simon & Schuster, Inc.
For information about special discounts for bulk purchases,
please contact Simon & Schuster Special Sales at
1-800-456-6798 or business@simonandschuster.com

Designed by Dana Sloan

Manufactured in the United States of America

5   7   9   10   8   6

Library of Congress Cataloging-in-Publication Data
Thomas, Evan, date.
Sea of thunder: four commanders and
the last great naval campaign 1941–1945 / Evan Thomas.
p.   cm.
Includes bibliographical references and index.
1. World War, 1939–1945—Naval operations. 2. World War, 1939–1945—Campaign—
Pacific Ocean. 3. World War, 1939–1945—Naval operations, American. 4. World War,
1939–1945—Naval operations, Japanese. 5. United States. Navy—History—World War,
1939–1945. 6. Japan. Kaigun—History—World War, 1939–1945. I. Title.
D770.T43 2006
940.54'26—dc22   2006047511
ISBN-13: 978-0-7432-5221-8
ISBN-10: 0-7432-5221-7

To Oscie

CONTENTS

In case signals can neither be seen or perfectly understood, no captain can do very wrong if he places his ship alongside the enemy.

—*Lord Horatio Nelson*

War is mainly a catalogue of blunders.

—*Winston Churchill*

The
Americans

Cdr. Ernest Evans

Adm. William Halsey

THE LAST SEA BATTLE ═══════

The
Japanese

Adm. Takeo Kurita

Adm. Matome Ugaki

SEA OF
THUNDER

CULTURE, CHARACTER, AND THE LONELINESS OF COMMAND

I N 1943, American sailors and soldiers entering the harbor at Tulagi, the front-line U.S. Navy base in the South Pacific, passed a billboard telling them to

Kill Japs, kill Japs, kill more Japs!

The billboard was signed by Adm. William F. Halsey, Jr., their commander. As the war progressed, newspapers quoted Halsey as saying about the Japanese, "We are drowning and burning them all over the Pacific, and it is just as much pleasure to burn them as to drown them."

To twenty-first-century ears, Halsey sounds like a racist monster or a sadist. In his own time, however, he was regarded by the public as a war hero, a little outspoken, too crude perhaps, but refreshingly blunt about the true nature of the enemy and the hard job ahead. In the wartime America of the 1940s, Halsey's attitude was unexceptional. Americans routinely referred to the Japanese as "Japs" and "Nips," and often as animals or insects of some kind (most commonly, monkeys, baboons, gorillas, dogs, mice, rats, vipers and rattlesnakes, and cockroaches). The Japanese were just as bigoted. They depicted Americans and other Westerners as reptiles, worms, insects

(rendered in cartoons with the faces of Franklin Roosevelt and Winston Churchill), frogs, octopuses, beached whales, and stray dogs. Dehumanizing the enemy to make it easier to kill them is an ancient practice between warring nations, but rarely has it been practiced with more depraved creativity than in the Pacific War.

The roots of mutual contempt between Japan and the United States were twisted and deep. The Americans, as historian John Dower has shown, regarded the Japanese as half-child, half-savage, to be pitied or condescended to but also to be feared. Before the turn of the twentieth century, newspapers and politicians warned of the "Yellow Peril," and when Congress set immigration quotas in the 1920s, Asians were excluded altogether. The Japanese copied the West by modeling their navy on the British Royal Navy, from uniforms to ships, but regarded Westerners as filthy "demons" who wished to defile the pure Yamato race. When the kamikazes flew off on suicide missions against the Americans in the spring of 1945, virgin schoolgirls holding cherry blossoms were mustered to the airfields to wave them goodbye.

Some historians see the war between Japan and the United States

as a grand tragedy of racial prejudice. It was certainly a cultural misunderstanding on an epic scale. Without suggesting moral equiva-
lence—Japan was the clear aggressor—it is fair to say that both sides
blundered into war. Blinded or warped by racial and cultural bias,
East and West consistently underestimated or misjudged the other.
Before the war, the Americans did not believe the Japanese capable
of great military feats, like attacking Pearl Harbor, in part because
Japanese were widely regarded in the West as "little people," near-
sighted, buck-toothed comical figures who made cheap toys and
bowed obsequiously. By the same token, the Japanese, whose faith in
their own master or divine "leading race" (*shido minzoku*) exceeded
Adolf Hitler's belief in German superiority, thought that Americans
would surrender quickly because they were weak and decadent, a
nation of frightened housewives, labor agitators, and greedy pluto-
crats. When the Americans did not give up but rather kept building
more planes and tanks, the Japanese responded with massive suicidal
attacks, believing that Americans, selfish and mongrelized, could not
stand up to such a show of national unity and self-sacrifice. The
Americans eventually decided, as a Fifth Air Force intelligence circular put it in July 1945, that "the entire population of Japan is a
proper Military Target . . . THERE ARE NO CIVILIANS IN
JAPAN." The Americans began burning Japanese cities—sixty-six of
them, finally obliterating Hiroshima and Nagasaki with atomic
bombs.

The degree to which cultural and racial stereotyping led to fatal
misjudgments is remarkable. The Japanese did not think that the
Americans had the stamina required for long stretches of submarine
duty. So they neglected antisubmarine warfare—with the result that
American submarines were able to cut the vital supply lines between
Japan and her oil-rich southern colonies. Similarly, the Japanese
were lax about changing their communication codes, in part because
they thought that the Americans were not smart enough to break
them.

In the war in the Pacific, misunderstanding and miscalculation
reached an apogee—or nadir—in late October 1944, at a naval engagement known as the Battle of Leyte Gulf. It was the biggest
naval battle ever fought. The conflict involved more ships (almost

300), more men (nearly 200,000), and covered a larger area (more than 100,000 square miles, roughly the size of the British Isles) than any naval battle in history. The fighting was horrific, dramatic, and courageous. And yet both sides missed their main chance.

For Admiral Halsey, the commander of the main American striking force, the battle beckoned as the dream of a lifetime. A brassy, rough-and-ready national hero, dubbed "Bull" Halsey by the press, he had overcome defeatism early in the war. He believed he was on the verge of the greatest naval victory since Trafalgar. And yet, misjudging the enemy, he fell for a Japanese feint and sailed off in the wrong direction.

For the Japanese navy, the battle offered the opportunity to die gloriously—and, possibly, to turn around the course of the war. Halsey's mistake opened the way for Adm. Takeo Kurita and the main Japanese battle fleet to descend upon Gen. Douglas MacArthur's landing force invading the Philippines. Up against smaller, weaker ships—destroyers and "jeep" carriers—the Japanese should have been wolves amongst the sheep. But confused, exhausted, and daunted by an unexpected show of American gallantry, Kurita turned his fleet around at the critical moment and limped home to quiet disgrace. In Japan today, naval scholars still debate Kurita's "mysterious retreat."

Curiously, in America, the Battle of Leyte Gulf has been largely forgotten. When Americans think of the victorious "Good War," they tend to think of D-Day and the liberation of Europe, not the Pacific War. Most people have heard of the Battle of Midway or seen the image of the marines raising the flag at Iwo Jima. But the Battle of Leyte Gulf blurs together with a dozen other battles fought in jungles or on coral reefs on the other side of civilization. Most Americans do not know when the Battle of Leyte Gulf was fought, where Leyte Gulf is, or even how it's pronounced (lay-TEE). They certainly don't know why the battle mattered.

For the Imperial Japanese Navy, the battle was a death knell. Never again would the Japanese be able to put to sea to engage the Americans in a fleet action. Without a fleet, the Japanese Home Islands were cut off, starved, and exposed to American attack. The battle was also, quite possibly, the last big naval battle. Fleets of ships and men have been fighting for thousands of years, but never before or since have they arrayed themselves against each other on such a scale. In the long history of fleet engagements, from Salamis, where the ancient Greeks fought the Persians, through the epic line-of-battle duels of the British, French, Dutch, and Spanish during the Age of Sail, to the modern clashes of the world wars, the Battle of Leyte Gulf stands as a kind of gory apex. The combatants used every kind of craft, from submarine to kamikaze plane, and employed every type of available weapon, and died every imaginable way—by fire, blast, exposure, drowning, and shark attack. At least 13,000 men, along with one of the two greatest battleships ever built, were lost.

This is the story of four commanders, two American, two Japanese, whose lives collided in the biggest sea fight of the worst war in modern history. My narrative will follow these men from the breakout of war in December 1941 to the day when they came together in the giant naval engagement in and around the Philippine Islands. The Battle of Leyte Gulf is the climax of this book, although not quite the end of the story for the three men who survived it.

Cultures clash; nations do battle. But in the end wars are fought, and won or lost, by the actions of individuals—heroes and cowards, the prudent and wanton, ordinary men reacting, not always predictably, to extraordinary circumstances. The characters of these men often reflect the cultures of their nations. A twisted national culture can corrupt even the purest souls. And yet, individual differences do matter, often critically and sometimes surprisingly.

The four men in the story that follows had to think, as all warriors do, about their own mortality. Japanese culture—or, more precisely, the national identity propagandized by the militarists who ran Japan during World War II—venerated death. In American war songs, as historian H. P. Willmott has noted, Johnny comes marching home again; in Japanese war songs, he marches off to die. But that does not mean that the human beings who fought for Japan were always heedless about wasting lives. Americans, on the other hand, celebrated the individual. The job of an American soldier or sailor, to paraphrase Gen. George S. Patton, was not to die for his country, but to make the enemy die for his. While Japanese commanders extolled "spirit," American commanders valued material superiority. But the Americans were no less brave than the Japanese—and, at times, no less foolhardy.

Illness, accident, fate all play a hand in deciding battles and determining the course of history. But the true story of any battle lies in the passage of individual character—a quirky, sometimes fragile and storm-tossed vessel—across the roiled, violent seas of national culture. Our journey begins aboard a ship in a bay on the coast of Japan, two months before the attack on Pearl Harbor.

CHAPTER ONE

DOUBTING SUPERMEN

"Across the sea, corpses in the water"

O N OCTOBER 9, 1941, the Combined Fleet of the Imperial Japanese Navy, some 200 warships, lay anchored in Hiroshima Bay. The early autumn day was clear and bright, the water on the bay was still and peaceful. Shortly after 9:00 A.M., all the captains of the fleet were summoned to the flagship *Nagato*. The broad deck of the battleship was cleared of enlisted men. Only officers above the rank of lieutenant commander were allowed to remain.

Adm. Matome Ugaki, the chief of staff of the Combined Fleet, addressed the officers. He was, as usual, unsmiling and severe. "It may be that this is the last meeting of all the Combined Fleet officers," he began. His booming voice uncharacteristically faltered. "We may not be able to see each other in this fashion." One of the destroyer captains, Cdr. Tameichi Hara, was taken aback by the slight crack in Ugaki's stern facade.

War against the West was coming, and Hara and the rest of the officers knew it. Most of them were not privy to the plan to strike the American fleet at Pearl Harbor, but it was clear that their relentless training would soon become actual combat. The Japanese trained day and night, in all weather; the Japanese naval week, the men lamely joked, was Monday, Tuesday, Wednesday, Thursday, Friday, Friday, Monday. Because they would be outnumbered and outgunned by the Americans, the Japanese high command had decreed, their forces would rely on *seishin*—spirit.

The Japanese empire was reaching far beyond its Home Islands. Imperial forces had struck north, absorbing Korea and Manchuria; west, into China; and south, annexing Southeast Asia as far as the Malay Peninsula. Now, in addition to attacking Pearl Harbor, Japan planned to conquer the British colony of Singapore and all of Dutch-controlled Indonesia with its vital resources, especially oil, and to build an outer defense of fortified islands through the Pacific.

Commander Hara had his doubts that *seishin* would be enough to defeat the American, British, and Dutch navies, and he went to see Ugaki in his cabin aboard the *Nagato* the next morning. Stone-faced as usual, Ugaki listened to Hara's reservations. The destroyer captain asked: Couldn't the Japanese avoid total war? Maybe strike south and take oil-rich Indonesia—but skirt the Philippines and avoid confrontation with the United States?

Too late, said Ugaki. Diplomacy was running out. Japan did not seek war with the United States, but it had no choice. America's refusal to sell the Japanese oil and steel was slowly choking the empire. Japan had to strike swiftly or die. Hara listened, groaning inwardly he later recalled, because he realized that further discussion was useless.

For all his pride, Ugaki was uneasy. A week after he deflected Captain Hara's questions, Ugaki sat down in his cabin aboard the *Nagato* and began writing a diary. He entitled it *Senso Roku*—"The Seaweed of War," or, as he also called it, "The Wastebasket of War." The title was curiously self-effacing. Ugaki was seen as a proud, even arrogant man. He was, in a culture that revered the military, a kind of war god. Naval officers had an elevated social status in prewar Japan. Eta Jima, the naval academy, turned away thirty applicants for every one it accepted. Its graduates were regarded as more gentlemanly, less crudely brutal than army officers, though brutality was a relative term. Japan was an island nation, isolated from the world for much of its history, until suddenly, in the twentieth century, it became hungrily expansionist. The navy was the empire's sword and shield.

Naval officers were modern samurai, the ancient warriors who could, with impunity, cut down disobedient commoners in the road. If an enlisted man failed to salute an officer in the Imperial Japanese Navy, the officer was required to strike the man five times with his fist.

Ugaki sometimes did not bother to return salutes from the lower ranks. Like a character in a Kabuki play, he revealed little, maintaining a kind of ritualized sternness and impassivity. His sailors called him "the Golden Mask," after a mysterious superhero in a popular comic book of the day. He was distant and aloof and seemed coldly confident. But he was deeply ambivalent about the coming war against the United States. Japan was already stuck in a bloody, undeclared war with China, a four-year quagmire that the Japanese pre-

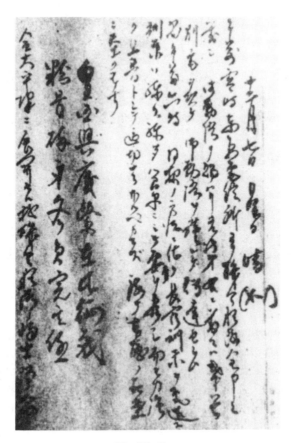

Ugaki's diary

ferred to call the "China Incident." Ugaki had been all for the ag-
gression into China—in the beginning. But now, writing in his diary,
he recorded his regret and guilt with the precise and elegant brushwork of an educated man writing in ancient Japanese: "Did the persons responsible for starting the incident ever dream or realize that it
would develop into the present state? We can't be proud of human
wisdom."

Ugaki was feeling ashamed of his own part in the run-up to a
much larger war. In the senior councils of the Combined Fleet—and
twice in private audiences with the emperor—he made the case for
annexing Southeast Asia for its natural resources. He had gone
along with Japan's formal alliance with Nazi Germany and Fascist
Italy, although against his better judgment. He had raised his glass
at a ceremony to mark the signing of the Axis pact, wondering, he
recorded in his diary, "whether this will turn out to be a victory cup
or a bitter dose for the future empire." He reflected, uncomfortably,
that he had been one of those "crying 'Wolf! Wolf!' for several years
in order to maintain and heighten the morale of the country." But
now, he regretted, "big wolves . . . are lurking around us." The coming war against America and its Western allies, he wrote, "will be
the greatest on record."

Ugaki's ambivalence, well hidden beneath a mask of command to
all but a few probing or perceptive souls like Captain Hara, was not
unusual among senior Japanese naval officers on the eve of the war
that would ruin Japan. A significant minority—including Ugaki's
boss, the commander-in-chief of the Combined Fleet, Adm. Isoroku
Yamamoto—held serious reservations about the coming conflict.
They understood that Japan lacked the resources to defeat America.
But like Ugaki, they raised their cups to victory and tried to ignore
the bitter taste.

Ugaki, like many well-educated, sensitive Japanese men of his
time, and all the times that came before, was accustomed to ambivalence. Americans needed certainty and tended to view the world in
simplistic terms. But Ugaki was used to living with contradiction. It
gave depth to a man. Ugaki was deeply read in Buddhist philosophy.
He did not smile, but he felt powerfully. Seeking to appreciate the
essence of the moment, he wrote small poems in his diary. As a sea-

man, he began every diary entry with the weather, but then often reflected on nature's beauty, recalling how the moon "hung on the edge of the mountain" or pining over the last fall of cherry blossoms in the spring.

Ugaki was caught in a web of obligations, sometimes conflicting, to his emperor, to his navy, to his family, to himself. Some of Ugaki's countrymen were paralyzed by a sense of duty that could not possibly be fulfilled. (The Japanese word for thank you, *arigato*, can also be translated, "you have placed me under a heavy obligation.") Ugaki accepted his obligations as the natural order of things. It did not bother him that conflict led to tragedy, to double or even multiple suicides. As a schoolboy, Ugaki, like all Japanese schoolboys, had taken to heart *The Tale of the 47 Ronin*, the true story of ancient samurai who killed themselves after committing murder to avenge their lord's honor. Many, if not most, of the great Japanese stories ended tragically; Ugaki, like most Japanese, enjoyed the drama and accepted the outcome as just, or in any case inevitable.[*]

Raised modestly in a small village by a family with samurai ancestors, Ugaki lived in a world balanced, often incongruously and a bit precariously, between old and new, East and West. His house in Tokyo was traditionally Japanese, with rice-paper screens and sleeping mats, but like most Japanese homes, it had a Western room, with heavy furniture and tassled lamps. Aboard the *Nagato*, lunch was Western and grand: from soup to dessert, eaten off silver and china and ending with finger bowls. Supper was Eastern and spare: sliced raw fish and boiled egg custard, consumed with chopsticks.

Japan had traveled from feudalism to modernity in less than a century. The navy's new fighter plane, the Zero, was a marvel of aeronautical engineering. But the planes were delivered from the factory in ox carts. The plane's name came from the double zero marked on its fuselage, for the 2,600th anniversary of Jimmu, the birth of the first emperor-god of Japan. Like all Japanese, Ugaki believed the saying, more or less true, that "for 2,600 years, our Empire has never known defeat." The Zero, faster and more maneuverable

---

[*]World War II movies in Japan, produced under strict state control, always ended with the death of most, if not all, the main characters.

than Western fighter planes, would show the Americans how far Japan had come. Only over time would the Zero reveal its Achilles' heel. Unlike the American planes, the unarmored Zero did not have self-sealing fuel tanks; they tended to burn or explode when hit by even a single .50 caliber round. The Japanese did not worry as much as Westerners about pilot safety—nor did they train enough pilots or build enough planes.

Ugaki was not unusual in concealing his feelings. Japanese can be very expressive when they speak, gesturing and exclaiming with loud sighs, but their eyes reveal little to Westerners. Adm. Shigeyoshi Inoue, the revered chief of the Naval Bureau, was a warmhearted, intelligent man, but he was also expressionless. Others adopted an expression of unwavering ferocity. Adm. Jisaburo Ozawa, Japan's best fleet commander, was called *Onigawara,* after a kind of stylized roof tile imprinted with the face of a devil to ward off evil spirits. The formal portraits of all Japanese admirals of the time are striking in their severity.

Impassivity, silent authority: these were qualities to be admired and emulated. When the emperor appeared for the "passing out" ceremony of young midshipmen at Eta Jima, he never spoke a word. The ceremony was conducted in complete silence. As an admiral permitted a rare audience at the Imperial Palace, Ugaki had bowed before the small, grave figure of Emperor Hirohito, whose expression was fixed, almost blank. The emperor was revered and worshipped as a true god. High school principals who failed to rescue the emperor's portrait when their wooden schoolhouses caught fire were so stricken with shame that they had been known to commit suicide. The last and most important duty of the captain aboard a sinking ship was to make sure the emperor's portrait had been taken from his cabin and safely bundled into a lifeboat. Then the captain would be free to go down with his ship.

In war councils attended by Ugaki, the emperor seemed optimistic, insisting that his troops could succeed if only they would try harder. On the other hand, the emperor would privately predict disaster. Word of imperial pessimism would seep back to navy headquarters from court gossip. It was one more contradiction, another of life's mysteries that Ugaki had to live with. His was not to question, but to recall the words of the navy's anthem, faithfully memorized in Eta Jima days:

> *Across the sea, corpses in the water;*
> *Across the mountain, corpses in the field*
> *I shall die only for the Emperor,*
> *I shall never look back.*

Writing in one of his first diary entries, on October 18, 1941, Ugaki turned his thoughts to the "extraordinary grand festival of Yasukuni Shrine," where the souls of some 15,000 fallen Japanese soldiers and sailors, killed in the China Incident, were being enshrined that day. Ugaki, like all military men, had worshipped at Yasukuni many times. The Shrine of the Righteous Souls was an inescapable presence in Tokyo. On the radio, over and over, blared the song:

> *You and I are cherry blossoms,*
> *Having bloomed, we're resolved to die*
> *But we'll meet again at Yasukuni,*
> *Blooming on the same treetop*

Ugaki had walked beneath the cherry blossoms in spring, past the old ladies selling "thousand stitches stomach wrappers" (good luck charms to stop bullets), to the top of Kudan Hill, the highest point in Tokyo. He had passed beneath the great *torii*, sacred gateways, and washed his hands, then washed out his mouth, before passing under the sixteen-petal gold chrysanthemum, the symbol of the emperor, into the simple wooden shrine. He had bowed low to the spirits of the fallen warriors, who never really die but go to Yasukuni, to rest, to be reborn, and to one day fight again. Purified, Ugaki had walked past the triumphal column bearing the statue of Masujiro Omura, the vice minister of war in the Meiji Restoration and great modernizer of the Japanese military. Omura had designed Japan's first Western-style warship and had often worn Western clothes. But on his European-style pedestal high above Yasukuni, Omura is garbed in a samurai's robe and carries the samurai long sword for battle and short sword for committing *seppuku*, suicide, better known to West-erners as *hara-kiri*, belly-cutting. Visitors did not remark (at least not in public) on the irony that he had been murdered by samurai swordsmen rebelling against modernity.

In his diary, Ugaki mused that if he could be so honored, if his soul would one day rest at Yasukuni, then he would be content. Ugaki was a deeply religious man. He read ancient Buddhist texts and, like most Japanese, at the same time worshipped Shinto, the na-tionalistic religion whose true god was the state. (Passengers on streetcars were required to stand and bow reverently when passing the Imperial Palace.) He knew from the ancients to accept suffering and impermanence, to laugh at privation. A hungry samurai, it was said, used a toothpick to pick his teeth after not eating.

As an admiral, former battleship commander, former operations chief of the Naval Bureau, now chief of staff to the commander-in-chief of the Combined Fleet, Ugaki was exalted by the growing mil-itarism of Japan. While subject to the emperor, the military had been elevated above all other branches of government by a flaw in the Meiji constitution, which gave veto power over the formation of a cabinet to the uniformed services. He had embodied the subtle dis-tortions of the samurai code, *bushido*, manipulated by the military government to make dying for one's country the glory and duty of all. He was, like the lowliest Japanese soldier, both honored and trapped. By military regulation, no Japanese soldiers or sailors were to be taken prisoner. They were to die first, killing themselves if nec-essary.

Ugaki's model—the ideal for all military men—was Gen. Mare-suke Nogi, the chief military adviser to the Emperor Meiji. After sending 58,000 men ("human bullets"), including his two sons, to their deaths in the 1905 Russo-Japanese War, he had asked the emperor's permission to take his own life. Meiji had asked Nogi to hold off until he, Meiji, passed away. On the day of the emperor's fu-neral in 1912, Nogi, dressed in white, helped his wife die—by plunging a dagger into her neck. Then he disemboweled himself with a short samurai sword. Hearing the news, his pupil, the young Prince Hirohito, who had addressed Nogi as "Schoolmaster," had wept, stunned into speechlessness. Hirohito was twelve years old, too young to see the perverse effect of Nogi's twisted morality on his nation, but many years later, he told an American reporter that Nogi's influence on him had been lasting and profound. At the time, there had been some grumbling in the newspapers. Hadn't *junshi*—following one's lord to his death—been outlawed in 1663 as antiquated and barbaric? But the complaints died away, buried by enthusiasm for the new *bushido*.

Sake, a rice wine with a high alcohol content, provided the only relief from this stern code. Drinking sake in large quantities was an acceptable release for Japanese naval officers. On joint maneuvers during the First World War, British naval officers—no slouches at imbibing spirits—were amazed by the quantities of sake consumed by their Japanese counterparts. The Japanese, as a people, were extraordinarily forgiving of drunks. Sake parties quietly ignored society's strict rules. At sake parties in Tokyo, men sat in one another's laps and sometimes wept. Ugaki was known to stay out all night drinking with fellow officers; it was the only time he dropped his mask. No one seemed to mind, or even notice.

Except, that is, for Ugaki's boss. Admiral Yamamoto thought that Ugaki was a drunk and, at first, barely spoke to his chief of staff. Ugaki hardly mentioned his commander-in-chief in the early days of his diary, but not because he felt confident about their relationship. Rather, in the Japanese custom, he was avoiding any criticism of his superior. In his diary entry for Monday, October 20, Ugaki noted, "the commander in chief bantered at me, 'You got up this morning at the time you went to bed last night, eh?'" Admiral Yamamoto may have been bantering, but with an edge. As Ugaki was uncomfortably aware, Yamamoto was not fond of his number two.

Isoroku Yamamoto was the most intelligent, most able officer in the Japanese navy, and it was America's misfortune (though ultimately Japan's) that he was able to disturb the conventional thinking of his fellow officers and forge the Imperial Japanese Navy into a formidable and daring striking force. Japan's warrior culture produced some great warriors, and Yamamoto was the most gifted of the Age of Showa, the reign of Hirohito.

He was by no means a prig. Though he did not drink, he loved to gamble—poker, mah-jongg, billiards, roulette (he joked about retiring to Monte Carlo). He engaged, avidly, in what Japanese officers called "S [for sex] Play." While Ugaki and his cronies had been downing sake, Yamamoto had slipped off to visit his geisha. His nickname among the geisha girls was "80 Sen," because it cost 100 sen to get a manicure from a geisha girl, and Yamamoto was missing two of his ten fingers.

Yamamoto's middle and index fingers had been blown off by an exploding gun at the Battle of Tsushima in 1905, when Yamamoto was a cadet serving on a battleship. He had played a small but sufficiently bloody role in Japan's most glorious of all victories—the

Yamamoto

smashing defeat of a Russian fleet that announced Japan's arrival as a twentieth-century great power. At five foot three, slightly stooped and with almost feminine features, Yamamoto did not look like much of a warrior. But he was a well-known daredevil, who, as a young officer, had performed handstands on the rails of ships. At fifty-seven, eight years older than Ugaki, Yamamoto was the navy's brightest star: outspoken, imaginative, and commanding.

Yamamoto's differences with Ugaki were not really over dissipation, which each enjoyed in his own way. The two men were opposites in more fundamental ways. Yamamoto was a creature of the future. He looked forward to an age of modern warfare—and recoiled at its implications for his homeland. Ugaki looked to the past with a fatalistic reverence—and not only accepted, but longed for his own glorious demise.

Ugaki had not been Yamamoto's choice as chief of staff. Ugaki had been imposed on him by the senior admirals of the General Staff, who, in Yamamoto's caustic reckoning, rated seniority and cronyism over skill. Yamamoto would later come to see Ugaki's more philosophical side, and Ugaki would come to recognize the martial realism of his commander-in-chief. But when Ugaki first took over as Yamamoto's chief of staff in August of 1941, the two men were badly matched; they did not understand each other.

To Yamamoto, Ugaki was one of those martinets who had spent too much time in Germany. Ugaki had studied in Berlin in the early 1930s, and, like many of his compatriots, he had been impressed by the totalitarian perfection of National Socialism, which, to men like Ugaki, seemed almost Confucian in its emphasis on obedience and loyalty. Ugaki admired German technology; at the same time, he felt a kinship with officers schooled with Prussian discipline and nationalistic fervor.

Yamamoto had no use for Hitler and had strongly opposed an alliance with Germany. He did not respect goose-stepping Prussians; his military ideal came from Great Britain. British naval officers, Yamamoto believed, were cosmopolitan and nimble, able to think on their feet. The Japanese naval academy, Eta Jima, had been founded by the imitative Japanese on the British model, patterned after the Royal Navy's training academy at Dartmouth. The red bricks to build Eta Jima's elegant, Georgian-style main building had been imported—each brick carefully wrapped—from England. A lock of Adm. Lord Nelson's hair was kept at Eta Jima as a sacred relic.

But more recently, Yamamoto feared, the British influence was wearing off. Eta Jima men were becoming automatons, their originality and initiative beaten out of them by the grueling regimen. The Eta Jima grads with the highest class rank—who were usually the most rigid and smug and inflexible—were given shore billets at headquarters and rose the fastest through the ranks. Yamamoto counted his chief of staff among these dogmatic paper-pushers.

Unlike Ugaki, who loathed "arrogant" America, Yamamoto was an admirer, or at least a respecter, of Americans. As a young officer, Yamamoto had studied at Harvard, and he had seen, firsthand, the automobile assembly lines in Detroit. He understood that Japan could never begin to match America, which every year produced twelve times as much steel as Japan, in an all-out arms race. Yamamoto had been frustrated by the naval officers who—like Ugaki—wanted to abandon naval disarmament treaties signed in the 1920s and try to outdo the Americans in a race to build the greatest fleet of leviathans.

Yamamoto had long worried that Japan's ambitions would eventually provoke a confrontation with the United States. Japan's cities were giant fire traps, made of paper and wood, Yamamoto warned. What if the Americans bombed them? Yamamoto subscribed to *Life* magazine and left copies of the American picture magazine about the wardroom for officers to see. One of those articles wrote glowingly of the new Anglo-American invention, radar. It's not clear that Yamamoto's subordinates paid much attention. They had faith in the superior eyesight of the Japanese race. The Japanese see better in the dark, the Japanese believed. So they trained extra-hard for night battle.

At least there were a few navy men who saw the recklessness of war with America, Yamamoto consoled himself. The army was hopeless. Far less cosmopolitan than the navy, the army generals were so in love with "spirit" over modernization that they were said to oppose the paving of roads "because it would damage the horses' hooves." As vice minister of the navy, Yamamoto had been blunt about the craze for a New Order, a blend of *bushido* and Asian imperialism that would dominate the East—and inevitably provoke war with the West. At a meeting of vice ministers in 1939, Yamamoto had demanded, "They talk of a new order, but what the hell do they mean by it?"

Yamamoto's bluntness was refreshing, especially in a society in which people made an art form of not saying what they really thought. He had a loyal following among some of the wiser heads in the navy. But the young hotheads in the army and not a few rabid junior officers in the navy wanted to kill him.

Assassination was becoming a tool of governance in Japan in the 1930s. Incredibly, Yamamoto—the navy's vice minister and the most respected naval figure since Adm. Heihachiro Togo, the hero of the Battle of Tsushima—had been made commander-in-chief of the Combined Fleet for his own safety. His friends and supporters needed to get him out of Tokyo. Officers were joking, "Better not get in the same car as the Vice-Minister," and a sinister order called the League for Carrying Out the Holy War had demanded his resignation. In Hirohito's reign, the Age of Showa, junior army and navy officers sometimes seemed to have more real power than the emperor. Denounced by the militarists as a "spy," Yamamoto was compelled to accept police protection; before he left for the fleet, machine guns were set up around the Navy Ministry.

It was a strange, paranoid time in Japan. The country was gripped with spy fever. In June 1941, a National Anti-Espionage Week was declared. A leading newspaper editorialized that Westerners living in Japan should be prohibited from owning carrier pigeons. In Tokyo, the Interior Ministry's Special Higher Police, also known as the Thought Police, patrolled for orthodoxy. Western ballroom dancing and golf were banned; baseball was not, though umpires were forbidden from using the English word "strike!" The government routinely lied about the stalemated war in China. Schoolchildren were taught to chant, "Brave Japanese! Cowardly Chinks! Brave Japanese! Cowardly Chinks!" Newspapers duly reported that Japanese officers were having contests to determine who could lop off the most heads of Chinese prisoners.

Ultranationalists demanded a holy war. Japan would liberate Asia and the Pacific archipelagoes from their white Western oppressors, though in the Greater East Asia Co-Prosperity Sphere, some Asians were more equal than others. The burden was to be divided according to racial and national ability: Japan, political leadership and heavy industry; China, light industry and manual labor; Korea, rice; Manchuria, animal husbandry. According to the Shinto faith, as shrilly propagandized in the early 1940s, Japanese were superior to all races. Soft and decadent, Americans were no match. A bestseller, *Why Fear the United States?*, concluded, "If at the outset Japan just seized Guam and the Philippines, we can fight with our bare fists if necessary."

Yamamoto knew this was poppycock. He had been stationed in America in 1927 when Charles Lindbergh flew the Atlantic; that was the real America, Yamamoto believed, scientific and adventurous. He repeatedly warned that a war against America would be suicidal. On September 29, 1941—only ten weeks before the attack on Pearl Harbor—he wrote the chief of the Naval General Staff that it was "obvious" that a war with the United States would be protracted, that the United States would "never stop fighting," that "ultimately we would not be able to escape defeat," and that "as a result of this war, people of this nation [will] be reduced to absolute poverty."

And yet, Yamamoto, like a true Japanese, was duty-bound—and, in his way, almost as fatalistic as Ugaki. "I find my position extremely odd—obliged to make up my mind and pursue unswervingly a course that is precisely the opposite of my own personal views," he wrote a friend on October 11. "Perhaps this, too, is the will of heaven." If war was inevitable he would fight it the best way he knew how. At Eta Jima, he had practiced *kendo*, a martial art that seeks to knock out the enemy in a single blow. Yamamoto proposed to try to do the same to the Americans.

Since his days as a naval attaché in Washington in the mid-1920s, he had been fascinated with the ideas of Gen. Billy Mitchell, who had insisted that the best way to sink ships was not with guns, but by bombing them with planes. As a rising commander in the Combined Fleet and as navy vice minister, Yamamoto had insisted that Japan build aircraft carriers, not battleships. Now, as commander-in-chief, his plan was to try to sink the American Pacific Fleet at its forward base in Hawaii with a surprise air raid—a bomb-and-torpedo attack against U.S. battleships and aircraft carriers at anchor in Pearl Harbor. It was to be a daring, brilliant, dramatic stroke, though Yamamoto was not confident that the blow would knock out America for good. "My plan is one conceived in desperation," he wrote another friend that October of 1941.

Ugaki had played little role in the planning for Pearl Harbor. Yamamoto had essentially cut out his chief of staff, preferring to rely on a senior staff officer, Capt. Kameto Kuroshima. A brilliant eccentric with a morbid turn of mind, Kuroshima was known for shutting himself in his cabin, closing the deadlights on his porthole, stripping naked, and smoking continuously while burning incense as he worked around the clock. Ugaki was left to handle other more routine fleet matters.

Ugaki was not a freethinker like Yamamoto. He was orthodox; he was a battleship man. He had been trained all his career to believe that victory would finally be achieved in a long-range gun duel fought primarily by battleships. Ugaki's faith was perfectly normal for a naval officer in the early 1940s. The Japanese navy—like most of the world's great navies—was almost cultlike in its devotion to a one-time shoot-out between giant battleships, or, as the British called them, "dreadnoughts."

Ugaki had briefly commanded a battleship, the *Hyuga,* and he had his eye on another, greater behemoth—the largest, most powerful battleship ever built. From the bridge of Yamamoto's flagship, the 38,500-ton *Nagato,* Ugaki had been watching the new superbattleship *Yamato*: 73,000 tons, painted silver-gray, with a giant gold Imperial Chrysanthemum adorning her bow, crashing through the waves at almost 30 knots. "Magnificent indeed!" Ugaki crowed in his diary on October 20.

The *Yamato* was hippy, belted with thick steel, but sleek, her smokestack raked and her superstructure towering like a modern skyscraper. *Yamato*'s nine 18-inch guns could lob shells weighing 3,200 pounds apiece (the *Nagato*'s standard 16-inch gun shell weighed 2,200 pounds). A single one of the *Yamato*'s gun turrets, weighing almost 3,000 tons, was heavier than the largest American destroyer.

Ugaki did not know these precise dimensions; the *Yamato* was a secret weapon, first planned in 1934 when international naval treaties restricted the size of Japan's warships. During her construction, she had been shielded by a rope screen so large that local fishermen had complained of a hemp shortage. Foreigners aboard trains passing the shipyard were ordered to lower their blinds until the train had passed. The *Yamato*'s vastness was designed with the Americans in mind. To match her, the Americans would have to build battleships that were too wide to fit through the Panama Canal.

The name *Yamato* had been carefully chosen to inspire national piety. Yamato was the cradle of Japanese civilization. A sister ship, launched shortly after the *Yamato,* was named the *Musashi,* after the ancient plain upon which Tokyo had been built.* When Japanese schoolchildren sang their traditional song "We're Children of the Sea," they now added a verse: "Let's go! Aboard the battleship! We'll defend the nation of the sea!"

---

*While Americans named their warships after states and battles and war heroes, the Japanese drew on myth and nature. Small destroyers, for instance, were named after flowers, fruits, and trees.

The Japanese were hardly alone in battleship worship. In 1901, Kaiser Wilhelm II of Germany had described the modern battleship as "a consummate expression of human purpose and national character." The kaiser, like the heads of state of all the great powers, had been reading the works of a retired American admiral named Alfred Thayer Mahan, who in the late nineteenth century preached a doctrine known as navalism: roughly, that the key to national greatness was to control the sea with large battle fleets. The British, who had ruled the seas for a century, celebrated Mahan, as did Teddy Roosevelt when he sent America's Great White Fleet around the world in 1907. Mahan's greatest believers were the Japanese. More of Mahan's books were translated into Japanese than any other language.

On the eve of World War I, the Germans had given a name to the fight-to-the-death fleet battle at sea: *Der Tag*, the Day. The Japanese called it *Kantai Kessen*, Decisive Battle. All great powers war-gamed for the final, all-out, ship-to-ship fleet engagement. The Americans called their plan—to send a fleet halfway around the world to defeat the Imperial Japanese Navy—War Plan Orange. The Japanese hoped they would come ahead, into an ambush. Under the Japanese

The Yamato

war plan (*Yogeki Sakusen*), cruisers and submarines would whittle down the advancing American fleet with torpedo attacks, then battleships would crush it in a final gun duel. The key to victory in this last naval Armageddon would be to simply outrange the Americans: the 18-inch guns of the *Yamato* and the *Musashi* could stand off and destroy the American ships, whose mere 16-inch guns could not shoot as far.

There was a historical flaw in the Decisive Battle doctrine, generally overlooked by its devotees. For much of naval history, massive fleet actions had been *in*decisive. Wind and weather and that bane of admirals, poor communications, disrupted the elaborate maneuvering of warships, or commanders broke off and sailed away to spare their fleets from annihilation. Mahan had been deeply influenced by Adm. Lord Nelson's victory at Trafalgar in 1805 over the French and Spanish fleets, which allowed Britannia to rule the waves in fact as well as song for the rest of the nineteenth century. Mahan's theories had been seemingly vindicated by the smashing victory of the Japanese over the Russians at Tsushima in 1905 and the American destruction of the Spanish fleet at Manila Bay in the Philippines and Santiago, Cuba, in 1898.

But the one great sea battle of World War I—between the British Grand Fleet and the German High Seas Fleet in the North Sea off of Jutland—was a stalemate. Thousands of sailors were killed in ship-to-ship bombardments, but because of missed signals, luck, and blunder, the Germans, seemingly trapped, were allowed to slip away. Jutland's muddled outcome in May 1916 did not stop the navies of all great powers from continuing to plan for Decisive Battle in the next great war. But it made more creative commanders wonder if the standard battleship duel could really turn the fate of nations in a day.

Over time, partly under the influence of Admiral Yamamoto, Ugaki would come to doubt the wisdom of a Decisive Battle strategy, especially as the day approached when he would actually fight in one. But in 1941, he was still a creature of conventional wisdom, a product of General Staff thinking. He was susceptible to the parochialism described by British historian B. H. Liddell Hart, who wrote after the war, "A battleship had long been to an admiral what a cathedral is to a bishop."

Admiral Yamamoto was free of such cant. He had opposed building the *Yamato* and the *Musashi*. In modern warfare, Yamamoto
warned, a battleship would be about as useful as a samurai sword. He
rejected arguments that torpedoes and bombs would bounce off the
Yamato's thick armor plate. "There is no such thing as an unsinkable
ship," he argued. "The fiercest serpent may be overcome by a swarm
of ants." Carrier-based airplanes, he foresaw, would be the deadly
swarm.

The old guard in the Imperial Japanese Navy demurred. One former commander-in-chief of the Combined Fleet, Adm. Zengo
Yoshida, refused to fly in an airplane. But Yamamoto surrounded
himself with brilliant young officers like the intense Captain
Kuroshima and Cdr. Minoru Genda ("Madman Genda"), a true genius who understood airpower and wryly joked, "the great follies of
the world were the Great Wall of China, the Pyramids, and the battleship *Yamato*." Not always patiently, they pointed out the simple
fact that the airplane had greater range than any gun on any battleship.

Yamamoto finally persuaded the reluctant admirals on the Navy
General Staff to go along with a carrier-based attack on Pearl Harbor by calling their bluff. Yamamoto did not yet trust Ugaki enough
to go to Tokyo to argue his case. He sent Captain Kuroshima to warn
the General Staff that unless they approved the Pearl Harbor plan,
Yamamoto would resign. Ready to plunge south to invade Indonesia,
unsure how to stop the American fleet from attacking its exposed
flank, the old admirals finally went along with Yamamoto and his
young Turks. Yamamoto was summoned to be given his orders, instructed to arrive at the Navy Ministry in Tokyo on November 3—
quietly, discreetly, "evading others' notice."

Ugaki was left minding routine business aboard the *Nagato*. He
was nursing an aching tooth and brooding. He went fishing in the
sunshine, which seemed to cheer him up. It was the birthday of the
Emperor Meiji, and all the ships in the fleet were "dressed" with
flags. Ugaki recorded in his diary, "The autumn sky was serenely
high and my reflections deep. Oh, this sacred Age of Showa! When I
reflect upon the great achievements of past heroes and the sacred
virtue of the emperor with his great and glorious works, they inspire

me with fresh courage." He expressed his exultation with a short
poem that is chilling in its sentiment and brevity:

> *You die,*
> *You all die for the sake of the land.*
> *I, too, will die.*

Ugaki terribly missed his wife, Tomoko, who had died the year before. A photo, taken in 1936, shows Tomoko looking young, slender,
and ethereal. A son, Hiromitsu, who would later become a naval doctor, stands in a cadet's uniform, round-faced and bookish. As Yamamoto planned for the attack on Pearl Harbor, Ugaki decided to
pay a rare visit to his extended family, various cousins and in-laws
living with his son at his house in Tokyo.

"All my family were surprised at my unexpected appearance,"
Ugaki wrote in his diary on November 6. "They all complained of

Ugaki's family

the shortage of food and the scarcity of necessities." Squeezed by the American embargo—no rubber, scrap iron, steel, aluminum, magnesium, copper, brass, zinc, nickel, tin, lead, airplane parts, or oil— Japan was looking threadbare and pinched on the eve of war. Fishermen had gone back to oars and sails and could no longer venture into deeper water. The fish markets now offered mussels and crabs, not tuna.

"But," Ugaki continued, "I didn't notice that anyone had lost weight!" He allowed that "after the death of my Tomoko, they have been experiencing considerable hardships," but briskly concluded, "they are getting along, and they will have to keep on somehow."

Ugaki returned to duty aboard the *Nagato*, where his thoughts were preoccupied with the coming attack on Pearl Harbor. On the morning of November 19, he was thrilled by the sight of a "queer-shaped submarine with no mark or number heading south." His eye was drawn to the tiny midget submarine cradled on the deck of the larger sub, which proved to be the *I-22*, flagship of the IJN's First Submarine Division. After a final sake party at the base at Kure, the submarines were headed down the Inland Sea, then to the east, toward Hawaii.

As Ugaki was well aware, they were on what was likely to be a suicide mission. On the morning of the Pearl Harbor attack, called "X-Day," five midget subs were to slip down the narrow, shallow channel into the harbor and torpedo anchored warships. At first, Admiral Yamamoto had rejected the attack proposal, arguing that the midget subs' two-man crews would never get out alive. The cruising range of the little subs was increased from five to sixteen hours, giving the subs at least a slight chance to get in, attack, and then escape to sea to find their mother ships. Grudgingly, Yamamoto assented to adding the midget subs to the attack force.

Ugaki was not worried about whether the subs could return. In his diary, he wrote of seeing the "young lieutenants" who would pilot the subs, standing on deck, smiling. "They expect never to return alive," Ugaki wrote, approvingly.

It is certain that Ugaki recalled, from his schooldays, an episode that had been seared in his consciousness. In April 1910, when Ugaki was a student at Eta Jima, a Japanese submarine—Submarine *No. 6*—

had sunk in the mud of Hiroshima Bay, just a few miles from where Ugaki was studying. Without an escape hatch, the crew of fourteen was doomed. But they kept at their duties until the end (when the sub was raised the next day, their bodies were found still sitting at their battle stations). The commander of the ship, Lt. Tsutomu Sakuma, wrote a letter as he slowly asphyxiated. "I am sorry that my carelessness sank the Emperor's submarine and killed the Emperor's sailors," the letter began. "We are willing to die for our country, but I regret one point, that our deaths might discourage the people of this nation. My sincere hope, gentlemen, is that the accident will give you material to study diligently the problems of submarine design and construction. . . . 12.30 very hard to breathe—gasping."

The letter was enshrined at the naval academy, where it is today. Lieutenant Sakuma was worshipped as a military martyr, along with Takeo Hirose, an officer who died in action while leading seventy-seven volunteers, chosen from 2,000, on a suicidal mission during the Russo-Japanese War. These models of self-sacrifice, both Eta Jima men, had a profound effect on young Ugaki. Along with the other cadets of Eta Jima, Ugaki had marched at the funeral of Sakuma and the rest of *No. 6*'s crew in the spring of 1910, as the cherry blossoms fell.

Ugaki had been shaped, or perhaps warped, by his years at Eta Jima. It was and still is a beautiful, sacred place, set on a bay, behind a mountain, on an island in the Inland Sea. Eta Jima men were instructed in table manners, introductions, and the making of toasts and speeches by teachers imported from Britain. They were told that an officer in the Imperial Navy must always travel first-class and never be seen carrying packages. On the other hand, they were brutalized. Captain Hara, the destroyer commander who had confronted Ugaki after he emotionally addressed the fleet officers on October 9, was a few years behind Ugaki at Eta Jima. He recalled being greeted by a senior cadet who punched him in the face a dozen times for failing to properly salute. Every Sunday, the freshmen lined up in the college yard and stood at attention in the broiling sun for four or five hours while the upperclassmen beat them. "After a few months of such treatment, the newcomers became sheeplike in their obedience," wrote Hara in a memoir.

Ugaki, like all freshmen, memorized the Imperial Rescript for Soldiers and Sailors, promulgated in 1882. Rule Number One: "The soldiers and sailors should consider loyalty their essential duty." He sang the academy song: "Our hearts throb more and more with the hot blood / Of the Sons of the Sacred Land / We shall never stop sacrificing ourselves." He was instructed in the meaning of valor, epitomized in the word *gyokusai,* which literally means "broken gem," from the proverb, "It is better to be a gem that is smashed to atoms than a tile that is whole."

And yet, as X-Day approached, he tossed and turned. The China war, "though it has been a sacred enterprise," had caused Japan great losses over four years, and the war Japan aimed to start now would be "bigger by far," Ugaki admitted in his diary. "War is a serious affair of state," he mused on November 23. "On the other hand," he wondered, when would there ever be a better chance to smite the enemy, to "push him down"? He tried to be Zen-like. "Whatever is to be, will be," he wrote. "We have to let the situation run its course; that's the way of the world, and I must live resignedly in the world without any peevishness. Let me give up such trivial thoughts and go to bed."

Cut out of the operational planning for X-Day, Ugaki had been given more ceremonial duties, like composing the commander-in-chief's message to the Pearl Harbor attack fleet. This was a grave obligation to Ugaki, and he turned to history. He borrowed from Lord Nelson at Trafalgar ("England expects every man to do his duty") and Admiral Togo at Tsushima ("The fate of our Empire depends upon this fight. Every man is expected to act with his utmost efforts"). Ugaki wrote: "The fate of the Empire depends upon this war. Let every man do his duty, exerting his utmost effort."

Ugaki showed this draft to Capt. Yasugi Watanabe, who was known as "Staff Officer for Chess," since his chief duty seemed to be playing *Shogi* (Japanese chess) with the commander-in-chief (Yamamoto usually beat Watanabe, but on at least one occasion he had bet and lost his entire uniform). Watanabe asked Ugaki to change a couple of words, which he said were too archaic. Ugaki went back to work, polishing the draft until it read: "The fate of our Empire depends on this expedition. Each of you will do his duty, wearing your-

selves to the bone." Ugaki's effort, as it appears in English translation, seems clunky and contrived, not up to his private poetry, but he
was typically trying to merge East and West, honor his ancestors,
and please his commander-in-chief. At any rate, he was pleased with
himself: "How this message will impress all the ranks and ratings on
their ships already deployed on the Pacific!" he crowed in his diary
on Sunday, December 7.

Ugaki would be safely aboard the Combined Fleet's flagship, in a
Japanese harbor several thousand miles away from the battle. Still,
he had already slipped a bit of hair and nail-parings into a closed en-
velope for his son as a warrior's final memento, to be opened upon
his death.

Ugaki's sleeping quarters were next to Admiral Yamamoto's in a
suite of rooms toward the stern of the *Nagato*. This "Flag Country"
included a large and formal conference room where the emperor's
portrait was kept and where Yamamoto and his staff dined (to the
accompaniment of the flagship's forty-piece band, lined up outside
on deck, at lunch). At three on the morning of December 8—
December 7 in Hawaii—Ugaki awoke, anxious to hear the news. "I
was having a smoke when [Air] Staff Officer [Cdr. Akira] Sasaki
hurried into my room and reported, 'At 0319 wireless TO is being
sent repeatedly.' "

"To" is the first syllable of *totsugeki*: charge. Admiral Yamamoto
was in the conference room, where he had been playing chess with
Captain Watanabe and dozing off. His mouth turned down at the corners as he asked, "Did you get that message direct from a plane?" Atmospheric conditions were unusually fine for wireless reception that
night. The radio operators aboard the *Nagato* could even hear the
first American distress signals. The reports from the Japanese pilots
came flooding in. "Surprise attack successful"; "Enemy warships torpedoed; outstanding results"; "Hickam Field attacked; outstanding
results." The American messages were confused and panicky. When
Yamamoto heard one of them—"Jap—this is the real thing"—he
smiled slightly.

The conference room aboard the *Nagato* was soon filled with jubi-
lant staff officers, though Yamamoto stood alone, oddly downcast.
Within a few hours, it was clear that the surprise attack had knocked

out at least four battleships. But as more reports trickled in, it was also apparent that the American aircraft carriers were not at their moorings in Pearl Harbor, and that the oil tanks had gone unscathed.

Ugaki was for going back and finishing the job, but more cautious minds prevailed. The American carriers were somewhere out there. What if they caught the Japanese fleet as it was launching planes? The Japanese fleet commander, Chuichi Nagumo, who had never been enthusiastic about the Pearl Harbor raid, wanted to sail for home. Yamamoto, perhaps already resigned to fate, did not countermand him. Ugaki spluttered in his diary that Nagumo's lack of daring amounted to "sneak thievery and contentment with a humble lot in life."

The Japanese people knew nothing of these internal doubts and squabbles. They were wild with joy over the Japanese onslaught throughout the Pacific. On December 8, Japanese forces swept south, invading the Philippines and Indonesia and sinking, on December 10, a British battleship, HMS *Prince of Wales*. The radio played "The Battleship March" over and over again, and a popular singer crooned, "More victory news on the radio! I can't sit still, the excitement, the joy. Aren't our men superb, divine heroes in action!" At the Imperial Palace, wrote the emperor's naval aide in his diary, "The Emperor wore his naval uniform and seemed to be in a splendid mood."

Yamamoto was depressed. He repaired to his cabin and wrote gloomy letters in response to the thousands of letters of congratulation that came pouring in. "A military man can scarcely pride himself on having 'smitten a sleeping enemy'; it is more a matter of shame, simply, for the smitten," he wrote in response to an overjoyed friend. "I would rather you made your appraisal after seeing what the enemy does, since it is certain that, angered and outraged, he will soon launch a determined counterattack." In another letter, he deplored "the mindless rejoicing at home. . . . It makes me fear that the first blow on Tokyo will make them wilt on the spot."

Even so, Ugaki was proud of the Japanese midget sub crews. He believed that at least two had penetrated Pearl Harbor and torpedoed American warships and that all the crewmen had perished gloriously. He was wrong: no Japanese sub did any damage, and one crewman had washed ashore and been captured and hence disgraced.

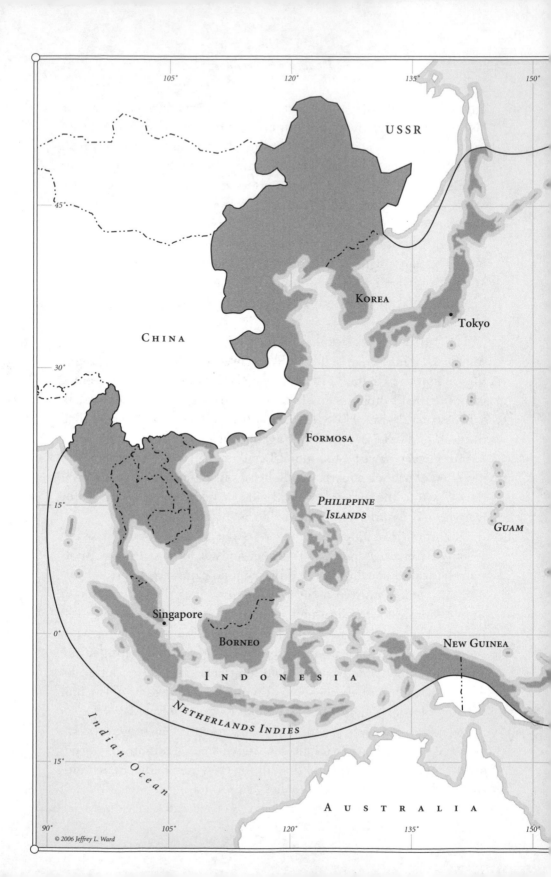

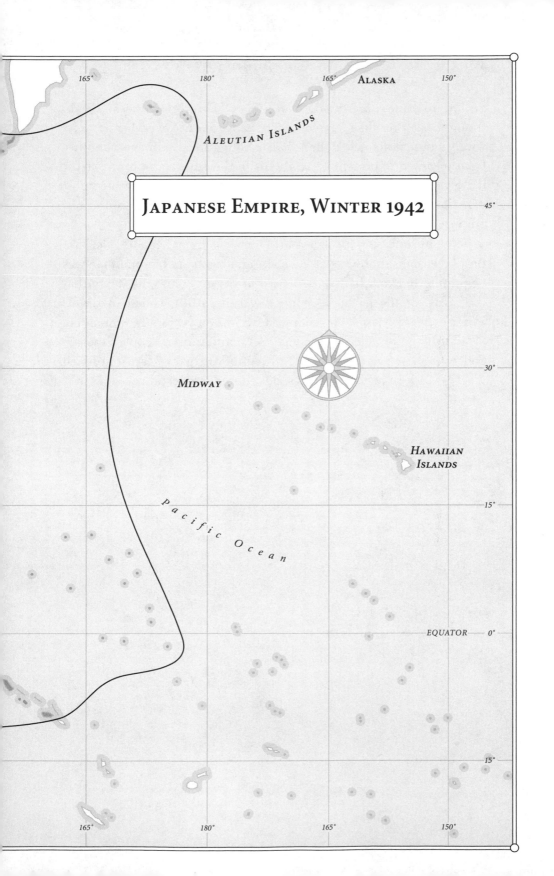

Still, the Japanese martyred the others as "The Nine Heroes." Ugaki thought back to their farewell party at Kure on November 17. The young lieutenants had signed their photographs with short mottos. Ugaki wanted to present their photos to the emperor one day. "Now it has really turned out to be the Second World War," he wrote in his diary on December 12. "The whole world will revolve around our empire."

Then his unease returned. Pearl Harbor had not been the Decisive Battle; perhaps there was no such thing, no sudden triumph. He was beginning to think like Yamamoto. On December 13, he wrote that the "zeal" of the Japanese people "will cool in the course of time." What if the war lasts "for as long as five or ten years?" he wondered. Would the nation's leaders be able to "maintain the people's morale and overcome every difficulty?" In public, Ugaki's face hardened with resolve. In private writings, he seemed less certain.

CHAPTER TWO

DAMN THE TORPEDOES

"We'll shoot first and argue afterwards!"

WILLIAM HALSEY had an enormous head. His caps were size 7⅞, specially made, and his expressions, both his sunny smile and fierce scowl, were outsized. He looked like "the figurehead of Neptune," according to the 1904 Naval Academy yearbook, the *Lucky Bag,* which also described him, at age twenty-one, as "a real old salt." Halsey could be theatrical and loved to play the role of "sailorman," a favorite term, but he had long since become the actor he played. He was never seasick. He was much happier standing on the bridge of a ship than sitting behind a desk, and when he used nautical lingo (the backseat of his limousine was "the stern sheets") he was not putting on airs. He spent most of his career at sea, more than two decades aboard swift but "wet" destroyers before graduating to higher commands. Unlike many sailors, he was not profane, but, like many sailors, he was superstitious. He filled his pockets with odd trinkets, feared Friday the 13th, and refused to fly in the same airplane as his boss, Adm. Chester Nimitz. "That's not superstitious," he explained. "It's common sense. Chester is bad joss in the air."

He was a squared-away naval officer, his buttons always brightly polished, his shoes shined. He seemed to spend hours in the bathroom in the morning, tending to his ablutions. But he was not other-

Halsey toasts

wise fussy or a stickler. He was informal with his officers, who reverently referred to him as "Admiral Bill," and he abolished neckties on
the uniforms of naval officers in the tropical South Pacific. He loved
parties and staying up all night carousing. "There are exceptions, of
course, but as the general rule," he proclaimed, "I never trust a
sailorman who doesn't smoke or drink." He cried easily. When he received letters, as many senior combat officers did during World War
II, from aggrieved families or ordinary citizens accusing him of
wasting the lives of young American men, he would mope for days.

Halsey was a bit of a mythmaker, but he was not a phony, and he
regretted some of the myths he had himself created. No one except
General MacArthur, an even larger mythical invention, directly addressed him as "Bull," a nickname Halsey insisted that newspapermen had made up. "I don't want to be remembered as 'Bull Halsey,'
who was going to ride the [emperor's] White Horse," he began his
memoirs, published in 1947. But after the war, he had posed astride
a white horse, and his ghostwritten memoirs contain, in at least a

few demonstrable places, the kind of slight elaborations that helped create the myth.

Halsey was a deceptive figure—rendered larger than life, at times almost buffoonish, by hero worship that verged on caricature. But he was also a sensitive man and smarter than he sometimes appeared to be. He could and often did sound like a hater, but he was more often good-hearted than bitter. His reaction and action on the first day of war illustrate some of his best and worst qualities.

On the morning of December 7, 1941, Halsey arose before 6:00 A.M.—0600 hours—to watch the launch of eighteen planes from his aircraft carrier, the *Enterprise*. They were bound for Ford Island, the navy airstrip in the middle of Pearl Harbor. Halsey had expected to enter the channel at Pearl Harbor at 7:30 A.M., but strong headwinds had delayed the refueling of his destroyers. Halsey's small task force, returning to Pearl after delivering some planes to the marine outpost on Wake Island in the Central Pacific, was running behind schedule. They were still 150 miles away from Hawaii. On a war footing, Halsey sent up a dawn search ahead of his fleet, with orders that the planes were to fly on ahead to Pearl, although without first notifying anyone at Pearl that the planes were coming.

After launching the planes, Halsey returned to his cabin, "shaved, bathed, and put on a clean uniform," he recalled. It was now a minute or two after eight. The phone rang, and Halsey's flag secretary, Lt. Douglas Moulton, took the call. After exclaiming "What!" he put down the phone and turned, with a look of shock of his face. The Japanese were attacking Pearl Harbor, he said. Halsey's first instinct was that it was all a big mistake, that jumpy defenders at Pearl had mistaken the unannounced arrival of Halsey's planes as Japanese attackers. In the first draft of his memoirs, essentially a dictated oral history, Halsey recalled, "I jumped to my feet and said, 'My God, they're shooting at our planes.'" In his published memoir, ghosted by Cdr. Joseph Bryan III, Halsey exclaims, "My God, they're shooting at my own boys!" Halsey may have thought of his boys. But Doug Moulton later told his family that what Halsey actually said was: "That joke's in lousy taste."

A moment later, Cdr. Harold "Ham" Dow, Halsey's communications officer, burst in with a dispatch:

FROM: CINCPAC
TO: All ships present
AIR RAID ON PEARL HARBOR X THIS IS NO DRILL.

Despite his momentary disbelief, Halsey had been expecting war. When the *Enterprise* had sortied from Pearl for Wake Island on November 28, he had asked the captain of the *Enterprise* to issue "Battle Order No. 1," which began, "1. The *Enterprise* is now operating under war conditions. 2. At any time, day or night, we must be ready for instant action." Halsey's operations officer, Cdr. William Buraker, protested, "Goddammit, Admiral, you can't start a private war of your own! Who's going to take responsibility?" Halsey recalled that he answered: "I'll take it! If anyone gets in my way, we'll shoot first and argue afterwards!" Halsey had been focusing on the threat from Japanese submarines. Even he did not expect a Japanese carrier task force to attack Pearl Harbor.

But it had, and Halsey was determined to find the Japanese fleet. Somewhere off the coast of Hawaii, possibly close by Halsey's ship at this very moment, were a half-dozen Japanese carriers. Providential headwinds had saved the *Enterprise* from destruction by the Japanese planes, which had hit Pearl Harbor shortly after 7:50 A.M., just when Halsey had been expected to drop anchor in the crowded harbor. Nelson's adage "No captain can go wrong who places his ship alongside an enemy's" had been "burned in my brain," Halsey related in his memoirs. But where were the enemy's ships?

Halsey was proudly, defiantly, offense-minded. He was also fond of invoking Confederate Gen. Nathan Bedford Forrest, whose simple rule of operation was: "Get there first with the most men." But Halsey, who lacked Forrest's conciseness, distorted General Forrest's words in a small but revealing way. "I think General Forrest's description is the best thing I know, to get to the other fellow with everything you have and as fast as you can and to dump it on him," Halsey said in December to a commission investigating the Pearl Harbor attack. Halsey had missed a subtle but important distinction.

When Forrest said "get there first with the most men," he meant get there with more men than the enemy had. In Halsey's sometimes imprecise mind, this became "get to the other fellow with everything you have."

Everything, in this case, meant one aircraft carrier, three cruisers, and nine destroyers. The Japanese First Fleet had six carriers and multiple battleships, cruisers, and destroyers. If Halsey had found Admiral Nagumo's striking force that day, Halsey's task force would have more than likely been annihilated. America had only three aircraft carriers in the Pacific at the time, the *Enterprise* and the *Lexington*, sailing out of Pearl Harbor, and the *Saratoga*, docked in San Diego. For the United States, it was a blessing of strategic magnitude that all three carriers survived the opening days of the war.

At the time, Halsey does not appear to have considered what might have happened if he had found the Japanese. He would later write, "I have the consolation of knowing that, on the opening day of the war, I did everything in my power to find a fight."

That day, and in the jittery days that followed as Halsey searched for the Japanese fleet after a brief stop in Pearl Harbor, Halsey's men thought they saw the Japanese lurking behind every wave. Whales became submarines, dolphins became torpedoes, floating broom handles became periscopes. Scores of depth charges were expended to kill fish. Halsey, increasingly frustrated, recorded his exasperation when a young officer aboard the *Enterprise*, watching the destroyer *Benham* run down a supposed submarine contact, cried out, "Look! She's sinking! There she goes!" Halsey snatched up his binoculars and looked out. The *Benham* was "hull down," momentarily obscured as she dipped into the trough of a wave. The destroyer arose again on the crest of the next swell. Halsey turned on the young lieutenant: "If you ever make another report like that, I'll have you thrown over the side!"

Halsey was gritting his teeth when the *Enterprise* sailed into Pearl Harbor at dusk on December 8. His attention was immediately drawn to the wreck of the battleship *Utah*—in the mooring space that would have been occupied by the *Enterprise,* had she not been delayed returning to Pearl. A pall of oily black smoke still hung over the harbor, and the silent, gaping sailors who lined the deck of the

Enterprise recoiled when someone recognized the acrid, still unfamiliar stench seeping across the water—burned human flesh. The *Enterprise* passed close by the battleship *Nevada*, beached in the channel as she tried to make a run for it during the attack. The once mighty battleship *Oklahoma* had rolled over, exposing her raw red bottom. The battleship *Arizona*, what was left of her, still burned. An exhausted soldier manning an antiaircraft gun along the shore yelled out, "Where the hell were you?"

Halsey growled, "Before we're through with 'em, the Japanese language will be spoken only in hell." It was the first, and most colorful, of his many avowals to kill as many Japanese as possible.

As darkness fell, the night was lit by streams of machine gun bullets, fired by strung-out antiaircraft gunners shooting wildly at anything they could imagine. Halsey was greeted onshore by a ghostly sight, Adm. Husband Kimmel, the commander of the Pacific Fleet, still in his Sunday-morning dress whites, now streaked with ash and mud. A large smoky blotch defaced the front of his uniform. A spent machine gun bullet had crashed through Kimmel's window as he was watching the attack and struck him in the chest. Picking up the bullet, Kimmel had murmured, "It would have been more merciful if it had killed me."

Halsey knew that Kimmel's career was over, and he felt for him. Kimmel was a friend in the tight, tiny world of Annapolis men that ran the prewar navy; he had been an usher in Halsey's wedding. But Halsey was irked by the beaten fearfulness of Kimmel and his staff. When a report came in that Japanese gliders bearing assault troops were landing nearby, Halsey laughed out loud. Kimmel wheeled on him and angrily demanded, "What in the hell are you laughing at?" Halsey explained that he had heard "many damn fool reports" in his life, but this was "the damnedest fool report" yet. The Japanese could not have towed gliders thousands of miles from their Home Islands, and they weren't about to waste their carrier decks on gliders. Kimmel smiled sheepishly. "You're right," he said.

Halsey was determined to present an unyielding, fierce, vengeful facade. Sensing that his own aviators were feeling a little skittish, he addressed them in their wardroom on the *Enterprise* on the morning of December 10. The war diary of the air group, "Fighting Six," does not record exactly what Halsey said, but it conveys the general impression he made on the pilots: "Those Japs had better look out for that man," it says.

Thus was a legend born that would grow until Halsey could not recognize himself, though he could not refrain from embellishing the myth. "Most" of his ancestors, he wrote in his 1947 memoir, "were seafarers and adventurers, big, violent men, impatient of the law, and prone to strong drink and strong language." Many of his forebears did go to sea, and one was even a pirate: Capt. Jack Halsey, an early eighteenth-century privateer whose exploits are described in *The History of the Lives and Bloody Exploits of the Most Noted Pirates.* But the rest appear to have lived ordinary middle-class lives.

Halsey as a boy

Halsey's paternal grandfather was an Episcopal priest who died when he fell out of a rectory window while experiencing a dizzy spell. Enticed by reading some true-life sea adventure stories, Halsey's father had attended the U.S. Naval Academy at Annapolis, Maryland, and made a moderately successful career in the navy. Young William wanted to go to Annapolis as well, but never a scholar, he failed to get an appointment on his first try and wound up at the University of Virginia.

Though Halsey spent only a year in Charlottesville, the impression made on him was lasting. "Mr. Jefferson's University" was a genteel place at the end of the nineteenth century, and Halsey, a natural charmer, was swept into the most aristocratic of the fraternities, St. Anthony Hall. There he developed a taste for whiskey and a romantic identification with the Virginia Cavalier, the beau ideal of the dashing gentleman soldier. He also absorbed a tinge of racial bigotry that undercut his generally open-minded and warmhearted nature. Halsey would cherish his fraternity brothers, though when a place opened up at the Naval Academy after his first year in college, he jumped at it.

The academy on the banks of the Severn had been a sleepy, backward-looking place for most of its nineteenth-century existence, imbuing naval officers with a sense of southern chivalry. Annapolis was beginning to break out of its torpor when Halsey arrived in June 1900. The impetus was the American navy's crushing defeat of two Spanish fleets in sea battles halfway around the world from each other, at Santiago Bay, Cuba, and Manila Bay in the Philippines, in 1898. The New World was pushing aside the old imperialists. A new order was arising, a kind of benign, less exploitive colonialism, though 3,000 American soldiers died suppressing a Filipino insurrection. The politicians and the jingoist press extolled the westward expansion into the Pacific. America was fulfilling its manifest destiny, and the U.S. Navy would lead the way. Every captain aboard the American warships in the Spanish-American War had been an Annapolis man. Suddenly, the navy was all the popular rage; Annapolis attained instant mystique.

To replace shabby, crumbling dormitories, Congress ordered the construction of a magnificent white marble-and-brick Beaux Arts campus. Midshipmen were to live and study in a shrine to naval glory. They were to absorb the myths of heroes past by memorizing sayings and lore and worshiping ancient relics, the tattered ensigns and iron cannon of battles won and lost. For a young midshipman with a sense of romance and history, the mix of old salt and almost overnight old grandeur was thrilling. Work commenced on the massive new main building, Bancroft Hall, in 1901, as Halsey was beginning his second year.

Annapolis men were hazed, though not nearly as cruelly as their Japanese counterparts at Eta Jima. Upperclassmen were forbidden from touching plebes (first-year students). If they violated this injunction, the plebe was free to hit back—an important cultural distinction from Japan, where the plebes were required to suffer blows in obedient silence. There was a certain amount of book learning at Annapolis, especially in engineering, but English was known as "Bull," and intellectualism was not the point. Midshipmen were abjured "not to appear unduly bright," according to an academy history.

Annapolis was about building character, which was fine by Halsey, who had low grades and told his father he'd rather "bilge" (flunk out) than quit football. Halsey graduated in the lower third of his class, but he was a great success at Annapolis, "everybody's friend," according to the 1904 *Lucky Bag.* Halsey and his classmates would remember their Annapolis days as demanding but euphoric. They felt they were joining a brotherhood for life, and they were not wrong.

During Halsey's day, the president of the United States was a familiar figure on the grounds of the academy, bustling about in his frock coat. Theodore Roosevelt, a fervent disciple of Admiral Mahan and himself the author of a naval history about the War of 1812, wanted to build a great navy and send it around the world. When the Great White Fleet arrived in Tokyo Bay in the fall of 1908, Ensign Bill ("Willie" and "Pudge" to his classmates) Halsey was a junior officer aboard the battleship *Kansas.*

Halsey, whose notions of Anglo-Saxon superiority were ingrained and never hidden, seems to have taken an instant dislike to the Japanese. He was not impressed by the great Admiral Togo, hero of Tsushima, who greeted the American officers aboard his flagship, the *Mikasa.* He regarded Togo as tricky and deceitful for having

Midshipman Halsey

staged surprise torpedo attacks on Chinese and Russian ships. Halsey and his mates were permitted to give Togo a "toss"—to follow the example of Japanese sailors tossing and catching their officers with a blanket to cries of *Banzai*. Since Togo was a "shrimp," Halsey recounted in his memoir, "we gave him three real heaves. If we had known what the future held, we wouldn't have caught him after the third one."

Though he arrived in England too late for combat in World War I, Halsey sought out the more dangerous billets. He was a "destroyer man" for much of his career, commanding low, sleek, torpedo-firing destroyers. He liked the cockiness and dash of the men who sailed the smaller, faster ships, more vulnerable than battleships but more gallant, too. "You could tell a destroyer man by the way he cocked his cap and walked down the street," recalled Halsey in his memoir. But by the early 1930s, he was farsighted enough to see that the navy's future lay with airpower. Slated to command an aircraft carrier, he was bold, or reckless, enough to earn his wings at the age of fifty-two. He was a dangerously bad flier. Refusing to wear his glasses, he could not read the instruments, and thus he often had no idea where he was flying, or how fast, or how high.

But he was always well liked by his men. For all his bluster, Halsey had a genuine self-deprecating streak. As an ensign, he had learned to get along well with enlisted men while patrolling whorehouses in foreign ports. He did not hold himself aloof; he mixed with the sailors (and apparently their consorts; there was much sniggering over Halsey's nickname "Big Bill"). In flight school at Pensacola, when Halsey cracked up his plane by plowing into a landing light on the runway, he was awarded a decoration called "the Flying Jackass," an aluminum breastplate shaped like a donkey. Winners were required to wear the Jackass until another neophyte pilot came along to do something stupid enough to win it away. Halsey, who held the rank of captain and was twice the age of the pilot cadets, dutifully wore his Jackass. When the time came to relinquish the decoration, he refused. He said he wanted to post it in his cabin aboard the *Saratoga*—the aircraft carrier he was slated to command—as a reminder of humility. "If anybody aboard does anything stupid, I'll take a look at the Jackass before I bawl him out, and I'll say, 'Wait a minute, Bill Halsey! You're not so damn good yourself.'"

Admiral Nimitz, Halsey's new boss as the chief of the Pacific Fleet replacing the disgraced Kimmel, was not Halsey's type. In contrast to the garrulous, boozing Halsey, Nimitz was a model of Germanic self-control. During the weeks and months after Pearl Harbor, Nimitz rarely, if ever, smiled. His lips were compressed into a thin, straight line. His eyes did not flash like Halsey's, but rather peered quizzically. A year behind the irrepressible Halsey at Annapolis, Nimitz had graduated in the top tenth of his class; "calm and steady-going," judged the *Lucky Bag*. But Nimitz believed in delegating and not second-guessing his line officers, and he needed Halsey.

He needed a hero to show the public and his own bosses back in Washington that he was fighting back. The newspapers were crying, Where is the navy? Why hasn't the navy fought back? The public had been panicked by the Japanese "sneak attack" at Pearl Harbor. For many months, Americans had sensed that war was coming, but not right away, and they had focused more on Europe, where Hitler had been rampaging for the past three years. Many—not just died-in-the-wool isolationists but ordinary citizens from around the country—wanted to avoid a world war, if at all possible. At the movies, before the double feature, they had seen newsreels of Japan's brutalization of China and its encroachment into Southeast Asia. Some were at least vaguely aware of the Rape of Nanking and other atrocities. But a lingering and unreasoning sense of racial superiority blinkered many Americans to Japan's military threat. Somehow, the Greater East Asia Co-Prosperity Sphere sounded like a joke, while the emperor—even well-educated Americans were led to believe—was a silly little man with a taste for jazz, scotch, and marine biology.

Pearl Harbor had been a terrible awakening. Overnight, the Japanese were transformed in the public eye from midgets to monsters. Angry crowds roamed the streets in Los Angeles, chasing the occasional Japanese immigrant who dared venture out, and better-off people began firing their Japanese gardeners and kitchen help and accusing them of spying. At the Jefferson Memorial in Washington, someone chopped down the cherry trees that had been planted as a gift from the Japanese people.

But amid the hysteria and rumors of imminent invasion a grim purposefulness quickly emerged. There were long lines outside recruiting centers all over the United States before dawn on December 8, and in Honolulu, where the oily smoke lay heavy over the palm trees, even prostitutes were volunteering to roll bandages. Isolationism vanished without a trace. A vast polyglot nation went to war, virtually as one. Victory Gardens were planted. Victory Bonds were sold. Victory Girls worked the train stations where the boys in their new khaki uniforms went to war or passed through on the way to military bases that were sprouting up overnight. Bankers' sons, farmers' boys, immigrants who could barely speak English signed up with Uncle Sam, a vast army of citizen soldiers, untrained but willing.

The military was not ready for them. For the first few months after Pearl Harbor, until the production lines began to churn in earnest, the new recruits trained by throwing eggs as grenades and wielding broomsticks as rifles. The peacetime military had been underappreciated and underfunded, ingrown and mediocre. Caught by surprise, the navy brass was demoralized, even defeatist. Annapolis men blamed the politicians and hunkered down for the inevitable blame game.

Halsey was a dazzling exception. He was, Admiral Nimitz appreciated, the answer to his problems—a bracing, effervescent cocktail of a man at a hand-wringing ladies' temperance meeting. Nimitz had been sent to Hawaii to restore shattered morale and bring some fighting spirit. His official title, in navy bureaucratese, was CINCPAC, commander-in-chief, Pacific. (His boss in Washington, Adm. Ernest King, was COMINCH, or simply commander-in-chief, a title shortened right after Pearl Harbor from its unfortunate predecessor, CINCUS, pronounced "Sink us.") Beneath Nimitz's steady-as-she-goes demeanor, he was fighting off his own sense of shock and demoralization. When he was given his appointment, his wife had congratulated him on "getting the fleet." Nimitz had responded, "The fleet, dear, is at the bottom of the ocean." But the carriers were still afloat, and Nimitz needed to show the Japanese and the American people that the navy could still fight.

Nimitz needed an aggressive fleet commander. The newly minted CINCPAC wanted to stage carrier raids on Japanese outposts in the Marshall and Gilbert Islands, coral specks in the mid-Pacific, to show that the navy had not taken Pearl Harbor lying down. Most of Nimitz's staff, largely inherited from Kimmel and still badly shaken by December 7, heatedly opposed Nimitz's idea as too dangerous. The fleet was not ready yet, they argued at a CINCPAC conference in early January 1942. To commit the carriers was to risk losing all that was left.

Halsey, back at Pearl after more fruitless searching for the Japanese at sea, came storming into the meeting and raised hell. The admirals were being defeatist, he charged. Yes, there were always risks in staging offensive operations, but to do nothing was unacceptable. Halsey's precise words were not recorded, but they carried the day, and they left a profound impression on Admiral Nimitz. In later years, when Halsey's critics demanded his head, Nimitz would remember how Halsey had stood up for him in those critical early days.

The *Enterprise* and another carrier, the *Yorktown*, sent around from the Atlantic to bolster the shattered Pacific Fleet, struck Japanese bases in the Marshalls and Gilberts in early February. Halsey was so nervous on the eve of battle that he repaired to his sea cabin so his men would not sense his anxiety. He smoked and read trashy novels and lay awake. In the morning, he listened on earphones as his pilots shouted out their successes at Kwajalein harbor in cocky American slang. "Get away from that cruiser, Jack! She's mine!" and "Bingo!" and "Look at that big bastard burn!" The pilots claimed to have sunk sixteen Japanese ships, including a cruiser, two subs, and even a small carrier. Halsey believed them, and he repeated their claims in his memoir. Their actual score was one transport and two smaller vessels sunk. It was not the only time Halsey was fooled by the boasts of his pilots.

Halsey came under enemy fire for the first time in his life off of Wotje Island in the Marshalls on February 1. Violating established doctrine by making his carrier vulnerable to shore-based bombers, he had brought the *Enterprise* in so close to the island that he could see antiaircraft fire bursting around his planes as they bombed and strafed Japanese shore positions. Five twin-engined Japanese bombers dived on the American carrier. Their bombs narrowly missed, but a wounded "Betty," its engines on fire, turned and dove right into the *Enterprise*. The plane seemed to be aiming for the planes parked on the carrier deck but clipped a wing and plunged into the sea, setting off a small fire that was easily contained. It was Halsey's first close experience with the Japanese warrior spirit. It did not intimidate him. Rather, he determined to be dismissive, to regard Japan's suicidal sacrifices as self-defeating, more pathetic than noble. As Halsey later explained in a letter, "the Americans fought to live; the Japanese fought to die."

On February 5, the *Enterprise* entered Pearl Harbor, flying her huge battle ensign, to an entirely changed mood. The ships in the harbor blew their sirens, and soldiers and patients from the Hickam Field hospital lined the shore to cheer themselves hoarse. On the bridge of "the Big E," Halsey choked up. "I myself cried and was not ashamed," he recalled. Nimitz came charging aboard, smiling now, exclaiming, "Nice going!" One of Nimitz's deputies, a doubter before, was excitedly wagging a finger in Halsey's face, "Damn you, Bill, you had no business getting home from that one! No business at all!" Back in the States, the newspapers, believing the pilots' wildly inflated claims of damage to the Japanese fleet, proclaimed, "Pearl Harbor Avenged!"

Americans had been desperate for good news. Although most Americans believed instinctively, as a matter of faith, that the United States would ultimately prevail, the headlines in the winter of 1942 were discouraging. The global war was not going well for the Allies. Hitler's armies were still on the march, deep in Russia at the gates of Moscow and in North Africa driving toward Suez. Japan seemed to be running wild through the Pacific and Southeast Asia. With a straight face, Americans described Japanese soldiers swinging from the trees as they marched through the supposedly impenetrable jungle of the Malay Peninsula to attack the British crown colony of Singapore. The British, having deemed such an advance impossible, had built most of Singapore's fortifications facing out to sea. The British garrison at Singapore, over 100,000 men, was on the verge of surrendering to a smaller, but far more aggressive Japanese army surging down from the north. The "Southern Movement," as the Japanese called their rapid conquest of Malaya and Indonesia, was moving ominously close to Australia.

America's only outpost in Asia, its quasi-colony in the Philippine Islands, was close to being overrun. On the Bataan Peninsula and its rocky outcropping, Corregidor, some fifty miles across the bay from Manila, an army of 80,000 men (20,000 American, 60,000 Filipino) under Gen. Douglas A. MacArthur had been encircled and trapped.

MacArthur's paralysis in the hours after Pearl Harbor remains a mystery. He was not the first great commander to freeze; even the legendary Confederate generals Stonewall Jackson and Robert E. Lee, so admired by romanticists like MacArthur and Halsey, had been overcome by a strange ennui at critical moments. But MacArthur's "daze," as one of his biographers, William Manchester, describes it, was catastrophic. Some nine hours after the attack at Pearl Harbor, Japanese bombers found MacArthur's air force mostly on the ground and destroyed it. In late December, a Japanese force invaded and began driving MacArthur's army into its final redoubt. An earlier plan to defend the beaches was abandoned, along with tons of supplies. Retreating onto the Bataan Peninsula, blowing bridges as they went, MacArthur's men were forced to leave behind the bulk of their food.

MacArthur was slow to appreciate what he was up against. The Japanese commander, Gen. Masaharu Homma, was an interesting example of Japanese ambivalence and ferocity. An Anglophile and Americanophile who had opposed the war, he was an amateur playwright. After the war, he would be executed by the Allies for war crimes. When MacArthur first saw the Japanese air force in action, he assumed the pilots could only be white mercenaries. MacArthur's own obsolete forces included one of history's last horse cavalry regiments, whose mounted troopers were strafed by those mysteriously able pilots in their surprisingly nimble and deadly Zero fighters. The Americans, stranded and surrounded on the Bataan Peninsula and bombarded in their rocky caves on Corregidor, allowed themselves to believe, for a while, in a dramatic rescue mission by the American navy. None was forthcoming. In his diary, Secretary of War Henry Stimson wrote, "There are times when brave men have to die." General MacArthur himself possessed some *bushido* spirit, and he resolved to die honorably, along with his wife and young child.

Against a backdrop of such strategic and human disaster, Halsey's raids against the Marshall Islands in the winter of 1942 did not amount to much. Even Halsey recognized that they were essentially pinpricks. But the American raids had a tremendous impact on the chief of staff of the Japanese Combined Fleet. On February 1, 1942, Admiral Ugaki wrote in his diary:

> Rain, later cloudy. Before 0700 a report came in of an air raid on the Marshalls. They have come after all; they are some guys!

Ugaki was not being facetious. He respected the Americans for their daring and defiance in sending carriers close-in to a Japanese airbase. Japanese forces had been running freely through Indonesia and Southeast Asia. Now they would have to watch their flank. "It seems we have been somewhat fooled," wrote Ugaki. "The incident was really 'a reproach that went to the heart.' . . . We must admit that this is the best way to make us look ridiculous. Adventure is one of their characteristics. . . . And the most probable move they would make would be an air raid on our capital."

Ugaki was learning to appreciate the true nature of his enemy. A common cliché in Japan at the time was that the fearful, spoiled women of America would not let their husbands fight. But Admiral Yamamoto's warnings about American resourcefulness were beginning to undermine Ugaki's smug sense of racial superiority and his disdain for weak American men and their frightened wives. Ugaki's views on racial purity would have been shaken further if he had known that an American warrior he would one day face in battle was a mixed-blood Cherokee Indian named Ernest Edwin Evans.

If homogeneity was Japan's strength—one race with one purpose under the hand of a divine emperor—then heterogeneity was America's. Compared to Japan, America was a wide-open society, but for a dark-skinned boy to get ahead took great resourcefulness and stubbornness—qualities that could be useful on a battlefield. The story of how Evans advanced from a railroad shack in Oklahoma to the bridge of a destroyer is testimony to the virtues of social mobility and strength of character.

The United States Navy in the years before World War II—Bill Halsey's navy—was reflexively racist and, at the senior level, insular and snobbish. The Naval Academy, which supplied every captain of every ship in the navy, was supposed to produce gentlemen, which by and large meant white Protestant ones. Blacks could only sail on navy ships as stewards serving officers in the wardroom. But there was room for a few ambitious young men of different or mixed races. After the Indian wars of the nineteenth century, some commanders admired Indians for their martial spirit. Teddy Roosevelt, for one, reminisced that when he was looking for fighters for his Rough Riders in the Spanish-American War, he especially sought out Cherokees. The occasional American Indian at Annapolis was subjected to ridicule and scorn, but then so were all plebes. The survivors brought cultural virtues that no military academy could teach.

Appointments to Annapolis in those days were generally made by Congress, but every year a few outstanding sailors were selected "from the fleet" for officer training. Ernest Evans was a poor Indian boy who had grown up in rural Oklahoma and joined the National Guard in 1926 after graduating from high school. He had quickly transferred from the guard to the navy and immediately applied, as an enlisted man, to the Naval Academy.

Applicants were given an aptitude test. The multiple-choice test asked students mathematical questions and proper word associations. Out of fifty questions, Evans made only two mistakes, both revealing. Question number 15 asked, "A meal always involves (?) . . . 1. a table, 2. dishes, 3. hunger, 4. food, 5. water." The correct answer was "4. food." Evans, whose answer was perhaps shaped by personal experience, chose "3. hunger." Question number 23 asked, "A contest always has (?) . . . 1. umpires, 2. opponents, 3. spectators, 4. applause, 5. victory." The correct answer was "2. opponents." Evans, a born warrior, put down "5. victory."

In the 1926 yearbook of Muskogee (Oklahoma) Central High School, Ernest Evans peers out of a senior photo, a proud, dark-skinned face in a sea of white classmates. His school activities were the usual ones (Scout Staff, Latin Club, Senior Pin and Ring Committee). There may have been other students in the class of '26 at Muskogee High with some Indian blood, but Ernest Evans was the only graduating senior who looked like a Native American.

Evans's singular status may seem surprising in a yearbook called the *Chieftain*, published by a public high school in the middle of historic Indian Territory. The town of Muskogee had for many years called itself the capital of the Five Civilized Tribes (Cherokee, Creek, Choctaw, Chickasaw, and Seminole). It was the seat of a huge Native American domain that had, in the years just before Evans was born in 1908, cherished dreams of American statehood. Cherokee leaders had wanted to name the nascent state Sequoyah, after the tribe's great early nineteenth-century chieftain. The Cherokees had once prized a highly developed culture with its own language and printing presses. But recent decades had been trying: driven west from their native lands east of the Mississippi along the "Trail of Tears," the Cherokee Nation had eventually settled in the vast grassy plains north of Texas. The land rushes of the late 1880s and early 1890s brought white settlers streaming in. Then, at the turn of the century, oil had been discovered. By 1907, Indian Territory had become a state—the white-controlled state—of Oklahoma.

Muskogee became a boomtown with a golf course and shingles hung for nearly 200 lawyers, the most lawyers per capita, the locals joked, outside of southern Manhattan. The lawyers were kept busy liberating Indians from their land. In return for ceding their communally held tribal lands, the Native Americans had been given small individual property allotments, from which they were quickly parted by legal sleight-of-hand and outright swindle. By the 1920s, the local Indians had lost 90 percent of their land titles. They were driven out of town or into shacks along the railroad tracks, the locale of Evans's boyhood home. In Muskogee, the few remaining Indian children went to the vocational Manual Training High School, not the all-white, or nearly all-white, Central High.

Evans lifted himself up. To do so, he had to break out of a vicious spiral of downward mobility. His paternal grandfather, George Washington Evans, who was mostly white, though with a dash of Creek blood, had exploited the local Native Americans. Evans was a southerner who had arrived in Indian Territory in 1887. He went into real estate and prospered, becoming the mayor of Okmulgee, a small town on the railroad line with a single telegraph wire and high hopes of cashing in on the land boom. On the day Oklahoma became the union's forty-sixth state, G. W. Evans was exultant. According to the local newspaper, he handed out cigars and drew a crowd around his brand-new car, the only one in town.

It was not uncommon in those days for white men to marry Indian women for the land allotments—and then divorce them. Under the property laws of the time, the ex-husband kept title to the land. George Washington Evans divorced his first two wives, both Creek

Indians, and disinherited his children. One of them—more Creek Indian in appearance than white—was William Charles Evans.

William Evans, an unemployed carpenter, moved to the wrong side of the tracks of Muskogee, and married a Cherokee woman, Anna Birdsong. On August 24, 1908, they had a son, Ernest Edwin Evans. He was born into a world of low prospects and ill will.

There were bad feelings between the Creeks, who often intermarried with blacks, and the Cherokees, who looked down on blacks and had once owned slaves. Whites generally looked down on all Indians. With his mixed blood—and noticeably dark skin—young Ernest Evans was caught somewhere in the middle. Possibly at his mother's insistence, he chose to be identified as a Cherokee. "Cherokees weren't discriminated against," observed Marian Hagerstrand, a Cherokee scholar who had grown up in Muskogee in the 1930s, a decade after Evans. "Cherokees discriminated against everyone else."

Anti-Indian bigotry was, relatively speaking, subtle in those days in Muskogee. There were no signs on stores saying "Indians and Dogs Stay Out," as there were in some places up north, but an Indian boy entering a store might be followed by a clerk, just checking to make sure he didn't steal anything. A local laundry could advertise, as one did in the 1926 Central High yearbook, that "We wash for white people only," and few people, if any, would object. The Muskogee schools were de facto segregated, but the occasional Indian boy could go to Central, especially if he was good at football or track.

Ernest Evans was not much of an athlete, but he did well in academics and activities, and he was serious and purposeful. In the yearbook, the inscription beneath his name—"the courage of his convictions"—hints that he was independent-minded, if not stubborn or rebellious. He was certainly self-reliant. Though proud, the civilized Cherokees learned to keep a low profile in white society. "The nail that stands up gets hammered down," was a Cherokee saying of the time. But young Indian boys of the Five Civilized Tribes identified with renegades, said Edwin Moore, a Creek who grew up near Muskogee in the 1920s. Their heroes were the Great Plains Indian chieftains Sitting Bull and Crazy Horse and, closer to home, Crazy Snake, who wouldn't take white money for his land and whose insurrection had to be suppressed by the National Guard in 1904. "If a boy had any spine," said Moore, a World War II veteran, "he wanted to be a warrior."

Despite their shabby treatment by the government, American Indians were intensely patriotic. Military service allowed Indians to win back their self-respect as warriors. In 1942, a year into World War II, U.S. Army officials stated that if the entire population enlisted in the same proportion as Indians, there would be no need for a draft. After graduating from Central High in 1926, Evans enlisted in the Oklahoma National Guard. Within a year he was a midshipman at Annapolis, a remarkable progression for someone without any political connections.

The Naval Academy in the summer of 1927 must have seemed like an otherworldly, enchanted place to a Native American boy from the hills of Oklahoma. Shimmering in the Chesapeake heat, cool and ghostly at night, the white marble of the Beaux Arts design radiated grandeur, tradition, pride. In the chapel, a new Tiffany stained glass window had been installed, showing a midshipman, Christ-like, in dress whites before a heavenly sea. (The artist's model, Thomas J. Hamilton, '27, had kicked the extra point to preserve Navy's undefeated season against Army the year before.) The academy was a temple to character and sportsmanship; constructed in Evans's time were a boathouse for the rowers and steel stands for the football field.

The source of that steel for the Thompson Field stands was a clue, however, that traditions were not quite as solid at the Naval Academy as they seemed. The steel came from battleships that had been dismantled under an arms control treaty designed to stabilize fleet building between the Great Powers at a 5 (U.S.)–5 (Britain)–3 (Japan) ratio. (This was the naval treaty Japan secretly broke to build the *Yamato*.) Fewer warships meant less need for line naval officers, and beginning in the 1920s, some midshipmen were being quietly advised not to accept their commissions upon graduation. Two years after Evans graduated, half the class was denied naval commissions and graduated as civilians.

The anchors-aweigh, full-speed-ahead spirit of Bill Halsey's day at Annapolis had given way to anxiety about the navy's future. The Depression forced the academy to fire 15 percent of its staff. Evans seemed unfazed by hard times, however, perhaps because he was still on the way up. Though he graduated fairly low in his class, 322 of 441, his yearbook epigraph was "never gripes, always ambitious." "The Chief" was described as "radical from birth," an allusion to his politics, possibly, though his just getting to the Naval Academy was radical enough. At the same time, he appears to have adopted a light manner. His "philosophy" was "life is what one makes it," according to his biographical entry in the *Lucky Bag*, which recorded that Evans preferred reading over studying, was "big hearted," and enjoyed a joke. "He was good company, he enjoyed life," recalled a classmate, John Colwell.

But he was dead serious about the essential spirit of the Naval Academy. The 1931 *Luck Bag* begins with a gold-embossed quotation

Midshipman Evans

in large print from John Paul Jones, "I do not wish to have command of any ship that does not sail fast, for I intend to go in harm's way." Judging from his later words and deeds, Evans was inspired by the example of the Revolutionary War hero, whose body was entombed in a magnificent sarcophagus beneath the Naval Academy Chapel, and whose sayings the midshipmen were required to memorize.

Evans, like Halsey, wanted to become an aviator, the most daring option offered a newly commissioned ensign. Like Halsey, he lacked good eye-hand coordination. Unlike Halsey, who was a captain with the command of a carrier awaiting him, Evans washed out of flight school. The late 1930s found him in command of a tugboat in San Francisco Harbor. But Evans did not complain. Indeed, he appeared to take some ironic pleasure in being underestimated. Among his duties was to serve as a harbor pilot, a job that allowed him to take the con of an aircraft carrier, USS *Saratoga*, as she navigated the tidal rips and traffic of San Francisco Bay. Evans had been wearing ordinary blue denim work clothes without officer's insignia, and when he showed up that night at the officers' club in dress blues, he saw the officers from the *Saratoga* eyeing him with puzzlement. "Doesn't that guy look familiar?" one asked, unable to quite believe the dark-skinned guy in denim that afternoon had been a naval officer. In later years, telling that story to one of his junior officers, Evans seemed more bemused than bitter. But the incident had stuck with him, a reminder that the best revenge against prejudice was skill.

In 1941, Evans finally won a place on a warship—as executive officer on an aging four-piper destroyer on the China station, an obsolete ship sailing in a backwater. Evans's ship, USS *Alden*, was near Singapore in early December when word came of the Pearl Harbor attack. The ship, along with three other four-pipers, was ordered to refuel in Singapore and head to sea to help defend two British warships in anticipation of an air attack at dawn. The captain's report of another destroyer, USS *Edwards*, describes a slightly comical departure scene. Problems with fueling delayed the squadron from getting underway, and the ship's men tripped over one another clearing the decks for action. "We made a good many mistakes in stripping the ship so hurriedly," reported the captain of the *Edwards*. "We dumped all our gasoline. We got rid of most of our paint." The captain did intervene to stop the men from tossing overboard "the loudspeaker for our movie machine" and record player because, he reasoned, "the use of phonograph records would do much to help the men pass the time later in the war."

The destroyers of the 57th Division finally arrived on station off the coast of Singapore a few hours after HMS *Prince of Wales* and *Repulse* had been sunk by Japanese planes. Evans's first taste of war was the smell of fuel oil on a windless Pacific night. All that was left of the mighty British battleship and cruiser was some charred flotsam; British destroyers had picked up roughly 2,000 survivors, while another 900 men had died.

The *Alden* joined a combined fleet of British, American, and Dutch warships, described by one naval history as "elderly and decrepit," to try to stop or slow the Japanese onslaught into the Dutch East Indies in the winter of 1942. The *Alden* was sailing under the overall command of a Dutch admiral, Karel Doorman of the Royal Netherlands Navy, when the motley fleet encountered a Japanese strike force advancing on Java in late February. The men of the Allied fleet were exhausted from weeks of false alarms; all dolphin trails were torpedo tracks; every masthead sighting was an enemy ship. Morale was very low. The Japanese had better ships and air cover. When Admiral Doorman announced that the Allies had the "possibility" of fighter protection, laughter could be heard on ship bridges around the fleet. In the wardroom of the *Alden*, the shortwave could pick up a female announcer on Radio Tokyo, taunting them in English:

> Poor American boys. Your ships are swiftly being sunk. You haven't a chance. Why die to defend foreign soil which never belonged to the Dutch or British in the first place? Go home, before the slackers steal your wives and girls.

In the late afternoon of February 27, the American-British-Dutch-Australian battle fleet, arrayed in ragged formation, confronted the Japanese strike force. Though destroyers are normally in the vanguard in a fleet action to loose their torpedoes, the four old American destroyers huffed along in the rear. Aboard the *Alden*, confusion reigned. Doorman's orders had to be translated from Dutch to English aboard an American cruiser, the *Houston*, and then transmitted to the destroyers by short-range radio. Apparently the transmitter was broken or blocked, because at first the *Alden* received no orders and just played follow-the-leader. Lieutenant Evans was standing on the bridge with his captain, Cdr. Lewis Coley, when they saw a British destroyer up ahead virtually vanish in a rain of Japanese shells. The ship sank in less than half a minute.

The sun was setting when the order, relayed by a blinker light, finally got through to *Alden*: DESTROYERS COUNTERATTACK. The aging four-pipers wheeled to face the enemy and steamed past the Allied cruisers toward the Japanese ships, whose guns could be seen flashing on the dusky horizon. But from the signal lamp on the *Houston* came another order from Admiral Doorman, presumably translated from the original Dutch: CANCEL COUNTERATTACK. Aboard the lead destroyer, USS *Edwards*, the squadron commander, T. H. Binford, was puzzled: was he reading Doorman's signals right? And then, rapid-fire, a third order: COVER MY RETREAT. But destroyer attack was the normal method of covering a retreat. "With no time for crossword puzzles," records a U.S. Naval Institute history of destroyer operations, "Commander Binford ordered a strike at the oncoming enemy." On the American destroyers came, trying to close within 10,000 yards before the Japanese cruisers could blow them out of the water.

On the bridge, Evans and the officers of the *Alden* watched in wonder as Japanese shells splashed around them. The water spouts were brightly colored—red, green, yellow. The Japanese had put dye in their shells to help them track the accuracy of each gun. The Technicolor display added an element of unreality to a scene that was already surreal. The World War I–vintage destroyers had labored, "straining every rivet," just to keep up with their own fleet at 28 knots. Now they were leading the attack. A man on the bridge of the *Alden* was heard to remark, "I always knew these old four-pipers would have to go in and save the day!" The laughter eased the tension, for the moment.

The torpedo attack was a failure. All forty torpedoes launched by the squadron either missed their targets or failed to explode (American torpedoes were notorious for malfunctioning early in the war). FOLLOW ME, signaled Admiral Doorman, and the destroyers turned to follow the main fleet into the night, unsure where they were going, their aged boilers barely able to sustain enough steam. Finally Commander Binford, on his own initiative, broke off from the engagement. "Realizing that I had no more torpedoes and that further contact with the enemy would be useless, since my speed and gunpowder were less than anything I would encounter . . . I retired," the squadron commander later wrote. "The old greyhounds panted into harbor," records the Naval Institute history. But the sea battle—the first fleet action of the Pacific War—kept raging through the night. It was a disaster for the Allied forces, with three light cruisers and three destroyers sunk and one heavy cruiser damaged. The Japanese had a single destroyer damaged.

However giddy that headlong, if futile, charge at sunset, Evans felt that he had participated in a fiasco. He was ashamed that the American destroyers had withdrawn from the battle, skulking into port while other ships in the Allied fleet were still taking fire at sea. It was doubly galling that one of the destroyers in the squadron was named the *John Paul Jones*, after Evans's hero. That night on the Java Sea, he would later tell his subordinates, he formed a vow never to retreat "from harm's way."

CHAPTER THREE

LONG JOHN SILVER AND CONFUCIUS

"To hell with it! It's Japanese!"

I T WAS KNOWN as the "victory disease." Japan's victories seemed so overwhelming, so easy, so divinely inspired, that the Japanese people became overconfident. They felt that nothing could stand in the way of the march toward global dominance by the leading race (*hakko ichiu*, the eight corners of the world under one roof). Despite his misgivings about the war, Admiral Ugaki was not immune. On February 24, 1942, when Admiral Halsey ran another one of his hit-and-run raids on Wake Island, sinking only a small patrol craft, Ugaki mockingly wrote:

> For the Americans, today is called Washington's birthday, and President Roosevelt was going to make a fireside talk. They had to do something, or the existence of the United States Navy would have been doubted.

In late February, the Japanese were still celebrating the collapse of the British army at Singapore earlier that month. In Tokyo, wearing the full dress uniform of a general, the emperor had appeared on his white horse, Snow White, on a bridge at the Imperial Palace. In early March, Rangoon and the Dutch East Indies fell before the Rising Sun, prompting a huge victory celebration in Tokyo. The popu-

The emperor on his white horse

lar euphoria made Ugaki uneasy. Suppose, he wrote in his diary, there was an American air raid "over the head of the rejoicing multitude?"

On April 18 came the raid Ugaki feared. Immediately after Pearl Harbor, President Roosevelt had begun agitating for a way to strike back at the Japanese, and the navy had come up with an audacious scheme to attack Tokyo. Carriers would transport army bombers, B-25s—so large they could barely fly off a carrier deck—to within striking range of Japan. The top secret plan called for a bold commander to get them there, and naturally Nimitz had called on Halsey.

Worrying about Japanese submarines every mile of the way, Halsey had sailed the *Enterprise* and the carrier *Hornet* across the Pacific to within 700 miles of Japan. There, in a 40-knot gale, the task force encountered a Japanese picket ship and sank it, but not before the Japanese flashed a radio warning to Tokyo. Rescued from the sea, a Japanese sailor reported that he had informed his captain of "two beautiful Japanese carriers passing by." The captain ran on deck and returned muttering, "Yes, they are beautiful, but they are not ours." Then he went to his cabin and shot himself.

The carriers were in range of Tokyo, but only barely. After hastily lugging extra jerricans of gasoline aboard their planes, Gen. Jimmy Doolittle and his men took off, their B-25s groaning and struggling off the *Hornet*'s pitching deck. On the bridge of the *Enterprise*, Halsey knew, as he later wrote, that he was witnessing "one of the most courageous deeds in military history." As the B-25s passed the Japanese coast, children and old men on bicycles waved cheerfully. They had never seen an American plane and could not imagine an attack on the homeland. Soon the bombers were over Tokyo (four bombers hit other cities), where they encountered no resistance from disbelieving defenders.

The bomb damage was light, and the brave fliers under General Doolittle, their planes out of fuel, had to crash-land in China. Captured by Japanese soldiers, three of them were tied to white crosses and executed. Amazingly, sixty-seven pilots and crewmen were rescued by the Chinese and smuggled out of Japanese-occupied territory. The Japanese retaliated by killing 250,000 Chinese civilians. Suspected of helping the Americans, one woman was wrapped in a kerosene-soaked blanket. At gunpoint, her husband was forced to set her afire.

The Japanese press joked that the American bombing of Tokyo was not a "Do-little" but a "Do-nothing" attack. But to Ugaki, this was just bluster. He was feeling shaken. His Eta Jima roommate had been killed by American planes on one of Halsey's raids. "Our homeland has been air raided and we missed the enemy without firing a shot at him," wrote Ugaki on April 20. "This is exceedingly regrettable."

His regret paled beside Admiral Yamamoto's. The commander-in-chief's steward later said that he had never seen his boss look so wan or depressed. For a day, Yamamoto retired to his cabin. Judging from the letters he wrote at the time, fretting about the vulnerability of Japan's paper-and-wood cities, he was imagining what Japanese cities would look like if the Americans ever came close enough to stage full-scale bombing attacks.

The Japanese war plans had always called for the Decisive Battle close to home waters, after wearing down the American fleet as it crossed the Pacific. But the Americans were sending out quick-hit raiders and then fleeing. Yamamoto was looking for a way to lure out the entire American fleet and defeat it once and for all—before American industrial power could crank out more and more powerful warships. He wanted to follow up a naval victory by seizing the Hawaiian Islands and, in effect, holding them hostage to win a favorable peace settlement. In his conference room aboard the *Nagato,* Yamamoto had been running tabletop war games for the Decisive Battle against the American fleet. The Japanese fleet would engage the Americans near a mid-Pacific island called Midway. "The children's hour," Yamamoto wrote a friend, was over. "Now comes the adults' hour."

The *Enterprise* and the *Hornet* slipped back into Pearl Harbor from the Doolittle mission on April 25. This time there were no cheers or marching bands. The raid on Tokyo had been staged in secret. President Roosevelt winkingly told reporters that the American bombers had come "from Shangri-La." On the bridge of the Big E, Admiral Halsey looked grim-faced and exhausted. He was sick. He had developed an itching rash over much of his body, and no amount of creams or powders or oatmeal baths seemed to cure it. He was sleeping only fitfully; his weight had dropped by twenty pounds, from 185 to 165.

Halsey was under enormous stress. The secret voyage across the Pacific had taken a toll. Halsey made a brisk joke of his hasty retreats from enemy waters; his staff nicknamed him "Haul Ass Halsey." But the tension was starting to show.

Halsey had no embracing and comforting family to return to. His wife, Fan, was in Wilmington, Delaware, with their daughter. Even if she had remained in Honolulu, she would not have offered much solace; she was mentally unstable, suffering from increasingly severe manic depression.

Frances Grandy had been a vivacious southern debutante when Halsey had first courted her. Actually, she had courted him—by throwing her hand muff at a handsome, if apparently overserious, young ensign as he drilled some sailors on a dock in Norfolk, Virginia. The muff knocked off Halsey's hat and drew his attention to a blond-haired young woman with a mischievous smile. Halsey soon learned that his flirtatious teaser came from a good Virginia family; she was the sister of one of his St. Anthony Hall brothers and the niece of a Confederate naval officer. He fell in love and asked for her hand.

At first Fan was lively and fun. But her mood swings became ever more severe. At dinner with other officers, she might be witty, or talk too much, or turn on Halsey and run him down in front of his fellow officers. Halsey took it all in good spirits, or tried to, but he was pretending. Fan's sickness had become noticeable to other officers when Halsey was stationed at Pensacola during his flight training in 1937. For all his joking about winning the Flying Jackass, Halsey had struggled in flight school. His weight had dropped from a somewhat pudgy 200 pounds to a very lean 155, which he blamed on poor mess hall food, though nerves were the more likely cause. Fan was not particularly sympathetic. She grabbed the loose skin under his chin and said, "What are these wattles? You look like a sick turkey buzzard."

Halsey felt that he could not really trust his wife, who referred to him loudly as an "old fool," not necessarily affectionately. In late November 1941, as he was about to sail for Wake Island to deliver the planes to the marine outpost there, he had confided to Fan that war might be close. She had become agitated and caused a scene in the dining room of the Halekulani Hotel on Waikiki, where Halsey and other officers were living. Halsey was relieved when she was packed off with other dependents and headed to their daughter's home on the mainland. But, from cryptic comments he made from time to time, and from the look on his face when he mentioned Fan, he worried about her. He was not the sort to talk much about his family life. He had no outlet or release, other than a bottle of scotch when he was in port.

Halsey hid his skin rash from Admiral Nimitz as long as he could. But when the *Enterprise* returned from a cruise in the South Pacific in May, Nimitz was shocked by the sight of Halsey, gaunt and hollow-eyed and covered with blisters (Halsey could not stop himself from scratching). Nimitz ordered his fighting admiral to report to the hospital. Halsey was lying under a single sheet, naked and swathed with ointments, when his successor, Adm. Raymond Spruance, led the American carriers, the *Enterprise* and the *Hornet*, to one of the greatest victories in the history of the U.S. Navy.*

Breaking pieces of the Japanese code, the Americans got the jump on Admiral Yamamoto's fleet off of Midway. Catching the Japanese as they were refueling and rearming planes, American dive-bombers sank the four main carriers of the Japanese striking force. The defeat spelled the end of Yamamoto's efforts to sink the U.S. Navy before America became too strong for Japan. From now on, Japan would be on the defensive, slowly retreating across the Pacific vastness to the Home Islands and Armageddon.

The American victory at Midway in June 1942 was instantly regarded as a turning point in the Pacific War. Halsey was bitterly disappointed to miss it. His rash worsened in the Pearl Harbor hospital. Halsey blamed a fine coral dust from a construction site a half-mile away, but his skin condition, described on the medical charts as "generalized allergic dermatitis," was probably psychosomatic (Yamamoto's agony was far greater; his biographer describes him after the Battle of Midway, "his face greasy with sweat from severe abdominal pains, retir[ing] to his private cabin, declaring that it was all his responsibility").

Halsey was flown back to the States to get special attention at a hospital outside Richmond, Virginia. Informed that he would receive allergy tests to determine the cause of his illness, Halsey declared, "Make sure the first test is a case of Scotch whiskey." What he

---

*The senior officer at Midway was Adm. Frank Jack Fletcher, who commanded from the *Yorktown* until his flagship was put out of action.

needed was rest. By the end of August, after briefly seeing his family, he was back to his old self. Traveling to Annapolis to appear before the Brigade of Midshipmen in their dress whites, Halsey, looking feisty and ready for war in his baggy khakis, declared, "Missing the Battle of Midway has been the greatest disappointment of my life, but I'm going back to the Pacific, where I intend personally to have a crack at those yellow-bellied sons of bitches and their carriers."

At noon on September 21, 1942, the aircraft carrier *Saratoga* limped into Pearl Harbor after taking a torpedo in the South Pacific. Nimitz came aboard and took the microphone aboard the flight deck to address the ship's weary men. "Boys, I've got a surprise for you. Bill Halsey's back!" Halsey stepped forward and the men on deck erupted. Halsey's eyes filled with tears.

Nimitz was watching Halsey closely. To steady his own nerves, the commander-in-chief of the Pacific Fleet had set up a horseshoe pit behind his quarters at Pearl Harbor, as well as a shooting range. That evening, Nimitz took Halsey out on the range and watched as Halsey plinked away at targets set out by the Filipino houseboy. Nimitz wanted to see if Halsey's hand was steady.

Halsey must have shot straight that night, because Nimitz made a momentous decision. The navy and marines were locked in the first great battle of the long, slow island-hopping campaign of the Pacific. After the hit-and-run raids on small mid-Pacific islands, the navy had begun to try to seize Japanese-held islands in the South Pacific, as stepping-stones on the long road to Tokyo.

The first was Guadalcanal. Not a canal, but rather a hilly jungle island, Guadalcanal was located in the Solomon Islands, in the Bismarck Archipelago northeast of Australia. First discovered in 1568 by Spanish explorers looking for King Solomon's fabled gold mines, it had become a British possession, but not a very valuable one. Some hardy colonialists harvested coconuts, but the island was a dank and eerie place, pestilential and fetid.

It was, however, strategically important. The Japanese were building an airfield there, a base to strike south against Australia and New Zealand. The Americans wanted to capture the airfield. With an airbase at Guadalcanal, the Americans could take a stand against the Japanese and turn the tide in the Pacific, pushing north.

American troops had landed on Guadalcanal on August 7, 1942, and, with only minor casualties, seized the nearly completed Japanese airfield, which they renamed Henderson Field after a marine bomber commander lost at Midway. But the Japanese counterattacked by land, sea, and air. The fight was not going well for the green American troops. The Japanese navy had outfoxed the Americans in a night battle off Savo Island in September, sinking four heavy cruisers in eight minutes, and the marines were struggling in jungle combat against die-hard Japanese forces. Nimitz had visited the overall commander in the South Pacific, Adm. Robert Ghormley, and found him weary and indecisive, his staff beset with defeatism.

Nimitz's answer was Halsey. On October 18, when Halsey received his orders to replace Admiral Ghormley as COMSOPAC (commander, South Pacific), he exclaimed, "Jesus Christ and General Jackson! This is the hottest potato they ever handed me!" Halsey felt badly about Ghormley, with whom he had played football at Annapolis. He also wanted to be prowling the bridge of a warship, not sitting at a desk mediating interservice disputes and wrestling with logistics. But while Nimitz knew that Halsey did not wish to be a detail man, fussiness had been part of Ghormley's problems. Nimitz wanted a fighter who would rally the troops.

The whole nation was watching Guadalcanal. The great campaigns against the Germans in Africa and Europe still awaited. A remote island in the South Pacific was providing the first test of American troops on the offensive, the first step toward regaining lost ground. Anyone reading a newspaper or watching a newsreel knew about the "Tokyo Express," the nightly convoys of Japanese destroyers bringing fresh men and supplies to the Japanese garrison, as well as "Iron Bottom Sound," the waters off Guadalcanal so named because of the many ships sunk there. "Guadalcanal," the *New York Times* editorialized on October 16, just before Halsey took over: "The name will not die out of the memories of this generation. It will endure in honor." The editorial sounded "ominously like an elegy," noted the leading historian of Guadalcanal, Richard Frank. In truth, the American marines holding the line on Guadalcanal were rattled by an enemy that cried, "Babe Ruth eat shit!" before making dead-of-the-night bayonet charges. Exhausted, frightened pilots back from their missions were crawling under the wings of their planes to sob. Marine air commander Gen. Roy Geiger "had to kick them—literally kick them—back into their cockpits," wrote Halsey in his memoir, not without a certain admiration, though his own leadership style was far more avuncular and jocular.

Halsey's reputation for rallying the troops was well known in the Pacific, and the mere announcement of his appointment to replace Ghormley seems to have had an electric effect. "Then we got the news: the Old Man had been made COMSOPAC!" recalled an air combat intelligence officer based at the marines' besieged Henderson Field on Guadalcanal. "One minute we were too limp with malaria to crawl out of our foxholes; the next, we were running around whooping like kids."

Halsey arrived aboard Ghormley's flagship, the *Argonne*, anchored in port at Noumea on New Caledonia, a French-colonized island 700 miles to the south of Guadalcanal, and set about making the sort of small changes that sent signals. His decision to dispense with the black neckties worn by naval officers seems minor; the army had already abandoned theirs. But as Frank noted, "to his command, it viscerally evoked the image of a brawler stripping for action." More bluntly, Halsey ordered painted on a large billboard at the naval base at Tulagi, across Iron Bottom Sound, his crude command to KILL JAPS. KILL JAPS. KILL MORE JAPS. Pretty soon, sailors and marines were penciling the exhortation on the walls of latrines.

Ghormley had lived and worked aboard the *Argonne* in cramped, stifling quarters. Halsey had no diplomatic inhibitions; he simply requisitioned the French consul's house on an airy hilltop and built a couple of Quonset huts for staff officers, promptly dubbed Wicky Wacky Lodge. Halsey disapproved of the French consul's furniture, Japanese-made seats so low to the ground that "we sat on our necks." When his Filipino steward dropped some of the consul's china, Halsey bellowed, "To hell with it! It's Japanese!"

Halsey would brook no retreat, but he tried to give commanders heart and to smooth over interservice rivalries by placing a bottle of scotch on the table. On October 23, the new COMSOPAC met with Gen. A. Archer Vandergrift, commanding the 1st Marine Division. Glass empty, fingers drumming the desk, Halsey asked Vandergrift if the marines could hold Guadalcanal. "I can hold, but I've got to have more active support than I've been getting." Halsey replied, "You go on back there, Vandergrift. I promise you everything I've got."

Halsey knew that he also had a sea battle brewing. By piecing together radio traffic analysis and search plane sightings, naval intelligence deciphered that Yamamoto was sending a carrier force south. Halsey hoped for another Midway. He sent a cable to Adm. Thomas Kinkaid, in command of the carrier task force that included *Enterprise* and *Hornet*: ATTACK REPEAT ATTACK.

But Kinkaid, at least in Halsey's view, fatally hesitated. Kinkaid would later blame poor communications (an excuse that would resonate two years later when the two men were miscommunicating at Leyte Gulf). But in any case, the Americans allowed the Japanese to get the jump. In a confused battle off the Santa Cruz Islands, the *Hornet* was sunk and the *Enterprise* badly damaged, leaving Halsey temporarily without any aircraft carriers to fight the Japanese. Halsey quietly moved to have Kinkaid relieved from carrier task command—an insult that Kinkaid would not forget.

In a letter to Nimitz on October 31, Halsey took ultimate responsibility for the navy's poor showing at the Battle of the Santa Cruz Islands. But he made some mild excuses and tried to put on his bravest front.

> As you may well imagine, I was completely taken aback when I received your orders [to relieve Ghormley] on my arrival here. I took over a strange job with a strange staff and I had to begin throwing punches almost immediately. As a consequence quick decisions had to be made. Since the action [off of Santa Cruz], I have about reached the conclusion that the yellow bastards have been playing us for suckers.

He vowed better strategies to, as he indelicately put it, "secure more monkey meat.

Unlike Ghormley, Halsey went to the front to visit the troops. His visit was "like a wonderful breath of fresh air," General Vandergrift said later. COMSOPAC bounced around in a jeep with the marine commander and stomped around in the mud. He was, as usual, dressed in unadorned khakis, "almost indistinguishable from a pfc's [private first class]," recalled his flag lieutenant, who urged him to stand by his jeep and wave to the troops. In a rare moment of restraint, Halsey declined, muttering, "It smells of exhibitionism. To hell with it." That night, he lay sleepless in Vandergrift's shack, listening to nearby artillery barrages.

Halsey returned to Noumea to be greeted with more ominous intelligence: the Japanese were mounting another major push from the sea. Halsey committed all the naval strength he had—the battered Big E, two battleships, and various cruisers and destroyers—to turning it back. He was full of trepidation as he sat in his cabin aboard the *Argonne* reading a trashy magazine, inhaling coffee and cigarettes, and awaiting word of the outcome. He knew he was violating Holy Writ at the Naval Academy by again sending capital ships into shallow, confined waters where they could not maneuver easily. But he had exposed his carrier and gotten away with it at Wotje, and he prayed that Nelsonic bravura would sustain him again.

His bet paid off. The Japanese were routed, their reinforcements destroyed or turned away. At what became known as the Naval Battle of Guadalcanal on November 12–15, the Japanese lost two battleships, one heavy cruiser, three destroyers, and ten troop transports. The Americans lost two light cruisers and seven destroyers. "We've got the bastards licked!" Halsey triumphantly declared to his staff. TO ALL SHIPS, Halsey messaged, like a Roman proconsul to his centurions: MAGNIFICENTLY DONE X TO THE GLORIOUS DEAD: HAIL HEROES, REST WITH GOD.

That month, Halsey won an extra star, making him a full, four-star admiral. He sent his two three-star collar bars to the wives of Admirals Dan Callaghan and Norman Scott, who were killed off Guadalcanal while carrying out Halsey's damn-the-torpedoes credo. Halsey wanted only officers like them, who would attack. After the Japanese torpedoed four cruisers at the Battle of Tassafaronga on November 30, Halsey censured a destroyer captain for sailing away after launching his torpedoes. The commander should have kept coming with guns blazing, Halsey decreed.

Halsey's favorite destroyer captain, his model fighting man, was Arleigh Burke, commander of Task Force 23, "the Gallant Squadron." Burke's standing orders were: "Destroyers to attack on enemy contact WITHOUT ORDERS from the task force commander." Here was a destroyer man after Halsey's heart. Burke instructed his captains: "If you make a mistake, for Pete's sake, make it on the radical side." Burke further endeared himself to Halsey by his quick thinking when Halsey questioned why Burke had detached a destroyer to Australia without permission from COMSOPAC. "Admiral," Burke explained, "we needed beer and whiskey." Halsey pretended to ponder this ridiculous excuse for a minute, then replied, "Burke, that's all right. But if you had sent her to Sydney for anything like repairs, I'd have your hide." The health fanatic Burke, who gobbled raw carrots to improve his vision for night battle, played the role of hard-drinkin', hard-lovin' sea dog for Halsey. The symbol of the Gallant Squadron was the cartoon character the Little Beaver, a little Indian boy, only drawn with an enormous phallus. Halsey affectionately teased his favorite destroyer man as "31-Knot Burke," not because, as popularly assumed, Burke was always full-speed-ahead, but rather because a faulty boiler slowed his *Fletcher*-class destroyer from 35 to 31 knots. Burke revered Halsey, although his veneration would be severely shaken at the Battle of Leyte Gulf.

Halsey had turned the tide at Guadalcanal. From now on the Japanese were on the defensive, in land battles as well as at sea. He had become a household name. His picture graced the cover of *Time*. "Halsey of the South Pacific," the magazine headlined, "When an attacker is attacked . . ." Under Halsey, American forces "hit hard, hit fast, hit often." Newsmen flocked to COMSOPAC, confident of a good quote. He did not disappoint. Touring New Zealand on New Year's Eve, he predicted that the Americans would be in Tokyo by the end of 1943 and made various unprintable aspersions, caught by the censors, against the emperor and Prime Minister Hideki Tojo. His prediction of a fast end to the war did not play well in Washington. "The production leaders at home put up a bellow that I could hear in Noumea. They were afraid that labor would take my word as gospel and quit their war jobs," Halsey later marveled. "The draft authorities also complained, as did a lot of other officials. They accused me of everything from recklessness to drunkenness." Tokyo Rose, the American voice who liked to taunt American GIs over Japanese radio, began listing the tortures that would be inflicted on Halsey when he was captured. Even Halsey's chums chimed in. When Halsey returned to Noumea, he found a couple of fellow admirals pretending to stir a giant pot——"of boiling oil," they cheerfully proclaimed.

Halsey never backed off his virulence toward the Japanese. In one private letter, he suggested that after the war, he would "advocate for the yellow bellies that are left—emasculation for the males and spaying for the females." Such wildly racist if not genocidal remarks are cringe-worthy, but they were not so uncommon at the time. (And not just aimed at the Japanese: FDR mused aloud to his advisers about castrating the German male population to prevent Germany from starting another war.) A popular song on American radio at the time was, "We're Gonna Have to Slap the Dirty Little Jap," and the most popular float at a day-long parade in New York in 1942 (entitled "Tokyo We Are Coming") showed bombs dropping on a frantic pack of yellow rats. Glowering for the cameras, growling about "yellow bellied bastards," Halsey was, especially during the first anxious months of the war, a reassuring figure to many Americans. He was not a model of War College professionalism, to be sure, and the top brass in Washington and later historians would regard some of his moves in the fall of 1942—such as sending two carriers to take on the Combined Fleet at the Battle of the Santa Cruz Islands—as reckless. Still, he was more than an inspirational figure. His leadership at Guadalcanal was resourceful, lucky, bold, and, most important, successful at turning around a near-disaster.

For all his spouting off, and despite enough nervous energy to cover him in rashes, Halsey was an instinctive leader who knew how to seize opportunity and get the best out of his men. The British Royal Navy's liaison officer, Cdr. Harold Hopkins, visited Halsey one day at his quarters in Noumea. Halsey, dressed in shorts, no socks, and a khaki shirt without insignia, sat on the veranda offering drinks and swatting at mosquitoes as he jawed and joked. "I remember thinking that he might well have been a parson, a jolly one, an old-time farmer, or Long John Silver," said the British visitor. "But when I left him and thought of what he had said, I realized that I had been listening to one of the great admirals of the war."

*   *   *

Four days before Halsey arrived in the South Pacific to take over from the beleaguered Admiral Ghormley in October 1942, the Japanese staged a raid that severely jarred the marines' tenuous grip on Henderson Field and demoralized the troops caught in the bombardment. Under cover of darkness, two Japanese battleships, the *Kongo* and *Haruna*, had sailed into range, ten miles off the Guadalcanal coast, and unleashed a terrific bombardment of high-caliber shells. A shell from the battleship's 14-inch gun was almost as long as a man and packed 1,400 pounds of explosives. At Henderson Field, planes erupted into flames and fuel dumps went off in fiery cataclysms as marines prayed in their foxholes. If the ships had been able to keep up the bombardment, they might have dealt the marines' air force a fatal blow. But the battleship commander in charge of the raid felt compelled to withdraw.

The commander's name was Adm. Takeo Kurita. Classically educated and civilized, and a great seaman to boot, Kurita was a living reproach to Halsey's racial jibes about "monkeys." Kurita was, as much as Halsey, the product of a great naval tradition. But he was, perhaps, a little gun-shy, at least in comparison to some of his more death-defying comrades in arms.

Admiral Kurita appeared to be a modest, amiable man whose innocuous presence concealed a strong character, though not one particularly suited to the brutal demands of total war. A formal portrait of Kurita, taken in 1944, shows a rather severe figure with a shaved head. It is a misleading picture. Kurita was suffering from dengue fever when the photograph was taken, his daughter, Shigeko Terada, recalled, and his face had been worn by defeat.

Kurita was a gentleman, quiet but kindly. Unlike the fierce Ugaki, he smiled easily. Like Ugaki, he was scholarly and had graduated high in his class, eighteenth of 149 students, at Eta Jima. Unlike Ugaki, he had no interest in administration, staff work, or naval politics. Top Eta Jima graduates tended to spend a great deal of time ashore at war colleges and on the General Staff. Kurita, by contrast, had spent nearly his entire career at sea, specializing in torpedo attack aboard destroyers and cruisers. During the war he had been continuously at sea except for two weeks when he was detached to the General Staff.

Kurita had long subscribed to the view that battleships, like men, should be preserved, not wasted. In this respect, Kurita was well within the mainstream of the Imperial Japanese Navy. While some commanders wanted to throw ships and men at the enemy, more—and especially more senior admirals—wished to preserve what was known as "the fleet-in-being." According to this school of thought, mighty ships like the *Yamato* and *Musashi* were national icons, quasi-religious symbols as well as weapons of destruction and strategic deterrents. They were to be treasured, like relics, never shattered or, it sometimes seemed, even scratched. In time, even the emperor would lose patience with the navy's reluctance to expose sacred battleships to the risk of being sunk.

This cautious streak in many Imperial Japanese Navy commanders conflicted with their oft-expressed longing for Decisive Battle and honorable death. IJN officers lived with contradictions that required tortuous rationalizations. The confusion over naval strategy is illustrative. Like Meiji-era architecture, Japanese naval doctrine was a strange mishmash of East and West, combining elements of the Chinese philosopher Sun Tzu (the emphasis on deception and surprise), ancient Sumaria (speeding, circular battle formations), and the disparate philosophies of various European navies. Tactically, in battle, the Japanese seemed to imitate British aggressiveness—Nelson's credo of attacking any enemy in sight. But when it came to overall strategy, the Japanese were influenced by the French and Russian navies, which were essentially defensive. A fleet-in-being man, Kurita had plenty of company, despite all the charging about and cries of *Banzai* by the stereotypical Japanese commander. Passivity was not exactly uncommon in the upper ranks, either. Brutalized and humiliated by the unbelievably harsh regimen of Eta Jima, a man could have his spirit beaten out of him. For many officers, passivity turned to fatalism. For Kurita, on the other hand, it meant avoiding pointless death.

Kurita was popular with enlisted men because they knew that he would look out for them. But he was an object of condescension by armchair admirals, who mistook his reticence for meekness and his avoidance of staff duty for dimness. He was regarded as a faithful old sea dog but not much more. True, he had seen a lot of action—in fact, more than almost any senior officer—and yet his promotions had been widely regarded as more a matter of seniority than talent. The mean, unfair joke about Kurita was that he was a *hiru andon,* a lantern in daytime, i.e., useless.

If Kurita was wounded by these slights, he never protested. Nor did he comment on the irony that he had been shot at much more than his detractors, who were usually safe in a headquarters bunker in Tokyo while he was dodging American dive-bombers in the South Pacific. Kurita was accustomed to cruel irony.

In classically contradictory fashion, Kurita had been raised to be both a fighter and a conciliator. The name Takeo means warrior. But his family lineage bred calm contemplation, kindness, and a wariness of foolish conflict. He had been born into a family of great scholars from the Mito prefecture, on the seacoast northeast of Tokyo. His grandfather had been an eminent professor at the University of Tokyo, the author of a famous history of Japan, written in classical Chinese characters. The shoguns who ruled Japan from the seventeenth into the mid-nineteenth century encouraged the study of Confucianism imported from China; its principles of loyalty and self-denial were blended into the warrior's code, *bushido.* Kurita's father was a scholarly man of independent means who lived in a large house, set behind an enormous gate, on the estate of a great landowner in Mito. Kurita never used terms of endearment like "dad" or "grandpa"; he was taught to use the more formal address, "teacher-father" and "teacher-grandfather."

Kurita had seven brothers. "My family had a rather strange tradition," recalled Kurita's daughter, Shigeko. "Because they were scholars, my family used women's names, taken from the classics, for the boys." But Takeo was given a manly name. "Without having a weak mind, I am giving the name 'To be a great warrior,'" Kurita's grandfather wrote at the boy's birth in 1890. "By having a name that means warrior, I hope this child will become the one who will live with courage."

Takeo was sent off to Eta Jima in 1905, the year of the Battle of Tsushima, when Japanese reverence for the navy was reaching a zenith. Like all midshipmen, he memorized the Imperial Rescript for Soldiers and Sailors, the collection of precepts which was taught like Holy Writ. The rescript emphasized loyalty, duty, and courage, but Kurita appears to have taken to heart passages that were often overlooked or slighted by Eta Jima's graduates:

> Those who appreciate true valor should in their daily inter-
> course set gentleness first and aim to win the love and esteem
> of others. If you affect valor and act with violence, the world
> in the end will detest you and look upon you as wild beasts. Of
> this you should take heed.

As a father, his daughter Shigeko recalled, Kurita would point to dusty volumes of Confucian philosophy, written in classical Chinese, and say, "You should read those." He had been required to read them by his own "teacher-father." As a boy, Kurita had been steeped in a concept from the Confucian classics called *jen*, a term that is difficult to translate, but combines kindness, charity, and civility, all aspects of treating people decently.

Mito, Kurita's home province, was known for both its emperor-worship over the centuries and its ties to the Tokugawa clan, whose shoguns ruled Japan in the seventeenth and eighteenth centuries. Reverence for the emperor, the mikado, and loyalty to the shoguns—who had effectively usurped the emperor's power—became irreconcilable when the Emperor Meiji moved to restore his power in the nineteenth century. Mito's ruling families at first tried to mediate, then became entangled in messy assassination plots as the Meiji Restoration drove out the old Tokugawa shogunate. Coming from a family of historians, Kurita was undoubtedly aware of the high price of divided loyalty. Kurita himself was not *mittopo*, the term used to describe the tendency of men from Mito to become riled up when vexed or thwarted. His family as well as his sailors considered him gentle, calm, and empathetic. His daughter Shigeko recalls being slightly awed by the return of the great sea warrior who was so often away from home, but also touched by his thoughtfulness. When his wife was hospitalized while they were stationed in China, and Kurita was called back to Japan, he worried about her becoming lonely and brought her a doll to keep her company. To Westerners, this may not sound like an act of great devotion, but to Kurita's family, it showed sensitivity and unusual consideration; in

Japanese, the second meaning for wife, *kanai*, is "woman in the back room."

At home, Kurita lived like a gentleman of an earlier era, dressing in a kimono, practicing archery in the garden. He was not unworldly; he had been to San Francisco on his midshipmen's cruise after Eta Jima. Raised to admire Chinese scholarship and revere the ancient cultivation of "the great country of T'ang," he did not have the flagrantly racist views of so many Japanese, who sneered at "pigtailed Chinks." But he was at the same time a true Japanese nationalist. He refused to eat tropical fruit because, he told his family, it "lacked Yamato spirit."

In the fleet, he was regarded as straightforward, unpretentious, down-to-earth. He was usually at sea and often in harm's way, or more accurately perhaps, *nearly* in harm's way. Kurita was a Zelig of sea battle, a witness to or participant in almost every major engagement fought by the Imperial Japanese Navy, though more often at a distance than in the thick of the fight.

In the opening days of the war, he had narrowly missed a gunfight with His Majesty's ships *Prince of Wales* and *Repulse*. His cruiser arrived on the scene after Japanese planes had torpedoed and sunk the British warships. Adm. Jisaburo Ozawa, the carrier commander, had been so moved by the destruction of the British ships that he had wept and ordered flowers dropped where they sank. But Kurita had merely smiled and looked pleased; his men had been spared a gun duel with larger, more powerful ships.

Kurita was a cruiser division commander at the Battle of the Java Sea and at Midway in 1942. He was criticized for not coming to the aid of two damaged cruisers at Midway, and at Java Sea he had the misfortune of operating on the fringes. At Midway, he had initially protested against advancing toward the beachhead without air cover. "There certainly appears to have been a disinclination to 'make for the sound of the guns' on the part of Kurita and his force," wrote naval scholar H. P. Willmott, who suggests that Kurita rose up the seniority list by keeping a low profile while more vocal opponents of the war, often able officers, were purged. Many of Kurita's sailors, on the other hand, appreciated that their commander sought to protect them from unnecessary risks.

Aboard the battleship *Kongo* at the Battle of the Santa Cruz Islands that October, he had come close enough to the American carrier *Hornet* to see her burn. Issuing orders as Combined Fleet chief of staff from 700 miles away in the island stronghold of Truk, Admiral Ugaki had wanted Kurita to take the *Hornet* under tow as a prize of war. Kurita was able to avoid the order; the American carrier, he cabled back, was too far gone.

At Guadalcanal, Admiral Yamamoto ordered Kurita to take the *Kongo* and her sister battleship, the *Haruna,* and sail in close enough to bombard the U.S. Marines' Henderson Field with their giant 14-inch guns. The maneuver was risky. It required the ships to steam back and forth in parade formation while their great guns belched. They would be vulnerable to attack by American PT boats or destroyers from Tulagi.

At first Kurita objected. The potential damage to the American airfield at Guadalcanal, he argued, was not worth the risk of losing two Japanese battleships. Under growing pressure from the emperor to produce results, Yamamoto insisted. Kurita tried a different tack. He asked for machine guns and rifles, tents and shovels for his sailors, so that if the battleships were badly damaged and sinking the men could run onto the beach and into the jungle. As always, he was thinking about the survival of his crew.

The bombardment of Henderson Field came on a tropical night so dark and menacing that a marine colonel called it a "purple night." The battleships used incendiary shells that turned the darkness into an inferno and destroyed scores of planes and almost all the aviation fuel of the dug-in marines. Though shelled from shore and attacked by PT boats, Kurita's ships escaped unharmed.

Henderson Field was badly chewed up and cratered. The marines' battered fleet of bombers and fighters, the so-called Cactus Air Force, had been 70 percent destroyed, but not annihilated. Some forty marines had been killed and many more had their eardrums blown out. General Vandergrift, the marine commander, admitted that he had been scared out of his wits. "A man comes close to himself in those times," he later wrote. It had been a terrible night—but not a decisive one.

Kurita had carried out his mission with serious damage for U.S.

forces. He had been ordered to pound Henderson Field for an hour and a half, but Kurita did not stay that long. After about an hour and fifteen minutes, he had turned his ships and headed for safety. He could not see the point in putting his ships and crews at risk for more than a minute longer than necessary.

CHAPTER FOUR

POP GOES THE WEASEL

"The navy is not supposed to lie"

A YEAR AFTER THE Pearl Harbor attack, Admiral Ugaki sat in his cabin aboard the *Yamato*, the superbattleship that was now the flagship for the Combined Fleet, and reflected on the progress of "the Great East Asia War," as he called it. The *Yamato* was at her moorings at Truk, an ideal anchorage snug by an atoll surrounded by coral reefs in the Western Pacific. Secretly and illegally fortified during the 1930s in violation of a League of Nations mandate, Truk was Japan's stronghold in her first line of defense. Safe behind torpedo nets in the glistening blue lagoon, the *Yamato* presided over her sister warships of the Combined Fleet like an empress dowager.

"I regret," Ugaki began his diary entry for December 8, 1942, "that we have not gained what we wished." He paid tribute to the 14,802 men and officers of the Imperial Japanese Navy who had died in battle that year. "We prepared an altar and a service was held at 0700," Ugaki recorded.

He was thinking about death, as he so often did. He was not quite ready to join the spirits of his fallen comrades at Yasukuni. "I'm not going to follow them in a hurry. I must make every effort possible until the last in order to break through this national crisis." He wanted to put the best face on the sacrifice of his dead compatriots. He listed all of the American ships sunk by the Japanese navy. "Battleships: 11 sunk, nine damaged. Carriers: 11 sunk, four damaged. . . ."

These figures were exaggerated. The Americans had lost four carriers. Ugaki had been perplexed to read, in intelligence and battle reports, about repeated sightings of American carriers presumed sunk. He chalked it up to American productivity. "The enemy builds and christens second and third generations of carriers, as many as we destroy," he wrote. This sort of reasoning was the source of considerable mirth to the Americans. Halsey's old carrier, the *Enterprise*, had been reported sunk so many times by the Japanese that her sailors now fondly referred to her as "the Galloping Ghost of the Oahu Coast."

Ugaki was wandering into the world of wishful thinking, a universe well populated by senior Japanese military commanders and the many men seeking to please them. In an entry the previous January, he had written, "The imperial headquarters announced last night that USS *Lexington* was considered sunk. . . . This morning's papers took it up with banners. I hope this sunken ship never appears in the paper or on the sea in the future. The navy," Ugaki had reminded himself, "is not supposed to lie."

But the navy did lie. The *Lexington* had not been sunk in January, though she was later destroyed at the Battle of the Coral Sea in May. As always, Ugaki was caught between his tough-minded sense of realism; his need to believe; and his rather mystical fatalism. He clung to his faith in Japan's spiritual superiority. He tried to rise above materialism. He had sent most of his two-month pay bonus for October and November 1942 to his brother, one-third to be used for religious services for his ancestors, two-thirds to be given to schools "as funds for moral training."

And yet, for all of the troops' brave bayonet charges, the Battle of Guadalcanal that autumn of 1942 had been a fiasco. He referred to it as "the place of bitter struggles" and agonized in his diary "about His Majesty's anxiety over the failure of Guadalcanal." On November 26, he had written, "it seems to be hopeless on all sides." He worried that the navy would be dragged into a quagmire by the army. He had, at first, wanted to believe in the army's fight-to-the-death spirit. Early in the battle, he had been moved by the final radio message of a cut-off army garrison: "We shall all die calmly." He could hear the echoes, from Eta Jima days, of Lieutenant Sakuma's doomed paean to duty, penned aboard the sunken submarine *No. 6,* as the oxygen ran out. But now he viewed the army with suspicion, as deceitful and as a dangerous drag on the navy. "We can't believe or trust what the army says," he wrote on November 8.

Ugaki had repeatedly allowed his hopes to rise, only to see them dashed. On Saturday, October 26, he had paced the weather deck of the *Yamato,* watching the full moon, awaiting word of a full-scale assault to capture the U.S. Marines' besieged Henderson Field on Guadalcanal. In the afternoon, he heard that the battlefield had been swept with a torrential rainstorm. Was this a "heaven-sent phenomenon"? Ugaki thought of the ancient battle of Okehazama, in which a Japanese hero achieved a brilliant victory by taking advantage of a rainstorm. Ugaki often composed poems by moonlight. "Beneath the moon," he wrote, "stretches a sea at whose bottom / Lie many ships." Just before midnight, he had been gazing "at the brilliant moon of the fourteenth night" when a messenger handed him an army telegram that read "2100 Banzai!" That was the signal for the capture of the airfield. Thrilled, relieved, Ugaki floated off to his bunk—only to be awakened at 4:50 A.M. and told that the airfield had not been captured after all. In his diary that night he dejectedly wrote, "The autumn full moon was not brilliant and no poem came to my mind. I went to bed early, placing a slight hope on tonight's army assault." That attack, too, failed.

Japan's strategic situation was worsening. The empire was slowly strangling. In his diary, Ugaki recorded shortages of steel, fuel oil, even rice, due to "the shortage of shipping bottoms." Japan had built mega-dreadnoughts for the Decisive Battle but not enough tankers and merchantmen for a prolonged war of attrition. Japan's material and technological inferiority was becoming obvious, though Japanese propagandists did their best to obscure it. Lying was not just a naval sin. In June 1942, the *Japan Times and Advertiser* had informed the Japanese people that the electric light bulb and telephone had both been invented by Japanese scientists in the Meiji era. Likewise, wireless radios and modern explosives were the creation of Japanese inventors. In May 1943, *Nippon Times* would tell its readers that the Japanese had invented the airplane.

By December 1942, Ugaki was no longer writing "the future is filled with brightness," as he had on New Year's Day, or gloating that the generals and admirals of the Allied nations "will soon be looking for some place to hide." A year before, he had casually approved of starving out the American garrison on Corregidor in the Philippines, noting that "starving the enemy has been a capital method of war for ages." At Guadalcanal, Ugaki knew, it was the Japanese who were starving.

Ugaki had been having reveries about the death of his friend and Eta Jima classmate, Adm. Tamon Yamaguchi, commander of a carrier division at Midway, whose flagship, the *Hiryu*, was sunk by American bombs and torpedoes. The story was deeply touching to an officer of Ugaki's sensibility; it was the sort of fate that both men had dreamed about as cadets at Eta Jima. As the *Hiryu* burned and shipped water after the American dive-bomber attacks, Yamaguchi gathered his men on deck, turned with them in the direction of the Imperial Palace, and led them in three cheers for the emperor. He then ordered the men to abandon ship. With his senior staff officer, Cdr. Seiroku Ito, Yamaguchi drank a silent toast. He handed Commander Ito his black cap, as a memento for Mrs. Yamaguchi. Then he turned to the captain of the *Hiryu*, Tomeo Kaku, and said, "There is such a beautiful moon tonight. Shall we watch it as we sink?"

Commander Ito, who survived, had described this scene in a letter to Ugaki. According to Ito's note, Yamaguchi "rejoiced in his good fortune of being able to die in the right place at the right time." In his diary, Ugaki wrote, "Those who can die at the right time and leave their spirit forever are fortunate. While having the heavy responsibility of deciding the fate of the country, I can hardly fulfill my duty by only losing ships and sacrificing many men. It's doubtful whether I can have the most appropriate place to die like Yamaguchi. The saying goes, to die is easy but to live is hard."

Ugaki envied Yamaguchi's death. Admiral Yamamoto reacted more soberly. In letters and conversation, he tried to discourage other captains from going down with their ships. Yamamoto was not unmoved by noble suicide, but he thought it was a waste. He knew that Japan could not afford to lose able commanders like Yamaguchi. During the Sino-Japanese and Russo-Japanese wars at the turn of the century, only one in twenty Eta Jima graduates perished. But as Japanese ships began littering thc bottom of Iron Bottom Sound in the fall of 1942, the Eta Jima death toll was creeping up (and would reach 95 percent of a class by the end of the war).

Ugaki could not help but notice, in the aftermath of Midway and in the months that followed, that his commander-in-chief seemed depressed. Immediately after Midway, Ugaki had cut his hair short, telling colleagues he was mourning the death of his dog, but in his diary he confessed that it was an act of renewal. "I was firmly determined to start over," he wrote. He worried about Yamamoto, who "seemed to be brooding over something and losing spirit."

All the senior officers who survived had been deeply shamed by Midway. Admiral Nagumo, the commander of the carrier strike force, had tried to go down with his ship, but he had been dragged off by his junior officers, who argued that he could not die until his last man had perished fighting. A veil of denial had been dropped over the defeat. To disappoint one's superior, to fail in one's obligation, was unbearable to the duty-bound Japanese. It was more acceptable to cover up and to dissemble. Prime Minister Tojo was not told the extent of the disaster for a week after the battle, and the public was informed that while Japan had lost a carrier, America had lost two. The actual totals were four Japanese carriers sunk to one American carrier. Officers from the sunken ships were confined to base; the sailors were sent back to the South Pacific, not even allowed to see their families.

The effect on Yamamoto was deeply demoralizing. He had failed to deliver the knock-out blow at Pearl Harbor and then lost the element of surprise at Midway. (By late July of 1942, Ugaki had figured out that the Japanese naval code, JN25, had been broken. The encipherment table [or "key register"] was subsequently changed, though American code breakers gradually cracked it again.) By autumn, Yamamoto could see that the Japanese navy was caught in a wasting war that it could not win. As he plotted the navy's moves at Guadalcanal from the distant perch of his flagship at Truk, he had become uncharacteristically tentative, slow to commit ships to battles a more aggressive commander, like Bull Halsey, might have won.

In this lonely, despondent time, Yamamoto had begun to open

himself up a little to Ugaki. The two men lived in close quarters aboard the *Yamato*, and eventually the distance between the extroverted Yamamoto and the introverted Ugaki was bridged by their shared predicament and, possibly, their sense of doom. Yamamoto surprised Ugaki by showing him his own poems, as well as poems by the Emperor Meiji about war and peace and the meaning of life. Yamamoto's favored senior staff officer, the intense, eccentric Captain Kuroshima, was in partial eclipse for designing an overly intricate plan of attack at Midway. Yamamoto began to turn more to Ugaki for tactical advice, as well as poetic communing.

Ugaki's daily existence was stressful, as he struggled for ways to stem the bad tidings from Guadalcanal. Whenever his nerves were on edge, his teeth and gums acted up, and his daily jottings often mention toothache. He complained in his diary of languor from "nicotinism" and briefly quit smoking. Small pleasures and consolations sustained him. Whenever he could, he went bird hunting on remote Pacific islands, with ten new shotguns given him, "with plenty of ammunition," by a friend. He missed his dead wife and dedicated his medals and decorations to her. He rejoiced in being able to wear pajamas after long days at sea. He and the other officers had time in Truk to visit the local "naval restaurant," i.e., bordello.

Ugaki lived in relative comfort. Officers on other ships groused about the "Hotel *Yamato*." The modern leviathan even had air-conditioning in the officers' quarters, though not for the enlisted men. Fuel was short, but not food for the officers: a visitor to Yamamoto's wardroom would be served broiled fresh fish and chilled beer on black lacquer tables. When the fleet secured eighty tons of sugar from Saipan, Ugaki was able to magnanimously suggest that it go to the children of Japan.

The luxuries of the wardroom became hard to enjoy as Japanese troops starved on Guadalcanal. On New Year's Day 1943, the *Yamato*'s orderlies made a mistake and served the traditional *okashiratsuki* (fish with head and tails intact) with the heads pointing in the wrong (i.e., nontraditional) direction. Was it an omen? Yamamoto tried to joke that it looked as if the fish, like the fortunes of war, had changed direction from the year before. Later, Yamamoto wrote a gloomy poem:

Looking back over the year
I feel myself grow tense
At the number of comrades
Who are no more.

Several hundred miles to the south, on that same January 1, 1943, the holiday ration for the remnants of the Japanese army huddled in remote corners of Guadalcanal was only caramels, two crackers, and a bit of grain. Soldiers were doubled over with dysentery, too weak to move as American artillery shells fell around them. The soldiers called Guadalcanal "Starvation Island." One soldier wrote a poem that ended:

... Our rice is gone
Eating roots and grass. ...
Covered with mud from our falls
Blood oozes from our wounds
No cloth to bind our cuts
Flies swarm to the scabs
No strength to brush them away
Fall down and cannot move
How many times I've thought of suicide.

Other soldiers worked out a mortality chart:

He who can rise to his feet	30 days left to live
He who can sit up	20 days left to live
He who must urinate while lying down	3 days left to live
He who cannot speak	2 days left to live
He who cannot blink his eyes	Dead at dawn

The evacuation of Guadalcanal was staged secretly and fairly swiftly by the navy in the first week of February. Of the original 30,000 Japanese soldiers, some 10,000 were rescued. A like number died in combat; another third died of starvation and disease. Very few were taken prisoner. The sailors were aghast when they saw their brothers in arms, their buttocks so emaciated that their anuses were completely exposed, their diarrhea uncontrollable, their only desire a cigarette as they stood in line for the reeking toilets.

In Tokyo, General Headquarters issued a statement that Japanese forces were "advancing by turning." When a prominent journalist giving a lecture at a university suggested that the withdrawal from Guadalcanal was a "strategic retreat," he was issued a warning by the Special Higher Police, the Thought Police. At the Imperial Palace, the emperor had worried that Guadalcanal might signal the beginning of the end, but as usual he gave off contradictory signals and pressed for more sacrifice. When Guadalcanal fell, he demanded a new offensive.

At Truk, Yamamoto and Ugaki planned a massive air attack on the advancing Americans. Halsey's forces were beginning to move up the Solomons. Yamamoto was short of carriers, but he still had island airfields. There was a serious catch: the Japanese were running out of planes and, especially, trained pilots. In 1942, the Japanese navy had lost almost 1,000 warplanes. Within a year, the navy would lose another 6,000—three times the number the navy started out with. Japanese factories were at this stage of the war still cranking out planes by the thousands, but the Americans were building them five times as rapidly. Yamamoto's superbly trained front-line pilots were joining the spirits of their ancestors at Yasukuni Shrine, and Imperial General Headquarters was forced to replace them with neophytes. The commander-in-chief was shocked to discover that of the latest batch of sixty pilots to reach Japan's forward base at Rabaul, only sixteen had ever flown a Zero before.

Yamamoto was tired of trying to direct battles from hundreds of miles away. On April 3, he and Ugaki and their staff left the comforts of their flagship at Truk to fly to Rabaul, there to direct a massive air attack on the Americans called *I-Go*, Operation I. Rabaul was the anchor of Japanese defenses in the South Pacific. The island bastion, with a superb natural harbor, had been strengthened with masses of poured concrete and five new airfields, but it was a pestilential hole. Misty squalls and smoky effusions from active volcanoes darkened the tropical light. Downpours turned the ash into goopy mud that mired trucks and swallowed cars. The heat was wet and deep, day and night.

Ugaki dealt with the oppressive atmosphere by entering his Zen mode, writing poems to his beloved Tomoko, on the third anniversary of her death:

> *Her beautiful face, like a flower out of season,*
> *Can never return, gone forever.*
> *Yet I cannot ever forget her*
> *Even in the middle of War.*

Camped in a hillside bungalow, Ugaki continued to draw closer to his commander-in-chief, who showed him his book of calligraphy and poems. Ugaki remarked on Yamamoto's "minute" handwriting—Ugaki, the scholar, used superior brushwork—but he was glad of the intimacy with his revered chief. Gone was the forty-piece ship's band outside the wardroom at lunch and the black lacquer trays. Yamamoto's orderlies tried to whip up something from the local foodstuffs—sea turtle sukiyaki, coconuts, vine of squash. "Quite tasty," pronounced Ugaki.

Malaria and dengue fever were rampant at Rabaul. Ugaki's mosquito must have bitten him shortly after he stepped off the plane, because by April 11, he was reporting in his diary, "first day of fever . . . I won't be beaten by dengue fever or whatever it may be!" Vomiting, weak, he was hospitalized the next day. Within five days, his body was covering with fever pustules.

The others were similarly stricken. Jinichi Kusaka, the theater commander, had been laid low by dysentery. Yamamoto himself seemed tired, ill, his hands shaking, his feet so swollen he was changing his shoes several times a day. Weather delays slowed Operation I, but waves of Japanese planes finally began seeking their targets on April 7. They returned, their numbers badly depleted, with the usual outlandish claims (they did sink one destroyer, USS *Aaron Ward*, in a bombing attack witnessed by a fresh young PT boat skipper, Lt. (j.g.) John F. Kennedy).

On April 17, Ugaki, his face and body covered with fever blisters, conferred with local commanders and got into a shouting match with one. Ugaki had criticized the commanders for failing to lead from the front. Naturally, it behooved Ugaki and Yamamoto to set an example.

Yamamoto had already decided that he wanted to visit an army camp full of battered survivors from Guadalcanal. The local air commander tried to dissuade them from flying to a small island south of Bougainville on April 18. Too dangerous, he said. His own plane had nearly been shot down by marauding American fighters on a similar trip two months earlier. Yamamoto ignored the warning.

On April 13, the C-in-C's Staff Officer for Chess, Commander Watanabe, personally carried the admirals' itinerary over to Eighth Fleet headquarters, instructing that it be messaged to Bougainville by courier. The communications officer said it had to be sent by radio. Watanabe objected: what if the message was intercepted and decoded by the Americans? No chance of that, replied the signals officer. The Japanese navy code had been changed on April 1.

Yamamoto's itinerary spelled out the precise time the C-in-C and his staff would leave and arrive, the type of plane they would fly in, and even the number and plane models of their six fighter escorts. The message was sent out by Eighth Fleet HQ late in the day on April 13.

It was intercepted by U.S. intelligence almost instantly. The Americans could not read the encrypted message, at least not right away. But they knew the cable was significant because of the variety and number of addressees. At Pearl Harbor, the code breakers—the same ones who had broken enough of the Japanese code to give the Americans the edge at Midway—went to work in their basement hive. Laboring through the night, they teased out bits of code (some not too difficult: Rabaul was "RR") and suddenly realized what they were deciphering. Marine Col. Alva "Red" Lasswell, the lead linguist-cryptographer, looked up from his work sheet in the early morning hours and cried out, "We've hit the jackpot!"

CINCPAC's intelligence chief, Cdr. Edwin Layton, was admitted to Adm. Nimitz's office shortly after 8:00 A.M. on April 14. He handed the message to Nimitz and remarked, "Our old friend Yamamoto." Nimitz's blond eyebrows raised. "Do we try to get him?" asked CINCPAC. Layton answered that Yamamoto was "unique," irreplaceable. Nimitz considered for a moment. "It's down in Halsey's bailiwick. If there's a way, he'll find it. All right, we'll try it."

Bougainville was 300 miles from Henderson Field at Guadalcanal. P-38 fighters, equipped with extra fuel tanks, could do the job, as long as Yamamoto was on time. The commander-in-chief of the Combined Fleet had a reputation for punctuality. Halsey did worry about compromising America's code-breaking ability. If the ambush succeeded, the Japanese would recognize that the sudden appearance of fighter planes boring in on Yamamoto's plane was not a coincidence. But Halsey lived for the main chance. He sent CINCPAC a can-do message. After checking with Washington (there is no record of formal approval by FDR, who was traveling, or from the Pentagon, probably for reasons of plausible deniability), Nimitz wired Halsey: "Good hunting."

Admiral Ugaki arose at five on the morning of April 18. The sky was clear and "the birds sang pleasantly in the trees," he recorded in his diary. Perfect flying weather, for a change. Ugaki donned a new green khaki uniform. There had been some talk of wearing the usual navy whites, but Ugaki felt that army green was more appropriate for reviewing the troops. "I looked gallant," he wrote. The C-in-C was also in his new green uniform. "It suited him fairly well," commented Ugaki.

Yamamoto and Ugaki were flying in separate planes, twin-engine bombers knows as Bettys by the Americans. The Betty bombers, recalled Ugaki's pilot, PO Hiroshi Hayashi, were called "one-shot lighters" because they "went up like a torch" when hit. Ugaki handed his sword to a staff officer and climbed into his seat, right behind the pilot's. The planes roared off, exactly on time, at 6:00 A.M. Ugaki could see Yamamoto's plane, close to his own plane's wingtip, and the six fighter escorts hovering protectively nearby.

Still recovering from his dengue fever, lulled by the throb of the engines, Ugaki dozed off. He later recalled being handed a note at about 7:30, telling him that the plane would be landing in fifteen minutes. According to Hayashi, Ugaki was still asleep when he put the plane into a sharp dive. Hayashi was following Yamamoto's plane, which had suddenly banked down toward the jungle below. "What's the matter?" Ugaki demanded. "Must be some mistake," answered the navigator.

A moment later the pilot spotted the first tracer bullet streaking by the cockpit. Afraid his own plane would break up if he dove too hard, pilot Hayashi eased up on the throttle. Ugaki, suddenly awake and alert, ordered Hayashi to follow the commander-in-chief's plane. Inside the bomber was pandemonium. The crew was wrestling open the gun ports and blasting away with machine guns at the American P-38s, which suddenly seemed everywhere. Ugaki estimated two dozen of them; the actual number was sixteen. The Betty bucked and weaved to get free of its pursuers. Ugaki desperately searched for Yamamoto's plane. He saw it—spurting black smoke and flame, about 4,000 meters ahead, flying just above the treetops. "My God!" cried Ugaki, gripping the shoulder of an air staff officer sitting at a chart table beside him. Ugaki's plane jinked again. When Ugaki looked back, all he could see was a dark smudge of smoke above the jungle.

Ugaki could see dogfights all around him, Zeros and P-38 Lightnings twisting and diving and climbing in acrobatic display. One P-38 made a rising half-turn and then swung at Ugaki's plane, cannon and machine guns blazing. Ugaki could feel the Betty shudder and vibrate as the bullets came smashing in. He looked over at the staff officer beside him—dead, sprawled across the chart table.

Pilot Hayashi took his damaged bomber, screaming at full throttle, down to the jungle tops, then over the wave tops as it raced out to sea. Suddenly, losing control as bullets ripped through his rudder, he tried to pull the nose up. The plane banked, a wing clipped the top of a wave . . .

Ugaki had stiffened his limbs, bracing for the impact. Ripped from his seat, he could feel seawater close around him. "This is the end of Ugaki," he thought to himself. His mind went blank. Darkness . . .

Then light, as he bobbed, gasping, to the surface. The wing of the bomber was jutting perpendicular to the water, burning furiously. The rest of the plane had vanished, along with its crew. Ugaki looked around him. The shoreline seemed about 200 yards away, so he began to swim, very slowly, breaststroking. A box floated by and Ugaki reached out to grab it. Nothing happened. He looked down his arm to see his hand bleeding and bent at a grotesque angle. With his other arm he pulled the box to him and used it as a float. Suddenly, he saw another man, another survivor, swimming furiously toward the shore. "Hey!" Ugaki called out, but the man didn't seem to notice him and kept swimming. The man was Petty Officer Hayashi, the pilot. He was miraculously uninjured.

As Ugaki neared the shore, the current caught him and he was swept along the beach. Ugaki felt strangely tranquil; he allowed himself to drift. Four Japanese soldiers appeared. One began firing his rifle at Ugaki. "Tell them to stop!" Ugaki cried at Hayashi, who was ahead of him in the surf. Hayashi managed to get the soldiers to put down their rifles, and one of the men swam to retrieve Ugaki. Spotting the braid on Ugaki's uniform, he called out, "He's a staff officer!" The soldier helped Ugaki into shore.

Ugaki managed to stagger along the beach for a distance, but collapsed and had to be carried on a door. He was taken to an officers' sickbay in a coconut grove. It was there that Yamamoto's grief-stricken staff officer, Commander Watanabe, found him later in the day. Ugaki was badly hurt—a severed artery and compound wrist fracture, bad bruises on his face and body. The doctors were pumping him with injections to ward off infection. Ugaki was able to crack a feeble macho joke with Watanabe. The injections were enough to cure his "R," he joked (navy slang for gonorrhea, *rimbyo* in Japanese). But when he saw Watanabe's eyes fill with tears, he told him, "The C.-in-C.'s 4.5 miles northeast of Point Camau. Get there quickly." In his feverish state, Ugaki had confused Point Camau, in far-off Indonesia, with Point Moila, near where Yamamoto's plane had gone down.

It took three separate search parties and two days more to find the wreckage of Admiral Yamamoto's plane deep in the jungle. It was said that the commander-in-chief was found sitting erect in his seat, his white-gloved hand on the pommel of his sword, his face at rest. This seems improbable for a corpse left moldering and exposed to wildlife for more than two days in the jungle, but Japan needed its myths, especially at this stage of the war. One report from the search party probably was true: soldiers found a wad of pure white toilet paper, a commodity in short supply, in his uniform pocket. "You get to use good paper when you get to be C.-in-C.," said one of the search party.

The first P-38 returning to Henderson Field after shooting down the most famous admiral in Japan did barrel rolls. POP GOES THE WEASEL was the cable sent to Halsey at Noumea. APRIL 18 SEEMS TO BE OUR DAY. It was the first anniversary of General Doolittle's air raid on Tokyo. When Admiral Halsey read the message the next morning in the conference room, Adm. Kelly Turner, the chief of amphibious operations, "whooped and applauded," Halsey recalled in his memoir. Halsey immediately slipped into his familiar role. "Hold on, Kelly," he interrupted. "What's so good about it? I'd hoped to lead that scoundrel up Pennsylvania Avenue in chains, with the rest of you kicking him where it would do most good!" But then Halsey reverted to competent naval officer. He ordered that the news be withheld from the press, lest the Japanese figure out that their code had been broken.

On May 21, the Japanese finally announced that Yamamoto had "met a gallant death on board his plane in an encounter with the enemy in the course of directing overall operations on the front line." Yamamoto's ashes were divided, half sent to his ancestral home, half buried alongside Japan's other great naval hero, Admiral Togo. A state funeral was held at Hibiya Park in the center of Tokyo on June 5, the same day of the same month as Togo's funeral nine years previously. As a million people lined the streets, staff officer Watanabe, bearing Yamamoto's sword, walked slowly behind the army caisson carrying his ashes.

Ugaki blamed himself, unreasonably and bitterly, for Yamamoto's death. He had told Watanabe that he was responsible; his diary does not make clear why, but perhaps he regretted urging Yamamoto to visit the front lines. Ugaki believed the story that Yamamoto had been found in the wreckage sitting erect, "in a state of great dignity," he wrote in a paean to his C-in-C. "He must really have been superhuman." Despite his earlier and correct guess that the Americans had broken the Japanese naval code at Midway, Ugaki determined that the shoot-down of Yamamoto had been "sheer luck." His

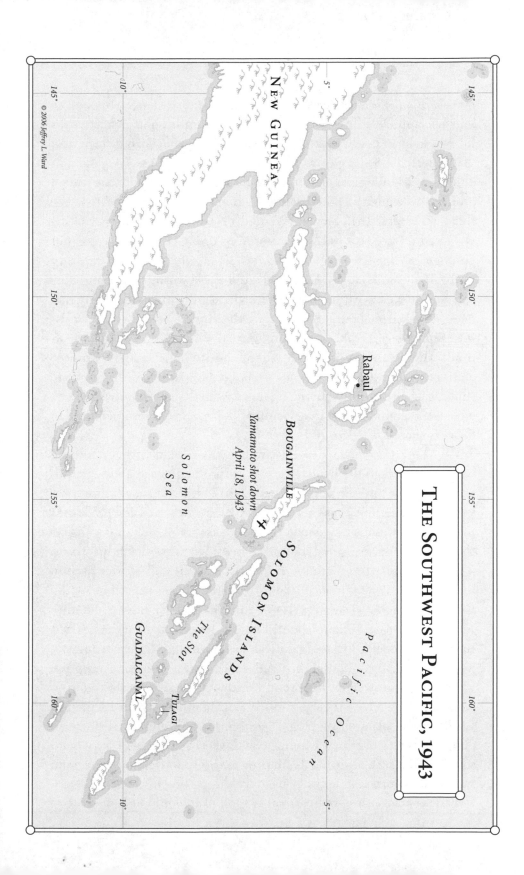

© 2006 Jeffrey L. Ward

NEW GUINEA

Rabaul

BOUGAINVILLE

Yamamoto shot down
April 18, 1943

Solomon Sea

SOLOMON ISLANDS

The Slot

GUADALCANAL

Tulagi

Pacific Ocean

THE SOUTHWEST PACIFIC, 1943

own survival he considered to be a miracle from God. Suppose he had not unbuckled his sword or worn Wellington half-boots, which he was able to easily kick off, instead of his usual formal lace-ups? "God must have done everything he could to save me," Ugaki concluded. Yet fate was so perverse. He had wanted to die for his leader, and yet his leader had died, while he had lived. Ugaki tried to make sense of it all: "I should be resigned to my fate, deeming it God's will, and do my best to live and serve to repay God by carrying out revenge."

Swathed in bandages, Ugaki dictated these words to a young officer, Ensign Kenzo Ebina. A graduate of Tokyo University, Ebina had been summoned aboard the *Musashi*, the *Yamato*'s slightly newer sister ship, where Ugaki was recuperating. Ebina had attended a famous middle school in Tokyo where the students learned Chinese characters and to write in ancient Japanese, the classical language that Ugaki used. Ebina found Ugaki in a small stateroom with a cot, a couch, and a table, in "Flag Country," the quarters reserved for flag officers aboard the *Musashi*.

Ebina was nervous when he saw Ugaki, or what little of him he could see through the bandages. The ensign had heard all the stories about Ugaki, how the admiral never smiled but instead wore a severe, expressionless mask. "I will speak, so you write down," Ugaki instructed, without any exchange of pleasantries. For many nights thereafter, Ebina returned to Ugaki's bedside to take down his words. The call usually came around midnight; Ebina did not ever dare to undress, lest he be unready. Ugaki complained that that none of the Eta Jima graduates could write in the classical Japanese style anymore. He seemed to appreciate Ebina's talents as his scrivener. Over time, Ebina decided that Ugaki was not the severe figure of legend, no martinet of command, but rather a warm, even kindly figure. Ugaki told Ebina about his proud family, his ten close relatives who were army or navy officers, and his family ethos, which seemed to Ebina to be admirably "frugal, strong, and manly." As Ebina, an eighty-six-year-old man when interviewed in 2004, recalled Ugaki some six decades after his death, he clearly felt affection for a man whom he regarded as a father figure.

Ebina's memories are heartwarming, but it would be a mistake to think of Ugaki as a sweet, avuncular figure as he lay recovering from his wounds in the summer of 1943. When Ugaki dictated to Ebina that he would "serve to repay God by carrying out revenge," he meant it. Vengeance was a sacred duty for a warrior who had been shamed by defeat. In premodern Japanese society, the murder of a lord or father called for a vendetta—*katakiuchi.* The classically educated Ugaki knew all the ancient legends, like the saga of the Soga brothers, who took seventeen years to track down and murder their father's killer. Ugaki knew that he had nothing like seventeen years left to him, but he was determined to avenge Yamamoto's death, no matter how many young men, Japanese or American, had to die.

CHAPTER FIVE

THE DEPARTMENT OF DIRTY TRICKS

Pondering "the Oriental mindset"

BILL HALSEY saw himself as a roving sea dog, not a shore-based military theater commander. His one fixed ambition was to lead a fleet against the enemy, preferably the entire fleet in a climactic battle, just as he had gamed in war college days, just as Nelson had done against the French and Spanish at Trafalgar in an earlier age. He would have to be patient. As commander, South Pacific, Halsey was required to be everything but a sea commander. From his island base at Noumea far from the front, Halsey had to play the role of diplomat/politician, strategist, and manager, with only occasional forays forward. Blunt, impetuous, careless about details, he was not particularly well suited to any of those roles. Yet by sheer force of personality and a peculiar mixture of good-heartedness and ruthlessness, he somehow managed to carry off the role of generalissimo. Halsey spent 1943 and the first six months of 1944 blustering about "killing Japs" while trying to figure out smarter ways to defeat them without getting too many Americans killed. Much of his time was devoted to engaging in the sort of factional politics that are inevitable in great undertakings involving competing philosophies and egos.

There were days in the Pacific War when, it seemed, divided command was a bigger threat than the Japanese fleet to the American war effort. Admiral Halsey was not alone in trying to dislodge the Japanese from their South Pacific bastions. A few hundred miles to the west, Gen. Douglas MacArthur was trying to do the same.

Though resigned to a warrior's death on Corregidor, MacArthur had escaped on a PT boat in March 1942. President Roosevelt valued him more as a commander than as a martyr, and he wanted MacArthur to survive in order to rally an army that could one day recapture the Philippines. MacArthur had responded with a burst of inspiring, if egocentric, rhetoric: "I shall return!" he had vowed from Brisbane, Australia, shortly after his escape. As attentive to public relations as he was to fighting, MacArthur had the words printed on matchbooks. Slowly and with great difficulty, MacArthur had set about fulfilling his vow, pushing a poorly equipped and green army through the jungles of New Guinea, a morass as unwelcoming as Guadalcanal. MacArthur's drive roughly paralleled Halsey's to the east. In Washington, the top brass drew a line between them; Halsey's command was SOPAC (South Pacific) and MacArthur's was SOWES-PAC (Southwest Pacific). SOPAC was actually a subdivision of Admiral Nimitz's larger area of responsibility, CINCPOA (Commander-in-Chief, Pacific Ocean Area), meaning that Halsey was Nimitz's subordinate and thus not MacArthur's equal. Cooperation between MacArthur and Halsey was not, at first, the order of the day.

Halsey was navy, MacArthur was army; they viewed each other with suspicion, if not active disdain.* Halsey, like most navy men, thought MacArthur was a fraud, given to grandiose declarations while enjoying the comforts of his hotel in Sydney, Australia. "The Commander-in-Chief has taken the field . . ." is how a typical press release would begin. MacArthur was actually a military genius, as he had proved in the First World War and would prove again in the Second, but he made Halsey seem almost humble by comparison. When Halsey, chronically short of airpower, asked to borrow some of MacArthur's planes to cut off the Japanese evacuation of Guadalcanal in February 1943, MacArthur sent a typically condescending

---

*In this respect, the Americans and Japanese were alike; the Japanese army and navy were so distant that admirals and generals addressed one another as "excellency," the formal honorific used for ambassadors from foreign lands.

message demanding to know Halsey's true intentions. Halsey wisely declined to take the bait, grumbling in a private letter to Admiral Nimitz, "I refuse to get into a controversy with him or any self-advertising son of a bitch."

But Halsey was too generous a spirit—and too much of a kindred soul—to dislike MacArthur forever, especially after he met him. The admiral and the general finally held a peace parley in Brisbane, Australia, in April 1943, and Halsey took an almost instant shine to his interservice rival. "I have seldom met a man who makes a quicker, stronger, more favorable impression," wrote Halsey afterward. Halsey was struck by the youthfulness of the sixty-three-year-old general. "His hair was jet black; his eyes were clear; his carriage was erect. If he had been wearing civilian clothes, I would have known at once he was a soldier."

MacArthur decided that he liked Halsey, too, especially after Halsey stood up to him. During one of their typical jurisdictional disputes over control of an airfield, MacArthur became offended by what he perceived as the meddling of Admiral Nimitz. Under the bifurcated command structure of the military, Admiral Nimitz, the navy's Pacific commander and Halsey's boss, reported to the overall navy commander, Adm. Ernest King. MacArthur reported to the Army chief of staff, Gen. George Marshall (leaving the conflict-averse president of the United States, Franklin Roosevelt, to referee). While Halsey was content with the title COMSOPAC (commander, South Pacific), MacArthur insisted on CINCSOWPAC (Commander-in-Chief, Southwest Pacific) in order to be a CINC, commander-in-chief, on the same level as Admiral Nimitz, who was CINCPAC-CINCPOA (Commander-in-Chief, Pacific Fleet and Pacific Ocean Area). MacArthur was exceptionally intolerant of any attempt by Nimitz to tell him what to do. MacArthur always made a point of mispronouncing Nimitz's name, "*Nee*-mitz."

When MacArthur huffed that "Neemitz" had offended his personal honor, Halsey had heard enough. "General," he said, "you're putting your personal honor over the welfare of the United States." This blunt impertinence shocked MacArthur's staff, and momentarily set back MacArthur. "My God, Bull," said MacArthur, the only man who could get away with addressing Halsey as "Bull" to his face, "you can't really mean that." But Halsey obviously did, and MacArthur backed off. MacArthur ultimately thought so highly of Halsey that when the navy, grudgingly, decided to provide MacArthur with his own fleet for amphibious operations, MacArthur asked Halsey if he would command the fleet. "How about *you*, Bill? If you come with me, I'll make you a greater man than Nelson ever dreamed of being."

Halsey wanted nothing more than to be the next Nelson, but he was too busy with his own South Pacific command to come over to MacArthur's theater. Halsey's advance northward in the summer and fall of 1943 after driving the Japanese from Guadalcanal was threatened by the Japanese bastion at Rabaul. The well-protected harbor, fortified by concrete aircraft bunkers, anchored Japanese forces in the Bismarck Archipelago, the strategic islands to the northeast of Australia. It was a formidable obstacle to the two-pronged American offensive in the South Pacific.

In November 1943, as Halsey's forces were clinging to a beachhead in Bougainville, a hundred miles from Rabaul, the code breakers in Pearl Harbor informed Halsey that a good portion of the Japanese Combined Fleet, including eight heavy cruisers, was bound for Rabaul, along with several hundred carrier-based planes. Their commander was Adm. Takeo Kurita, the man who had commanded the two battleships that shelled Henderson Field that heart-stopping night in October 1942. Kurita's task force was clearly planning to bombard the fragile American advance at Bougainville.

At the time, Halsey was at his forward base, Camp Crocodile at Guadalcanal. COMSOPAC and his staff anxiously debated what to do. Halsey had two carriers at his disposal, the old *Saratoga* and the new, but light, *Princeton*. As usual, his instinct was to strike first, to hit the Japanese before they could hit him. But he was fearful that the carriers would be trapped in the confined waters near Rabaul and sunk, while their airplanes were decimated by Rabaul's heavy defenses. "I sincerely expected both air groups would be cut to pieces and both carriers to be stricken, if not lost (I tried not to remember that my son Bill was aboard one of them)." Halsey's son, William F. III, a young Princeton grad, was a lieutenant, junior grade, aboard the *Saratoga*.

Halsey's chief of staff, Adm. Robert Carney, knew what few suspected, that Halsey was actually a very emotional man, and he was not altogether surprised when he found the admiral crying as he signed the order to attack. "He knew he was signing the death warrant of a hell of a lot of people. Yet it had to be done," Carney recalled. Halsey tried to be stoic about it. "Let 'er go!" he growled, as he handed Carney the signed dispatch.

The American attack was a surprising success. Ducking through a hole in the clouds, evading Japanese air cover, the dive-bombers and torpedo bombers from the two American carriers surprised the Japanese fleet at their moorings in Rabaul's Simpson Harbor, badly damaging four cruisers. The Americans only lost five of ninety-two planes.

The bold surprise attack was classic Halsey, and it helped cement his reputation as a hell-for-leather leader. It also helped quiet persistent grumbling in Washington about his somewhat careless ways and poor staff work. Word of Halsey's perhaps excessive informality had filtered back to Nimitz's Pacific Fleet headquarters in Hawaii and to the navy's overall commander, Admiral King, in Washington. Halsey, it was said, was having a martini or two before dinner and draining scotch bottles at parties. Halsey's officers adopted an air of irreverence—Halsey was

The Bull

teased as "Sir Butch" after the British gave him an honorary Order of the British Empire—and generally joined in the fun. At one medal awards ceremony, described in Halsey's memoirs as a "picnic," Halsey had to hold up a drunken New Zealand corvette captain as he pinned on a Navy Cross for ramming a Japanese submarine.

Admiral King was no slacker himself when it came to wine and women. Other naval officers learned not to have their wives sit beside him at dinner. "You ought to be very suspicious of anyone who won't take a drink or doesn't like women," King declared, sounding a lot like Halsey. But unlike Halsey, King was secretive and suspicious and had a fierce temper. "He was even-tempered," his daughter once observed, "always angry." Intolerant of sloppiness, King and Halsey had tangled over the slightly ridiculous issue of uniforms. King disliked navy whites (because they made officers easy targets), navy blue and gold (too gaudy and elitist), and navy khakis (too much like the army's). So he designed a dull gray uniform, which Halsey hated and refused to wear, on the grounds that it made naval officers look like "bus drivers."

A breaking point had come in January 1943, when the secretary of the navy, Frank Knox, had visited Halsey's headquarters at Noumea. Halsey's then chief of staff, Capt. Miles Browning, was brilliant but erratic. A champion carouser, after performing admirably at the Battle of Midway he had been caught in bed with the wife of a marine, who happened to be a champion boxer and cruelly beat up Browning. Intemperate in most ways and at most times, Browning somehow insulted Knox on the navy secretary's visit to SOPAC headquarters. Over Halsey's objections, Browning was relieved and a staff secretary with good political skills—Harold Stassen, the young ex-governor of Minnesota—was sent out to try to bring a semblance of order to Halsey's paperwork. Admiral Carney was imposed on Halsey as his new chief of staff in July 1943.

Robert "Mick" Carney had not wanted the job.* "It was a bitter pill," recalled Carney's daughter, Betty Taussig. Carney had com-

---

*"Mick" was his Annapolis nickname, given to him because of his Irish heritage. Annapolis nicknames were crude. Two Italian-Americans in Carney's class who later became admirals were known as "Wop," and a classmate who had accidentally shot his father at the age of four was called "Bagdad." In a 1995 speech, author Herman Wouk said he had used Carney as his model for Pug Henry, his fictional hero in *The Winds of War*.

mand of a cruiser off Guadalcanal and hopes of a bigger front-line sea command. He did not want to be ashore as the detail man for someone who had little use for detail. At first, Carney and Halsey were cool and distant. Carney liked formality; he dined alone off of silver, served by a marine orderly standing at attention. But he also had "a touch of Little Rascal," recalled his daughter. He liked to sing naughty navy ballads and strum the guitar, and he fancied himself a Viking and wished his mother had named him "Siegfried." Carney was intelligent, worldly, and well traveled. He could see that Halsey's bluster concealed shrewdness and sound instinct. And he was surprised and touched by Halsey's sensitivity.

Inevitably, he was drawn in by Halsey's charisma. Before long, Carney would be the ringmaster of a staff that was calling itself "the Department of Dirty Tricks." The staff prided itself on a loose, nonbureaucratic, freewheeling approach, though Carney observed that when the debate got too raucous, Halsey would quietly raise a finger, and the joking around would stop.

The Department of Dirty Tricks spent much of 1943 pondering what Carney called "the Oriental mindset." They found it "baffling" at first. "We couldn't put ourselves into the minds of the Japanese," recalled Carney. Japanese decision making seemed "irrational" and thus difficult to predict. Halsey's staff concluded that the Japanese just "thought differently." They seemed to favor complex, elaborate operations that, once started, could not be stopped or altered. "There could be no such thing as turning back once committed. Whether this was considered as cowardice or a violation of the samurai code, whatever it was, I don't know," recalled Carney.

The Japanese mind-set was puzzling to Carney, perhaps, because American soldiers were typically more willing to improvise or start over. Landed on the wrong beach on D-Day, Gen. Theodore Roosevelt, Jr., would famously declare, "We'll start the war from right here." But the Japanese were loath to concede that things might not be going according to plan. That would be tantamount to failing in one's obligation to headquarters, an unthinkable loss of face. So when things went wrong, as they often did in combat, the Japanese instinct was to go forward blindly, or sometimes to break down altogether.

Japanese stubbornness and inflexibility presented an opportunity, Halsey's staff eventually realized. The Department of Dirty Tricks began designing "trap operations," to lure the Japanese out with false signals and then ambush them. Using bogus radio traffic and even sound effects (like the clank of anchor chains being raised), Halsey's communications staffers pretended that ships were sailing and planes flying, in order to force the Japanese to lunge in the wrong direction. The feints and fakes did not always or even usually work, but they seemed to give a lift to the Department of Dirty Tricks.

There was one Halsey staffer "who came close to thinking like a Jap," Carney recalled, "and this was Captain Marion ['Mike'] Cheek." Cheek was the staff intelligence officer. "He sometimes came up with what seemed to be irrational conclusions which very frequently turned out to be correct," wrote Carney, "but he had a mentality which approximated the Oriental mentality in some ways and couldn't be rationalized." Cheek had won a Navy Cross for his intelligence work in the Philippines at the beginning of the war. A quiet, dour man, he did not fit in with the rollicking types in the Department of Dirty Tricks. He rarely spoke up at meetings, preferring to pass cryptic notes to Chief of Staff Carney. Halsey never warmed to his intelligence officer, with unfortunate consequences to be seen.

Halsey liked more voluble, self-confident officers. Though an Annapolis man, and very loyal to his alma mater, Halsey was not one of those "ring-knockers" who thought all naval wisdom resided on the banks of the Severn River, and that all reservists who had graduated from officer candidate school were hopeless landlubbers. There were not nearly enough "regular navy" career officers to fill even the most important billets in the mushrooming wartime naval service. Halsey welcomed the reservists—if they were resourceful and bold. Halsey had a particular soft spot for smooth Ivy Leaguers, who reminded him of his aristocratic St. Anthony Hall brethren at the University of Virginia. Halsey's staff aide, Bill Kitchell, like his own son, Bill, was a polished Princeton man. Halsey especially liked the slightly older Ivy Leaguers, men out of the law firms and investment houses of Wall Street who had been made into air combat intelligence officers under a program started by Artemis "Di" Gates, a Yale man who had helped create one of the first navy flying squadrons of World War I, the Yale Unit. Two of Halsey's air combat intelligence officers—John Lawrence and John Marshall—were Harvard men; a third, Carl Solberg, had been a Rhodes Scholar at Oxford.

Smart, inventive strategy was crucial to Halsey's success in the South Pacific. No one is sure who first came up with the "leap-frogging" or "island-skipping" idea. Victory has a thousand fathers, and this idea had been rattling around war colleges as early as 1940. But the "by-passing strategy," as Halsey called it, was an idea that saved thousands of lives and shortened a very long war. Rather than stage more bloody frontal assaults against die-hard Japanese troops, Halsey and his Department of Dirty Tricks began to think about end-running and isolating Japanese garrisons. Japanese forces could not stand to be cut off from headquarters. If they were, as Admiral Carney put it, they simply "withered on the vine." The by-pass strategy was first used by Halsey in mid-1943 when his forces simply went around a Japanese garrison as they worked up the Solomon Islands chain toward the Japanese bastion at Rabaul. Ultimately, the solution to Rabaul was not to storm it, but to blockade it and leave it to starve.

By Christmas of 1943, it was obvious that Halsey's command of U.S. forces in the South Pacific had been a triumph. The fighting was not over, but the Japanese were beaten in the Solomons. True, they were not giving up easily. In most battles, no more than one out of 100 Japanese surrendered. Halsey and his staff were hardened, if not dehumanized, by Japanese fanaticism. One way to deal with death is to belittle it. Just as the Japanese samurai warrior pretended to be carefree in the face of his own demise, Halsey and his men put on a mask of indifference to the carnage all around them. In such moments, there was no cultural divide between the Americans and Japanese; they were all debased.

Admiral Carney was cultivated. Yet he told reporters that "it would seem to be an unnecessary refinement to worry too much about" the sinking of a Japanese hospital ship because "they have been undoubtedly used for illegal purposes" and because "they are caring for Nips which we failed to kill in the first attempt." Carney was not wrong about the bogus Japanese hospital ships; an American destroyer stopped one to find it stuffed with 1,500 fresh infantry and ammunition. Halsey professed to delight in sinking Japanese barges full of troops, who on a few occasions were shot in the water. "It was rich, rewarding, beautiful slaughter," Halsey later wrote. During the war, he often ended his dispatches, KEEP 'EM DYING. How can one reconcile such bloodthirstiness with Halsey's better side, his sentimentality and warmth? Possibly, Halsey needed to treat the enemy as subhuman in order to keep on signing orders that were death warrants for them and for his own men as well. Or perhaps, not unlike his Japanese counterparts, he was a man whose human contradictions were sharpened and laid bare by the exigencies of war.

At Christmastime, Halsey went to San Francisco, then on to Washington to consult with his superiors about the war and his next move. He saw his wife, Fan, for the first time in sixteen months. It was not a completely happy reunion. Halsey's aides were stunned when Halsey interrupted a story she was telling and she barked, "Shut up!" One of Halsey's staffers, marine Gen. Bill Riley, laughed, "I never would have believed it, but there *is* somebody who dares to tell him to shut up." Halsey's comment was "Little did he know." Fan had continued to deteriorate. Her mania and their bickering now made it difficult for Halsey to be with her, even for short periods.

Halsey was still nurturing his true ambition, to go back to sea as commander of what the navy was calling its "Big Blue Fleet." American shipyards had been busy, stamping out a new class of large, fast carriers that would spearhead the drive across the Central Pacific and ultimately, it was believed, engage and defeat the Japanese Combined Fleet. This was War Plan Orange updated. In the prewar strategy games, the Japanese fleet was Orange, the American fleet was Blue, hence the Big Blue Fleet. Battleships were still essential components of the fleet—the "Gun Club," the fraternity of battleship commanders who still held considerable sway among the top brass, had not given up its dream of a climactic shoot-out—but carriers were now the most potent weapon, and Halsey wanted to lead them.

*   *   *

The U.S. Navy needed thousands of new recruits to man this armada. Between December 1941 and the end of 1944, the navy added 286,000 officers, less than one percent of whom had attended Annapolis. The reservists were almost all college grads, partly because the navy required technical know-how and partly because the officer corps demanded a certain social stratum. Still, most of the new officers had never stepped on a boat bigger than the Staten Island Ferry or more warlike than a yacht. Breaking in these landlubbers placed a great burden on the old hands of the regular navy. By and large, the reservists performed astonishingly well—indeed, in many cases, better than the Annapolis men, who sometimes were a little too respectful of hierarchy and showed less initiative than the citizen soldiers. Fortunately, there were Naval Academy graduates who could handle the inexperienced, if feisty, reservists with aplomb and skill. One of these officers was Ernest Evans.

The New Year 1944 found Evans, now Commander Evans, aboard a brand-new destroyer, headed west in the great American armada sweeping across the Central Pacific. After the debacle at the Battle of the Java Sea in February 1942, Evans had been given command of his creaky old four-piper, the *Alden*—but sent back east, far from the action in the Pacific. Before joining the scrap heap, the obsolete *Alden* served her final days seeking, though not finding, German U-boats in the Caribbean. Through 1942 and the first half of 1943, Evans had done his duty, but he had been bored and restless to return to the fight. He got his chance in the fall of 1943, when he was given command of USS *Johnston*, DD-557, a new *Fletcher*-class destroyer.

The *Johnston* was Evans's idea of a "fighting ship." The new destroyers were a testament to American industrial capacity. Between February 1942 and June 1944, American shipyards built, launched, and made ready for war 175 *Fletcher*-class destroyers. Long (376 feet), fast, and sleek, the destroyers were still known as "tin cans" because of their thin $3/8$ inch steel-plate hulls. They could be sunk by a single shell from a cruiser or a battleship, though their thin skins proved to be a blessing in disguise when struck by a giant armor-piercing shell. Rather than detonate, the shells would pass right on through. Destroyers were workhorses for antisubmarine patrol and antiaircraft defense, and their ten torpedoes, each packing a high-explosive charge, could be lethal to larger ships.

Evans dreamed of making a torpedo run that would erase his painful memory of the ignominious retreat aboard the *Alden* at the Java Sea. He was relieved not to have duds for torpedoes. He still fumed that, at the outset of the war, the Japanese had sunk ships with highly effective Long Lance torpedoes that didn't even leave a telltale wake. The American torpedoes had routinely bounced off ships without exploding or nosedived beneath them. The *Johnston*'s improved, more powerful Mark XV torpedo ran straight and true, and Evans was bent on putting a few into the hull of a Japanese warship.

At the commissioning of the *Johnston*, on October 27, 1943, at the Tacoma-Seattle Shipyard, Evans wanted to impress on his men the seriousness of their mission. As his officers and men, shipshape in dress blues on a bright fall day in the Pacific Northwest, gathered around, Evans invoked the spirit of his beau ideal from Annapolis days, the Revolutionary War hero John Paul Jones. "This is going to be a fighting ship," said Evans. "I intend to go in harm's way," he said, quoting the saying from Jones that had been inscribed in his Class of 1931 yearbook. The memory of the *Alden* still rankled. "Now that I have a fighting ship, I will never retreat from an enemy force," he went on. Anyone who did not want to go with him, he said, should get off now.

His men listened, some wary, some indifferent, some moved. Ed Takkunen, a nineteen-year-old sailor from Ely, Minnesota, didn't pay much attention to Evans's rhetoric. "It was the kind of stuff you hear from naval officers," he recalled six decades later. Bob Hollen-baugh, twenty-one, who had enlisted in the navy to avoid being drafted by the army, was also unimpressed. "It didn't ring true like something John Paul Jones would say," he recalled. But another young sailor, James Johnson, thought Evans was "inspirational," and Lloyd Campbell, a gunner's mate, remembered, "Nobody made a move. They knew he meant it."

At the formal Commissioning Ball that night, the ship's doctor

Commissioning the Johnston

made a punch, spiked with 180-proof grain alcohol, called a "Pink Lady." About 80 percent of the crew were teenagers who had never been to sea, and a significant portion of those had never drunk to excess before—until that night. By the time the Shore Patrol arrived, several brawls had broken out, and a couple of sailors from the newly commissioned DD-557 had to sleep off their hangovers in the brig.

The officers, including the captain, joined in the imbibing, though not the scuffling and punching. The gunnery officer, Lt. (j.g.) Robert Hagen, nearly broke his jaw when the wife of a petty officer hit him with her purse. One young officer, Lt. (j.g.) Ellsworth Welch, was startled to arrive at the party with a demure sorority queen on his arm just as the furniture began to fly. Captain Evans had a few drinks, and Hagen later claimed to have put him to bed. The next day, Evans exclaimed to Hagen, "Great party!" Then, recalled Hagen with a laugh, he saw the bill for $10,000 for damages to the hotel.

The officers and men of the *Johnston* respected and admired their captain, but they never did quite figure him out. A certain distance, dictated and enforced by the custom of the sea, always separates a captain from his officers and crew. A captain is an absolute authority aboard his ship, and he must be free to be ruthless. On eighteenth-century warships, the captain paced his own sacrosanct and inviolable territory along the windward rail of the quarterdeck. On larger modern warships, captains followed the ancient custom of dining alone, except when they asked officers (never members of the crew) to dine with them. Then they might be convivial, but never "mate-y." Destroyers were too small for such splendid isolation, and the captain dined in the wardroom. There was a saying at the time that you could always tell a captain by where he sat: at the middle of the table, Jesus Christ; at the head, a tyrant. Evans refused to be typed and sat anywhere.

Evans defied easy labels. He had an ineffable quality that made him at once a familiar, yet mysterious, figure. He could and did smile at sailors' high jinks—an Equator crossing ceremony or the Commissioning Ball, or "Commissioning Brawl," as it became known—and even shared in the fun. When Lieutenant Hagen, who could be a little prissy, became outraged at a sailor who had stolen a case of beer and drunk the whole thing, Evans made Hagen defend the man at "Captain's mast," an informal disciplinary hearing. "I think it amused him," recalled Hagen.

Evans identified with the underdog, but never in an aggrieved or angry way. Although he was an Annapolis graduate, the crew knew and appreciated the fact that he had once been an enlisted man, however briefly. Evans did not fit the ring-knocker mold in the least. The *Johnston's* first executive officer was an Annapolis man, a tall, lordly figure who seemed to condescend to reserve officers and enlisted men alike. Evans had little to do with him. Instead, he quietly encouraged Lt. (j.g.) Ed Digardi to defend some enlisted men charged with getting into a drunken brawl with the Shore Patrol in San Diego. The XO wanted to throw the book at the men, but Digardi, who after the war became a highly successful trial lawyer, got them off. Evans gave Digardi a quiet smile. There was some tension in the wardroom between the Annapolis men, who called the reservists "90 Day Wonders," and the reservists, who called the Annapolis grads "the Trade School Boys." The Annapolis men refused to join the penny-ante poker games of the reservists, most of whom had never been on a ship before.

Evans floated above the petty jealousies and rivalries. He would step in with a sharp look or a word when things got out of hand, as when the engineering officer once tried to choke Digardi, who liked to tease him. On the bridge, Evans did not say much, either to praise or to scold, and he kept an inscrutable half-smile on his face at most times. Only when action neared did he bark. Then there was no mistaking his meaning or his ferocity.

He was absolutely single-minded about victory at sea. Evans had a family, a wife, and two children, but he rarely saw them. When he was not at sea, his son, Ernest Jr., recalled, he was studying naval tactics. He would talk to his son, who was then a small boy, about the Battle of Jutland, the great World War I showdown between the British and German fleets. From studying Jutland, the junior Evans recalled, his father learned that a ship commander under fire in battle should "follow the splashes," i.e., steer his ship for the place where the enemy's last shell landed, on the theory that the enemy would be constantly shifting its aim. Aside from a game or two of father-son catch in the backyard, Evans was removed from the normal duties of fatherhood, except in the most atavistic sense, as a warrior role model.*

In November 1943, Captain Evans took the *Johnston* out for sea trials. He was visibly pleased with his new ship, a vast improvement in speed and firepower over the poky old *Alden*. To be sure, even a modern destroyer of that era offered few physical comforts. The *Johnston* would be a wet, rolling, confining home for her 310 men and twenty-one officers, only seven of whom had ever seen sea duty. As the *Johnston* plowed through heavy seas on her shakeout cruise to San Diego, many of the crew, officers and men, lined the rails to be seasick.

Longer than a football field but only thirty-nine feet wide, a *Fletcher*-class destroyer was basically a power plant inside a thin steel hull. Loaded and fueled, she weighed 3,000 tons, about the same as a single main gun battery turret aboard the *Yamato*. The two large engine rooms in the middle of the ship were hot and smelly (sailors would urinate in the bilge) and dangerous. The steam was heated to 850 degrees Fahrenheit. A pinprick in a pipe would unleash a jet of steam that could take off a finger. But the power pushing her two propeller screws could make the ship cruise along at 35 knots.

The men on a destroyer slept in bunks stacked four high in compartments that were hotboxes in the tropics. The twenty one officers lived a bit better in small staterooms, sharing two toilets, a urinal, and a shower. They ate off monogrammed china in the wardroom, but they were perfectly aware that their dining table, permanently lit by a surgeon's lamp, would become an operating table in combat.

Evans had two cabins, a tiny stateroom down below, and his sea cabin, with a bunk and a toilet, on the ship's bridge just behind the pilothouse. Sometimes Evans sat in his chair in the pilothouse, a surprisingly small space, with limited visibility through portholes, crammed with a dozen officers and men at battle stations. Other

---

*The younger Evans went on to graduate from Annapolis and become a colonel in the Marine Corps, seeing action in Vietnam.

USS Johnston

times, he stood out on the open-air bridge wings to either side. A small ladder at the back of the pilothouse led up into the gun director, a claustrophobic steel box where the gunnery officer, looking through an optical sight, could control all five of the ship's mounted 5-inch guns with hydraulics and a primitive computer.

The 5-inch guns, along with the batteries of 40-millimeter and 20-millimeter guns in tubs up and down the ship, were primarily useful for air defense or shooting up small craft. Depth charges were stacked on racks, poised to defend the ship against enemy submarines. The destroyer's most lethal offensive weapon—its ship killer—was the torpedo. The *Johnston* spent hours on mock torpedo runs, preparing for the day when it could unleash the full load of explosive-tipped underwater projectiles—all ten torpedoes—at a Japanese warship.

The greenhorn crew of the *Johnston* passed around the scuttlebutt about their skipper. They knew that he had seen action in the route at the Java Sea, and that he wanted revenge. "We thought maybe he was a little torpedo-happy," recalled Bill Mercer, who signed on to the *Johnston* as an eighteen-year-old. Most of the crew consisted of eighteen-, nineteen-, or twenty-year-olds who had never been to sea, much less seen action. But they appreciated that Evans showed none of the stiffness or haughtiness that marked some Annapolis men. The stewards—who were all Filipino or black and lived in separate quarters in the still segregated navy—especially liked Evans. He treated them like other sailors.

Evans was stern, in an evenhanded way, with his sailors. He was a stickler for drill, quickly earning the *Johnston* the nickname "GQ Johnny" because it was so often at General Quarters, the status that required every man to go to his battle station. He disapproved of profanity (used by officers or men) and he frowned on sloppy dress. He would correct sailors who rolled up their sleeves, warning them about flash burns. But his manner was good-natured, quiet, and confident. Lieutenant Hagen, the gunnery officer, was more high-strung with the crew, and Evans took Hagen aside to gently tell him to calm down. "Relax, Hagen," he would say, "there's a war on." Hagen had taken an instant dislike to the *Johnston*'s first chief boatswain's mate, a truculent sailor who wore his hat backward and kept his jacket unbuttoned when required to wear dress blues. "I don't like that son of a bitch," Hagen told Evans. "Now, Hagen, you've got to be tolerant," Evans replied. When the man went AWOL before the *Johnston* sailed, Evans did not rely on his haughty Annapolis executive officer to find a replacement but went ashore and personally recruited an excellent chief boatswain's mate named Clyde Burnett, who would be respected by the men.

With his officers, Evans was at once amiable and cryptic. He led with a light hand, by giving the officers responsibility, often wordlessly. Lieutenants junior grade Digardi and Welch recalled nearly identical experiences, of being suddenly given the con of the ship by the captain just as the *Johnston* was making a difficult harbor entrance or mooring. Evans did not say a word, except to override their orders when they made mistakes. He did not criticize or compliment, but rather let them learn by doing. Evans never explained himself, except once to say to Welch, "I'm paid for what I know, not what I do." Welch found Evans to be a somewhat mysterious figure, agreeable enough, but often alone in his cabin, reading mysteries.

Hagen, the gunnery officer and by his own admission the nervous type, envied Evans's cool. But Evans also seemed to envy Hagen's battle experience. Hagen had been aboard a destroyer at Guadalcanal, the *Aaron Ward*, badly damaged in an enemy bombardment. Evans, who knew all about the exploits of Arleigh Burke and the Gallant Squadron, was curious about the fierce fighting off Guadalcanal, the night actions against the Tokyo Express in Iron Bottom Sound during the fall of 1942 and winter of 1943. Wounded in action, Hagen had won a Silver Star for gallantry, a medal with real meaning to Evans. Hagen was modest about the award, not without reason. He had been cut up with shrapnel while sitting in the wardroom. Many years later, Hagen would recall with a chuckle that the captain of the *Aaron Ward*, a "screamer," had put Hagen in for the medal because he had felt guilty about the abusive way he had treated his officers. Hagen was relieved to have a low-key captain like Evans. But he had no doubt that Evans was eager to test his crew in battle.

In January 1944, the *Johnston* joined the great amphibious fleet rolling across the Central Pacific, taking small islands one by one on the way to Japan. The *Johnston*'s role was to provide gunfire support for landing operations. At Namur Island in the Marshalls, the crew had its first taste of battle. A Japanese 8-inch gun behind a thick concrete wall onshore was shelling the American landing craft, and no amount of bombardment seemed capable of cracking the protective wall. To get a better angle of fire, Evans took the *Johnston* into a lagoon close-in to shore and opened up with his 5-inchers, silencing the Japanese gun. As the nervous crew steamed close to shore, a wiseacre in the radio shack put a big band song called "Sleepy Lagoon" on the PA system. Evans just smiled.

From February to July 1944, the *Johnston* bombarded beaches in the Marshalls, Carolines, and Marianas, as the Americans island-hopped westward. At Guam in July, the *Johnston* sailed so close to the Japanese shoreline that the ship was able to spray the bushes with rapid-fire rounds from its 40-mm guns. Lieutenant Welch even pulled out his sidearm, a pistol, and opened fire. The ship was repeatedly straddled by Japanese return fire, but only one man was nicked with shrapnel, or possibly a stray bullet from shore. By now the men were learning to sleep through bombardments. In May, the *Johnston* was credited with the "probable" sinking of a Japanese submarine. Welch recalled that Evans regarded this success without a word. Sailors, no longer frightened and seasick, were now a little bored. On the long, slow days of steaming from island to island they made contraband torpedo juice. They tried to hide an outrigger canoe they had purloined from some islanders, but Evans made them get rid of it. With the cheerful profanity of sailors, they complained about the food and accommodations. Greasy salami was called "horsecock," chipped-beef-on-toast was "shit on a shingle," and the bunks stacked four high were "fart sacks." They had whiffs of the terrible fighting ashore. Ed Bloch, who was an "old" seaman at twenty-five, recalls his eyes welling up with tears when a landing craft pulled alongside, filled with badly wounded young marines. But others talked about wanting some real combat against a Japanese ship. "We were just dumb-assed kids," recalled Mercer.

The swift advance across the Central Pacific was the aircraft carrier's answer to the blitzkrieg. The planes from the carriers of the Big Blue Fleet dominated the skies over the islands and atolls while the marines splashed ashore. The fighting was sometimes hard—the first island conquest, at Tarawa in November 1943, had been a bloodbath. But the Japanese were fighting a rear-guard struggle. In 1943–44, the war tide had turned all over the globe: the Russians were driving back the Germans, and the Allies had defeated Gen. Erwin Rommel's panzer divisions in North Africa before launching the liberation of Italy in the summer of 1943. Although the Japanese continued to put up fierce opposition on their Pacific island strongholds, the American progress seemed unstoppable. The Big Blue Fleet rolled like a wave, westward toward Japan.

Admiral Halsey, by now a legendary figure in the American press, had hoped to lead the charge. He had tried not to be disappointed in the spring of 1943 when Nimitz had chosen instead Admiral Spruance.

Raymond Spruance and Bill Halsey, in the tight world of the Old Navy, were friends. They represented a vast cultural shift from the

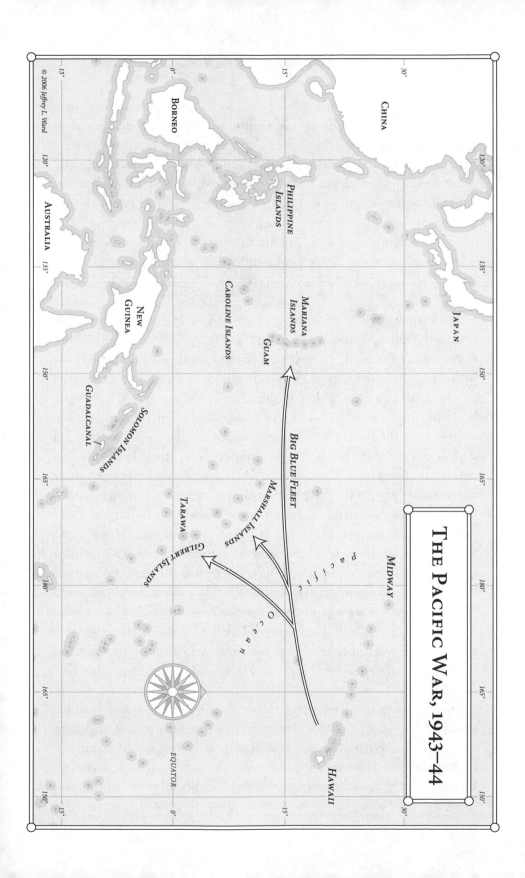

THE PACIFIC WAR, 1943–44

days of ship-to-ship combat, when a great sea warrior was the captain who took the fight to the enemy, to the era of massive fleet movements—sprawling, complex maneuvers that required close attention to numbing detail and equal measures of modern management techniques and old-fashioned leadership skill. The transition from one era to the next was neither simple nor sudden, and luck—and the actions of a mysterious and unpredictable foe—swayed and sometimes clouded the judgment of both Halsey and Spruance. Their experiences as battle commanders were almost mirror opposites. Each man reacted—and overreacted—to the mistakes of the other.

With their sharply contrasting personalities, Halsey and Spruance represent opposite models of naval leadership. At Annapolis, while Halsey was busy being "everybody's friend" and playing the old salt, Spruance was keeping to himself and studying. He graduated twenty-fifth in a class of 209, but the *Lucky Bag* described him, teasingly but unflatteringly, as "a shy young thing with a rather sober, earnest face and the innocent disposition of an ingénue. . . . A faithful supporter of the lee rail on all summer cruises" (he was seasick and threw up often). As a naval officer, while Halsey was taking chances and carousing with his staff, Spruance was cautious, remote, by-the-book, which, as a former instructor at the Naval War College at Newport, he had helped write. As Admiral Nimitz's chief of staff, Spruance lived like a monk, inhabiting a room "about the size of a destroyer's skipper's cabin," recalled Admiral Carney. Somewhat surprisingly, given their personalities, Halsey and Spruance were personally very close. They forged a bond commanding destroyers together. Spruance's ship once plowed into the stern of Halsey's in a freakish accident; neither man was blamed, and they remained friends. Spruance's son had married Halsey's daughter, further tightening the ties.

In the spring of 1942, when Halsey had been too sick to take his task force into battle, he had recommended to Nimitz that Spruance take his place. With the considerable help of Halsey's staff, Spruance (along with the *Yorktown*'s commander, Adm. Frank Jack Fletcher) had won the brilliant victory at Midway. Nimitz admired Spruance's modesty and immense organizational skills. He installed Spruance as commander of the Big Blue Fleet for the first big push across the Central Pacific in the fall of 1943 and winter of 1944. One by one, islands in the Gilberts, Marshalls, and Carolines fell or were cleverly end-run, including the Japanese Combined Fleet's forward base at Truk.

Nimitz, who had good judgment in men, could see that Spruance was perhaps better suited for the complex task of marshaling a great fleet than the more instinctive Halsey. Still, Halsey had performed well in the demanding role COMSOPAC. And Nimitz had not forgotten Halsey's loyalty, his performance in the dark days after Pearl Harbor, or his desire for fleet command. Running a carrier task force is an exhausting business, and even the careful Spruance, who rarely took a drink and rationed his energy, was worn down by the spring of 1944. Nimitz decided to substitute in Halsey and his staff, whose job was basically done in the South Pacific. Thus was created what became known as "the two platoon system." For the rest of the war, Halsey and Spruance and their staffs would rotate roughly every six months. When Spruance was in charge, the Big Blue Fleet was formally Fifth Fleet; when Halsey was in charge, it was Third Fleet. The name-switch was confusing to the Japanese, who assumed the Americans had two entirely different fleets.

Halsey arrived in Honolulu on June 17, 1944, to begin preparing himself and his staff for the August changeover. The Big Blue Fleet had just invaded the island of Saipan in the Marianas, a chain of volcanic islands about 700 miles south of Japan. Imperial General Headquarters regarded the Marianas as a critical line of defense on the road to Tokyo. The Japanese had been reluctant to commit the Combined Fleet to battle since the Midway fiasco, but with the Americans drawing nearer to the empire's Home Islands, the time had come to sally forth. American submarines picked up a large fleet movement heading out to do battle. It seemed that the Decisive Battle, the long-awaited fleet showdown, had finally arrived.

Halsey fretted that once again he would be ashore for the big battle and lose his last, best shot at lasting glory. But he did not miss out. When the smoke cleared from the Battle of the Philippine Sea on June 19–21, 1944, the Japanese battle fleet was still afloat, wounded but still intact. Admiral Spruance had been too cautious—too much the organization man—at least to a hell-for-leather type like Halsey. For Halsey, following the action from afar, the battle was instructive, though the lessons he took away were not necessarily the right ones.

As his Fifth Fleet provided air cover for the American army and marine landings at Saipan, and the Japanese fleet drew nearer, Spruance faced a choice. He could either hold back his carriers—and protect the invasion fleet, the transports, and supply ships anchored near the beach. Or he could head out to find and attack the Japanese fleet before it struck. The latter choice could potentially cripple the Japanese navy, but it involved the risk that a separate Japanese force could slip in behind the advancing American carriers and shoot up the transports at anchor. As Spruance understood his orders, his primary responsibility was to support the invasion, not to go looking for the Japanese fleet.

Spruance was influenced by some important intelligence. That spring, the Americans had captured a top secret Japanese document, called Plan Z. The document had been a windfall. In March 1944, almost a year after Admirals Yamamoto and Ugaki were shot down over Bougainville, planes carrying Yamamoto's successor, Adm. Mineichi Koga, and his chief of staff, Adm. Shigeru Fukudome, had gone down in bad weather in the Philippines. Koga died, but Fukudome survived. The chief of staff dropped a briefcase full of top secret documents as he flailed in the water. Fearing reprisals, local Filipinos, who hated the Japanese, let Admiral Fukudome go free, but they kept his briefcase and turned it over to the Americans.

Inside was a document entitled "Z Operation Orders." The plan was actually a series of options and contingencies, but it called for the use of diversions or bait. The Japanese, fond of intricate plans involving multiple fleet movements, imagined various stratagems and flanking manuevers. One involved engaging American carrier forces with air attacks from afar—and then sending in battleships to pummel an American landing fleet as it lay vulnerable at anchor.

Spruance was an old battleship man, a member of the Gun Club that had war-gamed through the 1930s for the big-gun duel with the Japanese. To achieve his stunning carrier-based victory at Midway in

June 1942, he had followed the recommendations of Halsey's old staff aboard the *Enterprise*, especially the advice of the brilliant but unruly Capt. Miles Browning. Spruance's lifelong ambition, as it was for any Gun Club member, was to send out the battle line—the big battleships with their 16-inch guns—to take on the *Yamato* and the *Musashi* and the rest of the capital ships in the Combined Fleet. The former instructor at the Naval War College was essentially prepared to refight the Battle of Jutland or the Battle of Tsushima. Unlike Halsey, he did not consider himself a carrier man; he did not have the same faith in carriers as offensive weapons.

As the Japanese battle fleet approached the Marianas on June 18, Spruance wanted his battleship commander, Adm. Willis "Ching" Lee, to take his fast battleships and engage the Japanese in a night action. But when Lee balked—he had seen enough night action against the Japanese in Iron Bottom Sound to be appropriately wary—Spruance held back altogether and waited for the Japanese to come to him.

Aboard the *Lexington*, the commander of the fast-carrier strike force, Adm. Marc Mitscher, was quietly seething. Mitscher was the quintessential carrier man. He had been with Halsey to launch the Jimmy Doolittle raid on Tokyo in the spring of '42, and he had commanded carriers across the Central Pacific as the Big Blue Fleet island-hopped. Wizened, with a pointy jaw, he was unassuming and quiet for long periods of time. (One newsman said he looked like "the village grocer.") He always rode facing the stern, so he could watch carrier landings and so he wouldn't have to look into the wind. His men, especially the fliers, loved him because he so obviously cared about their well-being. At launch, he could be seen using his body language to get each and every plane airborne.

In the Marianas, Mitscher wanted his Task Force 58 to attack the Japanese fleet. So did his chief of staff, Capt. Arleigh Burke, the ex–destroyer commander of the Gallant Squadron idolized by Halsey at Guadalcanal. Resentful that a noncarrier man had been forced on him as his chief of staff, Mitscher had initially refused to confer with Burke, but by the Marianas campaign he had recognized Burke's fighting spirit. Examining the estimated size and location of the Japanese fleet off the Marianas on June 18, Mitscher turned to Burke and said, "It might be a hell of a battle for a while, but I think we can win it." But Admiral Spruance turned down Mitscher's request to venture forth. The carriers would have to play defense, protecting the beachhead.

The Japanese attacked first, launching wave after wave of carrier planes. Very few got through. The American pilots were now much better trained than the Japanese, and they flew better airplanes. They benefited from radar coverage and superb fighter control. "Hell, this is just like an old-time turkey shoot!" exulted one American pilot. The Japanese lost more than 300 planes, the Americans fewer than twenty. The air battle became known as "the Great Marianas Turkey Shoot."

Gently prodded by Admiral Nimitz in Honolulu, Spruance finally gave Mitscher the go-ahead to launch against the Japanese carriers late on June 20. Darkness was approaching and the planes were at the limits of their range, but off they went. Then the Americans learned, from a new sighting, that the Japanese fleet was sixty miles further away than they had first thought. The usual radio intercom chatter died out as the pilots realized their predicament: after bombing the Japanese, they would have to locate their darkened carriers on a pitch-black sea on a cloudy, moonless night—that is, if their fuel supplies lasted long enough—and land. Most believed they would have to ditch.

The raid on the Japanese fleet was not hugely successful—only one carrier out of seven was sunk—but the heroic recovery made Mitscher's name and legend. As the planes straggled back toward the carriers, their gas gauges dropping toward empty, Mitscher decided to help out the pilots. He ordered every carrier lit up, with searchlights blazing, star shells exploding, a Fourth of July of lights, and to hell with any Japanese submarines lurking nearby. From 216 planes launched, sixteen pilots and thirty-three airmen were lost, but the toll could have been much higher. In three days of fighting, the Japanese lost 475 planes they could not afford to lose. From then on, newsmen no longer compared Mitscher to a grocer; he was the "Ferocious Gnome" or "Admiral of the Ocean Air."

But there was much grumbling aboard the American carriers. "The enemy had escaped," Arleigh Burke bitterly concluded in his battle report. "His fleet was not sunk." That was the toned-down version; Mitscher had made Burke soften his explicit condemnation of Spruance. Back at Pearl Harbor, where Admiral Halsey had been intently watching the battle, poring over the charts and radio messages, the second-guessing was already in full cry, led by Adm. John Towers, the Pacific Fleet's air chief.

Towers represented the Brown Shoe Navy. Regular naval officers who served on ships wore black shoes. Aviators wore brown shoes and felt themselves to be a breed apart. Towers was their "crown prince," wrote Clark Reynolds, Towers's biographer. Towers and his kind believed that carriers should always be under the command of aviators who understood airpower. Brown Shoe Men mocked Black Shoe Men as "buffalo hunters" because they were so backward-looking they might as well have been Indian fighters. To the Brown Shoes, Spruance was a charter member of the old Gun Club, caught in the hazy past of the battleship era. "I told them not to send him out there," Towers complained to an army logistics man at CINC-PAC, when he learned that Spruance was holding Mitscher back in the Philippine Sea. When Spruance relented the next day and allowed Mitscher to unleash Task Force 58 against the Japanese carriers, Towers changed his mind: "I was wrong. Spruance is a great man," he said. But he soon returned to his original opinion.

Halsey kept his opinions about his friend Spruance to himself. His memoirs render no judgment on Spruance's actions at the Battle of the Philippine Sea. But there can be no doubt from his strongly expressed views on the use of carrier power—and his later actions at the Battle of Leyte Gulf—that Halsey sided with Towers.

As a winner of the Flying Jackass award who had barely earned his wings well into his fifties, Halsey was not a true member of the Brown Shoe fraternity. To the younger aviators, he was a "JCL" (Johnny Come Lately) or a "synthetic." But he was with them in spirit and attitude and he believed in the primacy of the carrier. He and Towers were natural elitists; they carried in their minds an aristocratic ideal of the bold cavalier, the well-born knight whose natural nobility conferred confidence. Like Halsey, Towers had a soft spot for Ivy Leaguers, the bankers and lawyers plucked from Wall Street to serve as air combat intelligence officers. Some regular navy men were suspicious of the "Quonset Point swells," the reserve officers who had trained at Quonset Point at Newport, Rhode Island, but Halsey and Towers appreciated the confident judgment of the Harvards and Yales and Princetons. Towers was regarded as a bit of a snob who was a little too partial to the well born (once asked for her Social Security number, Towers's wife, Pierre, produced a Social Register).

Towers had made the mistake of tangling with Adm. Ernest King, the skirt-chasing, hard-drinking commander-in-chief of the navy. At a party in Washington, after King had too much to drink and leered at Pierre, Towers called him a "penny whistle," a noisemaker. Towers later said that this small sneer was the worst mistake of his career. Wearied by Towers's single-minded zeal for aviation, King kept Towers behind a desk, not at sea where the glory lay. Towers wanted to command the Big Blue Fleet, but he was stuck as a staff officer at CINCPAC in Honolulu. But if he could not lead the carriers against the Japanese fleet, then his choice was Halsey, who would soon start his rotation as Third Fleet commander. Towers thought Halsey could be a bit of a loudmouth at times, but he believed that Halsey would know what to do when the time came.

The muttering by the Brown Shoe Navy against Spruance and the other "non-air" men became so persistent that Nimitz had to put out the word in July that everyone should hush and get back to fighting. But the divisions between the Brown and Black Shoe Men, just like the age-old rivalries between the army and navy or the academy grads (the ring-knockers) and the reservists (the 90 Day Wonders), would not go away. The result was often a failure to communicate, always a problem in large organizations, and in war, fatal.

In July, Halsey was temporarily called back to the mainland. Fan had had a nervous breakdown so serious that she was summoned to Delaware, where she was living with Halsey's daughter (and Ray Spruance's daughter-in-law), Margaret Halsey Spruance. When Halsey returned, he settled down to plan what he would do when he took command of the Big Blue Fleet in August. Halsey's chief of staff, Admiral Carney, had long been in touch with Towers and his staff, and had spent hours talking to Halsey about their shared philosophy. "I found that our views were pretty much in line with Admiral Towers's concept of a far bolder, wide-ranging utilization of carrier air," Carney later recalled. At Pearl Harbor in the summer of 1944, Halsey and Towers had many meetings of the minds. Halsey's staff—now the Third Fleet staff—worked on contingency plans that were always, Admiral Carney recalled,

> based on the assumption, Admiral Halsey's assumption, that the prime purpose of the any operation whatsoever in the Western Pacific was to bring about a climactic battle, to settle the question of supremacy in sea power. This he brought out again and again and again . . . that always, no matter what else we were doing, there must always be ready at hand a plan for the showdown.

CHAPTER SIX

THE SHATTERED GEM

"Isn't there someplace we can strike the United States?"

B Y FEBRUARY 1944, Admiral Ugaki had recovered from his injuries in the plane crash. He was given command of the First Battleship Division, including the behemoths *Yamato* and *Musashi*. Ugaki had hoped for something even grander, but he was glad to be going to sea again. He knew that in Japan's shrinking navy, there were only so many good commands.

Sacrifice was the order of the day. Banquets and even geisha girls had been banned in Japan, where slogans on billboards read "Luxury is the enemy." Tokyo was becoming ever more shabby and threadbare. The iron railings had been removed from park benches, along with the gongs and great hanging bells in temples, for scrap metal to build armaments. Men now wore something called "the national civilian uniform," drab gray trousers and tunic, while women wore *monpe*, peasants' pantaloons.

"My inside doesn't feel well," Ugaki wrote on March 22. "It's best to eat less. Under the present circumstances, our food is too much of a luxury." Ugaki was more worried about oil than food, and he fretted that American submarines were sinking Japanese tankers before they could reach Japan from the south. Only belatedly was the Navy General Staff looking into better protection for convoys.

When he wished to be, Ugaki was an intelligent critic of Japanese naval strategy and a sober realist. On April 27, he went aboard the aircraft carrier *Taiho* to participate in tabletop maneuvers pushing small model ships around a large table in a conference room. The American navy now had roughly twice as many carriers as the Japanese. To compensate, the Japanese rigged their war games, making assumptions that favored the Japanese. Ugaki could see the folly of this, and in his diary he privately chided his superiors (though not by name) for setting up the exercise "with developments too favorable" to the Japanese fleet. He had learned by bitter experience: as Yamamoto's chief of staff refereeing war games before the Battle of Midway, he, too, had arbitrarily changed outcomes to forecast a Japanese victory.

Ugaki was no longer a dyed-in-the-wool battleship man. His service with Admiral Yamamoto had undermined his faith in conventional doctrine. He was even beginning to question the holy of holies, Decisive Battle. "I wonder why they don't give enough consideration to attacking enemy elements easy to destroy, instead of always seeking a decisive battle," he wrote on April 27. Ugaki would continue to have doubts about Japanese strategy, and from time to time he bravely spoke up about them. But then he would succumb to martial fantasies or retreat into a naturalistic dreamworld suffused with the spirit of Yamato, the ideal of ancient Japan that shimmered as a refuge from the harshness of war.

Ugaki clung to memory. He wrote lovingly of his wife, Tomoko, on the fourth anniversary of her death ("I owe her soul a great deal") and he memorialized the anniversary of Admiral Yamamoto's death and his own near-death. He was still looking for a way "to fight so gallantly that one's name goes down in history and commit harikari when nothing is left to one." He reread Yamamoto's poetry, though perhaps not quite appreciating the self-effacement of his late chief. "Mikado's shield I shall always strive to be," Ugaki wrote, quoting Yamamoto, "never caring for my fame or life."

Reality kept intruding. He was "appalled at the condition of the supply ships." At target practice, the *Yamato*'s gunners were scattershot. Most discouraging was the sight of Zeros crashing as they tried to land on carriers moored near the *Yamato*. The green pilots were better at takeoffs than landings. There were so many accidents that

Admiral Ozawa, the overall fleet commander, called off training in May.

Typically stern, unusually tall, striding with a strange loping gate, Adm. Jisaburo Ozawa was eager for Decisive Battle. As the commander of the Mobile Fleet, the carrier strike force, he was under pressure from the Imperial Palace to seek out and destroy the American navy as it swept across the Pacific. "Isn't there someplace we can strike the United States?" demanded Emperor Hirohito, increasingly petulant with his admirals, who sometimes seemed more interested in preserving their own ships than attacking the enemy's. "When and where on earth are you [people] ever going to put up a good fight?" he railed at a palace conference in early 1944. "And when are you ever going to fight a decisive battle?"

Ozawa had devised a plan to try to overcome the Americans' roughly two-to-one edge in ships. The Japanese carriers would use their island bases to extend the range of their planes and put the Americans in a vise. Shuttling back and forth between carriers and land bases on Saipan in the Marianas, Japanese planes would bomb the American ships in between. This so-called shuttle bombing had merit as a tactic, but it overlooked the growing superiority of American planes and radar. The new, armored Grumman Hellcat was more than a match for the Zero; it could climb higher and absorb much more punishment. Ugaki had heard stories of Hellcats, hit with Japanese fire, emitting smoke but then flying safely away, while Zeros hit by the Americans had burst into flames. "Why can't we get planes that can't be shot down?" lamented Ugaki.

Ugaki was dubious about Ozawa's battle plan, called Operation A. He never criticized Ozawa by name, but he wrote a sarcastic poem, awkwardly phrased but clear enough in its meaning:

> *In the land of the south, where green trees cover isles*
> *Lies an armada impatient to go to sea*
> *Time for the showdown is close at hand*
> *At a loss who is to do with Operation "Fool"*

Ugaki was making a bitter pun about Operation A. The word "Aho" in Japanese means "damn fool."

And yet, as Admiral Ozawa's fleet sailed for the Marianas in mid-June, Ugaki's blustery mix of wishful thinking and fatalism returned. Ugaki was sailing ahead of the carrier strike force in a vanguard of four battleships, including the two biggest under his command, *Yamato* and *Musashi*, eight cruisers, and three carriers. He wrote in his diary: "Can it be that we'll fail to win with this mighty force? No! It can't be!" He prepared for battle, as he had before Midway, by getting a haircut and saving a lock of hair "in case of my death," and taking a bath, he recorded in his diary, "so I'm well prepared for the worst."

But at the Battle of the Philippine Sea, Ozawa's shuttle bombing strategy failed. On June 19, Ugaki anxiously waited on the bridge of the *Yamato,* cringing at a series of blunders. Ugaki's ships opened fire by mistake on Japanese planes flying overhead. An American submarine torpedoed Ozawa's flagship, the brand-new carrier *Taiho.* Attempting to air out the gasoline fumes collecting belowdecks, the *Taiho*'s crew only spread them. Then a spark ignited the fumes, and the ship erupted, splitting its flight deck wide open. The final moments of the *Taiho* are emblematic of the warped priorities of the late-war Imperial Japanese Navy. On the bridge, the proud Admiral Ozawa engaged in spirited debate with his subordinates over the proper way to show honor. Talked out of going down with his ship, Admiral Ozawa rescued the emperor's portrait from his stateroom. But in the confusion of going over the side, he forgot his codebook—and lost communication for a time with headquarters in Tokyo. Ozawa had thrown caution and his pilots to the wind in a final assault on the American carriers. Most of the Japanese planes were shot down in the Great Marianas Turkey Shoot before they could reach their targets.

At day's end, Ugaki recorded, "Not only did we fail to inflict damage on the enemy, but we sustained heavy damage. Is it," he wondered, "that heaven still does not side with us?" It is perhaps revealing that Ugaki was blaming heaven for Japan's shortcomings while the Americans, who had shot down far more aircraft, were blaming themselves for failing to win a more resounding victory.

Admiral Mitscher's planes from Task Force 58 found Ugaki's battleships and the carriers they were escorting the next day, June 20, just before dusk. The scene was almost eerily beautiful. As the sun, a giant red ball, hung on the horizon, the American planes came wheeling and diving, machine guns spitting, as they skirted giant cumulus clouds piled on a darkening sea. Heeling, helms hard over, the *Yamato* and her sister ships threw up a multihued display of flak, bursts of red, blue, yellow, pink, and lavender. Ugaki watched from his bridge as his ship and the rest of the vanguard slew around, making 90 degree turns almost in unison to dodge the American dive-bombers and torpedo planes. One carrier, the *Chiyoda*, was not quick enough, and Ugaki spied a pillar of black smoke rising from her fantail. The carrier was not sunk, but another carrier sailing with the main body of Ozawa's fleet, the *Hiyo*, was hit and slowly rolled over. The men of the *Hiyo* raced to abandon ship, but a young ensign, wielding a sword, stopped them. He made the crew sing several patriotic songs until, as the water swirled around their legs, the men swept by him and jumped over the side. The ensign could be seen waving his sword and still singing as the ship went down.

The battle was not quite over. Before the war, Admiral Ozawa had traveled to Germany to study the Battle of Jutland. To him, the lesson of Jutland was to never stop pursuing the enemy. So he ordered Ugaki's battleships and the rest of the Mobile Fleet's vanguard to head east and seek a night battle against the Americans. Planes were sent forward to find the enemy. But as darkness fell, the lead scout plane radioed back, "No enemy sighted, so I shall return." The fleet was ordered to turn about and head west to safety. Ugaki was by now thoroughly demoralized. The next day, he wrote:

> *Utterly awakened from the dream of victory,*
> *Found the sky rainy and gloomy,*
> *Rain clouds will not clear up,*
> *My heart is the same*
> *When the time for battle's up.*

Ugaki lamented, "The result of the decisive battle on which we staked so much was extremely miserable."

* * *

At the Battle of the Philippine Sea, Admiral Ugaki reported to Adm. Takeo Kurita, the overall commander of the Second Fleet, which was serving as Ozawa's battleship vanguard. Given Japan's extreme aggressiveness in the Pacific War, its premium on sacrifice and the willingness to die, it is perhaps puzzling that Admiral Kurita rose as high as he did in the Imperial Japanese Navy.

Kurita was not a forward-leaning commander. In June 1942, at the Battle of Midway, when two of the cruisers under his command had collided as they were evading a submarine, Kurita had left them behind as he retired from the battle. Faced with a difficult choice, he elected not to risk the rest of his fleet to protect the disabled cruisers. After one of the cruisers, the *Mikuma*, was sunk, and the other, the *Mogami*, was badly damaged by American planes, Kurita was criticized for not standing by the cripples. At Imperial General Headquarters, the gossip was that Kurita would only attack when directly ordered—that he "needed his butt kicked" (*shiri o tataubekida*). And yet, by June 1944, he had been given a great command, overall responsibility for the IJN's heaviest guns, a fleet comprised of most of the navy's battleships and cruisers.

At the end of the Battle of the Philippine Sea, on the night of June 20, Kurita had not wanted to pursue the American fleet; he was content to withdraw and live to fight again another day. Kurita was as ever quiet, composed, considerate of his men—but not bold. His attitude had not changed since that "purple night" in October 1942 when he had taken two battleships in close to shell Henderson Field at Guadalcanal, then withdrawn into the safety of the night. He had been thinking all the while how *not* to make martyrs of his men and sacrifice his ships. Since Guadalcanal, Kurita's career had continued to advance—but not because he was a great warrior spirit. Rather, he was a beneficiary of the IJN's rigid seniority system, and he had been wise to avoid admiralty politics, thereby making fewer powerful enemies.

Kurita was a torpedo-and-gun man, part of the old fraternity of admirals who only grudgingly accepted the primacy of airpower. As other senior admirals were wounded or killed in action, or chose to go down with their ships, or were sidelined by internecine rivalry, Kurita kept bobbing, like a cork, up the chain of command. By the spring of 1944, Kurita had been made commander of the Second Fleet, the force of four battleships, eight cruisers, eight destroyers, and three light carriers that at the Battle of the Philippine Sea had formed the vanguard for Ozawa's Mobile Fleet, the main carrier task force. Ugaki's battleship division, the superbattleships *Yamato* and *Musashi*, provided the heaviest firepower for Kurita's Second Fleet. Ugaki answered to Kurita; his fate was largely in Kurita's hands.

Kurita, now fifty-four years old, had been two years ahead of Ugaki at Eta Jima. The two men were longtime acquaintances, though not friends. Their careers had followed essentially different paths, Ugaki often at headquarters, Kurita almost always at sea. Though their fates were intertwined in the last great sea battles of the war, the two men would stand apart as different models of leadership in a losing cause.

On the eve of war, on November 20, 1941, Ugaki had written in his diary that he had been favorably impressed by Kurita. As the commander of a cruiser division heading south for the invasion of Singapore, Kurita had come by the quarters of the C-in-C of the Combined Fleet to say goodbye. At the time, Ugaki had written approvingly that "Rear Admiral Kurita, who is supposed to meet the most dangerous situation, was the most calm. He is most trustworthy." As the war dragged on, however, Ugaki revised his opinion. He came to regard Kurita as complacent, more passive than steady, lacking in the ardor required to fight a materially superior foe. As always, Ugaki was careful not to criticize his superior by name in his diary, but his feelings about Kurita are not hard to detect. In private conversation, Ugaki was less discreet. According to Kenzo Ebina, the young ensign who had acted as Ugaki's scrivener, Ugaki held Kurita in low regard.

Kurita was widely criticized for being tentative at the Battle of the Philippine Sea. After the war, senior captains in the Second Fleet told a leading popular historian of the Japanese navy, Kazutoshi Hando, that Kurita had not pushed boldly eastward when he first received the order for a night attack from Ozawa. He had stalled and zigzagged instead; he had not displayed the fighting spirit that Ozawa himself possessed.

Interrogated by the Americans after the war, Kurita was laconic and defensive. Communications in the Battle of the Philippine Sea had been poor, he said. He had lost most of his air cover by the last day. Kurita was not blinded by delusions of miraculous victory. He did not think the Americans were weak or easily intimidated. Ever since Guadalcanal, he told his interrogators, he had known the Japanese were heading for defeat. Kurita never came right out and said it to his American inquisitors, but the implication was that a lost cause was not worth dying for.

By the summer of 1944, Kurita presented a stark contrast to Ugaki. While Ugaki believed, as he often wrote in his diary, that the purpose of life for a warrior is death, Kurita believed that dying was never the purpose of life—that duty was important, to be sure, but that to die needlessly served no greater glory. Kurita had admired Admiral Yamamoto for urging captains *not* to go down with their ships.

Kurita's model after Yamamoto's death was Adm. Shigeyoshi Inoue, the most forceful and articulate philosopher of preserving lives and avoiding pointless sacrifice. Admiral Inoue had been Yamamoto's close friend; he would become Kurita's mentor. At the Navy Ministry before the war, Inoue had tried to protect Yamamoto from the right-wing hotheads who wanted to depose him, if not kill him. As the war spun toward an ever more nihilistic climax, Inoue stood as an increasingly solitary voice of reason in the Imperial Japanese Navy. His voice did not carry. Accused of being gun-shy in early sea battles, Inoue had been marginalized and given shore-based commands. Ground down by war and naturally reticent, Kurita kept his admiration for Inoue to himself.

Kurita dutifully stayed out to sea and in the fight. But he was seared by a near-death experience at Rabaul, the Japanese bastion in the South Pacific, toward the end of 1943. He had been sent—over protest and against his better judgment—to bombard the American landings at Bougainville with a squadron of cruisers. This was the Japanese raid, detected by American code breakers, that prompted Admiral Halsey to tearfully sign orders for a daring preemptive attack by the carriers *Lexington* and *Princeton* in November 1943. Kurita's cruisers were fueling in Simpson Harbor at Rabaul at 9:30 on the morning of November 5 when the American dive-bombers and torpedo planes broke through the cloud cover and began raining bombs. The harbor was a chaos of geysers from exploding bombs and churning wakes, as ships tried to unmoor and escape, only to be strafed and bombed and set on fire. Kurita was watching on the bridge of his flagship, the heavy cruiser *Atago*, when a bomb fragment ripped out the abdomen of the ship's captain, Nobuyoshi Nakaoka. As he was being carried below on a stretcher, Captain Nakaoka, gushing blood, smiled at Kurita and said, "Banzai." Then he died. Masanori Ito, a journalist who knew Kurita, would later write that Nakaoka's horrific, smiling, pointless death profoundly affected Kurita. It "strengthened his feeling of resistance toward any useless sortie," wrote Ito.

There is no record of Kurita's inner thoughts at the Battle of the Philippine Sea in June 1944. But a lookout aboard the *Atago*, Kosaku Koitabashi, recalled seeing Kurita as he stood on the bridge watching planes land on a carrier a few thousand yards away. The pilots, young, green, untrained for battle, and inept at flying, were having great difficulty placing their planes down on the deck of the carrier. The planes would rise and sink, wings dipping and wobbling, as the anxious, exhausted pilots tried to line up a proper approach. Often they would break off and come around. Some crashed on deck or plunged into the sea. Quiet disgust played across Kurita's face.

At the end of June, Admiral Ugaki sailed back to Japan aboard *Yamato*. At his hotel at Kure, the great Japanese naval base near Hiroshima, he noticed that the citizens seemed grave and even downcast. The seriousness of their country's plight was beginning to sink in, notwithstanding years of propaganda. Privations were becoming more severe. That summer of 1944, the government instituted a seven-day workweek. Prostitutes were being pushed into factory work; they were chided as "accomplices of the Anglo-American ideological struggle." Trains were now so crowded that a number of infants had suffocated, and coffins were so scarce that they had to be reused.

As a senior naval officer cosseted by the privileges of rank, Ugaki did not feel the pinch himself. He was able to find some relaxation at a geisha house that had renamed itself the Hanazono Service Corps, sewing buttons by day and "offering services" at night. He showed two of Yamamoto's geisha girls examples of their late lover's calligraphy.

On July 4, Ugaki went aboard Admiral Kurita's flagship, the cruiser *Atago,* and spoke to the Second Fleet commander's chief of staff, Adm. Tomiji Koyanagi, who had just visited Tokyo. The chief of staff reported that headquarters was "in turmoil," but still "optimistic" and planning to shift to "guerrilla warfare." Koyanagi did not elaborate on what, exactly, guerrilla warfare might entail, but Ugaki picked up the notion and began ruminating in his diary about "new ideas" and "new weapons."

In fact, work had already begun on "new" or "special" ways of attacking. In the grandly euphemistic lexicon of the Imperial Navy, "special" meant suicidal. In the Imperial Palace, the emperor's naval aide, Capt. Eiichiro Jo, began pushing suicide as an official strategy of war, apparently with the emperor's approval or at least his acquiescence.

Captain Jo was a direct descendant of a well-known thirteenth-century samurai warrior who had been saved when a divine wind (the *kamikaze*) providentially swept away a Mongol invasion fleet. In June of 1943, Jo had drawn up a plan for a "Special Attack Corps" that would fly planes equipped with 550-pound bombs into American ships. At the same time, a pair of navy designers began work on a one-man suicide torpedo, the *Kaiten,* or "Heaven Shaker." By shaking the heavens, the *Kaiten* would turn around the course of the war and reestablish the natural order of things, with Japan at the center of the universe.

The idea of "body smashing" and *Kesshi* ("dare to die") tactics was centuries old. From the very first hours of the war, Japanese warriors had voluntarily and spontaneously sacrificed themselves for their emperor. In April 1944, a young pilot plunged his airplane into the path of a torpedo launched by an American submarine, saving a Japanese warship and winning a posthumous promotion to lieutenant. Told of the pilot's heroism, Emperor Hirohito granted the man's spirit a place at Yasukuni.

But until the summer of 1944, the emperor and his senior commanders had stopped short of requiring pilots to die. The American invasion of the Marianas and the defeat of Japanese forces on the island of Saipan in June and July were the tipping point. The Marianas were supposed to be Japan's defensive perimeter in the Pacific. Once the Americans were installed on Saipan, they would be within long-distance bombing range of Japan. Such a setback could not be concealed, and Japanese public discontent, for the first time, began to show. Dissent was a relative term. No one spoke openly about the failures of the government, or about surrendering, or even publicly conceded that the war was not going well (much less acknowledged that it was a disaster). There was nothing like a resistance movement; only some scrawled graffiti in bathrooms and the occasional lonely scholar or journalist, trying to slip by the Special Higher Police carefully worded double meanings of veiled protest.

Still, there were quiet rumblings within the government; in the past, vague murmurings of disquiet had preceded violence from the shadows. Hirohito's prime minister, Gen. Hideki Tojo, took most of the blame for the surprising developments in a war that, according to the newspapers, Japan had been gloriously winning. Threatened with assassination, Tojo stepped down and a new government was formed in July.

The fall of Saipan might have been the moment to seek peace. The emperor added a well-known dove, Adm. Mitsumasa Yonai, to his cabinet. Along with Admirals Yamamoto and Inoue, Yonai had argued against going to war with America in the first place. If Hirohito had really wanted to spare his people and his sacred islands from destruction, he might have looked for ways to begin negotiating with the Americans in July 1944.

But Hirohito often seemed to be traveling on two tracks—in opposite directions. Just as he was including a dove in his cabinet, the emperor adopted the policy of *gyokusai,* or broken gem ("better to be a gem that is smashed to atoms than a tile that is whole"). Japan was the gem; Imperial General Headquarters documents of the time speak of the "*Gyokusai* of the One Hundred Million." (Like almost every other aspect of Japanese strength, the empire's population was officially exaggerated; it was actually 70 million people). The *gyokusai* policy was not, at least in the beginning, nihilistic. The Japanese high command continued to believe that the Japanese

could simply outlast America—that the decadent liberal individual-
ists of the West would fold in a test of wills with the Yamato spirit.
Scholars have argued about whether the emperor was the pawn of
the militarists or their goad. The best evidence suggests he was a bit
of both, a deeply passive-aggressive figure overwhelmed by unbearable destiny. In any case, the Showa throne was entering deep twi-
light in the summer of 1944.

Some of the steps required of the One Hundred Million were pathetic. In schoolyards, children began making 30,000 balloon bombs
that were supposed to drift 5,000 miles across the Pacific and wreak
havoc on the West Coast of the United States. At least 9,000 balloon
bombs were launched between November 1944 and April 1945; a few
made it, killing some trees and an unfortunate adult and five children
who found a balloon and accidentally detonated it in Oregon in May
1945. The Japanese populace did not all toe the line; black markets
were popping up here and there. But the Thought Police pounced on
social deviance, arresting movie patrons who failed to remove their
hats when the emperor's image appeared in a newsreel.

From the Imperial Palace, Captain Jo unleashed the madness in
more significant ways. The emperor's aide-de-camp had been aboard
Admiral Ozawa's flagship, the *Taiho*, sunk at the Battle of the
Philippine Sea. He had seen with his own eyes a pilot crash-dive his
plane into a torpedo heading for the carrier. For months, he had been
discussing "body-hitting" tactics with Adm. Takijiro Onishi, the
IJN's leading advocate of airpower. Onishi was a brilliant (seventh in
his class at Eta Jima), hard-drinking, hard-living man who had
caused a minor scandal before the war by publicly slapping a geisha
girl for being sullen. In late June, Captain Jo wired Onishi: "No
longer can we hope to sink the numerically superior enemy aircraft
carriers by conventional attack. I urge the immediate organization of
special attack units to carry out crash-dive tactics."

Onishi had some reluctance to order mass suicide, but he over-
came it. He was infamous in the navy for his unyielding treatment
of seven Japanese airmen who had escaped from an American prisoner of war camp. Because they had violated standing orders to die
rather than be taken prisoner, the men were stripped of rank and ordered to fly daytime reconnaissance over Port Moresby, New Guinea;

in effect, to go out and die, which they did. In the autumn of 1944, Admiral Onishi began organizing the first suicide, or kamikaze, squadron of pilots.

The palace blessing on suicide set into motion a veritable assembly line. First came the *Ohka* ("Cherry Blossom"), a piloted rocket bomb, very fast but hard to aim (the Americans rechristened the bomb the *Baka*, "Stupid"). Then the *Kaiten* human torpedo was put into production, along with the *Shinyo* ("Ocean Shaker") suicide speedboat. Eventually, suicidal frogmen, called *Fukuryus* ("Crawling Dragons"), would be wired with bombs and sent crawling across the sea bottom toward American ships. It would be October before the suicide units were sent into action, but they would make an already horrific war more terrifying.

Admiral Ugaki welcomed the spirit of required sacrifice. In July, he faithfully recorded the farewells of the doomed garrison on Saipan. "I am going to charge into an enemy position. Banzai!" wired one commander before losing every one of his 3,000 men, some armed only with sticks, in a suicidal night attack on July 6. On July 11 and 12, hundreds of Japanese civilians on Saipan leaped to their deaths over the cliffs onto the rocks below or blew themselves up with grenades. American sailors and marines watched, appalled, yelling, "Surrender! Don't jump!" But the Japanese had been told they would be raped by the Americans or flattened by tanks. Japanese newspapers extolled the mass self-extinction. One Tokyo daily headlined: SUBLIMELY WOMEN TOO COMMIT SUICIDE ON ROCKS IN FRONT OF GREAT SUN FLAG; PATRIOTIC ESSENCE STUNS THE WORLD.

Reading about the mass suicide, Ugaki was "moved to tears" and wrote in his diary, "What a tragedy!" It was "only to be expected that servicemen should be killed in action," he went on, but he was amazed to read about "women, children and old men" killing themselves. "No people but the Yamato nation could do a thing like this," he wrote proudly on July 29. "I think that if one hundred million Japanese people could have the same resolution . . . it wouldn't be difficult to find a way to victory."

Ugaki himself was feeling under stress from so much thinking about new and better ways to kill and be killed. Though no longer in an influential staff position to affect war policy, as commander of the superbattleships his voice carried some weight—or so he hoped. He spent hours stewing over the war situation and writing memos to the admiralty in Tokyo. He didn't feel well. His bad teeth were acting up, and he reported in his diary that he was suffering from piles and a bladder infection. Though an avid hunter, he declined an offer to go shoot wild boar. "As the war situation is deteriorating and my health is not so good, I couldn't feel like going out to shoot. 'Thou shalt not kill' for me for a while," he wrote, without apparent irony, on August 6. He was dreaming of death on a far larger scale. "I'm in agony trying to discover the way to win by all means," he wrote that same day.

At Imperial General Headquarters in Tokyo, Ugaki's superiors were also looking for a way. The emperor was still demanding a decisive battle, a splendid victory like Tsushima. He sulked over the loss of Saipan and demanded that his forces stop the next likely step by the Americans, an invasion of the Philippines. By taking back the Philippines, the Americans could cut off the sea lane between Japan and her oil-producing colonies to the south. Japan would slowly strangle.

On August 1, 1944, Combined Fleet Top Secret Operations Order Number 83 directed Japanese forces "to intercept and destroy the invading enemy at sea in a Decisive Battle." The plan was called *Sho-Go* ("Victory Plan") Number One. The plan would evolve and mutate and become increasingly complex until it was really not a plan at all, but rather an expression of frustration and longing. By mid-October, at Imperial General Headquarters, the navy's chief operations officer would melodramatically declare the Sho Plan's ultimate and true purpose: "Please give the Combined Fleet the chance to bloom as flowers of death. This is the navy's earnest request."

Throughout the planning process, the top brass juggled the honor of dying for the emperor with practical concerns, like a drastic shortage of planes and pilots. Japan's high command was slowly being forced to face the prospect of defeat. Reality was too much for them; posturing, bureaucratic gamesmanship, and apocalyptic fantasy became an excuse to avoid facing harsh truths. The complex maneuvering at the top of the Imperial Navy's chain of command in the summer and fall of 1944 is complicated to unravel, but it is essential background to understanding the terrible dilemma that would face the striking force commanders at sea—Admiral Kurita and his battleship commander, Admiral Ugaki—when they finally encountered the enemy in late October.

Interrogated after the war, the navy's top man, the commander-in-chief of the Combined Fleet, Adm. Soemu Toyoda, confessed that he had felt tremendous pressure to defend the Philippines at all costs, even if it meant sacrificing his entire fleet. The public was beginning to question why the navy had failed to prevent the loss of the Marianas. Toyoda was not sanguine about the outcome, but he was willing to gamble.

Toyoda exemplified the strange psychosis that gripped that Japanese military in the last days of empire. In less than five years, he had progressed from opposing a war with the United States to a kind of suicidal fatalism. The only constant was a fanatical notion of the navy's honor.

Admiral Toyoda was a precise, strict, prickly, bitter man. The story was told of his bathing with his young son. The little boy urinated in the water, and when Toyoda senior confronted him, the child denied it. Toyoda called his son a liar and bullied him until the boy confessed. The moral of the story, it was said, was never piss in Toyoda's pool; in other words, never question his authority or try to duck his commands. Toyoda hated the army as much or more than he hated the Americans; he blamed the army's political meddling for dragging Japan into the war. Secretive and suspicious, he moved Combined Fleet headquarters off a cruiser moored at Yokohama, Tokyo's port city, into a bunker at the Navy War College, the IJN's senior command school, in the suburb of Hiyoshi. He rarely left and when he did, he traveled incognito.

Toyoda's direct subordinate was Adm. Jisaburo Ozawa, the tall, dynamic, headstrong commander of the Mobile Fleet, the navy's carrier task force. The Japanese navy had its own Gun Club, but the battleship commanders had finally, grudgingly, recognized the preeminence of aircraft carriers. At the Battle of the Philippine Sea, the Mobile Fleet was the main force; Kurita's battleships and cruisers, the so-called Second Fleet, had been under Ozawa's overall direction. Ozawa was a very able officer, but he, too, had been reduced by the unthinkable—the likely defeat of the empire—to contemplating the proper way to die.

At first, Toyoda was counting on Admiral Ozawa to produce a miracle. He badgered Ozawa to take his carriers and sail south to Lingga, near Singapore, where Admiral Kurita had moved with the battleships and cruisers of the Second Fleet to be close to a ready oil supply. Toyoda wanted Ozawa to take over the overall battle plan. But there was a catch: after the carnage of the Great Marianas Turkey Shoot in June, the navy was woefully short of planes and pilots with enough experience to both take off and land on carriers. Ozawa, who was known as very independent-minded, resisted Toyoda's request to go south. He argued that he needed to stay in the Home Islands to train his pilots. Besides, Ozawa wanted to know, if this Decisive Battle was to be the last gasp of the Imperial Japanese Navy, if the navy was really planning to throw the entire Combined Fleet at the Americans, then why didn't Admiral Toyoda—the C-in-C himself—go to Lingga to lead the way?

Both men were stubborn. While their staffs worked on an intricate battle plan, the commanders argued. It was not entirely clear who was in charge. It appeared that Ozawa would be willing to take his

Ozawa

Mobile Fleet to Lingga and join forces with Kurita's battle ships *if* he could muster enough planes and trained pilots. But that might not be until November or December. Toyoda was worried that the American invasion would come as early as September, perhaps even in August.

In that case, if the Americans attacked before the Japanese were ready to fight them head-on, Ozawa said, his carriers would act as a diversion. Sailing down from the Home Islands, they would try to draw the American carriers north. The Japanese knew that the American carrier task force was commanded by Admiral Halsey, and they knew, from reading Bull Halsey's own brash talk in the American press, that he was the sort of commander who liked to charge.

The Japanese would, in effect, drag their capes in front of the bull in hopes of luring Halsey into battle off Cape Engaño, which in Portuguese means Cape Deception. With Halsey charging north, the way would be open for Admiral Kurita to attack the relatively unguarded American transports as they unloaded troops onto the Philippine beaches. The Sho Operation would be essentially carrying out one of the options of the Z Plan, the document the Americans had captured before the Battle of the Philippine Sea. In that battle, Admiral Ozawa had followed a different tack, the attempted shuttle bombing. But now Ozawa proposed a classic use of deception to clear the way for a battleship attack on the American landing force. Of course, the deception was tremendously risky, since by coming close enough to tempt Halsey, Ozawa would be exposing his fleet to Halsey's warplanes. Ozawa knew that he would not have enough trained pilots and planes to put up much of a defense. That Ozawa was willing to use Japan's remaining carriers as the bait suggests how far gone he was on the road to self-annihilation.

Whether the suicidal gambit would work was unclear. Coordinating the movements and timing of different fleets over thousands of miles is difficult, even with good communications, which the Japanese lacked. Ozawa and Toyoda were barely speaking to each other— and no one was speaking to Admiral Kurita, commander of the Second Fleet, who would actually command the main battle fleet if Ozawa failed to come to Lingga to take charge.

*　*　*

Aboard the *Atago*, Admiral Kurita's chief of staff, Adm. Tomiji Koyanagi, wondered why his boss was not consulted on the Sho Plan. Koyanagi asked Tokyo to send the Combined Fleet's chief of staff to Lingga for "open and frank" discussions of the plan to repel the American invasion of the Philippines. But headquarters refused. Instead, Koyanagi was instructed to fly to Manila to be briefed—to be informed, not consulted—by a Combined Fleet operations officer, a mere captain.

Koyanagi did not protest. The Second Fleet's top staff officer, who would play a critical role advising Admiral Kurita in the coming battle, was an enigmatic figure. In the Japanese fashion, he was a master of indirection, rarely saying what he meant, but persistent nonetheless in getting his way. Well educated, near the top of his class at Eta Jima, he was a close observer of the scene; his postwar recollections are revealing of the inner workings of the Imperial Japanese Navy, though Koyanagi was careful not to offend.

He was regarded as a gentleman by his fellow officers, though by some as a "sea lawyer" who could twist the facts ever so subtly, if necessary. Koyanagi had the manners of a diplomat, but he had seen plenty of action, and his experiences had filled him with abhorrence for futile struggle. In contrast to his superiors Toyoda and Ozawa, Koyanagi was *not* a fatalist. Like Kurita, he believed in survival, though he was willing to pose as a death-defying zealot to preserve his chances of survival. His postwar writings about the Battle of Leyte Gulf have a slightly schizophrenic quality. He writes thankfully about being given the opportunity to die while, in the same sentence or the next, subtly conveying his true feelings, that sending men on a doomed mission was a waste.

During the first year of the war, he had been the captain of the battleship *Kongo*, and at Guadalcanal he had commanded a destroyer squadron. His destroyers had pulled off the successful evacuation of thousands of starving troops. Koyanagi later recalled the dead expressions on the faces of the soldiers as they spooned in bites of porridge, the only food they could hold down.

At his destroyer base at Bougainville in 1943, Koyanagi had tried to make light of American air raids, so frequent they were dubbed *teikibin*, scheduled runs. At the sound of the air raid alarm, the destroyers would cast off their moorings and violently jerk their bows back and forth to present a moving target. Koyanagi nicknamed these evasive maneuvers the *"Bon* dance" because they reminded him of the rhythmic swinging of dancers at the annual *Bon* Festival of the Lanterns. But by the Battle of the Philippine Sea, Koyanagi's lightheartedness had turned to despair. He recalled watching an American reconnaissance plane lazily turning above the range of antiaircraft guns as it tracked the movements of the Japanese fleet. The Japanese had no more planes left to shoot it down.

At the Kure shipyard after the battle, Koyanagi had watched as workmen welded hundreds of 25-millimeter machine guns onto every bit of available space of his ship. The machine guns were supposed to shoot down or ward off attacking planes. Battleships now carried an extra ninety machine guns, cruisers an extra sixty, and destroyers an extra thirty. They would not be enough, Koyanagi was well aware. Without proper air cover, Koyanagi realized, with a weary and bitter heart, the next battle of the great warships of the Combined Fleet would be the last.

On August 9, Koyanagi and Kurita's chief operations officer, Capt. Tonosuke Otani, flew to Manila. They were put up in a grand suite that had once accommodated General MacArthur, but at breakfast the next day, they were served hard rice and, as Koyanagi recalled, "soup with nothing in it." Even naval officers were now feeling the food shortages. After this meager repast, the Navy General Staff captain sent down from Tokyo gave them their orders: as soon as the American invasion force was detected off the coast of the Philippines, Kurita's Second Fleet—seven battleships, thirteen cruisers, and nineteen destroyers—would swing into action. Now dubbed the First Diversionary Striking Force, it would "rush forward and destroy the enemy transports on the water before they disembark their troops," Koyanagi recorded. "If this fails and the transports begin landing operations, the attack force will engage and destroy the enemy in their anchorage within at least two days of the landing, thus crippling the invasion effort."

Koyanagi was full of questions. Shouldn't the Japanese battle fleet be seeking out and destroying the American carrier task force? After all, weren't the American carriers the real threat? Sink them and the

Combined Fleet would stop the Americans on their path to Tokyo. Koyanagi was given somewhat vague reassurances that Ozawa's Mobile Fleet would take care of the American carriers, although how was not made clear, since Ozawa had few pilots and planes at his disposal. Koyanagi wanted to at least leave open the possibility that Kurita's battleships could attack the American carrier fleet if the opportunity arose. He carefully and diplomatically posed a question, conceding his duty but leaving open the possibility for more glorious action: "According to this order the primary targets of the First Diversionary Striking Force are enemy transports, but if by chance carriers come within range of our force, may we, in cooperation with shore-based aircraft, engage the carriers and then return to annihilate the transports?" Koyanagi later wrote,"This question was answered affirmatively by Combined Fleet Headquarters." Koyanagi, the sea lawyer, had just written a loophole wide enough to steer a fleet through. In the battle to come, he would use it as an escape clause.

Koyanagi flew back to Lingga to report to Admiral Kurita. He found the commander of the newly created First Diversionary Striking Force in his cabin aboard the cruiser *Atago*. The admiral, Koyanagi observed in a memoir of his service, *Kurita Kantai* (The Kurita Fleet), "rarely states his opinion. He does not get agitated or moved easily." But this time, Koyanagi noted, "Kurita showed his surprise in his expressions." Kurita's reaction was mild compared to that of his captains. Koyanagi later wrote:

> On the following day, the report [of the Manila meeting and the Sho Plan] was conveyed to all the main officers of the fleet. Everyone of Kurita's fleet expected that there were going to be some interesting and exciting tales from the meeting. They were taken aback and disappointed to learn that their job was to charge into the enemy's bay and smash the transport fleet. They complained: why couldn't they fight face-to-face with the U.S. main fleet? But the order was the order . . .

Orders are orders; still captains want to know. As Ozawa had asked, why didn't Admiral Toyoda come down to Lingga and take command of this last great sortie by virtually all of the battleships and cruisers of the Combined Fleet? What if Japanese scout planes failed to detect the American invasion fleet while it was still at sea, and as a result, the First Diversionary Striking Force arrived too late, after the transports had unloaded? What good would it do to sink empty transports? The American carriers, they were the real game. If the Japanese battleships ignored them and sailed for the invasion beach, American carrier-based planes would rain bombs on them, sinking them before they could even reach the beachhead.

On and on the questions came. As chief of staff for Admiral Kurita, Koyanagi's job was to listen patiently and betray no personal bias or favoritism or sympathy. "Outwardly," wrote Koyanagi, "I rejected all complaints of this nature, but inwardly I understood and sometimes even agreed with my officers."

One of the officers watching and listening as the debate raged was Admiral Ugaki. As commander of the First Diversionary Striking Force's biggest battleship division, including the *Yamato* and *Musashi*, Ugaki was the most senior officer after Kurita. As Yamamoto's former chief of staff, Ugaki was a voice to be reckoned with. But he remained silent as more junior captains raged and fulminated.

Ugaki was, in his own more fatalistic way, almost as ambivalent as Koyanagi—and just as careful about not revealing his true feelings to his fellow officers. Ugaki had at first welcomed the Sho Plan. "Now we have something to study," he wrote on August 13. "Whether the plan is adequate or not," he went on, "let's bind ourselves together tightly for one object and seek the last decisive battle once and for all." But then, his doubts about Decisive Battle, which had begun to nag at him before the Battle of the Philippine Sea, began to return. He became downcast and began to brood. On the last day of August he wrote one of his melancholy poems, "Gone is the sun, and the mountain / Of the Clouds loses its color."

For all his invocations of the Yamato spirit, he realized that in the Sho Operation, an inferior force would be attacking a superior force. Such a decisive battle, he knew, left "little chance of winning a victory." He began thinking about a sumo wrestler who beats five opponents in a row. "I realized that one couldn't win if one grappled and exerted too much effort with each of the five. One had to win four of the five by just pushing them out or outwitting them. A case where [the sumo wrestler] was really matched in earnest occurred only once or twice." The lesson for the outmatched Japanese navy was to avoid Decisive Battle, and instead chip away at the enemy with surprise attacks on the flanks.

Alone, away from the other commanders, Ugaki presented his views to Admiral Koyanagi. The chief of staff said he would pass them along to fleet headquarters in Tokyo. Ugaki patiently waited for some kind of response. None came.

Ugaki swallowed his frustration by going hunting. He roamed the hot sands around Lingga searching for pigeons. Caught in rain squalls, he did not have much luck. "Though I got all wet, the bag was small," he recorded on September 20. His *Banzai* spirit would return, then fade. An American carrier task force was spotted near the Philippines. Land-based planes went looking for it. "If the planes are to be expended anyway, attack the enemy and perish!" Ugaki wrote, favoring for the moment a last all-out spasm of violence. His mind was full of contradictory thoughts, at once wild and prudent. On September 24, he had a reunion with some Eta Jima classmates. "Who can guarantee that this will not be the last reunion at the battle front?" he wrote.

Night and day, the First Diversionary Striking Force trained for the Sho Operation. Ugaki's superbattleships took turns playing aggressor. Some days, the *Yamato* would stage a mock attack on Lingga anchorage, while the *Musashi* played the role of defender; other days, the roles would be reversed. Often, the maneuvers took place at night, the preferred hour of battle. The Japanese no longer believed that superior Oriental eyesight was enough. Learning from early defeat in night battles at Guadalcanal, the Americans had begun using radar. After much delay, the Japanese had finally responded by installing radar in their warships, though it was crude and not yet very effective. But in the tepid waters off Lingga, the war games went on. Exhausted, the men were granted shore leave in early October. Ugaki balked at letting the men go into the fleshpots of Singapore. He was worried that the fleet would not be ready to sortie when the time came. The Americans had been bombing Manila, and the American Third Fleet—under Admiral Halsey—had been sighted near the Philippines. On October 3, Ugaki wrote in his diary, "Halsey's forces are powerful indeed."

CHAPTER SEVEN

BIG BLUE FLEET

"These kids aren't Japs"

O N SEPTEMBER 12, the day of his first action as commander of the Third Fleet, Admiral Halsey came striding onto the flag bridge of the USS *New Jersey* to watch the dawn launch, an air strike against the central Philippines. Lt. Carl Solberg, a junior staff officer, was struck by Halsey's vitality and his disproportionate features. "His eyebrows, more black than gray, seem to jut ahead of him," Solberg later wrote. Although Halsey was "not a big man," his shoulders and head were so large that he almost seemed "to lurch as he walked." Halsey advanced "like a boxer, rising on the soles of his feet" with "a spring in his step." The sixty-two-year-old Halsey, Solberg observed, was "like a man going to a tryst."

Halsey's fleet was so vast that he could not see it all. Stretched out across the Pacific in regular cruising formation, the 200-odd ships of the Third Fleet occupied an area forty miles long and nine miles wide. In the panicky hours after Pearl Harbor, Halsey had sallied forth in a task force that consisted of one carrier, three cruisers, and nine destroyers. Now, two years and nine months later, he commanded the largest, most powerful fleet of warships ever assembled: eighteen carriers, six battleships, seventeen cruisers, and sixty-four destroyers. The only limit on the reach and endurance of the Big Blue Fleet was human exhaustion. By a miracle of ingenuity, the At

Sea Logistics Service Group—some thirty-four fleet oilers, protected by eleven small escort carriers, nineteen destroyers, and twenty-six smaller destroyer escorts—a giant floating Texas oilfield—accompanied the Third Fleet, delivering the two to three million barrels of oil and three to four million barrels of aviation gasoline it needed every month.

Halsey's flagship, the battleship *New Jersey*, stretched 888 feet, about three football fields. Its crew of 2,000 men slept in bunks stacked four high, but they lived better than Japanese sailors, who slung their hammocks wherever they could and were motivated by "spiritual bars"—wooden bats used as nightsticks by petty officers. The *New Jersey* was a luxury liner compared to the typical Japanese warship. Since 1905, ice cream makers had been installed in American battleships to promote "clean living and good fun." Officers fared well. Halsey lived in "Flag Country," a warren of staterooms for his staff of fifty officers in the ship's forward superstructure. His staff officers were handed a notice when they joined the ship. It read, one of them later noted, "as if written for a country club": "Your room boy will collect your laundry Monday and return it to you Wednesday. Laundry, cobbler service, tailoring services and haircuts are free. Medical and dental services are available to officers at all hours at Sick Bay, located at Frame 85 on the third deck." The wardroom served fresh steaks and chops, tossed salads, and Baked Alaska every Sunday. Aboard the *New Jersey*, Halsey had his own private flag bridge, beneath the ship's main bridge. He could watch his fleet, stretching from horizon to horizon, while sitting in one of four elevated chairs reserved for him—two on each side of the ship, one behind glass, one exposed to the sea air.

Halsey had first wanted an aircraft carrier as his flagship, but he decided that a carrier was too vulnerable. Admiral Spruance had modestly raised his flag on a cruiser, but Halsey chose a swifter (33 knots) and more formidable brand-new *Iowa*-class battleship. Though not quite as large as the *Yamato*, the *New Jersey* could throw nine tons of munitions almost fifteen miles in a single broadside. The recoil from its main battery pushed the 45,000-ton ship ten feet sideways. The concussion, one gunnery officer recalled, was "rather like being hit by a slow truck wrapped in a sofa."

Customarily, the fleet commander received his captains aboard his flagship; he did not go visiting them. But Halsey was eager to see one of the new *Essex*-class "fast carriers." Halsey's first act upon joining the Third Fleet was to call on his carrier task force commander, Adm. Marc Mitscher, aboard his flagship, USS *Lexington*. In a sense, Halsey was showing his respect for Mitscher. But Mitscher, who had been at sea for almost a year leading the carriers of the Big Blue Fleet across the Pacific, was not cheered by the arrival of Halsey.

Mitscher gave no outward sign and received Halsey royally. Men are transferred from ship to ship at sea by breeches buoy, a chair on a pulley. Mitscher provided Halsey with a handsome chair, fitted out with a surrey fringe on top and an ashtray. Mitscher was all smiles,

Halsey and Mitscher

but he knew that Halsey's arrival meant an end to, or at least a cur-
tailment of, Mitscher's freewheeling authority. Excepting the first
day of the Battle of the Philippine Sea, when he reined in Mitscher,
Admiral Spruance had quietly given his carrier commander great
leeway. The more domineering Halsey would want to call the shots.
Mitscher appreciated that Halsey would be hard-charging, but he
also knew that Halsey had not stepped aboard a carrier in nearly two
years and that Halsey's staff knew little about carrier operations—
certainly, far less than Mitscher's own staff.

Halsey wasted no time testing the Japanese. Halsey visited the
Lexington on September 12. On September 12 and 13, the Third
Fleet's warplanes struck the Philippines. They encountered surprisingly little resistance. Halsey was puzzled. The fliers of the Big Blue
Fleet claimed to have shot down 173 planes and destroyed 305 more
on the ground, all at a loss of only eight planes. A downed aviator,
rescued by the natives, reported hearing that there were no Japanese
on Leyte, at the center of the Philippine archipelago. This somewhat
slender evidence was good enough for Halsey. He announced to
Mick Carney, his chief of staff, "I'm going to stick my neck out.
Send an urgent dispatch to CINCPAC."

The invasion of Leyte in the Philippines was not set for another
three months, in December. Halsey recommended that the date be
pushed up to October 20. At the time, Admiral King was in Quebec
at a war-planning conference with the other military chiefs and
Roosevelt and Churchill. The assembled brass debated for only
ninety minutes before approving Halsey's suggestion. Halsey's im-
pulse, while just that, was brilliant. As it turned out, the downed
pilot, or his Filipino rescuers, was wrong about Leyte. This island
was crawling with Japanese, and reinforcements were on the way.
But by pushing up the invasion date from mid-December to October
20, Halsey guaranteed that Japan would not have enough planes and
pilots ready to mount a decisive air-sea battle against the Third
Fleet. Though he did not know it, Halsey was forcing the hand of
Admiral Toyoda and the Combined Fleet before they were ready.

Halsey was as ever impatient to get at the Japanese fleet. On September 15, Lieutenant Solberg observed Admiral Halsey sitting on
his bench in Flag Plot as the Third Fleet provided protective cover

for a marine landing at the Palau Islands. Flag Plot, a deck above Halsey's living quarters, was the nerve center for all Third Fleet operations. It was a "teeming place," recalled Lt. Cdr. John Lawrence, who, like Solberg, was an air combat intelligence officer evaluating threats, targets, and the effectiveness of raids. Officers pored over a large chart table while sailors wrote on clear plastic plotting boards with grease pencils and relayed orders over a cluster of voice tubes. Airless, windowless, stuffed with men and machinery, Flag Plot reeked of a strange stew of smells: the acrid odor of radio tubes; the ever-present, bittersweet warship smell of paint, lubricants, and a sealing solution called Cosmoline mingled with tobacco smoke and male sweat. Radio transmitters filled the stuffy room with the excited chatter of pilots on their bombing and strafing missions.

Throughout this commotion, Solberg noted, Halsey was calmly, though "ostentatiously," reading a dime-store paperback. Solberg wondered at this staged picture of repose. He guessed that Halsey was making a show of confidence in his men—going into battle, the admiral was so serene he could read novels. But he also suspected that Halsey was unhappy with his assignment, a costly and unnecessary diverson. (Halsey was right; the Palaus had little strategic significance, and the marines ran into more than 10,000 well-dug-in Japanese on one of the Palau Islands, Peleliu.)

Halsey was chafing at the very nature of the Third Fleet's duty that day. The Big Blue Fleet's job was to cover the marines' beachhead from air or sea attack, yet there was little threat of that; the Japanese fleet was nowhere nearby. Halsey didn't want to baby-sit the marines. After all, he reasoned, the amphibious landing force had its *own* navy—small escort carriers, whose planes could fly over the beaches, strafing and bombing, and old, slow battleships (several of them salvaged from the bottom of Pearl Harbor), perfectly suited to shore bombardment. Such passive, stationary duty, Halsey believed, was wasted on the new fast carriers and fast battleships of the Big Blue Fleet.

Halsey saw the Third Fleet as a kind of modern cavalry force. After the war, Halsey's operations officer, Capt. R. E. "Rollo" Wilson, described in a war college speech how Halsey wanted to use "typical cavalry tactics to strike hard at many sources of enemy

strength in a fashion unpredictable to the enemy." Even in the
Palaus, Halsey positioned his aircraft carriers so they could go
chasing after the Japanese fleet at a moment's notice. Halsey's freewheeling, take-'em-by-surprise tactics were bold and often effective, like those of the Confederate generals Halsey revered, dashing
figures like Nathan Bedford Forrest and J. E. B. Stuart. But later
events would suggest that Halsey shared the weaknesses of his heroes. When Gen. Robert E. Lee arrived at Gettysburg for the South's
own decisive battle against the North in July 1863, the Confederates
had badly needed scouting intelligence on the Union Army. J. E. B.
Stuart's cavalry was off joyriding, nowhere to be found, and Lee was
deeply disappointed. The day would soon come in the Pacific War
when Admiral Nimitz would be similarly frustrated about Bull
Halsey.

Halsey wanted to make sure he was not tied down the way Admiral Spruance had been in the Marianas, tethered to the beachhead
while the Japanese carriers taunted him from afar. In September,
CINCPAC prepared the Third Fleet's orders for the coming invasion
of the Philippines. The Big Blue Fleet was to cover the invasion, just
as it had supported earlier landings in the Gilberts, Marshalls, and
Marianas. But then there appeared some language that had *not* appeared in earlier operations orders:

> IN CASE OPPORTUNITY FOR DESTRUCTION OF MAJOR PORTION OF
> THE ENEMY FLEET OFFERS OR CAN BE CREATED, SUCH DESTRUC-
> TION BECOMES THE PRIMARY TASK.

It is not clear who wrote this proviso, which was to have dramatic
consequences—a fatal "tail that wagged the dog," as the great naval
historian of World War II, Adm. Samuel Eliot Morison, later wrote.
But the hunting license for Halsey expressed the clear intention of
Admiral Towers, the air chief back at CINCPAC, who was always
searching for ways to make aircraft carriers into offensive weapons.
Towers, ever the champion of the Brown Shoe Navy, wanted to free
the Third Fleet commander from the chore of covering troop landings. That September, Towers wrote in his diary, "Thank Heavens
Halsey and Mick Carney have slipped into the driver's seat." Halsey

was quick to grasp the meaning of his broad writ. After reading the operations plan, Halsey wrote Admiral Nimitz at CINCPAC:

> In as much as the destruction of the enemy fleet is the principal task, every weapon must be brought into play and the general coordination of these weapons should be in the hands of the tactical commander responsible for the battle. . . . My goal is the same as yours—to completely annihilate the Jap fleet if the opportunity offers.

By "tactical commander responsible for the battle," Halsey meant himself. Halsey reported to Nimitz, who at the time did not object to Halsey's license to roam. Unfortunately, Nimitz was not the only commander with a stake in Halsey's operations. The reoccupation of the Philippines was to be a joint army-navy operation. The invasion itself would be staged by General MacArthur, fulfilling his vow to return to the Philippine Islands he had been forced to abandon in the first months of the war. The amphibious landings would be covered by the Seventh Fleet under Adm. Thomas Kinkaid. The Seventh Fleet, also known as "MacArthur's Navy," with its small escort carriers and aging battleships on loan from the Pacific Fleet, was fine for shelling and bombing Japanese shore positions. It was less well equipped to hold off an attacking fleet, the task assigned to the Third Fleet. Kinkaid reported to MacArthur, just as Halsey reported to Nimitz. The chains of command stayed separate all the way to the commander-in-chief, President Roosevelt. Halsey's operational orders, with their seeming carte blanche to break off from supporting the landings, say nothing about getting permission from General MacArthur or consulting with Admiral Kinkaid. Halsey was not even required to notify them. This was a grave oversight, born of the folly of divided command.

Halsey's staff prepared constantly for their commander's longed-for collision with the Japanese fleet. A board for war games was built on the deck in Flag Country. Halsey's men pushed about model ships, creating and re-creating battle scenarios. After the dinner plates were cleared in the wardroom, the old Department of Dirty Tricks—Halsey's staff had followed him from Noumea to Hawaii to the *New*

Jersey—would debate the best way to set a trap for the Japanese. "We felt it was a poor day," recalled Halsey's chief of staff, Admiral Carney, "when we couldn't think of something that would bitch up the enemy's plans and intentions." The atmosphere in the wardroom was informal, proudly so. When the staff had moved from Noumea to Pearl Harbor, they had resisted the CINCPAC dress code. A sign was posted by Rollo Wilson, the operations chief and "staff poet," outside Halsey's office:

> *Complete with a black tie*
> *You do look terrific*
> *But take it off here:*
> *This is still South Pacific!*

Halsey had no use for "timid subordinates," recalled Carney. "Things were hammered out. They were hammered out with a degree of informality, which I think raised some eyebrows around the world, and certainly around the navy, from time to time. Sometimes these things were purple slugging matches." Halsey called Carney "a god-damned stubborn Mick" and worse. Carney pushed back. But when Halsey decided, he would point his finger and announce that he had made up his mind. That was it. There were no appeals. His subordinates, long accustomed to the absolute power of captains, knew not to press a point.

In order to allow debate to go on, Halsey would sometimes withdraw from the wardroom into his day cabin next door, where he would "pretend not to listen," recalled Lieutenant Commander Lawrence, his chief air combat intelligence officer. But the admiral would jump in if he heard something he didn't like. One night, a new arrival on the staff, a regular navy officer who was a little too smug about his Annapolis class ring, made the mistake of condescending to Cdr. Doug Moulton, Halsey's air ops officer, who was a reservist. "You, a reserve officer, dare to argue with me!" the ring-knocker sputtered at one point. Halsey "came storming into the room," Lawrence recalled, and chewed out the startled and abashed Annapolis man.

Halsey's staff returned his loyalty. "The staff was devoted to

Halsey. He was the most marvelous man to work for. He had a temper, but he was kind," Lawrence recalled. "And he had extraordinary charisma." Every day, Lawrence played "cutthroat" deck tennis with Halsey and two other staff officers, stripped to their shorts, on a court created on the foredeck next to a 16-inch gun turret. Lawrence partnered with marine Gen. Bill Riley, Halsey's bluff chief of plans, whom Halsey's critics at CINCPAC regarded as a weak planner but an ironfisted partier. Halsey's partner was his doctor, Carnes "Piggy" Weeks.

Halsey met Dr. Weeks at a cocktail party in Pearl Harbor at the end of 1943 and had been charmed by him. Wisecracking and determinedly, if somewhat manically, upbeat, Weeks functioned as a kind of all-purpose morale officer for the staff. He wrote funny, ribald diagnoses of their various ailments, which usually seemed to center around sexual deprivation. Weeks also controlled the wardroom liquor supply. Drinking alcohol had been banned aboard navy ships since World War I, but Weeks and Halsey had a benign view of the medicinal properties of drink. When he heard that stressed-out pilots were being given sedatives, Halsey ordered that the pilots' Ready Room be supplied with bourbon instead.

Judging from the quantities of bourbon and scotch that Halsey bought for his wardroom liquor stores every month, some spirits may have been consumed in the wardroom as well.* Lawrence could recall only one drinks party aboard ship, after a stressful series of air raids against Japanese bases on Formosa in October, but he suspected that Dr. Weeks gave his patient a shot or two at bedtime. Weeks was very sensitive about Halsey's emotional as well as his physical health. "We all were," recalled Lawrence. Everyone in the wardroom knew about the psychosomatic rash that had put Halsey into a hospital and kept him out of the Battle of Midway.

Lawrence, a genial Boston Brahmin educated at Harvard, loved the free-flowing, relaxed, often entertaining banter and debate of

---

*The admiral's "wine mess" shows 221 bottles of scotch and 198 bottles of bourbon on hand as of October 31, 1944. In the month of October, when Halsey was entirely at sea, seven bottles of scotch and six bottles of bourbon were withdrawn, mostly "for flavoring and for Admiral's birthday," according to Halsey's records.

the Dirty Tricks Department. But he was uneasy about the tension he felt with Capt. Mike Cheek, the staff's chief intelligence officer. Cheek outranked Lawrence, but he was not as comfortable with the give-and-take in the wardroom. Cheek rarely went to Flag Plot, preferring to maintain an office in his stateroom. "Cheek was a very tense person," Lawrence recalled. Cheek seemed to the Ivy Leaguers to have a chip on his shoulder. An Annapolis graduate, he had been passed over for promotion and left the navy in the 1930s. As a businessman in the Far East, he had learned a great deal about the Japanese by playing poker with them. He had rejoined the navy before Pearl Harbor, not as a line officer on a warship, but in the Office of Naval Intelligence. Cheek had little "command presence," and his insights rarely broke through the hubbub around the wardroom table. "Because of his poker face, it was very hard to know what was on his mind," Lawrence recalled. "His inarticulateness made him his own worst enemy."

Although Carney, the chief of staff, turned to Cheek for his read on the "Oriental mindset," Cheek "could not stand up to the flyboys," recalled Solberg, who also found Cheek to be "one of the most phlegmatic men I've ever known." The "flyboys" were the air combat intelligence officers—on paper, subordinate to Cheek, who was in charge of overall intelligence, but in fact freewheeling Brown Shoe Navy Men. "Flyboys" and deck officers alike tended to look down on men from the Office of Naval Intelligence, on the dubious proposition that only a man who couldn't get a ship command or fly airplanes would settle for intelligence work. Air Combat Intelligence derived its aura of superiority and even snobbery in part from the social prominence and natural confidence of officers like Lawrence, as well as ACI's affiliation with the aviators, the true "flyboys," whose missions Air Combat Intelligence evaluated.

It took a strong voice to thrive in the Department of Dirty Tricks. One belonged to Halsey's staff man for communications, Ham Dow. Carney relied on Dow for what he called "communications hornswoggles," for sending the Japanese false signals. Dow went to great lengths to fool the Japanese. Convinced that Japanese radio interceptors could identify the individual "fists" of American telegraph operators, Dow was known to move an operator from ship to ship—to confuse the Japanese, making them think that the man's ship itself was in a different location.

Halsey delighted in deception, and he would use any means necessary, even the weather. On October 9, Halsey sent a group of destroyers and cruisers to attack Marcus Island, northeast of the Marianas. The American warships laid down smoke screens and floated dummy radar targets and filled the sky with star shells and tracer fire. They were only pretending to be the Third Fleet. The next day, 1,500 miles to the west, the actual Third Fleet hit the Ryukyus, including Okinawa—the island chain closest to the Japanese Home Islands. Halsey had not come this close to Japan since the Doolittle Raid in '42. Halsey's carrier planes flew 1,396 sorties, shooting up ships in harbor and planes on the ground and serving notice on the Japanese that the U.S. Navy had arrived at their doorstep. Halsey caught the Japanese completely by surprise. The Big Blue Fleet had snuck up on Okinawa behind an advancing typhoon, which the wardroom wags dubbed "Task Force Zero," because it grounded all Japanese planes.

As the typhoon veered north, Halsey swung south to approach the more formidable target of Formosa, coming in so close the lookouts could see snow-capped mountains. The huge island south of Japan had fifty Japanese airfields. "They knew we were coming," recalled Admiral Mitscher, who had spotted Japanese "snooper" planes circling over the Third Fleet. On the morning of October 12, Halsey launched 1,378 sorties at "Fortress Formosa." By coincidence, the C-in-C of the Combined Fleet, Admiral Toyoda, happened to be visiting an airbase on Formosa. He was taking a bath when the first wave of American planes came over the field. Smelling of soap, wearing a bathrobe and rubber-soled *zori* sandals, he ran into the operations room yelling, "Chase them! Chase them!" The commander of the Sixth Base Air Force, Admiral Fukudome, ordered more than 200 planes into the air. He could see his Zeros diving on the oncoming American planes and puffs of smoke and flame as planes plummeted out of the sky. "Well done! Well done!" he cried, clapping his hands. "A tremendous success!" But then he realized that almost all the falling planes had been Japanese. He took cover as the bombs began to fall.

Most of the young Japanese pilots had never seen combat or even flown much. To save fuel and time, they had trained to identify and attack by watching a movie of six-foot-long models of American ships floating in a Japanese lake. The first wave of American planes shot about a third of the greenhorns out of the sky. By the third wave, no more Japanese fighters rose to meet the enemy.

By now, however, Admiral Toyoda was out of his bathrobe and into the fight. He sent out orders mobilizing air groups all over the empire, including an elite group of torpedo pilots, the "T-Force," trained to fly their torpedo planes at night and in poor weather. Based in Kyushu, the southernmost of the Home Islands, the T-Force ("T" stood for Typhoon) was ordered to attack Halsey's fleet at dusk.

Toyoda's orders were intercepted by American code breakers and relayed to Halsey. Solberg and Lawrence were analyzing pilot reports in Flag Plot when the communications officer handed Halsey the red folder containing top secret intercepts from the ULTRA code-breaking program. They all knew what to expect when darkness fell; the Japanese had used the same tactics at Guadalcanal, sending in torpedo attackers at last light.

In the hour between sunset and nightfall, the Japanese torpedo planes came skimming at wave-height toward the American fleet. A ghostly flare illuminated the American ships, presenting them as targets. From the bridge of the *New Jersey*, at the center of the fleet's battle formation, Solberg could see tracer rounds arcing out toward incoming twin-engined Betty bombers. Red flashes streaked across the deepening darkness as the destroyers opened up with 5-inch guns. Then hundreds of small- and large-caliber guns on the cruisers and battleships joined the cacophony. Solberg could see the Japanese planes suddenly light up, then cartwheel into the sea. None made it all the way to the *New Jersey*.

The Japanese raid was a failure; near-misses but no hits. But the battle was just beginning. On the second day, October 13, Halsey launched another 947 sorties against Formosa, and once again, the Japanese struck the Third Fleet at dusk. Mick Carney was watching the radar screen as a blip became a blob, an armada of planes closing on the American carrier groups. But when American interceptors, flying cover for the carriers, climbed above the Japanese formation and began calling out the different types of attacking planes, Carney noticed something else. The attackers were more of a mob than a formation; a motley odd-lot collection of planes patched together from different units and airfields. Carney wondered if the Japanese were starting to scrape the bottom of the barrel.

Even so, several torpedo planes got through the Third Fleet's formidable defenses on October 13, and one of them left the cruiser *Canberra* dead in the water, its engine room flooded. Halsey was faced with a choice: scuttle the cruiser or try to tow it to safety. He chose to save the ship—but at the risk of losing more ships. Another cruiser began towing the wounded *Canberra* at a painfully slow 4 knots, with no ability to maneuver against air attacks. On October 14, the Japanese attacked again, and once more a cruiser, the *Houston*, took a torpedo amidships. The captain ordered "Abandon Ship," then changed his mind, but the badly holed cruiser was wallowing and listing. Halsey ordered the *Houston* put under tow as well.

Halsey later described his agony over the decision. Was he "throwing good ships after bad?" Halsey fretted and paced, chain-smoking, in Flag Plot. "Every 15 minutes I glanced at the pin that represented the two cripples on my chart and cursed because they had inched no closer to safety," some 1,300 miles away at Third Fleet's island base, the atoll of Ulithi. He was, he later admitted, on the verge of giving the order to sink them both and "run beyond the range of the Japs' shore-based air before a worse disaster struck us."

But Carney, his chief of staff, and Rollo Wilson, his ops man, had an inspiration. They had been listening to the English-language broadcasts of Tokyo Rose, piped into Flag Plot. There were actually several Roses, American-born or educated women who broadcast on a propaganda show out of Tokyo called *Zero Hour*. One was a UCLA graduate of Japanese descent who had been visiting her sick aunt in Tokyo when the war broke out. This evening's Rose was in a state of ecstasy. The Japanese navy was claiming that it had sunk a dozen American carriers. People in Tokyo were dancing in the streets. Now that the empire's intrepid fliers had nearly annihilated the American ships, a Japanese fleet was sailing down from the Home Islands to finish the job. An ULTRA intercept confirmed the last part of Tokyo Rose's boast: at 12:16 in the afternoon on October 14, Imperial General Headquarters had ordered a task force of cruisers and destroyers to sail east of Formosa to mop up the "remnants" of the American fleet.

Gathering the Dirty Tricks Department in the wardroom, Carney and Wilson argued that this was just the moment to set a trap—to use the damaged cruisers as a lure to draw out the Japanese fleet and pounce on them. Halsey was feeling torn by his responsibilities. To Carney's worried eye, Admiral Halsey seemed worn out. It was one of the few times, Carney recalled, that Halsey was guilty of "thinking tired." The invasion of the Philippines was scheduled to begin in five days, and General MacArthur was counting on the Third Fleet to provide cover. Carney produced a copy of Halsey's orders for the Philippines operation—and pointed to the loophole that read, "In case opportunity for destruction of major portion of the enemy fleet offers or can be created, such destruction becomes the primary task."

This seemed to arouse Halsey from his uncharacteristic moroseness. The saucy spirit of the Department of Dirty Tricks returned. A plan to deceive was concocted. In the acronymic jargon of the navy, a battleship division is known as BATDIV, followed by a number. The wardroom jokers had defiantly named the two crippled cruisers under tow and their escorts CRIPDIV 1. Now a new moniker was chosen: BAITDIV 1. The commander of the ships, Adm. Lloyd Wiltse, was ordered to send out urgent "distress signals," prompting one of his captains to say: "Now I know how a worm on a fishhook must feel." Meanwhile, one of Halsey's carrier groups hovered a hundred miles away, ready to spring the trap.

The ingenious plot fizzled. A Japanese snooper spotted the lurking American carriers, and the Japanese fleet turned and ran for home. Still, the Battle of Formosa was deemed a smashing success. In three days, the Third Fleet had shot down or destroyed on the ground some 600 Japanese planes—roughly a third as many as all the German Luftwaffe planes shot down in the Battle of Britain. Halsey mocked the wildly exaggerated reports of Radio Tokyo, which by now was claiming that almost all the American carriers had been sunk. Halsey sent a dispatch to CINCPAC in Hawaii and COMINCH in Washington: THE THIRD FLEET'S SUNKEN AND DAMAGED SHIPS HAVE BEEN SALVAGED AND ARE RETIRING AT HIGH SPEED TOWARD THE ENEMY.

Halsey's pluck amused President Roosevelt, and as a morale booster, he released Halsey's message to the general public, adding more luster to the Bull Halsey myth.

Incredibly, the Japanese continued to celebrate their wholly imagined victory at sea. "Greater than Pearl Harbor!" the newspapers shouted. "As Great as Tsushima!" The emperor declared a day of national celebration and the radio broadcast a congratulatory message from Hitler in Germany. Imperial General Headquarters claimed that the effectiveness of the U.S. Navy had been reduced by 60 percent and that 26,000 American sailors had perished. Halsey, whose racist boasts had not gone unnoticed in Japan, came in for special attention. The keeper of the National Zoo in Tokyo was quoted saying that he had reserved a special monkey cage for the admiral of the Third Fleet.

"At first," Halsey wrote after the war, "I thought that this jubilation was merely more of the Japs' familiar self-hypnosis, but its extreme hysteria convinced me that they really believed we had been crushed." Casting about, Halsey came up with a seemingly plausible explanation: "All through the nights of the twelfth and the thirteenth, Jap planes burned on the water around our fleet, and when one of our ships was momentarily silhouetted against the blaze, it was hard to realize that she herself was not afire. No doubt the Jap pilots who escaped had the same illusion and reported our 'annihilation' in all sincerity."

Halsey was onto something. The chain of errors did begin with pilots calling out "Pillar of fire!" (*hibashira*), a commonly used term, as they darted away from the scene of battle. But more revealing is the way those excited shouts were hardened into damage assessments that were believed (or at least half-believed) by the high command. An unofficial Japanese war history published in 2002, *The Illusive War Results: The Truth of the Imperial Headquarters Reports*, describes the debriefing of pilots who attacked the Third Fleet on the night of October 12. One pilot described seeing a "pillar of fire," possibly an oil tanker or a carrier burning "at a far away place." A senior officer demanded, "Wasn't that an aircraft carrier?" The pilot responded, "It could have been." The chief officer pressed: "It was an aircraft carrier, right?"

This photo shows how easy it was for pilots to overestimate their damage reports. Only one of these American transport ships (the one on the left) was actually burning. The smoke rising from the other two comes from burning planes downed near the ships.

The pressure to exaggerate or lie seems hard to understand. Surely, accurate intelligence was essential. But interviewed after the war, pilots said they could not bear to disappoint their superiors, who in turn felt an overwhelming obligation not to disappoint *their* superiors, and on and on all the way to the imperial throne. Recalled Kosaku Koitabashi, a lookout aboard Admiral Kurita's flagship, "In those days, an order by the superiors was absolute. Also, it was our obligation to make sure that the morale (*shiki*) of the Japanese people should be maintained high even by false reports." The Japanese never used the word "defeat." They spoke of *tenshin*, changing the course. A "divine nation" could not be defeated.

The Japanese were not the only ones guilty of hyping their battle reports. Especially early in the war, when the pilots were green and the American public was desperate for good news from the front, the heroic claims of returning aviators were more fiction than fact. The cultural cues were a little different from the Japanese, but the initial results were nearly the same. Adm. James Holloway, later the chief of naval operations, recalled the one-upsmanship between two of his Annapolis classmates, fliers in an air battle in the South Pacific in 1942. The first pilot claimed a "close" hit on a carrier. The second pilot claimed a "direct" hit. The first pilot went back to the combat air intelligence officer: "I've been thinking it over," he said. "I got a direct hit." Recollected Holloway, laughing: "They were classmates, competitors." Just as subordination and duty could make the Japanese see things that never were, American individualism led to distortion, sometimes on a grand scale. Neither the Japanese nor the American pilots were willful liars or cynics; men under fire sometimes need to believe they are accomplishing great deeds just to keep going.*

The crucial question was whether their superiors believed them. Generally speaking, the American commanders were more skeptical of their pilots' reports. They benefited from code-breaking as a reality check, and, as the war progressed, American pilots probably became less hyperbolic than their Japanese counterparts. While some Japanese officers used a rough rule of thumb to discount pilots' claims (divide by two was a common equation), most U.S. Navy commanders were more exacting. Admiral Spruance, in particular, had been made skeptical by some of the woollier claims. One Army Air Corps pilot, for instance, had preposterously claimed to have sunk a Japanese cruiser in fourteen seconds, when he had in fact bombed an American submarine, the *Grayling*, which had crash-dived. Spruance refused to believe his own aviators' claims unless there was proof.

But some air combat intelligence officers were more lenient—and more credulous. Accuracy was a paramount consideration, but not the only one, recalled John Lawrence, Halsey's chief ACI staffer. "We had to think about the morale of the fliers when we were questioning the veracity of their reports," said Lawrence. "The pilots

---

*Pilots were not the only combatants to exaggerate their kills. At the Battle of Tassafaronga in November 1942, the American fleet commander claimed two cruisers and seven destroyers sunk. In fact, one Japanese destroyer was sunk.

were under enormous strain," risking their lives on every mission. "We wanted to encourage the pilots to go back and attack." The ACI staffers were faced with a dilemma. "The great question," said Lawrence, "was to what extent you could water down the pilots' reports without killing morale. Sending these pilots back out . . . ," said Lawrence, pausing as he recalled those feelings, still with him a half-century later. "That was very tough to do." Admiral Halsey cared for his pilots, said Lawrence, and his concern was contagious. "He felt very deeply about those under his orders. He had enormous personal feeling about each and every one. He flew every mile with them."

By late October 1944, the pilots of the Third Fleet were under tremendous strain. A brief respite at the atoll of Ulithi early in October had been cut short by a typhoon. Unable to take on provisions, ships sailed with their storerooms half-full, and normally well-fed pilots were subsisting on Spam and beans. After months of action, some pilots could hardly bear to crawl back into their cockpits. Aboard the fast carrier *Bunker Hill*, Adm. Gerry Bogan sent Halsey a "sad picture . . . Fighting Squadron 8 is practically 100% suffering from combat fatigue. Of 44 fighter pilots including four recent replacements, 20 grounded on recommendation of two flight surgeons." Admiral Mitscher, the carrier task force commander, fretted to Halsey that the air groups were losing their edge, that their response times were dangerously slowing. Mitscher was well known for his sensitivity to the pilots. He knew that a pilot could not be simply ordered to dive on an enemy ship or shamed into it. "We don't hypnotize them," he wrote: "These kids aren't crazy. They know we don't want them to commit suicide. He, himself, has to feel he has a chance of getting out or he won't bore in. These kids aren't Japs."

After storming across the Pacific for the past ten months, Mitscher himself was badly worn. When he was tired, he would go quiet, and lately, his silences had been lengthening. Halsey had not been at sea nearly as long as Mitscher, but he, too, was feeling the stress. The admiral and his staff were feverish and ill—the flu had swept through Flag Country aboard the *New Jersey*, as the overworked staffers watching the progress of BAITDIV 1 failed to get any rest. But, painfully, Halsey resisted requests for relief of overstretched fighter squadrons. He issued a stern order that "responsible seniors instill and maintain a resolute spirit in overworked pilots when stakes are high." Aboard the *New Jersey*, Lieutenant Solberg recalled,

> Some of us could see how unhappy he was when next he heard that *Lexington* [Mitscher's flagship] pilots were near the end of their tether. He was seen pacing the bridge nervously until he blurted out to no one in particular but just thinking out loud, "Damn it all, I know they're tired and need a rest. So do all the carriers. I'd like to give it to them but I can't—the morale of the whole fleet would be gone."

There was far too much to be done. The Third Fleet had to prepare to cover, along with Admiral Kinkaid's Seventh Fleet, General MacArthur's invasion of the Philippines on October 20 (by an amphibious force second in size only to the D-Day landings at Normandy). Intelligence was beginning to pick up stirrings of activity by the Japanese fleet. Halsey was aware that a large number of Japanese battleships and cruisers were assembled at Lingga, at the tip of the Malay Peninsula, roughly two days' sail from the Philippines. Radio intercepts picked up significant tanker movements, suggesting that the Japanese fleet was preparing to sortie. American eavesdroppers even heard references to an "S" operation. The "S" stood for *Sho* they were hearing Admiral Toyoda send Admiral Kurita the signal to prepare to execute the last-ditch "Victory Operation" against the American invasion. But the code breakers did not know what tricks the Japanese had in store for the American invaders.

Halsey was not sure what to believe. He wanted to be aggressive. He chafed at covering the MacArthur landings, and requested permission from Nimitz to go barging through the San Bernardino Strait, from the east side of the Philippines, where the landings were being staged in Leyte Gulf, to the west side, where Japanese battleships might be lurking. But Nimitz reined him in, at least until the invasion was safely done. Halsey could not argue that the lunge after the enemy would be worth it—that this was the "opportunity" to destroy the Japanese fleet provided for in the escape clause of his operational orders to cover the Philippine landings. He didn't know where the fleet was.

Halsey and his staff spent hours debating and guessing at Japanese intentions in the third week of October. Halsey predicted that some Japanese ships would come up from their bases in the south to try hit-and-run raids. At the same time, he salivated over bigger game. He particularly "obsessed" about the Japanese carriers, recalled Mick Carney. He had heard reports that the Japanese had been building new carriers at their bases on the empire's Inland Sea. Like Captain Ahab in his quest for Moby-Dick, Halsey was fixedly intent upon finding and destroying those carriers—delivering the final deathblow, he believed, to the Japanese navy and turning the key to ending the war.

But he didn't think the Japanese would be rash enough to commit their entire fleet to a decisive battle until they had built up their air strength, which had been decimated at Formosa. Halsey misread the Japanese. He thought they would take foolish risks, but he believed that they were cowardly at heart. He failed to appreciate their almost apocalyptical spirit.

On October 22, Halsey put down his thoughts in a long personal letter to Admiral Nimitz. He told CINCPAC that Admiral Mitscher believed that "Jap naval air was virtually wiped out." Mitscher had reached that conclusion after observing the poor skill of the Japanese pilots and their odd-lot planes in the battle off Formosa. But Halsey was not so sure. He assumed that the enemy "still had some carrier air strength up his sleeve." He acknowledged he had no hard information. But he believed those carriers and their planes were out there, somewhere.

As General MacArthur's vast armada prepared for the invasion of the Philippines in early October, Capt. Ray Tarbuck, a navy officer attached to MacArthur's G-3 (planning staff), had been studying the map and making some crude calculations. From captured documents and radio intercepts, he knew that Admiral Kurita's fleet was based at Lingga Roads near Singapore. By moving to Brunei Bay, the Japanese base on Borneo, Tarbuck realized, the Japanese fleet could be a day's sail from the U.S. Army's landing beaches in Leyte Gulf. Tarbuck had a "seafarer's hunch" that the Japanese would try to make a run at attacking the American invasion force from the sea. He guessed that the Japanese ships would divide into two prongs, one passing through the Surigao Strait to the south of the landing beaches, the other passing through the San Bernardino Strait to the north. The two columns of battleships would create a pincer movement and attack MacArthur's troop ships as they off-loaded on the beaches of Leyte Gulf. Tarbuck had no special intelligence, just intuition, some charts, and a navigator's compass, but he had correctly guessed at the Japanese Sho Operation. He even predicted, presciently, that the Japanese would try to lure away Admiral Halsey's carriers with a diversionary force to the north.

Worried, unable to sleep, Tarbuck took his prediction, complete with an estimated "chart track" of the enemy ships, to his boss, Gen. Stephen Chamberlin. A regular army man and member of the tight circle around MacArthur, Chamberlin ignored Tarbuck's concerns. "Listen, General," Tarbuck said after stewing for a few days, "you have four army divisions abreast and four more floating in reserve, and you're going to have a quarter of a million men swimming in full packs if you don't send that up"—pass his warning up the chain of command. Grudgingly, Chamberlin forwarded the plan to MacArthur's chief of intelligence, Gen. Charles A. Willoughby. A rigid Prussian (he had changed his name from Karl Weidenbach) and an admirer of Spain's Fascist dictator Gen. Francisco Franco, Willoughby, known as "Sir Charles" by his staff, was rigidly turf-conscious. He told Tarbuck to mind his own business—planning (G-3)—and stay out of intelligence. Willoughby and the intelligence staff of MacArthur's navy, the Seventh Fleet under Admiral Kinkaid, had made their own estimate of Japanese intentions:

> Though the capability exists, the probability of a major Orange [Japanese] Task Force sortieing against Blue [American] shipping or naval vessels East of the Philippines seems unlikely and a venture involving more risk than the Japanese are believed ready or able to assume.

Like Admiral Halsey, General Willoughby and the intelligence staffers for MacArthur's landing force were making the assumption that the Japanese would behave cautiously or prudently, the way most American commanders would act under similar circumstances. How they might have believed this after nearly three years of war against an increasingly fanatical foe is testament to a cultural divide wider than the Pacific Ocean.

CHAPTER EIGHT

SHO-GO

"There are such things as miracles"

ADMIRAL TAKEO KURITA, faithful to the ancient arts of his ancestors, sometimes practiced archery on the foredeck of his flagship, the heavy cruiser *Atago*. His sailors would watch as the commander of the Second Fleet, straight-backed and silent, fired arrows into a target. Kurita had spent his more than three decades at sea perfecting the art of firing torpedoes, modern arrows, that could sink warships from a range of up to eleven miles (twenty miles at a low-speed setting). He was regarded as one of the Imperial Navy's leading experts in night torpedo attacks. And yet, despite seeing considerable action since the war began, he had never had the chance to fire a torpedo against an American ship. Mostly, his war had consisted of being bombed by American warplanes—at Midway, Santa Cruz, Rabaul, the Marianas. Perhaps, in the Philippines, his luck would change and he would destroy the enemy in a surprise torpedo attack at night. That was his official position, at least. Privately, he was full of doubts.

On the evening of October 15, as the sun set over the flat, sandy islands of the Lingga anchorage, Admiral Kurita appeared on the foredeck of the *Atago*, alone and looking lost in thought. From the bridge, quartermaster Kosaku Koitabashi watched as the admiral sat down in a folding chair that had been placed in front of a gun turret.

Drafted as a young man at twenty, now a battle-tested sea dog at twenty-four, quartermaster Koitabashi had spent many hours standing by the admiral on the bridge, and he knew his commander's moods. Koitabashi turned to a signalman, Nagaoka, and asked, "Why is the admiral so tense?" The two petty officers watched as Admiral Kurita slowly and deliberately looked around the anchorage at the thirty-nine Imperial Japanese Navy warships swinging at their moorings in the last rays of daylight.

The firepower of the Imperial Japanese Navy had been concentrated in this one calm, tepid bay at the tip of the Malay Peninsula, a thousand miles from the homeland but close to the so-called Southern Resources Area, the oil-rich islands of the East Indies that provided their fuel. The colossal *Yamato* and *Musashi* loomed at anchor. Almost three years into the war, they had never seen action against an enemy ship. Their 18-inch guns, the largest naval guns ever forged, had never been fired in ship-to-ship combat. The sacred behemoths had been saved, preserved, protected for the final Decisive Battle. Around them, gray and leaden in the shimmering turquoise waters, were five more massive battleships, eleven heavy cruisers, two light cruisers, and nineteen destroyers. It was an armada for the ages, though with one glaring weakness: there were no aircraft carriers anywhere to be seen. Japan's few remaining flattops were still in the Inland Sea of the Home Islands, awaiting planes and pilots with at least enough training to take off, if not land.

As Kurita sat quietly on *Atago*'s foredeck, he seemed to be looking from ship to ship, as if to take their measure. Suddenly, Kurita's chief of staff, Admiral Koyanagi, appeared at his elbow and whispered into his ear. Watching from the bridge, quartermaster Koitabashi and signalman Nagaoka looked at each other knowingly. The long-awaited day of Decisive Battle, they felt sure, was at hand.

The two sailors, both noncommissioned officers, fancied that they were in on all the scuttlebutt. Every day, after breakfast or lunch or dinner, a gaggle of NCOs would gather by the tobacco "bon," a large metal ashtray set on the fantail, behind the toilets, to smoke and gossip. Koitabashi and Nagaoka were in the Seventh Division, the bridge detail of quartermasters (who keep the charts and the logs), signalmen, and lookouts, and they were particularly welcome at the bon. Signalmen could show off by leaking the contents of decoded cables to their fellow petty officers—a forbidden practice, but routine nonetheless. "We were the first to know what the bridge was up to," recalled Koitabashi. Like every sailor in the fleet, they had been told they were training for Decisive Battle, but not where or when. Then, in early October, coded telegrams had begun arriving from Combined Fleet headquarters in Tokyo. "We knew from leaks that this battle would decide the fate of Japan," Koitabashi recalled. "We knew this would be the last sea battle."

Koitabashi and his mates would gossip about their superior officers. "I never heard a negative word about Admiral Kurita," Koitabashi recalled. "He was an expert in torpedoes. I thought he was a great man." (His opinion was more mixed about Admiral Ugaki. "Men loved or hated him," recalled Koitabashi. "He was seen as arrogant.") On the right wing of the main bridge of his flagship, Admiral Kurita sat in a large swivel chair, which the sailors called *saru no koshikake*, the flat mushroom—the place where the top monkey sat in the jungle. Behind him stood the operations officer, Captain Otani. Garrulous, confident, Otani was a commanding figure, though a bit officious. He did most of the talking, consulting with Admiral Koyanagi, the low-key, quietly bitter but gentlemanly chief of staff, who would in turn seek Kurita's final judgment. The admiral of the fleet barely spoke. He would swivel in his chair and nod and smile slightly.

On the eve of battle, the petty officers cadging their postprandial smokes on the fantail were fairly upbeat, eager for action. Noncommissioned officers like Koitabashi were the heart of the Japanese navy, "spirited, diligent, faithful to orders, and well-trained . . . the best in the world," according to British naval historian Arthur Marder. True, they could hardly avoid seeing that the war was not going well. Even if the Japanese press lied about the illusory victories, the sailors could see that the Combined Fleet was gradually retreating—or in the approved lexicon, changing course—westward, closer to home. Koitabashi had seen the human cost, badly wounded sailors from sunk or burning ships, laid out on makeshift operating tables in the *Atago's* wardroom. At the Battle of the Philippine Sea, it had been disheartening to watch the young pilots veering and crashing as they tried to land their planes on the decks of carriers. And what had become of those carriers? When would they rejoin the fleet?

Even so, Koitabashi and his mates could see with their own eyes that the epicenter of Japan's naval might—the literal and figurative soul of the navy—was still intact. Since schoolboy days, Koitabashi had believed that the key to national greatness, celebrated in poem and song in the classroom and on the radio, was the battleship. Majestic castles of steel, the *Yamato* and *Musashi* strained at their anchor chains just a few hundred yards from Koitabashi's post on the bridge of the *Atago*. At night, in practice, the great guns of the superbattleships flowered with orange blossoms, flinging massive shells for miles in the dark. Surely, Koitabashi and his fellow smokers reassured themselves, the American fleet could not withstand such power.

The men did notice, however, that their superior officers seemed worried, even downcast. Their normally amiable commander, Admiral Kurita, was notably somber. The admiral, still suffering from the lingering effects of dengue fever, had shrunk into his leathery skin. Kurita was always wizened and weathered, but now he looked exhausted and careworn.

Kurita had much to worry about. He did not believe the reports from Tokyo of a smashing victory over the American fleet off Formosa, the claims that twelve or more carriers had been sunk. As was his customary practice, Kurita divided all claims by Japanese pilots in half, but even that, he could guess, was a generous estimate.

Kurita was on his own, isolated and cut out of the *Sho-Go* planning. He was facing a Decisive Battle—possibly, one that really would be decisive. Japan could no longer trade space for time as it backed across the Pacific. Kurita was well aware that the Philippines had to be defended or the empire would be cut off from its fuel source in the Southern Resources Area. But the commander of the Second Fleet, or as his fleet had now been named, the First Diversionary Striking Force, had heard very little from headquarters, save orders to prepare for a coming battle. His fleet's new name was loaded with irony. It clearly suggested that Kurita's battleships would act as a decoy or diversion while Admiral Ozawa's Mobile Fleet of aircraft carriers delivered the main attack. But without planes, Ozawa's carriers were powerless. They could only play the part of decoy. Kurita's force would not be "diversionary." His battleships and cruisers would be the main event, the navy's hope to repel the American invaders in the Philippines.

In some of the early Sho planning, the admirals in Tokyo had discussed sending two or three carriers down to escort Kurita's battleships and provide air cover. Kurita had never been directly or formally informed of this planning; he had to rely on rumor and speculation. In August, Combined Fleet headquarters had condescended to Kurita by sending a mere captain to brief Kurita's fleet on the Sho Plan. Kurita was being told, in effect, do your duty; we do not need your advice. It was understood or expected that Kurita would accept his fate and his obligation.

Some Japanese naval historians cast the appointment of Kurita in a cynical light. He was, after all, a rather lackluster choice to lead the fleet into decisive battle. It may be that Kurita was being set up as a fall guy, a kind of grand strategic patsy. For all the brave rhetoric, the less deluded of the top command could have guessed that the Sho Plan was doomed to fail. They may have figured that Kurita would go down without protesting, or that in any case he would be easy to blame.

Kurita may or may not have suspected that he was being badly used. He never complained. But he was a realist. He understood that he would be steaming into battle with only spotty air cover, if any at all. The Philippines had dozens of airfields that might be used to support Kurita's fleet. But Kurita knew from battle reports that the navy's land-based air fleets had been decimated, fed to the slaughter by Admiral Toyoda at Formosa. The army still had several hundred planes in the Philippines, but Kurita, like most naval officers, never counted on the army for help. Army pilots had not been trained to navigate over water. Besides, the army and navy, by tradition, barely communicated.

Kurita had little faith in his own service's planning for battle. Interrogated by the Americans after the war, Kurita would say that Imperial Navy Headquarters lacked a "sureness of touch," but he was being diplomatic. He understood before he sortied from Lingga Gulf that his fleet was being sent out as a kind of offering, to appease the war gods and show the Japanese people that the navy, too, would sacrifice to protect the homeland. He wondered whether his objective under the Sho Plan was worth the cost. Was sinking some American troop transports really worth risking the *Yamato* and the *Musashi* and their crews? His hope, his devout wish (he would later say), was to encounter the main American carrier fleet and sink them in a proper sea battle. Conceivably, the elaborate diversion plan would work, and the American carrier fleet would be fooled and take the bait, but Kurita was not counting on it. He assumed that he would encounter American warships along the way. He had trained all his life to fight enemy warships in a surface battle and hoped this would be his chance.

But Kurita could not control his fate. He had to accept it. On October 16, the day he was seen sitting on the foredeck, staring across the anchorage, seemingly lost in thought, he was preparing for battle. He had canceled orders to dry-dock two cruisers and began making plans to sortie. Fuel was a gnawing concern. Though the fleet was close to its fuel source in the East Indies, the navy lacked enough tankers to transport the oil. American air raids and submarines were taking their toll on the Imperial Navy's supply chain. Kurita had to figure out a way to make sure his ships had enough fuel to sail to the Philippines. Kurita's superiors in Tokyo may not have worried whether Kurita's fleet would

Last sortie of the Japanese fleet

be able to sail home from battle. But Kurita did. He was prepared to lose half his fleet—but not all of it.

At 8:55 on the morning of October 17, the order came from Combined Fleet headquarters in Tokyo: stand by to execute *Sho-Go Dai Ichi*, Victory Operation Number One. An advance force of U.S. Army rangers was landing on Suluan Island, at the mouth of Leyte Gulf. The American invasion of the Philippines was clearly imminent. Kurita gave the order to strip the fleet for action. Anything flammable or movable had to go: furniture, decorations, clothes. Sailors were to go into battle with only the shirts on their back.

At one o'clock in the morning on October 18, the First Diversionary Striking Force hoisted anchor and filed from the warm protective bay at the tip of the Malay Peninsula. The night was fair, and the great ships, with their distinctive pagoda superstructures, formed shadowy silhouettes in the gloom. One by one they went into the open sea, the last time the Imperial Japanese Navy would ever be able to muster such a force for battle.

"We sailed quietly east in the dark of night," recorded Admiral Ugaki, who was at his post on the bridge, high in the towering superstructure of the *Yamato*. The next day, as the fleet steamed northeast along the coast of Borneo, Ugaki recorded that a young hawk had perched atop the gray-metal gun director of the *Yamato*'s main batteries. Some sailors had captured the hawk and caged it as a

mascot. To Ugaki, this was an omen. He was looking for signs in the sky and in the beauty of nature. Later, he wrote, "a faintly illuminated layer of auspicious air" hung near the surface of the sea.

Ugaki had drifted into the realm of the mystical, as he often did, to escape his conflicting impressions of reality. He had faithfully recorded Tokyo's claims of carriers sunk off Formosa—and then written that he didn't really believe them. He doubted that the fleet could get to the landing beaches in time to do real damage to the American invaders—yet he was somehow confident of victory. "We are not afraid of a million enemies or a thousand carriers because our whole force shares the same spirit," Ugaki wrote in elegant ancient Japanese characters, illuminated by the red light of the battle lamp above his desk.

The mood below decks in the ships of the First Striking Force was, like Ugaki's, at once giddy and fatalistic. "We knew we would lose our lives," recalled Hiroshi Yasunaga, a pilot of a floatplane (used for scouting) aboard the cruiser *Chikuma.* Rejected by Eta Jima at age seventeen, Yasunaga had gone to flight school and bounced around the Pacific War as a reconnaissance pilot, logging more than 3,000 hours in the air. "We were ready to die, to scatter like jade," he recalled, invoking the "shattered gem" imagery used by the propagandists for national sacrifice and self-immolation. "I didn't think we were going to win the battle. But I was a survivor. I'd survive somehow." Word of the hawk settling on the conning tower of the *Yamato* spread quickly through the fleet. A sign from the gods, proclaimed senior officers to their men. "We laughed at it," recalled Yasunaga. He and his mates aboard the *Chikuma* were a little cynical about their commanders. Why did Admiral Kurita choose the cruiser *Atago* as his flagship instead of the mighty *Yamato?* Because the *Yamato* was easier for enemy planes to spot, joked Yasunaga and his buddies.

Aboard the *Atago,* Petty Officer Koitabashi had heard all the jokes but defended his commander. It was traditional, he knew, for the fleet commander to fly his flag from a cruiser, which was faster and more maneuverable than a battleship and would lead any night torpedo attacks, the opening blow in battle (and Kurita's specialty). Still, Koitabashi took the talk of omens with a grain of salt. "We heard all kinds of stories—that the hawk had landed on the thumb of the captain of the *Yamato*. We just laughed," recalled Koitabashi.

The great fleet steamed into Brunei Bay on the coast of Borneo, a day's sail from the Philippines, at noon on October 20. Aboard the *Atago,* Kurita received news that the invasion of the Philippines had begun in Leyte Gulf, just as predicted. Thousands of American troops were streaming ashore. Combined Fleet headquarters in Tokyo had wanted Kurita's force to barge into the American anchorage on October 22, to catch the invaders while they were still at their most vulnerable. But it was impossible, Kurita protested in a cable to Combined Fleet Headquarters.

Kurita was never one to rush into anything, including battle, as he had shown with his zigzagging and stalling on the last night of the Battle of the Philippine Sea. Kurita had reason to slow his pace toward the Philippines. When he arrived at Brunei Bay for refueling, there were no tankers awaiting them. The battleships fueled the destroyers from their own tanks and waited for the empire's supply chain, always its weakest link, to provide the necessary oil to sally forth and, Kurita hoped, return with at least half their strength intact.

As his fleet idled in a bay surrounded by mountains rising 12,000 feet out of the jungle, Kurita received some more bad news: he was to send all but four of his thirty-two floatplanes to the Philippines. The floatplanes, seaplanes stored on the stern or amidships of his cruisers and battleships, were the fleet's eyes over the horizon, used to spot enemy ships and particularly submarines. Apparently Southwest Fleet Headquarters in Manila needed the planes for its own reconnaissance purposes. There was considerable bitterness among Kurita's officers as the floatplanes went winging off on the afternoon of October 20. "I'd hate to be responsible for this decision when enemy submarines attack," remarked a staff officer, who could guess at what lay ahead for Kurita's fleet as they drew near the Philippines.

While the Japanese bickered and dithered, the American invasion ground ahead. General MacArthur himself had waded ashore at Leyte Gulf, as triumphant as Caesar across the Rubicon. "People of the Philippines," the former field marshal announced into the microphones arrayed for him on Red Beach on "A-Day" (Eisenhower had already appropriated "D-Day" for the Normandy landings). "I have returned. Rally to me!" With his father's derringer in his pocket in case he was captured alive, MacArthur staged his return with a showman's brio. He was supposed to arrive high and dry at a jetty, but the landing craft delivering him ran aground a hundred yards shy of the beach, forcing the general and his staff to slosh in water above their knees. A cameraman caught MacArthur angrily grimacing. He was angry at a navy aide, not the Japanese, but the picture looked so heroic that he waded ashore again the next day for the cameras.

Within twenty-four hours of the October 20 landings, American forces pushed inland past the first line of Japanese defenses. By October 22, nearly all the troops would be ashore. The only targets left at the beachhead for the Japanese attacking from the sea would be cargo and ammunition ships and mostly empty troop transports. Sinking them could cause some temporary havoc, but it would hardly delay the advance of an American armada toward Japan. MacArthur's invasion force of 700 ships had stretched over a hundred miles. Sink even 100 of those ships and American shipyards would just crank out 200 more. Indeed, it is hard to see how *any* blow struck by the Imperial Japanese Navy could strategically slow the Americans. At this stage, the Japanese were fighting for honor.

On the morning of October 21, as his battle fleet continued to idle in Brunei Bay, Kurita received his final orders from Combined Fleet headquarters in Tokyo. He was to "break through" into Leyte Gulf at dawn on October 25 "after first destroying the enemy's surface forces" and "cut down his landing forces." The First Diversionary Striking Force had trained to fight at night, a time when American planes usually did not mount attacks. The idea of a daylight action appalled most of Kurita's officers and Kurita, too, though he tried not to show it. The final orders from Tokyo gave Kurita little realistic hope of air cover. None of Ozawa's carriers would be coming south to join forces with Kurita's battleships; they would all be staying in the north to act as a lure to draw away Halsey's carriers. The true nature of their orders began to sink in with Kurita's staff and his senior commanders: they were on a suicide mission.

A few may have welcomed it. Ugaki, as usual, greeted the prospect

The invasion force

of doom philosophically. "Well," he wrote, "if you dare to act, the devil may avoid you." Just maybe the fleet would surprise the Americans and escape, Ugaki reasoned. If not, then the First Diversionary Striking Force would perish memorably. Ugaki was moved by the spirit of some of his more zealous fellow admirals. The navy's First Air Force, based in the Philippines, had fewer than a hundred planes left to support the Sho Operation. But Ugaki recorded in his diary that Admiral Onishi was going to organize "a Kamikaze Special Attack Corps" with twenty-six fighters, "of which 13 are suicidal ones," to attack the enemy carriers. "Oh, what a noble spirit this is!" exulted Ugaki.

Onishi was the brilliant, volatile air expert who had once slapped a geisha and dispatched Japanese POWs to their deaths, each for the same crime—insufficient attention to duty. His frequent discussions about *tokko* (body-slamming) tactics with Captain Jo, the emperor's military adviser, were finally nearing the execution stage. Onishi had been thinking about putting together a suicide squadron since the Battle of the Philippine Sea, which had cost so many pilots and planes back in June. Now the time had come. The shortage of planes and the desperation of the moment in the Philippines moved Onishi to introduce kamikazes to the Pacific War just when Japan's defeat was about to be sealed. The reasoning was essentially circular nihilism. As Admiral Toyoda, the Combined Fleet's commander-in-chief, explained to American interrogators after the war, Onishi reckoned that if Admiral Kurita's fleet was taking "such desperate measures," then he, too, as the champion of the air force, "must take similarly desperate measures."

Kurita did not put much hope, if any, in the kamikazes (he made no mention of them during his postwar interrogation). With hundreds of miles of open ocean to cross, then a narrow strait to navigate, he would have to forge ahead—with or without air cover. His ships bristled with antiaircraft guns. Perhaps they could raise a curtain of fire, though chances were practically nil it could keep out hundreds of determined American pilots. Kurita had been under sustained air attack before—at Rabaul, when he had stood silent on the bridge as his captain, nearly disemboweled by shrapnel, was carried below, shouting *"Banzai!"* as his intestines fell out.

On the afternoon of October 21, he briefed his captains on his plan of attack. The main force would leave the next morning, October 22, at 0800, 8:00 A.M. They would proceed west of Palawan Island toward the Philippines at 16 knots. This slow speed would conserve fuel, allowing, Kurita hoped, for a return voyage. At the same time, however, the plodding pace would make the fleet more vulnerable to American submarines, which ran on the surface at about 20 knots. After reaching the Philippine island of Mindoro on the morning of October 24, the fleet would pick up steam and snake eastward through the islands of the Sibuyan Sea at 24 knots. At about sunset, the fleet would enter the San Bernardino Strait, a narrow, tide-ripped passage that connected the island-filled Sibuyan Sea on the west side of the island of Leyte to the open Philippine Sea on the east. Emerging from the San Bernardino Strait, Kurita expected to encounter enemy ships, defeat them in a night action, and sail down the east coast of the island of Samar, to arrive at the mouth of Leyte Gulf by dawn. The orders were a little vague about the enemy ships Kurita might encounter and defeat by night. Halsey was out there somewhere, and so were dozens of American submarines. Presumably, they would lie in wait to ambush Kurita as his ships debouched from the San Bernardino Strait on the evening of October 24. In any case, after Kurita stormed into Leyte Gulf, it was a certainty that American warships and planes would try to trap Kurita's fleet inside the gulf. That battle would have to be fought in broad daylight.

Kurita's battle plan picked up a new wrinkle before he sortied. The Striking Force detached two older, slower battleships, the *Yamashiro* and *Fuso,* as well as a cruiser and four destroyers, to approach Leyte Gulf through Surigao Strait to the south. The two fleets—Kurita's main body of five battleships, twelve cruisers, fifteen destroyers and the second, smaller group under Adm. Shoji Nishimura—would create a pincer movement, joining after dawn on October 25 to bash into the American invasion fleet's anchorage. The idea behind splitting the fleet was to further confuse the Americans, to add an additional decoy that would draw off the more numerous American defenders and allow Kurita's battleships to slip by. The concept of a two pronged attack was not Kurita's. It had been suggested by headquarters, which seemed to delight in devising ever more intricate plans, regardless of faulty communications and the inevitable fog and friction of war.

On the eve of the legendary naval battle at Trafalgar, in October 1805, Adm. Lord Nelson announced his battle plan to his adoring captains. As Nelson wrote his lover, Lady Hamilton, "Some shed tears, all approved—it was new—it was singular—it was simple!" On the eve of the last and largest naval battle in history, Kurita's captains reacted less enthusiastically. Kurita was bombarded with complaints. Kurita's own operations officer, Captain Otani, worried that the overall Sho Plan—with Ozawa maneuvering in the north and Kurita dividing his fleet in the south and each element dependent on the other for close timing—was "too complex and too inflexible to work."

In his cabin aboard the *Atago*, Kurita sweated in the tropical heat as he read through the notes piled on his desk. His captains were in open revolt. They assured him that they did not mind death. It was the honor of the navy they feared for. If this was to be the last great sortie of the fleet, the last gasp of the Imperial Navy, how could they justify its sacrificial altar: shooting up a fleet of empty cargo ships? Surely their ancestors must be weeping in their graves. What would the great Togo, hero of Tsushima, think of sacrificing battleships for such paltry targets?

At sunset on October 21, Kurita summoned his captains for a final banquet. From ships all around the fleet, motor launches emerged with stern men in dress whites sitting silent and erect, their minds on the coming battle. The small boats clustered around the *Atago*, not a capital ship in the class of the *Yamato* or *Musashi*, but a formidable warship nonetheless. With her peculiarly Japanese features—a raked-forward smokestack, towering pagoda superstructure, Long Lance torpedo tubes, and not two but three gun turrets on the foredeck—*Atago* was more powerful than any American cruiser of its type. (Officially, *Atago* was a 10,000-ton ship, but the Japanese had cheated on the arms limitation treaties of the 1920s and built her at 13,000 tons, about one-fifth the weight of the *Yamato*.)

The officers gathered in *Atago*'s wardroom, now stripped of furnishings for the modest banquet; food stores were low. Only the emperor's portrait remained on the bulkhead walls. Under Hirohito's imposing stare, the senior officers of the First Diversionary Striking Fleet raised their sake cups to the victory none of them thought possible. It was Kurita's time to speak. Never one for orations, he knew he had to say something to comfort and inspire his restless and anxious commanders.

"I know that many of you are strongly opposed to this assignment," he began honestly. "But," he went on with equal forthrightness, "the war situation is much worse than you imagine." Several of his listeners noticed that Kurita's tone of voice was different. Normally, he was benign or taciturn or just silent. Now he seemed both stern and passionate. He advanced the official line, the nihilistic reasoning of Admiral Toyoda in Tokyo. "Would it not be a shame to have the fleet intact while our nation perishes?" Kurita made a somewhat ambiguous nod to his superiors. "I believe that Imperial General Heaquarters is giving us a glorious opportunity," he said.

In Japan, there is an important distinction between what one says (*tatemae,* public talk) and what is left unsaid—usually, what one really means (*honne,* private thoughts). In the sudden tropical night of October in Brunei Bay, Kurita's officers understood what he really meant. According to another, less literal translation, what Kurita said, or perhaps what he really meant, was "I think the HQ wants to give us a place to die. We are pressured into it."

Glorious chance or death sentence, it was their duty. "You must all remember there are such things as miracles," said Kurita, who did not believe in miracles. "What man can say there is no chance for our fleet to turn the tide of war in a decisive battle?"

Kurita was mouthing all the platitudes. He went on: "We shall have the chance to meet our enemies. We shall engage his task forces. I hope that you will not carry your responsibilities lightly. I know that you will act faithfully and well."

Some heard, between the lines and in the subtlety of his language, a more ambiguous message: "Be cautious and fight" is another translation of the words Kurita used that night—not quite the ringing damn-the-torpedoes rallying cry that captains of the First Striking Fleet might have heard from a more gung ho commander—Admiral Ozawa or Admiral Ugaki—or for that matter, Admiral Halsey.

The captains stood and cried, *"Banzai! Banzai! Banzai!"* Their true feelings may have been less fervent. That night, the petty officers of the fleet had their celebration in their mess hall. Koitabashi recalled the dreary scene:

> On the last evening before departure, there was an order to provide us with a little sake. All the personal belongings were removed and there were tables with stains and long benches. Even these were going to be removed from the ship. It was kind of a bare and sad room where petty officers were drinking cold sake in tea cups. One was carrying a kettle of cold sake and pouring it into the tea cups of young ones. "You may die tomorrow. Drink up, drink up, while you can."

* * *

At 8:00 A.M., the first elements of the First Diversionary Striking Force sailed from Brunei Bay. Kurita was in the lead in *Atago*. He did not wish to be aboard her. The jokesters belowdecks and in the officers' mess who mocked him for staying away from the bigger and more prominent target, *Yamato*, had it wrong. Before the coming battle, Kurita had wanted to transfer with his flag and staff to a superbattleship, either *Yamato* or *Musashi*, both of which had better communications gear than the *Atago*. But tradition, as always, ruled: Kurita was reminded by headquarters that the proper flagship for a striking fleet was a cruiser, to lead night torpedo attacks. Never mind that the battle plan, as now conceived, did not specifically call for such an action.

At the tip of Borneo, the great fleet divided. Admiral Nishimura, the southern arm of the *Sho-Go* pincer, turned east with his detachment of two battleships, a cruiser, and four destroyers and made for Surigao Strait, the southern entrance to Leyte Gulf. Kurita and the main body continued north on its slow and winding journey to the San Bernardino Strait. Kurita's course on the first day took him just west of Palawan, a long thin island where Japan kept (and abused, starved, and eventually incinerated) American prisoners of war. The commander of the First Striking Force had to be careful not to stray into waters called the Dangerous Ground because of their shoals and reefs. The Palawan Passage, as it was called, was only about twenty to thirty miles wide. Perfect for a submarine ambush.

That night, two American submarines were waiting. The *Darter* and the *Dace* were sitting quietly on the calm surface of the Palawan Passage in the cloudy, moonless dark. Their commanders had been given no specific intelligence about Kurita's fleet movements, but they knew about the invasion of Leyte Gulf, and the submarine captains figured that if the Japanese fleet was to sortie, it would likely come through the Palawan Passage. Not long after midnight, at 1:16 on the early morning of October 23, a radar operator in the conning tower of the *Darter* called up to Cdr. David McClintock that he had a contact at 30,000 yards. Probably just a rain cloud, said the radar man. *Rain cloud, hell*, thought McClintock. *That's the Japanese fleet.*

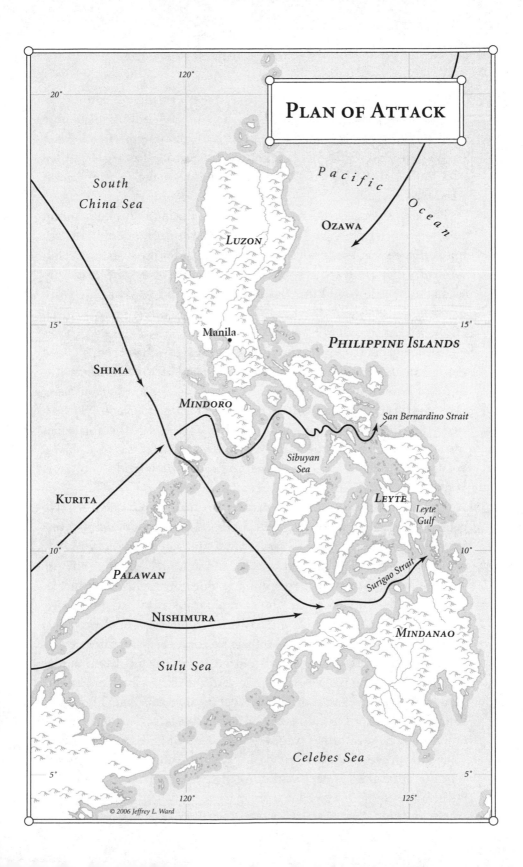

PLAN OF ATTACK

*South
China Sea*

P a c i f i c

O c e a n

OZAWA

LUZON

PHILIPPINE ISLANDS

Manila

SHIMA

MINDORO

San Bernardino Strait

*Sibuyan
Sea*

LEYTE

*Leyte
Gulf*

KURITA

PALAWAN

NISHIMURA

Surigao Strait

MINDANAO

Sulu Sea

Celebes Sea

© 2006 Jeffrey L. Ward

The *Darter*'s captain went below to have his suspicions confirmed. Numerous blips began appearing on the screen. Climbing back onto the conning tower bridge, he grabbed a megaphone and called out to his partner, Cdr. Bladen Clagett of the *Dace*. "Let's go!" yelled McClintock to Clagett, who had been his classmate at the Naval Academy.

The two subs ran south on the surface through the dark night, submerging before dawn. At first light, McClintock peered through his periscope and saw gray shapes forming in the mist. It was a column of Japanese warships. McClintock waited until the lead ship was almost on top of him, less than a thousand yards away. "Fire one!" he ordered. He could see that his target was a heavy cruiser. He hoped she was the flagship.

He was in luck. Out of carelessness or fatalism or perhaps out of habit, Kurita had put his own ship at the head of the column, without a sufficient destroyer screen. Aboard the *Atago*, a lookout sang out: "Six torpedo tracks, coming dead-on. No time to evade." The officers of the flagship could only watch as four of the torpedoes buried themselves in the hull of the *Atago*. Speaking to a friend years later, Admiral Kurita recalled the sound they made as the torpedoes struck, one after another. *Dong! Dong! Dong! Dong!*

The admiral knew almost instantly that his ship was doomed. He could hear the deep grinding roar of bulkheads breaking, of rivets popping and bursting as steel gave way to the sea. As the *Atago*'s bow began to settle and she heeled over, he announced, "This is it." There was no foolish discussion of the captain going down with the ship. Kurita turned to Captain Araki, the commanding officer of the *Atago*, and said simply, "It's time to go." As Kurita later recalled, he took off his shoes and was the first one over the side and into the water.

Below the surface, a few hundred yards away, Commander McClintock swung his periscope to look at the cruiser he had just torpedoed. It was "the sight of a lifetime," he later relished. The *Atago* filled his periscope lens. She was billowing black smoke and already down at the bow. Bursts of bright orange flame shot from her decks.

Quartermaster Kosaku Koitabashi was deep in the bowels of the flagship, sitting at his duty station by the gyro compass on the lowest deck, when the first torpedo struck. He heard a loud bang, then another, and at first thought the *Atago* must be attacking an enemy ship. Then came a third and a fourth explosion, which threw him from his seat and against a bulkhead. The lights flickered and went out.

Plunged into complete darkness, Koitabashi realized that his ship had been badly hit, but he was unsure what to do. A Japanese sailor's first rule of combat was never to leave his duty station. On the other hand, he could hear water rushing somewhere nearby, and he could feel the ship begin to heel. For ten long seconds he deliberated; then he decided to try to save himself.

He had to feel his way down a maze of passageways, through heavy bulkhead doors and up narrow ladders, heaving open steel hatches and closing them behind him as he struggled in the darkness to the main deck. He arrived gasping and barely able to stand up. Already, the *Atago* was listing 30 degrees. He hurried to the bridge to find it almost deserted. His friend Nagaoka was still there. "What's going on?" Koitabashi asked. Nagaoka pointed in the early morning light to a scene of chaos on the surrounding sea.

Hundreds of heads—"like watermelons," Koitabashi recalled— were bobbing in the water as the *Atago*'s officers and sailors swam for the lives. About 200 yards away, a destroyer, the *Kishinami*, was picking up survivors. The two petty officers decided to join them. *Atago* by now was heeling 70 degrees, close to capsizing. Koitabashi was able to walk off the slanting deck into the water. But before he went, he noticed an odd detail. Dozens of pairs of shoes had been neatly lined up along a bulkhead, left there by the fleeing crew of the sinking cruiser. Koitabashi recalled a cultural peculiarity of his people: if a Japanese man commits suicide, leaping off a bridge or a cliff or out a window, he is always careful to first take off his shoes.

In the water, sailors were doing their duty. Two officers struggled to swim while awkwardly holding aloft portraits of the emperor and empress, rescued from the officers' wardroom. A seventeen-year-old seaman held a rucksack over his head as he swam, but he began to flail and go under. He yelled out, "Here are coded messages, coded messages from the HQs. Please take this!" Hands reached out to help him.

Admiral Koyanagi, Kurita's chief of staff, was in the water, laboring to swim the last few yards to the *Kishinami*. He had hurt his leg and his arms were heavy with exhaustion. He could see dozens of ropes dangling off the side of the destroyer and oil-soaked sailors grasping for them and trying to hold on as sailors topside heaved. Koyanagi swam amidst a group of four of five sailors waiting their turn. An officer spotted him and commanded his men, "Get away, get away, let the chief of staff go up first. Sir," the officer formally addressed Koyanagi, as they bobbed in the warm sea by the steep side of the destroyer, "please go up and continue the battle." Koyanagi was moved by the officer's sense of duty and protested, "Never mind, let the first one go on up, just go on," but the officer insisted. Koyanagi grasped the rope and was hauled to the deck, like a large, oily fish.

Koyanagi found Admiral Kurita on the bridge. The commander of the First Diversionary Striking Force was trembling. The officers around him looked anxious; they knew the admiral was still recovering from dengue fever. Kurita's first words when arriving on the bridge of the *Kishinami* were: "Do you have whiskey?" A bottle was found; the admiral took two or three swigs and his trembling seemed to stop. Kurita also needed some shoes. The only pair that fit was some white sneakers taken from an enlisted man. Kurita made a joke about being an admiral in sneakers. He looked seaward and did not see his flagship. She was gone, sunk in nineteen minutes.

Aboard the *Yamato*, Admiral Ugaki had been on the bridge at General Quarters since an hour before dawn. He had watched, with horror, as the submarine attack unfolded. The fleet had picked up radio transmissions overnight suggesting that American submarines might be lurking nearby, and the ships were zigzagging to make it more difficult for an unseen American sub to get a firing solution on a Japanese ship. The *Yamato* had just swung its enormous bow to port at 6:25, Ugaki recorded in his diary, when "all of a sudden I saw . . . the flame of an explosion and what seemed like a spread water column on the dawn sea. I shouted involuntarily, 'Done it!'"

Ugaki could only watch as *Atago* staggered and began to sink. Suddenly, another cruiser, the *Takao*, went dead in the water and began to stream white smoke. A few minutes later came a spectacular explosion. The *Maya*, a 10,000-ton cruiser steaming right in front of the *Yamato*, blew up and disintegrated. "Nothing was left after the smoke and spray subsided," wrote Ugaki.

There was pandemonium throughout the fleet. False sightings of periscopes began pouring in. Ugaki estimated that the fleet was under attack by a wolfpack of four American subs. Ships violently changed course and picked up speed. In the *Dace*, submerged nearby, Commander Clagett had been watching as he lined up his shot on the *Maya*. "It looks like the Fourth of July out there," Clagett exulted to his crew. "The Japs are milling and firing all over the place. What a show!"

With Admiral Kurita swimming for his life or dead, Ugaki assumed command of the overall fleet, but there was not much he could do. The Dangerous Ground, with its uncharted rocks and shoals, threatened just to the west, while Ugaki could see the mountains of Palawan silhouetted against the eastern sky. He had little room to maneuver.

For the rest of the morning, destroyers raced about dropping depth charges and responding to seven more submarine alarms, all false. Finally, at 1540, 3:40 in the afternoon, the *Kishinami* was able to come alongside the *Yamato* and transfer Admiral Kurita, dried out and fortified by a couple of belts of whiskey, and his staff.

On the bridge of the *Yamato*, Ugaki greeted Kurita with an uncharacteristic smile. "Ugaki-kun," Kurita said to his number two, using the "kun" address for a subordinate, "we were pretty well beaten up." Ugaki responded, "Commander, the battle has just begun."

Ugaki had to make an effort to appear glad to see his commander-in-chief. He did not have a high opinion of Kurita, and his own place was diminished by Kurita's arrival. He had to relinquish his "monkey seat"—the top commander's chair—on the right side of the bridge to Commander-in-Chief Kurita. Quartermaster Koitabashi, along with most of the enlisted men from the *Atago*'s bridge detail, had accompanied Admiral Kurita to the *Yamato*, which now became the fleet's flagship. Koitabashi recalled the feeling of tension as the staffs of the two admirals awkwardly mingled and sorted out duties and accommodations. Now that the *Yamato* was the flagship, Ugaki and his staff would be effectively marginalized. Ugaki would still command the First Battleship Division, but as a practical matter, Kurita and his staff would be in control on the crowded bridge.

Not all of Kurita's staff had made it to *Yamato*. Some critical signals specialists had died on board or drowned or been rescued by other ships. For communications, Kurita would have to rely on Ugaki's staff. The radio and telegraph equipment on Japanese ships was often poor; the unfamiliar staff would add to the fog of war.

Writing in his diary that night, Ugaki stiffly acknowledged his "changed circumstances." "This may be fate," he wrote, though his feelings were best expressed by the question he used to open his diary entry for October 23: "Could there be any worse day than today?"

The mood among his fellow officers was no better. Muffled derision greeted a cable that arrived shortly after 5:00 P.M. from Combined Fleet headquarters. Tokyo concluded that "it is very probable that the enemy is aware that we have concentrated our forces." That was darkly amusing to the assembled officers, some of them in borrowed dry clothes after their morning's swim. The cable went on to predict, in essence, disaster. The enemy would "probably" concentrate submarines in "the San Bernardino and Surigao Straits area"—the two straits the Japanese would have to force to gain entry to Leyte Gulf. The Americans would "plan attacks on our surface forces, using large type planes and task forces, after tomorrow morning" and "plan decisive action by concentrating his surface strength" to the east of Leyte Gulf.

A warm welcome. And the Japanese plan? "Carry through with our original plans," Combined Fleet headquarters ordered. The IJN staff officers safe in their bunker in a Tokyo suburb emphasized the importance of the deception—luring the American carriers north with Admiral Ozawa's decoy operation—and called for "an even stricter alert against submarines and aircraft." Tokyo also called on "shore-based planes" to "destroy enemy task force." That was also good for a stifled laugh. What shore-based planes? Most of the officers knew that the air force had been fairly well obliterated, though few were aware of Admiral Onishi's plan to turn some of the few that remained into kamikazes. Ugaki caught the mood. He ended his diary entry, "A bad day is a bad day to the end."

CHAPTER NINE

A FATAL MISUNDERSTANDING

"Where in the hell are those goddamn carriers?"

T HE MESSAGES FROM the *Dace* and the *Darter*, warning of the advance of Kurita's fleet, began arriving in Flag Plot aboard USS *New Jersey* at 6:20 on the morning of October 23. Halsey had arisen at 5:00 A.M., after no more than a couple of hours of sleep, and performed his normal and elaborate morning ablutions. He had been served breakfast (powdered eggs; the real ones had run out) by his Filipino steward, Benedicto Tulao, and he appeared tieless but crisp in pressed khakis, showered and freshly shaved with his hair slicked back. After six weeks of more or less constant combat operations, he was tired. Judging from the letters his doctor, Carnes "Piggy" Weeks, was sending home describing the admiral's health, he was not feeling well. Halsey and most of his staff were suffering from, or were just recovering from, the flu.

Smoking Lucky Strikes from his first of two to three packs a day and sipping his second or third of ten daily cups of muddy coffee, Admiral Halsey spread the messages in front of him on the wardroom table. The first "SECRET URGENT" signal from the submariners reported three "possible" battleships. The next sighting reported nine ships and "many radars." Then: "Minimum eleven ships. Same course same speed." Halsey told his staff lieutenant, Bill Kitchell, to summon a meeting of the Department of Dirty Tricks.

Halsey and his staff pondered the significance of the sightings by the two submarines. Was it possible that the Japanese fleet was coming out to challenge the American invasion after all? The half-dozen officers around the table, weary middle-aged men worn by strain, illness, and lack of sleep, their faded khakis already showing sweat stains in the dense humidity, were doubtful. It was hard to imagine that the Japanese would be so rash, not after their air forces had taken such a beating over Formosa just the week before. Halsey still lusted for the chance to wipe out the Japanese fleet. But he had a hard time believing that Tokyo would be brave or foolhardy enough to give him the opportunity.

Even so, eleven ships—at least three of them battleships, if the submariners were right—amounted to a formidable force. And yet . . . the combined wisdom of the intelligence analysts working for General MacArthur and Admiral Nimitz had predicted that the Japanese navy would not seriously challenge the American landings at Leyte Gulf. What to make of the battlewagons spotted by the *Darter* and the *Dace*?

Halsey was not the only fleet commander tracking the Japanese movements. The Seventh Fleet—"MacArthur's Navy"—of old battleships and small "jeep" carriers floated off the invasion beach, supporting the landings with gunfire and strafing and bombing runs. Aboard his flagship at anchor in Leyte Gulf, Adm. Thomas Kinkaid, the commander of the Seventh Fleet, weighed in with his prediction. In a message to all commanders (MacArthur, King, Nimitz, and Halsey) sent shortly after 10:00 A.M., Kinkaid suggested that the Japanese warships were headed to the Philippines to stage what Kinkaid called a "magnified Tokyo Express," the old Japanese standby from Guadalcanal days. The Tokyo Express had been essentially an armed troop train. Many nights, like clockwork, the Japanese had run troop-filled destroyers down the Slot from the Japanese citadel at Rabaul to reinforce the Japanese troops besieging Henderson Field. Kinkaid guessed the ship movements detected by the *Dace* and *Darter* presaged more of the same. Kinkaid suggested that by sea, under cover of night, the Japanese were planning to run reinforcements to their troops battling the invading American forces at Leyte.

The mood of the Dirty Tricks Department was anxious, but not overly so. A Tokyo Express, even a "magnified" one, would be a nuisance, everyone in Halsey's wardroom agreed. But it would not greatly test a navy that had mushroomed since those precarious first innings in the South Seas. At Guadalcanal in the late summer of 1942, the U.S. Navy had withdrawn its three carriers from the invasion area for fear of losing them. A little more than two years later, Halsey's task force boasted eighteen fast carriers, as well as half a dozen battleships. And that did not count the six old battleships and eighteen small auxiliary or jeep carriers of Admiral Kinkaid's Seventh Fleet. At this stage of the war, the American navy had more destroyers than Admiral Ozawa's carriers had warplanes—while American factories were turning out planes at the rate of about one every five minutes. Halsey and his men did not quite understand the extent of their superiority, but they were confident, if not cocky, about their ability to outgun the Japanese. The more difficult question was whether they could out-think an enemy they did not fully understand.

In the smoky wardroom of the *New Jersey*, dankly hot by 10:00 A.M. despite the droning of the forced-air blowers, Halsey's chief planner marine Gen. Bill Riley hazarded a more ominous guess. Riley was known as Halsey's drinking buddy, but he was also the officer most likely to ask creative questions. Riley was the first one to figure out the Japanese plan. He wondered aloud: What if the Japanese aimed to attack the American transports sitting in Leyte Gulf?

There was some history to suggest that the Japanese might try. In the early days at Guadalcanal, the Japanese had sent a battle fleet steaming toward the invasion beaches, apparently intent upon shooting up the landing forces. In a classic night action, the Battle of Savo Island, the Japanese fleet had sunk four Allied (three American, one Australian) cruisers. After the battle, the Japanese had inexplicably withdrawn, rather than press ahead to sink the vulnerable transports. But what if this time was different? What if the Japanese aimed to send heavy gunships right at the beachhead?

Halsey could remember how the Japanese brazenly shelled Henderson Field in October 1942. On several other occasions, the Japanese had sent ships in close to shore to bombard American forces. Still, to try anything like that now, given the strength of the navy's defenses, Halsey reasoned, would be madness.

Halsey's chief of staff, Adm. Mick Carney, spoke up last. What if the Japanese decided to shoot the works? Send the entire fleet to take on the American naval forces in a great and final sea battle?

Halsey said he didn't think so. He did not state his reasons, but Halsey's views on the Japanese did not need an airing. The Japanese may have been crazed, they may have mounted *Banzai* charges with bamboo sticks, but they were not the supermen of America's post–Pearl Harbor imaginings. To Halsey, the Japanese were still little people. They lacked a capacity for greatness. Halsey concluded that the Japanese were running some kind of Tokyo Express. At the same time, he wondered, not for the first time: where were the Japanese carriers? The submarines had spotted battleships—but no flattops, the greatest threats and, to aviators like Halsey, the true heart of Japan's remaining naval power. The Japanese carriers had been last reported in Japan's Inland Sea. But had they sallied forth?

Watching from his chair, Lt. Carl Solberg, the Oxford-educated air combat intelligence officer, noticed that chief of staff Carney had a way of pushing up his glasses on his balding forehead when there was nothing left to be said. The Department of Dirty Tricks quieted. Scowling, pushing up his glasses, Carney summed up the situation. Japanese battleships were approaching the Philippines. At the very least, the Third Fleet needed to gird for some kind of confrontation.

Worried about his pilots, so exhausted that many were cracking up or on the verge, Halsey had ordered two carrier groups to retire to Ulithi, the sandy atoll where ships could resupply and the men could drink a warm beer or two and go for a swim. Now Halsey canceled those orders for one of the carrier groups—Adm. R. E. Davison's Task Group 38.4, comprised of the carriers *Enterprise, Franklin, San Jacinto,* and *Belleau Wood*—but he allowed another, Adm. John S. "Slew" McCain's Task Group 38.1, with carriers *Wasp, Hornet, Hancock, Monterey,* and *Cowpens,* to continue on to Ulithi for resupply and R&R. McCain's five ships carried roughly 400, or two-fifths, of the Third Fleet's 1,000 warplanes. Their absence would seriously diminish Halsey's resources and limit his flexibility. Still, Halsey felt confident that he had enough left to handle a "magnified Tokyo Express," if one was coming their way. Halsey ordered the remaining carrier groups to close on the Philippine shore and prepare for action.

At dawn on the morning of October 24, the Third Fleet sent search flights racing to the west, looking for the Japanese ships. Aboard the *New Jersey*, Flag Plot was "noisy, crowded," Lieutenant Solberg recalled, "and tense." Halsey, Carney, "and a dozen others listened to the pilots' voices piped into the room on loudspeakers." Anxiously, "men kept looking at their watches and saying, 'It's about time.'" Where was the Japanese fleet? Weather was not helping. The remnants of a front still lingered south of Manila, and the pilots were reporting cloud cover.

Then, at 8:20, came the break. Lt. Bill Verity, flying a Grumman fighter from the aircraft carrier *Cabot*, shouted out, "I see 'em!" He was flying off Mindoro Island at the edge of the Sibuyan Sea, an inner sea in the Philippine archipelago—the likely passage a Japanese fleet would take to advance toward the American landing beaches on the other side of Leyte.

"Big ships!" yelled Verity. Everyone in Flag Plot quieted and listened. Two minutes later came the voice of Cdr. Mort Eslick of the *Intrepid*'s Bombing Group 18. The pilot's voice, Solberg recalled, was "loud, clear, and very cool." Eslick gave a count: "Four battleships, eight heavy cruisers, and 13 destroyers, course east, off the southern tip of Mindoro."

The Department of Dirty Tricks quickly did the math: twenty-five ships—not the eleven reported by the *Dace* and *Darter*. This was no "magnified Tokyo Express." The Japanese appeared to be committing their main battle fleet. (Eslick's count was close; Kurita's fleet at that moment numbered twenty-eight ships, including five battleships.)

Halsey took no time in deciding what to do. Officially, Halsey was overall commander of the Third Fleet, but "tactical" control of the fast carrier task force belonged to Adm. Marc Mitscher. If Halsey had been following proper procedure, he would at least have consulted with Mitscher before giving an order. But Halsey was not a by-the-book man, and there was no time to waste. In one swift motion, he cut Mitscher out of the chain of command. At 8:37, picking up a radiophone receiver for a communication net known as TBS (Talk Between Ships), Halsey commanded, in what he called his "best radio voice": "Strike! Repeat: Strike! Good luck!" Halsey, not for the first time, was being self-conscious about his own legend. As Solberg later wrote, Halsey's order was "greeted with cheers on all the ships of the force. Everyone caught the resounding echo of his famous radio to his beleaguered carriers as he took command at Noumea in the South Pacific's darkest hours, 'Strike, repeat, strike!'"

At 8:46 Halsey ordered Admiral McCain's carrier group to reverse course and prepare to refuel at sea. Halsey realized he would need all of his carrier planes. McCain's force was already 600 miles away. It would take him more than a day to return.

The search planes from Halsey's fleet appeared as blips on the *Yamato*'s radar screen at dawn. As the sun rose, the heavy cloud cover blew away, and the ocean turned a brilliant blue, a kind of deep, almost iridescent turquoise. Fluffy clouds floated by, dappling the water. A steady but gentle breeze raised the occasional whitecap. The islands of the Philippine archipelago, lush and green, rose out of the sea in volcanic cones. Both the Japanese sailors and the American fliers would remember the incongruous beauty of the day.

At 8:20, standing on the bridge of the *Yamato*, Admiral Kurita sighted three American planes to the north (the search planes flew in groups of three, two fighters and a bomber; one of them was Lieutenant Verity's plane). The "tension rose" on the bridge, recalled Admiral Koyanagi, Kurita's chief of staff, who was standing behind his commander. Everyone on the bridge was already exhausted. After the sinking of the *Atago* and the *Maya* the day before, lookouts were on edge and saw periscopes everywhere. Destroyers had raced about all day and all night, dropping depth charges on phantoms. The crew of the *Yamato* had been called to General Quarters at dawn, interrupting their simple breakfast of rice and dried fish. Most the men would not eat again until nightfall, when they would be fed rice balls as they stood at their battle stations.

At last, shortly after 10:30 A.M., the Americans arrived in force.

From the east, thirty planes—fighters (Hellcats), dive-bombers (Helldivers), and torpedo bombers (Avengers)—could be seen, breaking tight formation as the bombers commenced their runs. From the bridge of his superbattleship, Petty Officer Koitabashi watched in awe as the *Yamato*'s 150 antiaircraft guns, sticking up like needles on a porcupine, spewed out 12,000 shells a minute. Red tracers filled the sky. The rain of shells was so thick it reminded Koitabashi of a tropical storm.

In their proper circular formation, with the destroyers forming an outer ring and the larger cruisers surrounding the battleships at the center, Kurita's fleet could put out a nearly impenetrable screen of fire. But as the ships began to twist and turn to evade torpedo tracks, the curtain parted. The American planes fearlessly bore in, juking and bombing or just flying low and straight on their torpedo runs. Pressing its attack, one dive-bomber flew right between the *Yamato*'s towering forward superstructure and the ship's huge, swept-back smokestack. Koitabashi was stunned. "We had been educated that the Americans had no guts," he recalled. "But my goodness! They came so close." Aside from hearing the gossip at the tobacco bon, Koitabashi had depended for news of the war on Radio Tokyo and Japanese newspapers faithfully delivered, a few weeks late, to the fleet. Any newspaperman who praised the enemy's performance was officially branded a traitor, so the Japanese press never reported American success or improvement. Sailors like Koitabashi had to learn firsthand. The effect, especially when the Japanese compared the performance of the Americans with their own, was disillusioning and demoralizing. After the submarine attacks on *Atago* and *Maya*, staff officers had been heard grumbling, "It's too bad our own subs can't pull off an attack like that."

And yet, the superbattleships, at least, seemed indomitable. So many times, Koitabashi and the other petty officers, like Japanese schoolchildren everywhere, had sung the rousing "Battleship March" ("Defending or attacking / like a floating fortress of steel . . . so dependable"). The crews of the *Yamato* and *Musashi* had been told repeatedly that their ships were unsinkable. On the *Musashi*, sailors learned a litany that perfectly captured Japan's lethal brew of overconfidence and fatalism: "The *Musashi* is unsinkable. If it sinks,

Japan will sink with it. And if Japan falls, we should all go down with it." When Koitabashi had come aboard *Yamato* after swimming off the *Atago* and riding cooped up with other survivors aboard a destroyer, he had immediately seen why the ship had acquired the moniker "Hotel Yamato."

Bullets from strafing airplanes seemed to rattle off the ship's armor plating. Koitabashi watched as machine gun bullets from the buzzing American planes chewed up the wooden planks on the main deck. They barely dented the battleship, except to expose the steel plating beneath. Still, there were casualties. A lookout standing on the wing of the bridge took a bullet and slumped over. Koitabashi, held in reserve along with the rest of the bridge detail from the sunken *Atago*, stepped into his place, taking over the high-powered binoculars. Koitabashi had been to sea for six years, but he had never been in an attack like this. He was frightened, he recalled many years later, but, at the same time, he was thrilled.

The officers maintained their usual impassive expressions. Admiral Ugaki's diary entry for that morning reflected an almost haughty disdain, like the hungry samurai picking his teeth: "At 1040, when I was thinking it was about time for the guests to come, twenty-five of them came in. . . . We shot down a few SB2Cs [Helldivers], F6Fs [Hellcats], and TBFs [Avengers] and thought nothing of them."

At noon, the Americans came again. Enormous geysers erupted around the *Musashi* as a pair of torpedoes buried their heads in her bow. Unshaken, she plowed ahead at 24 knots. But from the *Yamato*, Kurita and the other senior officers noticed something odd. Her bow wave was now a giant cataract of water, a rooster tail that spewed up and out. The commanders did not know it at that moment, but they were watching blood pour from an Achilles' heel. The superbattleships were like citadels wrapped in thick steel belts. But the heavy side armor stopped abreast the foremost main battery turret, making the bow, affixed with the proud Imperial Chrysanthemum, vulnerable to the Americans' high-explosive torpedoes (the duds of the early war had been fixed). Aboard the *Musashi*, steel plate had been bent out by the force of the explosion, creating the telltale bow wave. Water was slowly flooding the *Musashi*'s forward compartments.

Aboard the *Musashi*, known to her crew as "the Palace," the gunnery officer asked permission to open up on the American planes with their giant 18-inch guns. The guns had been supplied with shells, called *sanshiki dan*, filled with tiny incendiary bombs that would scatter and explode amidst attacking planes. But the captain of the *Musashi*, Adm. Toshihira Inoguchi, refused the request. The antiaircraft shells might damage the smooth bores of the giant guns. He wanted to save his firepower for a truer test, shooting against enemy ships.

From the high bridge of the *Yamato*, Admiral Kurita watched wordlessly as the American planes broke off their attack and disappeared back over the eastern horizon. He knew that more were coming. He had little useful intelligence the weather front had interfered with Japanese scout planes flying out of Manila. But Kurita had no doubt that Halsey's task forces were out there somewhere, and it was apparent from the bombs exploding around him that the Americans had found their enemy. Admiral Nishimura, commanding the smaller, southern arm of the First Diversionary Striking Force's pincer movement, scheduled to advance on Leyte through the Surigao Strait, was reporting that he, too, was under attack. Kurita had not heard a word from Admiral Ozawa, whose decoy fleet was supposedly luring away Halsey's carriers somewhere to the north—though not very effectively, judging from the swarms of American carrier planes descending on Kurita's ships.

Kurita had been radioing Combined Fleet headquarters in Tokyo and First Air Fleet headquarters in Manila since eight o'clock in the morning, requesting air cover. He had received no response. The answer, he bitterly understood, was all too clear. The empty skies overhead—not a sign of a Japanese plane—were an open invitation to the Americans to return and attack at their leisure. Kurita could hear his staff grumbling that, if the attacks kept up, the fleet would be reduced by half before it ever reached its target. Already, one cruiser had been sent limping back to port, escorted by two destroyers. The operations chief, Captain Otani, was discussing, in a tentative way, the possibility of turning around and withdrawing, at least to get out of range of the Americans and regroup while the rest of the Sho Plan had time to do its job—to divert Halsey's fleet with Ozawa's half-empty carriers or attack it with shore-based planes.

Kurita decided to send a message to his superiors. It was a request for information intended, in a classically Japanese roundabout way, to shame them:

> WE ARE BEING SUBJECTED TO REPEATED ENEMY CARRIER-BASED AIR ATTACKS. ADVISE IMMEDIATELY OF CONTACTS AND ATTACKS MADE BY YOU ON THE ENEMY.

Kurita received no answer. After the war, Admiral Fukudome, commander of land-based air forces, admitted that he "turned a deaf ear" to Kurita's requests.

Lt. Nick Fellner, a young American navy pilot, was captivated by tension, fear, anticipation, and, oddly, by beauty, as he pushed his dive-bomber along at 12,000 feet above the green islands and deep blue water of the Sibuyan Sea—the snaking inland sea that confined Kurita's ships as they struggled eastward toward the elusive Decisive Battle. A pilot in a bomber squadron off the carrier *Franklin*, Fellner was flying in a wave of thirty planes, the fourth attack to hit Kurita's force that day, and the second in less than an hour.

The surrounding scene was peaceful. Fellner could hear nothing but the sleepy drone of his engine. Then, ahead, beyond a few fleecy white clouds, he could see a strange, almost festive sight: thousands of tiny puffs of colored smoke—red, blue, green—and yellow and red streaks and sparks. He was looking at the Japanese fleet's antiaircraft barrage, lofted by more than a score of ships, each with about a hundred guns pointed skyward. "A rainbow rain of death," he thought to himself, and pointed his nose down for the 70 degree dive into the maelstrom. The time was 1426, 2:26 in the afternoon.

Below was a magnificent, dramatic sight. The white wakes of great gray warships swirled and twisted as the ships maneuvered to evade the American bombs and torpedoes. Fellner fastened on the biggest ship, a ship he had never seen before, not even in a photograph. Few Americans had. The Office of Naval Intelligence had printed "artist renderings" of the superbattleships, which the pilots used to practice ship identification. Dive-bomber pilots are supposed to fly straight down, but Fellner spiraled and twisted to keep the massive ship in his gunsight as she made a tight turn. As his altitude gauge passed 1,000 feet and colorful blossoms violently exploded all around him, he "pickled" his bomb, releasing it. Almost as an after-thought, he fired his machine guns and 20-millimeter cannon, not really to do any damage, he later recalled, but for "the sheer sense of elation." Then he pulled back on his joystick, and like all dive-bomber pilots, passed out for several seconds from the intense g-forces as his plane clawed above the antiaircraft fire and leveled off. When the Helldiver pilots returned to their carriers, the wings of their planes were smoldering from bits of the phosphorus used in Japanese shells.

Fellner's 1,000-pound bomb pierced the deck of the *Yamato* near the bow and penetrated through five decks. When it exploded, it blew two holes below the waterline in the side of the ship, six square feet on one side, twenty-four square feet on the other. The great ship shuddered and began to heel slightly but did not slow. As one of the bow compartments filled with water, a damage control officer opened valves to flood a compartment on the other side with 3,000 tons of water. The *Yamato* righted and plowed on.

The crew of the *Yamato* did not flinch. The days and nights of training, reinforced by petty officers wielding spirit bars, worked to maintain discipline. Morale among the enlisted men did not flag, even though their casualties were mounting. Jiro Iwasa, a young re-connaissance pilot, had gone to the deck to watch the action and had been wounded slightly in the thigh. He watched as some sailors gathered up body parts and placed them in a large bathtub. An or-derly was carrying a bucket filled with rice balls (*onigiri*) which he handed out to sailors as they stood at their battle stations. Iwasa re-coiled as he saw one sailor hungrily eat a rice ball that had somehow become coated with human blood. Iwasa, without any duty to per-form, decided to go lie in his bunk in the gun room.

The *Musashi* was in worse shape. Her torn bow was plowing up water in a great geyser. The bombs that nearly missed the ship still threw sheets of water and shrapnel across her decks and into exposed gun tubs. The great ship had been torpedoed nine times. She began to slow and drop behind, struggling to maintain 12 knots while the rest of the fleet pushed ahead at 22 knots. From the bridge of the flagship, Ugaki watched, stone-faced, as *Yamato*'s great sister ship began to lose the fight. Across the bridge, Admiral Kurita was not sentimental. He gave the order for the *Musashi* to retire from the fleet and withdraw to Coron Bay, a safe harbor, if there were such places, in the western Philippines. All along the *Yamato*, men were ordered to come to attention as the *Musashi*, the unsinkable symbol of national pride, turned her lowering bow and retreated toward safety.

It was too late. At 3:10 in the afternoon, a fifth wave of American planes descended on the Japanese fleet. It was the biggest attack yet, about a hundred planes. They circled the *Musashi*, like wolves finishing off a straggler from the flock. Bomb hits sprayed shrapnel across the decks, cutting down sailors who wore *hachimaki* "victory" headbands, patterned after the white cloths that ancient samurai wore around their heads, signifying their expectation of death. (American sailors, by contrast, wore metal helmets.) Fragments "like steel popcorn" ricocheted off the bridge. Ten more torpedoes thudded into the sides of the great leviathan. Finally, with his ship's life at stake, Admiral Inoguchi gave his gunnery officer permission to use his massive 18-inch guns as antiaircraft guns. They had never been fired at a ship, and now they never would. They were not very effective against airplanes. From the *Yamato*, Ugaki watched as the *Musashi*'s three turrets wheeled and their gun barrels belched flame. "It was regrettable to see that the number of enemy planes shot down was small," he would write in his diary that night.

The great ship was listing to port. A battleship can keep an even keel by flooding compartments, but the damage control officer was reporting that he was running out of available space to fill with seawater. Admiral Inoguchi decided to flood one of his engine rooms, even though it meant killing scores of men trapped in an inner compartment. Fires were breaking out all over the ship. The sickbay filled with carbon monoxide, snuffing out the wounded.

A bomb tore through the bridge of *Musashi*, killing most of the officers. Admiral Inoguchi was spared. He was standing atop the bridge on a special platform used by commanders aboard Japanese ships under air attack. They would point with a baton, like the con-

Musashi down by the bow

ductor in an orchestra, to direct the ship's evasive maneuvers. But shrapnel swept across the observation tower, slicing into Inoguchi's shoulder. The ship was by now almost helpless, decks awash. Suddenly, for no apparent reason, sailors—those who were still alive— began to cry *Banzai!* Someone had started a rumor that the entire American fleet had been destroyed, and it quickly spread through the ship.

On the bridge of the *Yamato*, Kurita's staff knew the fleet was in trouble. Captain Otani, Kurita's operations officer, had been quietly but persistently badgering his commander to turn around the fleet, to withdraw, at least for a time. Before darkness fell in two hours, Otani reasoned, the Americans could launch another three attacks. It was time to pull back.

Kurita was not ready to abandon the mission, though the futility of it was becoming increasingly obvious. Perhaps, his staff argued (or rationalized), withdrawing temporarily would work as a feint to convince the Americans that the Japanese were retreating. Just as important, it would send a signal to Combined Fleet headquarters in Tokyo that unless a way was found to provide air cover, the whole mission was doomed. Kurita listened impassively to his staff's argument and finally nodded his assent. Otani dictated a message to a signalman to be sent to Tokyo. The fleet was turning around—"to temporarily retire beyond the range of enemy planes and reform our plans." Otani's message described the heavy air attacks and the damage that had forced the *Musashi* and a heavy cruiser, the *Myoko*, to limp for port. The operations chief, writing for Kurita's signature, explained in unusually graphic terms:

UNDER THESE CIRCUMSTANCES IT WAS DEEMED THAT WERE WE TO FORCE OUR WAY THROUGH, WE WOULD MERELY MAKE OF OURSELVES MEAT FOR THE ENEMY, WITH VERY LITTLE CHANCE OF SUCCESS.

Kurita and his staff later claimed that they were completely without air cover throughout the slaughter in the Sibuyan Sea, and it may have seemed that way to them. From airfields in the Philippines, a total of ten Japanese planes had flown out to protect Kurita's fleet. Four of them were shot down.

One of the others was piloted by Cdr. Iki Haruki. At the very beginning of the Pacific War, Commander Haruki had been one of the pilots who dropped the bombs that sank the British dreadnought *Prince of Wales* and the battle cruiser *Repulse*. Haruki had a sentimental streak, and after he had helped destroy the British capital ships, he had flown back out over the sea to the spot, a smear of oil and flotsam, where the British warships and 840 of their officers and sailors had perished. Looking down from the cockpit of his plane, Haruki had dropped a bouquet of flowers to honor his fallen comrades—four Japanese planes had been lost—and the enemy dead.

How long ago that day seemed, Haruki thought—how distant were those noble feelings of elation and gallantry. Now, as the afternoon shadows lengthened, Commander Haruki flew far above Kurita's fleet as it twisted in agony beneath the attack of the marauding Americans. Haruki could have sacrificed himself as a final gesture. Instead, he turned the nose of his plane and flew away.

From his bunker at Combined Fleet headquarters in Tokyo, Admiral Toyoda had, not unreasonably, wanted to go on the offensive with what little airpower he had left. He had made only a handful of planes available to defend Kurita's fleet. But the navy had cobbled together about 200 planes, based at airfields around Manila, to attack Halsey's carriers as they floated, in three separate groups spread over a hundred miles, in the warm waters of the Philippine Sea. The northernmost group, Task Group 38.3 under Adm. Frederick C. Sherman, was preparing to launch its planes to attack Kurita's fleet when, shortly after 8:00 A.M., radar picked up a large blob of bogeys, enemy planes, to the northwest. Adm. Marc Mitscher, the overall commander of the carriers in Halsey's fleet, was aboard his flagship, the *Lexington*, attached to Sherman's Task Group 38.3. He sent out the signal, "Hey Rube!"—the old circus cry for help, adopted by the navy when its ships came under attack. The carriers in Sherman's group scrambled to launch fighters to repel the invaders.

The Japanese pilots were a motley crew, mostly inexperienced and undertrained, and a single American pilot, Cdr. David McCambell off the *Essex*, was able to cut out and shoot down no fewer than nine Japanese planes (his wingman got six). But at about 9:30, a "Judy" bomber dropped out of a rain cloud and deposited a 500-pound bomb on the flight deck of the light carrier *Princeton*. The blast started a fire that set off a string of torpedoes in the bomb bays of Avengers waiting to take off. The carrier burned and then blew apart, slaughtering dozens still aboard and more than 200 men on a cruiser, the *Birmingham*, which had come alongside to help.

Aboard the *New Jersey*, sailing fifty miles to the south with Adm. Gerry Bogan's Task Group 38.2, Admiral Halsey did not know that the planes attacking Sherman's carrier group had been land-based. He guessed, wrongly, that they had flown from Japanese carriers. As always, Halsey was fixated on finding and sinking the Japanese carrier force. His staff was no less impatient and determined. Again and again, Halsey's top staffer for air operations, Cdr. Doug Moulton, pounded the table in Flag Plot and demanded, "Where in the hell are those goddamn carriers?" (During the course of the day, Moulton must have said this "fifty times," Halsey later wrote.)

The intelligence on the Japanese carriers was thin. That morning, an aide handed Halsey a red top secret folder containing ULTRA material, decrypts of Japanese signals sent from the code breakers at Pearl Harbor. By monitoring the messages sent to Japanese oil tankers, the code-breakers had determined that Admiral Ozawa's carriers had left their safe haven of the Inland Sea in Japan and sortied through the Bungo Straits into the Pacific . . . but where? The best estimate was "the Formosa-Philippine Sea area," not a very precise description.

The Department of Dirty Tricks pondered this intriguing scrap. Halsey's self-effacing naval intelligence officer, Mike Cheek, studied the document, and, in his reticent way, wrote Halsey a little note, rather than speak up at the table. Cheek's note predicted that the Japanese carriers were coming south looking for Halsey's Third Fleet. Cheek's quiet assessment was lost in Moulton's bellowing about finding "those goddamn carriers."

As the Dirty Tricks Department was trying to find Ozawa, Admiral Ozawa was trying to be found. His force—a heavy carrier, three light carriers, and two "hermaphrodites," battleships with short runways attached to the stern—was making as much noise as possible. Following the vast deception that was at the heart of the Sho Plan, Ozawa was trying to lure Halsey away to the north. He needed to get Halsey's attention by nightfall, in order to allow Admiral Kurita's remaining battleships and escorts to slip in behind, through the San Bernardino Strait and down the east side of Samar Island into Leyte Gulf.

Ozawa was committing suicide with his fleet. He had brimmed with self-sacrificing spirit when he bade farewell to Admiral Toyoda. "I shall disregard any damage which may be inflicted upon my force in this operation," he had announced to the C-in-C before setting sail on October 20.

Ozawa was flooding the airwaves with telltale radio signals, or rather he thought he was. He did not know that the radio antenna on his ship, the carrier *Zuikaku*, was broken. Though American carriers were only about 200 miles away, they could not hear any radio signals from Ozawa, and so far, their search planes had not found the Japanese carriers.

Ozawa's men had no illusions that they were anything other than cannon fodder. The carriers, once the heart of Japan's naval might, were now decoys. Their decks were more than two-thirds empty of planes. Ozawa had managed to put together an odd-lot collection of 108 fighters and bombers, many flown by pilots who could not return because they did not know how to land on a carrier deck. Shortly before noon on October 24, Ozawa launched seventy-six of his planes against the American carriers bombed earlier that morning by the Philippines-based planes. He also ordered his two hermaphrodite battleships, the *Ise* and *Hyuga*, to steam south and engage the enemy. The orders reveal the Imperial Navy's willful, almost pathological, denial. The two Japanese ships were instructed to mop up the "remnants" of the American fleet.

As the Japanese planes took off from the *Zuikaku*, Admiral Ozawa stood on the flight deck in the bright midday sun and saluted. Then he looked away. He ordered the planes to make for bases on land, though he knew that many of them would never get that far.

Ducking in and out of rain showers, Admiral Sherman first spotted the Japanese attackers at 1:31 that afternoon. He radioed Halsey that the planes were approaching not from land—not from the Philippines in the west—but rather from the northeast—suggesting that they had been launched by carriers at sea. Aboard the *New Jersey*, Halsey was increasingly convinced that he would be engaging his long-sought foe in a matter of hours—if he could only find the carriers.

At the same time, he had to worry about Admiral Kurita's fleet coming through the San Bernardino Strait and descending on MacArthur's landing ships, as General Riley had warned the day before at the war council of the Department of Dirty Tricks. Halsey's first responsibility was to safeguard the invasion fleet. True, he had a loophole. His orders specifically stated that if the opportunity to destroy a "major portion" of the Japanese fleet presented itself, "such destruction becomes the primary task." To Halsey, the carriers qualified as the "major portion" of the Japanese fleet. But he needed to prepare for all eventualities—to be ready to plug the San Bernardino Strait, as well as to plunge north to engage the carriers.

At 1512, 3:12 in the afternoon of October 24, Halsey issued a message that would be the cause of a fatal misunderstanding. The message was labeled "Battle Plan." It instructed Adm. Willis Lee to form a battle line, made up of four of the Third Fleet's six battleships, the *New Jersey, Iowa, Washington*, and *Alabama*, together with five cruisers and nineteen destroyers. The battle line, dubbed

Task Force 34, would "engage the enemy at long ranges." The coded telegram was sent throughout the Third Fleet, as well as to Admiral King, the navy's commander-in-chief in Washington, and to Admiral Nimitz, the Pacific Fleet commander, based at Pearl Harbor on the island of Oahu.

It was not addressed to Admiral Kinkaid, the commander of the Seventh Fleet, who was floating on his flagship, the *Wasatch*, in Leyte Gulf. Halsey was not obliged to contact Kinkaid; indeed, he was prohibited from direct communication with the Seventh Fleet's commander, who was in General MacArthur's chain of command. Ever jealous of his power, MacArthur did not want any back channels between old navy mates. Halsey and Kinkaid communicated with each other through a clumsy, maddeningly slow process designed to make sure that MacArthur saw all the message traffic. If Kinkaid wanted to pass information to Halsey, or vice versa, he had to send it to a radio station on the island of Manus. From there, it was retransmitted on something called the "Fox Schedule" that went to all ships and all headquarters. Commanders were expected to decode messages only if they carried the call sign of their ship or force.

The fact that Halsey did not send Kinkaid his Battle Plan to create Task Force 34 did not stop Kinkaid from finding out about it. He intercepted the message and, in essence, eavesdropped. It was common practice among ship and fleet commanders to pull down and decode messages addressed to others, and so Kinkaid had no scruple about listening in on Halsey's communications. Indeed, Kinkaid was delighted to read Halsey's message. It suited his own plans perfectly.

Earlier that morning, planes from Halsey's carriers had spotted Admiral Nishimura's small fleet making for Surigao Strait. From his command post at Leyte Gulf, Admiral Kinkaid had quickly grasped that the Japanese intended a pincer movement—Kurita's large fleet coming through the San Bernardino Strait to the north, and Nishimura's smaller force—two battleships, a cruiser, and four destroyers—coming through Surigao Strait to the south. It was obvious that they planned to converge in Leyte Gulf to attack MacArthur's invasion ships.

Kinkaid immediately sent word to the commander of his gunships, Adm. Jesse Oldendorf, to take his fleet and prepare for a night battle. Of Oldendorf's six battleships, four—the *Pennsylvania, Tennessee, West Virginia,* and *California*—had all been badly damaged or sunk at Pearl Harbor on December 7, 1941. Salvaged from the mud and repaired, they were old and slow, and not much use for anything more than bombarding beaches during invasions. But they had a score to settle, and they could be arrayed across the Surigao Strait to blast any Japanese ship that tried to come through.

Kinkaid decided that he did not need to worry about San Bernardino Strait to the north. Halsey had that covered with his Battle Plan. Or so Kinkaid assumed.

In war, as in almost everything else, assumption is the mother of error. Kinkaid did not know it, but Halsey had not actually given a formal order to form Task Force 34. Rather the Battle Plan was only a *contingency.* Halsey sent out another signal a few minutes later, telling his commanders that "Task Force 34 will be formed when directed by me"—in other words, if and when it was necessary, and only at Halsey's further command. But he sent this message by TBS (Talk Between Ships)—by short-range radio. Kinkaid never heard it.

Nor did Nimitz nor King. And these commanders, too, believed that Halsey was forming Task Force 34 and intending to position it at the mouth of the San Bernardino Strait as a welcoming committee for Admiral Kurita's fleet. Kinkaid was no more guilty of making assumptions than his superiors. This misunderstanding was caused, or at the very least exacerbated, by poor grammar. The Battle Plan read like a command (Task Force 34 "will be formed"). But in the navy, as naval historian Tom Cutler has pointed out, verb tenses are sometimes misused for effect. "Good discipline will be maintained" doesn't mean sometime in the future, it means *now.* Since Halsey specified no exact time to form Task Force 34, Kinkaid—and Nimitz—assumed that he meant right away. Halsey could be loose with his language. His staff, particularly his chief of staff, Admiral Carney, should have guarded against such imprecision. He surely should have sent Halsey's clarifying follow-up message—"Task Force 34 will be formed when directed by me"—to Nimitz, King, and Kinkaid. But Carney, a fairly literate man, was sick and exhausted, just like his boss.*

Halsey's poor staff work was partly to blame. Even so, Kinkaid and his staff showed a startling lack of curiosity, an odd passivity in not communicating with Halsey to make sure that the San Bernardino Strait was covered. Personal feelings may have come into play.

Kinkaid did not like Halsey. Aside from the fact that both men had bushy eyebrows and graduated in the bottom half of the class at Annapolis, they were opposite types. Kinkaid avoided newspaper reporters. He was neither flamboyant nor brilliant. In Halsey's estimation, he had botched the handling of a carrier task force at the Battle of the Santa Cruz Islands off Guadalcanal in October 1942. After the battle, Halsey had quietly relieved Kinkaid, reassigning him to command a squadron of cruisers. Kinkaid was bitter about getting shoved aside, especially when Halsey refused to see him afterward. Kinkaid had rehabilitated his career by competently handling army-navy amphibious operations in Alaska, and when the time came to find a commander to run a fleet reporting to General MacArthur, Kinkaid had been given the job. But he had not overcome his resentment of Halsey. MacArthur need not have worried about back channels between old navy cronies. Kinkaid wasn't speaking to Halsey.

In hindsight, it is apparent that Admiral Nimitz should have stepped in and made sure that Halsey and Kinkaid were properly communicating and that Halsey's intentions were clear. But Nimitz was a successful commander-in-chief in part because he trusted and stood by his subordinates. Nimitz himself had been second-guessed by the profane and bullying Admiral King at the outset of the war; he was not about to repeat the mistake. Nimitz was not unaware of Halsey's freewheeling ways. But he believed in him as a leader. The

---

*Staff work in the navy was historically weaker than in the army. Ambitious naval officers avoided staff jobs if at all possible; the route to advancement and fulfillment was command at sea, not serving as an admiral's aide. Halsey's staff was argumentative and boisterous, and not as careful as it might have been. Carney had been chosen by Nimitz to be a check on Halsey's sloppiness, but the chief of staff seemed instead to have been imbued with Halsey's devil-may-care spirit. Carney was a very sociable man, but in the Department of Dirty Tricks, sociability sometimes got in the way of substance.

Kinkaid

navy has a long tradition of letting captains run their own ships and fleet commanders run their own fleets. Command meant solitary responsibility; it had been so in Western navies since the time of Sir Francis Drake. The modern age of communications, the complexity of vast fleet movements over hundreds of miles of ocean, the delicate and intricate dance between landing forces and supporting fleets—all of this cried out for careful coordination. But ego and tradition, mingled with fatigue and the fog of war, got in the way.

CHAPTER TEN

SHIPS IN THE NIGHT

"Mea culpa, mea culpa"

ALL THROUGH THE bright, breezy afternoon of October 24, Admiral Halsey and his staff sat in the gloom of Flag Plot, listening. From speakers on the wall, they could hear, through the crackling static, the voices of exultant young pilots masking fear with bravado. The pilots told of torpedo after torpedo hitting "*Yamato*-class" battleships, though how many torpedoes and how many battleships remained unclear. They reported frequent near-misses and direct hits on "*Kongo*-class" battleships, though again, with so many different pilots and strike groups, it was hard to keep them all straight. One pilot described a "light cruiser" capsizing, although, in fact, none did.

Then, at 1640, 4:40 P.M., a pilot reported that the Japanese battle force, which had been circling and milling to elude American air attacks, had regrouped. The ships had turned 180 degrees. The Japanese fleet was heading *west*, away from San Bernardino Strait and its passage to Leyte Gulf.

A cry went up in Flag Plot: "We've stopped 'em!" The Japanese fleet appeared to be retreating under the onslaught of more than 270 American planes in five successive attacks over six hours. There were smiles of relief among the Department of Dirty Tricks. Still, they wondered, as Commander Moulton had been demanding all day long: Where were the carriers?

217

Within a few minutes, the answer came. A search plane from Admiral Sherman's carrier group, the furthest north, had spotted a force of Japanese ships—it wasn't clear what types—steaming south. Then one of Sherman's pilots got a "good look," and there they were, like so many figments of Halsey's imagination, Japanese carriers heading right for them, less than 200 miles away.

The scout plane counted three carriers—apparently, heavy fleet carriers—four to six heavy cruisers; and six destroyers. Halsey had been yearning to battle Japan's carriers since the morning of December 7, 1941, if not long before. His enthusiasm was tempered by the dilemma of confronting not one but three enemy fleets. He called for a meeting of the Department of Dirty Tricks.

On the broad chart table where the Japanese ships were tracked with blue pencils and marked with pins and symbols, a pattern was emerging. The main Japanese battleship fleet had been advancing, at least until very recently, on the San Bernardino Strait. A smaller Japanese force was heading toward the Surigao Strait to the south. And the Japanese carriers were coming down from the north. Steaming at a slow pace—about 15 knots—they had all seemed to be converging on the American invasion force at Leyte Gulf. Halsey's men quickly named the pieces of the three-pronged attack. The larger battleship fleet that had been aiming for San Bernardino Strait was tagged "Center Force." The smaller battleship fleet steaming toward Surigao Strait was called "Southern Force." And the carriers heading toward them through the Philippine Sea were labeled "Northern Force."

The Japanese were advancing from the north, south, and west. Halsey's three carrier groups were arrayed to the east. It was time for Halsey to decide where to send his ships. He had on hand a huge and powerful fleet—twelve carriers and six battleships. Should he keep them concentrated? Or divide them? And where should he direct them?

One option was to use the entire Third Fleet to guard the San Bernardino Strait, in case Kurita's Center Force turned around again and came through in the dark. Cdr. Rollo Wilson, Halsey's operations officer, strenuously argued against that course of action. It would be like sitting and watching "a rat hole, waiting for the rats to come out," he said.

The lesson of the last battle hung over the teeming, smoky room. Everyone at the table was conscious of the way Admiral Spruance had played it safe six months earlier at the Battle of the Philippine Sea, sitting close to the invasion beaches at Saipan rather than venturing forth to take on the Japanese carrier fleet. This was no time for the "Spruance nuance," as the Department of Dirty Tricks mockingly described Spruance's caution. Nimitz's instructions had been clear—and clearly reflected regret over Spruance's missed opportunity back in June. If Halsey had the chance to destroy the "major portion" of the Japanese fleet—meaning the carriers—he should grab it.

The second option was to divide the fleet. Halsey could form the battle line, Task Force 34, and send it to guard the San Bernardino Strait, while his main carrier force steamed north to confront the Japanese carriers. This seemed, at first, the prudent choice. But dissenting voices rose. The chief of staff, Mick Carney, invoked a cardinal rule of sea battle: never divide your forces. Keep power concentrated. Halsey did not need reminding. The lesson, articulated by the great naval thinker Alfred Thayer Mahan, had been drummed into him at Annapolis and again at the Naval War College at Newport. A divided force, warned Mahan, can be defeated "in detail," piece by piece, by a smaller force.

Dividing the fleet could be dangerous, Halsey agreed. His dozen carriers were six short of full strength. He was shy about 400 warplanes out of his full force of over a thousand. The absent aircraft were mostly with Admiral McCain's five carriers, detached to Ulithi for resupply and R & R on October 22. (A sixth carrier, the *Bunker Hill*, had been sent back because its air crews were exhausted.) That morning, Halsey had ordered McCain to return, but McCain and his planes were not expected back until the next day.

The battle line guarding San Bernardino Strait would need air cover, Halsey knew. That would mean leaving a couple of carriers behind. Suddenly, Halsey's strength did not seem so overwhelming. Halsey was left wrestling with some tricky math. Two light carriers could put aloft fifty fighters. Was that really enough air cover for the battleships? On the other hand, if he detached a whole carrier group, he would seriously deplete his firepower against the Japanese carrier force to the north. Halsey knew that his forces had shot down hundreds of Japanese airplanes, but he did not know how few planes the Japanese had left. He was worried about shuttle bombing— carrier planes bombing the American ships, flying to land bases to refuel and rearm, then flying back and hitting the Americans on the return trip. He was also concerned that other carrier groups might be lurking behind the three carriers the scout plane had spotted. Halsey had received top secret intelligence documents reporting that the Japanese had as many as six fleet and five light carriers, and he knew that the Japanese often ran intricate, hydra-headed operations. The sinking of the *Princeton* that day had been a warning that Japanese airpower could still bite.

The so-called American Way of War was to overwhelm the enemy with superior firepower. With big factories and technical know-how, Americans could expend money and metal, instead of lives, to achieve victory. The Big Blue Fleet was, in some ways, a magnificent exercise in overkill. Halsey didn't want a fair fight against the Japanese. He wanted all the odds on his side.

The chance to wipe out the Japanese carriers in a devastating stroke argued for the third option, taking the entire Third Fleet to the north to engage the Japanese carriers. Halsey also may have harbored a personal motivation. Task Force 34, the battle line, included Halsey's flagship, the *New Jersey*. If the battle line were left guarding the strait, and if Kurita's fleet was already truly beaten, Halsey would be left to float idly about, watching, as Rollo Wilson had put it, "a rat hole." Meanwhile, 150 miles to the north, his fleet might be fighting what promised to be one of the climactic naval battles of history. *Without him.* He never mentioned his private ambitions during the discussions in Flag Plot that evening, but he did not need to. His staff understood that Halsey, having missed the Battle of Midway, was not about to sideline himself from the contest of his life. Admiral Toyoda may have preferred to follow the progress of the Decisive Battle from Tokyo, but Admiral Halsey wanted to be in on the kill.

Among Halsey's staffers, there was also consensus that Admiral Kinkaid and the Seventh Fleet could handle both the Center Force, if it did rally and come through the San Bernardino Strait, and the

Southern Force, recently spotted on course to enter the Surigao Strait by midnight. Even if the Japanese battleships now retreating in the Sibuyan Sea turned around and came through San Bernardino Strait, they could not reach Leyte Gulf until about 1100 hours, at eleven o'clock the next morning. Halsey's staff had read the messages sent by Admiral Kinkaid, ordering his line commander, Admiral Oldendorf, to form a "welcoming committee" for the Japanese entering Surigao Strait that night. Halsey's staff reasoned that Oldendorf's six battleships and numerous cruisers and destroyers would have plenty of time to knock off the Southern Force—two aging Japanese battleships and a cruiser—before heading north to block the Center Force as it descended on Leyte Gulf. The Japanese "will never make it," to Leyte Gulf, confidently predicted Commander Moulton.

There was a certain casualness to these assumptions, especially considering that Halsey had made no effort to keep Kinkaid in the loop. Halsey's staff took little, if any, notice of some uncomfortable facts about Admiral Oldendorf's old, slow battleships. They had been armed with munitions for bombarding beaches, not shelling enemy ships. About three-quarters of the shells in the magazines of the Seventh Fleet were high-explosive, packing shrapnel that could cut a swath through soldiers on a battlefield, but only about a quarter were armor-piercing—necessary to punch through the steel of a battleship. In the confined waters of Leyte Gulf, Oldendorf might hope to trap Kurita's battleships. But if the Japanese broke out, the old battleships of the Seventh Fleet were not well suited to fight a running sea battle.

In later years, one of Halsey's staff officers vaguely remembered that, a day or two before the battle, the Seventh Fleet had asked for armor-piercing rounds from the Third Fleet, and that Halsey had made an ammunition ship available. But the recollection was probably faulty; no record of such a request or delivery was ever found. In any case, it was presumptuous and unwise for Halsey's staff to be making assumptions about Admiral Kinkaid's intentions and capabilities. No one, it appears, suggested to Admiral Halsey that he simply communicate and *ask* Kinkaid what he planned to do.

In the end, the Dirty Tricks Department was deceived by its own eagerness. The excited chatter of the pilots piped over the loud-speaker in Flag Plot and the "flash reports" from the combat information centers in the three carrier groups had convinced Halsey's men that the Center Force was essentially finished. Assistant Air Officer Jack Hoerner argued that the air strikes had dropped so many bombs on the topsides of the Japanese ships that their fire control systems had been wrecked, meaning that the Japanese could no longer accurately aim their guns. Hoerner had no evidence, and his guess was incorrect. But in the heady atmosphere of Flag Plot, Hoerner's assessment was just another untested assumption accepted as fact.

At 1830, 6:30 P.M., just after sunset, Lt. Cdr. John Lawrence, the air combat intelligence officer, recorded a flash report from Adm. Ralph Davison's carrier group. It toted up an impressive list of Japanese ships sinking or out of action: a *Yamato*-class battleship bombed and torpedoed, left afire, and down at the bow; a *Kongo*-class battleship left smoking and badly damaged; another battleship bombed and torpedoed two or three times; and a light cruiser "torpedoed and seen to roll over." Lawrence wrote, in his report distributed through the fleet and to CINCPAC, "Enemy force on easterly course when first sighted and when last seen, on westerly course." Mauled by air attacks, the Center Force seemed to be retreating.

Some sixty years later, Lawrence, a gracious, elderly gentleman sitting erect in his imposing house on Boston's North Shore, recalled the moment. "There was a sense of elation," he said. "I shared it." Lawrence paused and slowly raised his hand to his face. "Mea culpa," he said, "mea culpa."

As Kurita's fleet swung back to the west in the slanting light of late afternoon, the *Yamato* passed her crippled sister ship, *Musashi*. She was listing to port and barely moving. Her "miserable position" was a "sorrowful sight," Admiral Ugaki recorded. The foredeck was nearly awash, and water lapped at the imperial crest at the bow. Desperate to do something, Ugaki had radioed her commander, Admiral Inoguchi, instructing him to try to beach the great ship on a shoal where she might be repaired and salvaged. But, her steering damaged, she was doomed to turn slowly in circles. "At the moment, I couldn't even think of words to cheer them up," wrote Ugaki.

On the wing of the bridge, where he was scanning the surface looking for submarine periscopes, Petty Officer Koitabashi felt "a strange anxiety" watching one of Japan's two great battleships founder. He wondered if his own ship was next. "I wasn't losing my fighting spirit, but I asked myself: does this mean that the *Yamato* is not perfect?" he recalled. Silence had fallen over the bridge. "We couldn't talk," said Koitabashi.

Jiro Iwasa, the young reconnaissance pilot who had been shocked by the sight of a crewman eating a bloody rice ball, grew restless lying in his bunk, nursing his slightly wounded thigh. He wandered up onto the bridge. Before he was turned back and warned not to come too close to the senior officers, he saw Ugaki staring at the *Musashi*, looking grave and, through his grim features, a little sad. Across the bridge, Admiral Kurita, his jaw thrust out, was staring straight ahead. Iwasa noticed, as he quietly watched from the rear of the bridge, that Ugaki and Kurita, though separated by no more than thirty or forty feet, seemed remote from each other, not speaking or exchanging glances.

Years later, recalling the battle, Kurita told a young naval cadet that his "heart ached" to leave the *Musashi* to her fate. Telling himself, "This is war, this is war," he began mustering the will to turn back and face the enemy. A thousand considerations, from the profound to the practical, weighed upon him. His destroyers had just enough fuel to make it all the way to Leyte Gulf and back again. He did not want them to end up as target practice for the Americans, helpless because their tanks were dry. If he was going to complete his mission to Leyte Gulf, he had to turn around and venture back to the east now, toward San Bernardino Strait. The time was 1715, 5:15 in the afternoon.

"All right," Kurita announced, shedding his characteristic reticence, "let's go back." His chief of staff, Admiral Koyanagi, seemed taken aback. "Are we turning?" he asked. Another staff officer spluttered that they had received no answer to their pleas for air support. "That's all right, let's go," Kurita responded.

There was barely concealed disgruntlement among Kurita's staff officers. Earlier that afternoon, Combined Fleet headquarters in Tokyo had sent another message:

> PROBABILITY IS GREAT THAT ENEMY WILL EMPLOY SUBMARINES
> IN THE APPROACHES TO SAN BERNARDINO STRAIT.
> BE ALERT.

The message might have been "humorous," wrote Japanese journalist Masanori Ito, who interviewed Kurita's staff officers after the battle; "instead it was ludicrous and infuriating." The anger turned to derision shortly after 6:00 P.M., when the following message came from Admiral Toyoda, the commander-in-chief of the Combined Fleet, by wireless, to be decoded and handed to Admiral Kurita:

> TRUSTING IN DIVINE GUIDANCE, RESUME THE ATTACK.

Interrogated after the war, Toyoda explained that Admiral Kurita was to continue on the attack into Leyte Gulf, even if it meant the loss of every ship in the fleet.

Kurita's staff officers understood perfectly well that they had been ordered to their deaths. There were jeers in the operations room behind the bridge. "Leave the fighting to us. Not even a god can direct naval battles from the shore," protested one officer, while another mockingly rephrased the order. "Believing in annihilation, resume the attack!" If Kurita heard these rumblings from his monkey seat in the forward corner of the bridge, he said nothing.

Once more headed eastward, Kurita's ships filed past the stricken *Musashi* one last time. She was in her death throes. High in the pagoda superstructure, Admiral Inoguchi was writing a letter of apology to the emperor. It had been a mistake, he wrote, to believe in the gun power of great battleships. Inoguchi's executive officer wanted to stay and die with his commander, but Inoguchi ordered him off the ship, so that he could live to seek revenge. As the ship began to settle for its final plunge, Inoguchi gave the order to abandon ship. A sailor named Kiyoshi Watanabe was scrambling up from his duty station belowdecks when he heard a shout. "The Emperor's portrait! Move aside!" Two petty officers carrying the portrait, draped in a white sheet, pushed him out of the way. Watanabe was bitter; he hated the petty officers for regularly beating him, and he had no more reverence left. He angrily thought to himself that he might die because he had to get out of the way for a picture.

With a rattling, roaring groan, the leviathan dipped and began to roll over. In the fading light, sailors on a nearby destroyer watched, transfixed, as hundreds of desperate men ran and slipped and slid across the *Musashi's* slowly rotating hull (encrusted with razor-sharp barnacles), like mice on a treadmill. The stern of the great ship rose straight up out of the dark sea and plunged down, hissing, taking more than a thousand men with her. Another thousand swam for their lives, trying not to be sucked down by an enormous whirlpool that forced even the attending destroyer to steer clear. Voices could be heard across the water, crying for help, but also singing marching songs and the national anthem, and finally, as dusk turned to night, a popular tune, "Shanghai Gal."

That evening, as he wrote in his diary by the light of the red battle lamp, Admiral Ugaki grieved for the *Musashi*, which, he felt, "had sacrificed herself for *Yamato*." He was as fatalistic as ever. "I therefore finally made up my mind to share the fate of the ship without reservation, having decided to have *Yamato* as my death place."

He recorded the "telegram from the Combined Fleet to keep on advancing, convinced of heavenly guidance." He also noted a scrap of intelligence about what awaited them, not much or very precise information, but enough to at once disappoint him and arouse his fevered hopes. The American invasion fleet at Leyte had mostly "gone out," he wrote, "leaving a few big ships in the bay," slim pickings after such an arduous journey. But there was an enemy task force floating somewhere out there on the other side of the San Bernardino Strait. Perhaps the enemy would close and engage in a Decisive Battle. "It was my idea at the time that once we got out of the channel we should search for an area where an enemy would most likely be found and attack it." He was being wishful, he knew, hoping his battleships could get close enough to the American carriers, whose planes could outrange his guns. Reality intruded, as he recalled the incessant bombing of the past day in the Sibuyan Sea.

Without air cover, Ugaki wrote bitterly, "all of our fighting strength will be reduced to nothing at the end." Yasukuni Shrine beckoned from beyond. Ugaki pledged himself "to be reborn seven times to serve the country."

In the gathering darkness, a lone American night search plane flew high above Kurita's battered fleet. The pilot radioed his carrier, the *Independence,* that the Japanese battle fleet had turned around once again and now was headed on a southeasterly course—headed toward the San Bernardino Strait. The message reached Flag Plot aboard the *New Jersey* at about 8:00 P.M.

Admiral Halsey was just going to bed. A few minutes earlier, he had made a great show of striding into the crowded room, leaning over the chart, and stabbing with his finger at a point in the Philippine Sea where the Japanese carriers had been sighted late that afternoon. "Here's where I'm going," he announced. "Mick," he said, turning to his chief of staff, Mick Carney, "start 'em north." Carney immediately began writing up orders sending all three carrier groups to a rendezvous point for the northward charge. By the time the messages were transmitted at 2020 (8:20 P.M.), Halsey had already retired to his cabin one deck below Flag Plot, not to be disturbed. He had been awake for almost all of the past forty-eight hours. He desperately needed a few hours of rest if he was to rise in the middle of the night and command what he expected to be the defining sea battle of the war.

It is not clear from contemporaneous records whether Halsey was told, before he retired, that the Center Force had turned back toward the strait. Many years later, Halsey—who, to his dying day, never conceded that he had erred by taking his entire fleet north—told his old battle line commander, Adm. Willis "Ching" Lee, privately that he was sorry he had not been awakened with the report that Kurita's remaining force was remounting its attack. Halsey's remark suggests that he went to bed unawares and that he felt at least a hidden twinge of regret that he had not had the chance to rethink his strategy.

If Halsey had been warned as early as 8:00 P.M. that Kurita was coming through, might he have left the battle line to guard the San Bernardino Strait? Possibly, though it seems more likely that he would have kept on steaming after the carriers, assuming all the while that Kinkaid was defending Leyte Gulf. Halsey had made his name by bold actions, not by hedging. He had come to believe the newspaper headlines about "Bull" Halsey. And he had for years nurtured his Ahab-like pursuit of Japanese carriers. "We were obsessed with the carriers," said Lawrence, using the same word Mick Carney employed to describe Halsey's fixation.

Halsey's staff felt free to argue with Halsey—but only up to the moment when Halsey made a decision. Then, in the rigid tradition of naval command at sea, argument ceased. Changed circumstances—Kurita's reversal of course—should have been enough to reopen the debate, but Halsey's staff by then had saluted and determined to carry out his order. Halsey did not have the opportunity to reconsider his decision until much later—until he arose after midnight, by which time his fleet was well along on its course toward the enemy carriers.

Halsey's staff deferred not just from obedience, but out of concern for his physical and emotional health. They were worried about the man they affectionately called "Admiral Bill." Many years later, John Lawrence recalled the enormous tension in Flag Plot as information about Japanese fleet movements came pouring in from disparate and sometimes conflicting sources. "It was unbelievable, everyone was wound so tight," said Lawrence. The staff remembered that Halsey had succumbed to stress once before—in April 1942, when he had come down with the psychosomatic skin rash after the frantic hit-and-run raids in the Pacific and on Tokyo. "I'm perfectly sure that the disease was the result of the Doolittle raid," Lawrence recalled. "Everyone had this on their mind."

Throughout combat operations that September and October, Halsey's doctor, Carnes "Piggy" Weeks, tried to put Halsey at ease with ribald jokes and a nightly shot or two of whiskey. After the war, Weeks told his son Carnes Weeks, Jr. (also an MD), that he routinely used alcohol to help Halsey sleep. In those days, sleeping pills were powerfully narcotic, knocking a person out for eight hours. Weeks used whiskey as a lighter drug to induce relaxation and drowsiness.

"He told me that he tried to make Halsey 'comfortable,' as he put it," said Carnes Weeks, Jr.

Dr. Weeks may have used alcohol as a mild sedative and then, in effect, collaborated with Mick Carney and the rest of the staff to hang a "Do Not Disturb" sign outside Halsey's cabin. "I have no doubt that Piggy Weeks gave Halsey something to drink that night," said Lawrence.

Dr. Weeks also knew that Halsey, like many of his staff, was under the weather. On October 26, 1944—less than two days later—Weeks wrote his wife, Margaret, that "Adm. Bill, Mick, Harold and others have all been laid low with the flu. Pretty sick, but all now recovering—pretty ticklish as this was right when things were hot." "Mick" was Carney, "Harold" was Harold Dow, the communications officer, and their illness may help explain why Halsey's staff work was inadequate at this critical moment. On this of all nights, Halsey's communications were sloppily worded and imprecise. One wonders if Ham Dow was so feverish that he simply overlooked crucial details, like making sure Kinkaid was kept informed. "Harold was quite ill—just beginning to get around," Weeks wrote his wife on October 26.

Dow was not bedridden. Others remember seeing him in Flag Plot that night. No one could afford to be incapacitated "when things were hot," and it was unmanly to admit to feeling poorly to anyone but the admiral's doctor. But Weeks knew who was sick and who was well, and he understandably wanted to give Admiral Bill as much chance to rest as possible.

Not everyone on Halsey's staff agreed that the admiral had made the right decision by heading north en masse. Mike Cheek, the chief intelligence officer, had never fit in with the boisterous Dirty Tricksters. During the discussion of the possible options around dusk on October 24, Cheek had stood in the back of Flag Plot and said nothing. When Halsey's staff went down to the wardroom to continue the discussion over dinner, Cheek went to his stateroom to rest before coming back on watch.

Still, he tried to do something. In Flag Plot, after Halsey had given the order to head north and then retired, a "furious" argument broke out between Cheek and Doug Moulton, the air operations officer. With some bitterness, Cheek regarded the sometimes pompous Moulton as "Halsey's favorite." Cheek had just seen the report from the *Independence*'s night search plane that Kurita's Central Force had reversed course and was headed for the San Bernardino Strait.

Armed with this information, worried that Halsey was leaving the strait unguarded, Cheek accosted Moulton. Normally, Cheek wrote crabbed little notes to the chief of staff while Moulton expostulated, but this time Cheek stood his ground. "They're coming through, I know," said Cheek. "I've played poker with them." ("That was, for Mike Cheek, an outburst," commented Lieutenant Solberg. "He'd never let on to any of us that he had even been to Japan.")

But Moulton was unpersuaded. He brushed off Cheek's arguments by saying that orders had already gone out. Besides, he told Cheek, the Central Force was "finished. It can't do any damage."

Cheek was not the only doubter in Flag Plot that night. Lt. Harris Cox, Cheek's deputy intelligence officer, was deeply bothered by Halsey's decision to "head 'em north." Cox was just a junior officer, and he said nothing as he manned his duty station, a stand-up desk piled with intelligence documents, in the corner of Flag Plot. After he came off watch at 8:00 P.M., he returned to his small cabin and told his roommate, Lieutenant Solberg, that he was appalled. Halsey, he told Solberg, had just done what the Japanese hoped he would.

Cox was preoccupied with a captured Japanese document. It was titled "Z Operation Orders: Secret Combined Fleet Orders Operation No. 73." These were the secret orders lost by Admiral Fukudome, the Combined Fleet chief of staff, when he was shot down in March of 1944. The twenty-eight-page document was a series of contingency plans for thwarting American invasions of Japan's defensive perimeter. The plan clearly stated that the "primary objective" of the Japanese surface forces was to sink the American troop transports at the invasion beach. The Japanese carriers were supposed to hover over the horizon and make a flank attack.

Admiral Spruance had been influenced by the captured Z Orders during the Battle of the Philippine Sea. He had stuck close to the beach lest Japanese battleships slip behind and attack the invasion force while the Third Fleet was off chasing carriers. Apparently determined to do the opposite of whatever Spruance did, Admiral Halsey's staff had not seemed to pay much heed to the Z Orders, except to note that they recommended the tactic of shuttle bombing, sending planes between carriers and land bases.

Cox was frustrated by his superiors' indifference to such an important blueprint. "He kept the document in our quarters and was forever pulling it out of a drawer and talking with me about it," recalled Solberg. "He also went over it with Capt. Cheek, our chief." But while Halsey and his top men had endlessly debated and tried to guess Japan's next move, the reticent, tongue-tied Cheek had been unable to get the attention of Halsey or the rest of the Department of Dirty Tricks.

As the *New Jersey* vibrated from her giant turbines, barely rolling as she slashed northward through the calm Philippine Sea, the two young intelligence officers wondered what to do. Finally, Cox decided to go to Captain Cheek one last time, to persuade him to go up the chain of command and warn that the Japanese were luring the Americans in the wrong direction.

Cox and Solberg were unaware of Cheek's earlier run-in with Commander Moulton. Neither man had been in Flag Plot at the time; they had heard about it later from an assistant operations officer who had witnessed the "furious argument."

Now, shortly before 2200—10:00 P.M., Cox and Solberg found the gaunt, worn-looking Cheek in his cabin. Cheek listened wearily. He had seen that the Japanese seemed to be gathering to hit the transports at Leyte Gulf, he told Cox and Solberg. But, he said, he had not necessarily concluded that the Japanese carriers were decoys, being used to lure away the Third Fleet. Still, he had not been sitting idly. He had tried to persuade Commander Moulton that the Center Force was not finished, merely retreating as a bluff. Moulton had rebuffed him, said Cheek.

Cox and Solberg urged their boss to try harder—to go up a notch on the chain of command and appeal to Mick Carney. If Cheek could just persuade Carney, then the chief of staff could awaken Admiral Halsey before it was too late to avoid falling into a trap.

Mike Cheek was not as timid as he seemed. He had barely escaped the Japanese onslaught on Manila at the beginning of the war, and he had been through typhoons at sea, once aboard a destroyer that rolled almost 90 degrees. While inarticulate, Cheek was smart, and he—unlike his colleagues in Halsey's wardroom—had some understanding of the Japanese. This was the moment to use his insight, to play the role of intelligence officer and provide the information that his commander needed to correct his judgment.

Cheek disappeared into the suite of rooms shared by Carney and Halsey, just off the wardroom below Flag Plot. A few minutes later, according to Solberg's account, Cheek returned to report disappointing news. He said he had made their case to Admiral Carney, but that Carney had replied that Halsey was asleep, not to be disturbed.

More than two decades later, Cheek gave a slightly different account in a letter to naval historian Clark Reynolds. Carney had gone to bed, ill and exhausted, but Cheek woke him up. Carney could not have been too pleased to be roused, but according to Cheek, he said, "Since you feel so strongly, you have my permission to awaken the Admiral, but I do not believe it will do any good. As you know, he has had little or no sleep in the past 48 hours." Carney made a reference to another staffer (Cheek did not reveal the name; his identity remains a mystery) whose dissenting views earlier that evening had been overridden by Halsey.

Cheek did not have the heart to take on Halsey. "I silently agreed that any effort on my part would be useless," Cheek recalled. Cheek was deeply worried that the Third Fleet was being led astray. But he had never felt comfortable directly addressing Halsey, and he could not bring himself to do it now.

Cheek's sense of alarm—and resignation in the face of Halsey's bullheadedness and guard-dog staff—was shared by more powerful men. Indeed, almost all of Halsey's top commanders had misgivings about his course of action. But, out of fatigue or deference, they did not push their objections. Halsey was not a cruel or frightening figure, but he exuded such cockiness and lust for command that he overawed even the most confident men, especially men who had been more or less continuously at sea for months and even years. In a seaborne world of absolute authority, Halsey had become too much the Pirate King; no one dared cross him.

Aboard the battleship *Washington*, the commander of the battle

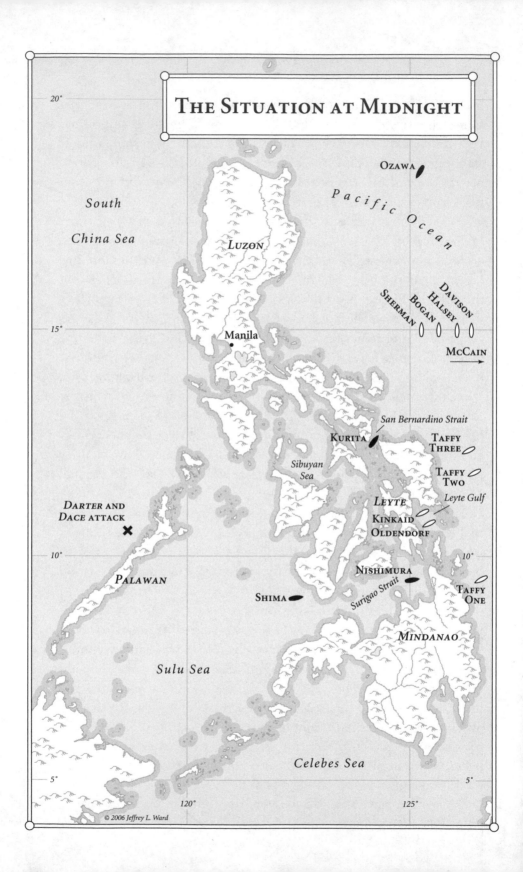

THE SITUATION AT MIDNIGHT

South

China Sea

LUZON

Pacific Ocean

OZAWA

DAVISON
HALSEY
SHERMAN BOGAN

McCAIN

Manila

San Bernardino Strait

KURITA **TAFFY THREE**

Sibuyan Sea

TAFFY TWO

LEYTE *Leyte Gulf*

DARTER AND DACE ATTACK

KINKAID
OLDENDORF

PALAWAN

NISHIMURA

SHIMA **TAFFY ONE**

Surigao Strait

MINDANAO

Sulu Sea

Celebes Sea

© 2006 Jeffrey L. Ward

line, Adm. Ching Lee, had guessed before the sun went down that the Japanese carriers were decoys, and he sent a signal to the *New Jersey* expressing his views. From someone on Halsey's staff, he received a perfunctory "Roger." Again, when Lee saw a report from a snooper night fighter aboard the *Independence* that the Center Force had turned east again, he signaled the *New Jersey* warning that the Japanese were setting a trap. Again, a "Roger," and nothing more. Lee, a hero at Guadalcanal for sinking a Japanese battleship in a night action, was tired after two years of combat operations at sea. He did not press his opinion.

The *New Jersey* was sailing in a carrier group under the command of a gruff Irishman named Gerry Bogan. Flying his flag from the carrier *Intrepid*, Admiral Bogan was communicating by short-range TBS with Capt. E. C. Ewan of the carrier *Independence*, whose night search planes were keeping a watch on Kurita's fleet. Ewan told Bogan that Kurita's fleet was headed for the San Bernardino Strait. His pilots had reported that, for the first time in weeks, navigation lights had been turned on in the narrow, twisting strait—an ominous sign that the Japanese were coming through.

Bogan later recalled that he thought Halsey was making "one hell of a mistake" by leaving the strait unguarded. Bogan drew up a recommendation that Task Force 34, Admiral Lee's battle line, be detached, along with a couple of carriers for air cover, to await Kurita's fleet. Bogan drafted a message to Halsey saying that the navigation lights were shining brightly in the San Bernardino Strait and that Kurita's Center Force was heading right for it. Taking the TBS phone handle, Bogan personally read the message to one of Halsey's staffers aboard the *New Jersey*. "Yes, yes, we have that information," came the response. Bogan later recalled that the Halsey staffer (never identified) spoke to him in a "rather impatient voice." Bogan felt he was being given the brush-off. He did not bother to try to persuade the commander of the Third Fleet to detach the battle line. He didn't think that Halsey or his staff would listen.

Aboard the *Lexington*, Adm. Marc Mitscher was, in theory at least, the commander of all four carrier groups of the Third Fleet. Mitscher had his own ideas about how to handle the Japanese. Before sunset, he had discussed them with his staff. Mitscher wanted to

Mike Cheek and Harris Cox

Mitscher and Burke

send the battle line racing north to attack the Japanese carriers, then quickly bring them back to catch Kurita's Center Fleet, either before or after it arrived in Leyte Gulf the next day. Carrier planes could finish off the remants of Ozawa's Northern Force at dawn. If everyone moved right away, there was just enough time to, in effect, kill two birds with one stone. But Mitscher hesitated; he was reluctant to press the plan on Halsey. At about 8:30 P.M., Mitscher received Halsey's command to take all the carrier groups and the battle line north. "Admiral Halsey is in command now," Mitscher told his subordinates. From his flat tone of resignation, it was clear he was disheartened; carrier commander Mitscher was, in effect, being pushed aside. A fellow officer once joked that Mitscher "didn't look a day over 80." Lately, he had been sleeping more and more and speaking less and less. Bone-weary, Mitscher went to bed.

Meanwhile, Mitscher's chief of staff, Arleigh Burke, stewed impatiently. "31-Knot" Burke, the gallant destroyer man from the Solomons unwillingly drafted to be Mitscher's number two, had made peace with his boss and immersed himself in carrier operations. He had keen instincts, and they all told him that his former hero Halsey and his staff were about to commit an epic blunder.

Burke had closely observed the one-sided air battle off Formosa just ten days earlier. He could accurately guess that Japanese airpower had been badly depleted. Notwithstanding the loss of the *Princeton*, he thought the Japanese air attacks over the past day had been poorly coordinated and weak. If the Japanese carriers were out there, they didn't present much of a threat. Like Admiral Lee, Burke suspected that the carriers were being used as decoys.

At the same time, Burke guessed that the Japanese battleship fleet now making for the San Bernardino Strait was more powerful than Halsey assumed. The air combat intelligence officers on Mitscher's staff were more experienced with carrier operations than Halsey's team. They understood how often and how much pilots exaggerated their claims. Burke discounted the damage report on Kurita's fleet. He predicted that the Japanese would still have plenty of firepower when they emerged from the strait and headed for Leyte Gulf.

Burke had explained his views to Admiral Mitscher. "Well, I think you're right, but I don't know you're right," replied the beaten-down Mitscher. "I don't think we ought to bother Admiral Halsey."

But Burke continued to fret. As Mitscher slept, Burke studied the reports coming in from the *Independence*'s search planes. At 2305, 11:05 P.M., the last dispatch showed the Central Force about to enter the San Bernardino Strait. Burke decided to awaken Mitscher, to get him to implore Halsey to detach the battle line to plug the gaping hole.

Burke and his operations officer, Cdr. James Flatley, knocked on the door of Mitscher's cabin. The admiral was lying in his bunk. "Admiral," said Flatley, "we better tell Halsey to turn around."

Mitscher raised himself on one elbow as Flatley described the report from the search plane tracking Kurita's fleet. "Does Admiral Halsey have that report?" he asked.

"Yes, he does," said Flatley.

"If he wants my advice," said Mitscher, "he'll ask for it." Then he rolled over and went back to sleep.

About a half-hour before midnight, a dive-bomber off the *Independence*, piloted by Lt. Bill Phelps, flew high above the narrow western entrance of the San Bernardino Strait. There, in solemn single-file procession, were more than a dozen Japanese warships, including four battleships. Lieutenant Phelps could see the ships playing their searchlights off the high cliffs at the entrance of the strait as the column crept through the narrow waters. It was the last look at Kurita's fleet that Phelps, or any American pilot, would get that night. All search planes were commanded by Halsey's staff to head north—to search for the Japanese carriers.

CHAPTER ELEVEN

SURPRISE AT DAWN

"Never give a sucker a chance"

IT WAS A STRANGE NIGHT," recalled lookout Kosaku Koitabashi. From high atop the superstructure of the *Yamato*, he stood watch, peering through high-power binoculars while trying to ignore pangs of hunger and waves of fatigue. A dim half-moon shone through a milky sky as Kurita's fleet entered the San Bernardino Strait at about 11:20 P.M. The fleet, diminished but still lethal, navigated the treacherous ten-mile channel against an 8-knot tide. Rain squalls swept in, "but it didn't seem like the tropics," remembered Koitabashi. "It was foggy. There was no visibility." When a dark shape loomed up behind the *Yamato*, Koitabashi and the other lookouts cried out a warning. The battleship *Kongo* came surging out of the murk, nearly staving in the *Yamato*'s stern. The two behemoths swung apart at the last moment. The squalls passed, and the night cleared as the fleet entered the empty Philippine Sea at twenty minutes past midnight on the morning of October 25.

Koitabashi had been at his battle station for most of two days. Going without sleep was a test of spiritual strength, but most of the officers and men just looked grim and exhausted. Koitabashi and his mates had grabbed rice balls from a bucket passed around the bridge, and they had been given occasional cigarette breaks. The gossip at the bon had turned gloomy. "We expected to be torpedoed in the

237

morning," Koitabashi recalled. The signalmen reported that Tokyo had sent a message ordering the fleet to charge ahead, "with divine assistance." But requests for air support had gone unanswered. "We kept saying, 'Where are our airplanes?'" recalled Koitabashi.

Admiral Kurita had plunged into the strait without much idea of what he would find on the other side. His request for scout planes had been greeted by silence. He had not heard anything from Admiral Ozawa. With Ozawa's radio transmitter broken, Kurita had no way of knowing that Ozawa was successfully luring the American carriers off to the north. Kurita tried to keep a brave face on. "Chancing annihilation," he had radioed headquarters at 2213, 10:13 P.M., his fleet was "determined to break through" to the American anchorage at Leyte Gulf "to destroy the enemy."

Optimistically, given the circumstances, or possibly just by rote, Kurita's staff drew up a schedule and plan of attack. The admiral wanted to arrange a rendezvous with the southern arm of the pincer movement, Admiral Nishimura's force, at 0900, 9:00 A.M., near Suluan Light, at the mouth of Leyte Gulf. He need not have sent the order. To any objective observer, the rendezvous was doomed, given the mismatch of ships and firepower between Kinkaid's warships defending Leyte Gulf and Nishimura's last-gasp fleet approaching from the south.

As he sailed through the Sulu Sea 200 miles to the south of Kurita's force, Admiral Nishimura was paying no attention to schedules. Shortly after 10:00 P.M., he wired Kurita that he planned to break through to Leyte Gulf at four that morning. But rather than slow down to delay his arrival until Kurita could join forces, he speeded up. Nishimura may have assumed, correctly, that he would not live to see the dawn. His ships were old and slow; indeed, his two battleships were virtually obsolete, relegated for use as training vessels in the Inland Sea. He had been given as well the most weakly armed cruiser and the oldest destroyers—clearly, a fleet assembled as cannon fodder. The Combined Fleet was holding nothing back; essentially, anything that could float was being thrown into the attack.

Shoji Nishimura was, like so many of his brother officers, a fatalist. He had lost his beloved only son, who had graduated at the top of his class from Eta Jima, in a seaplane accident in the first weeks of the war. He had no interest in politics. Like Kurita, he avoided shore duty. When Kurita made him the commander of the small southern force for the attack on Leyte Gulf, Nishimura made no attempt to make the acquaintance of the captains of the ships under his command. He had been present, with a smile fixed on his face, when Kurita gave his pep talk on the evening of October 21, saying, "You must all remember there are such things as miracles." But he had not bothered to attend a final conference of captains and staff at Brunei before the fleet sortied on October 22. There was no real point to it, except to exchange farewell toasts. "We were told to look out for a shoal in the northern part of Leyte Gulf," recalled the captain of the destroyer *Shigure*, who did attend the meeting—and whose ship would be the only one of Nishimura's seven warships to return. "We determined to do our best. Then we had a few drinks."

MacArthur's navy, the Seventh Fleet, was waiting. Admiral Kinkaid's fleet was organized to support invasions by bombarding beaches, not to fight attacking fleets—that was Halsey's job. Even so, the coming battle promised to be more like target practice. The Seventh Fleet packed enough firepower to cripple Nishimura's two battleships, one cruiser, and four destroyers as they tried to break through the narrow mouth of the Surigao Strait. There had been ample time to prepare. After receiving reports that Nishimura was in the Sulu Sea steaming east toward the strait that morning, Admiral Kinkaid had issued an order to prepare for night battle.

Admiral Oldendorf, the commander of the American ships lining up to greet Nishimura, was an unapologetic practitioner of the American way of war. He believed in massed firepower and overwhelming force. Or, as he later explained to the *New York Times*: "My theory is that of an old-time gambler: *Never give a sucker a chance.*"

To that end, Oldendorf arrayed his "welcoming committee." First, thirty nine PT boats would attack. Then twenty-eight destroyers would make torpedo runs or fire their 5-inch guns. Then four light cruisers and four heavy cruisers would open up with 6-

inch and 8-inch guns. Then, steaming in line abreast across the
northern neck of the Surigao Strait, six battleships armed with 14-
inch and 16-inch guns would finish off anything that was left. Salvaged from the wreckage of Pearl Harbor and equipped with
modern radar and fire control, the old battlewagons would gain
sweet revenge. They would, as the Naval War College textbooks dictated, "cross the T." For centuries, the goal in a sea battle was to
place a line of battleships broadside to the bows of the enemy,
thereby bringing more guns to bear. Admiral Togo had crossed the
T of the Russian fleet at Tsushima in 1905. Now, for the last time in
history, battleship would face battleship in a classic crossing-the-T
engagement.

The sea was glassy as Nishimura's ships approached the Surigao
Strait in the deepening night. The moon was due to set after midnight; the sky would become inky black under low clouds and passing squalls. At 2236, 10:36 P.M., Ensign Peter Gadd's *PT-131* picked
up the Japanese on radar and, along with two other PT boats,
charged at 24 knots. Wooden speedboats were rarely effective against
steel warships, but their warning set off a night of fireworks and appalling slaughter.

Nishimura made little attempt at evasive action. He plowed
straight ahead into a murderous crossfire of torpedoes and crashing
heavy guns. "The arched line of tracers in the darkness looked like a
continual stream of lighted railroad cars going over a hill," recalled
a destroyer captain who watched in awe as the fire poured down on
the luckless Japanese. The Japanese tried to fire off star shells to illu-
minate the enemy, but the bursts of white light just added to the sur-
reality of the carnage. Tons of shells rained down; more than a
hundred torpedo wakes crisscrossed the water. Most of the flying
metal was American. The only real damage done to an American
ship, the destroyer *Albert W. Grant*, came mostly from other American ships' friendly fire.

Two Japanese destroyers were quickly sunk. The battleship *Fuso*
was cut in half. Admiral Nishimura's battleship, the *Yamashiro*,
burned brightly from stem to stern. The admiral sent a last command to his vanishing fleet: "We have received a torpedo attack. You

are to proceed and attack all ships." Then, shortly after 4:00 A.M., his ship blew apart and capsized.

Into this inferno, a second, separate Japanese fleet of two cruisers and four destroyers came steaming—or blundering. In the smoke and darkness, the advancing flagship *Nachi* collided with one of Nishimura's battered vessels, the cruiser *Mogami.* "Sorry!" cried the *Mogami*'s gunnery officer, who had taken over for the dead captain and dead executive officer. The story of this orphan fleet, under the command of an admiral who had spent most of his career as a courtier and shore-based staff officer, is a pitiful footnote to the Combined Fleet's Götterdämmerung strategy. Some ten days earlier, Adm. Kiyohide Shima of the Second Diversionary Striking Force had been ordered to mop up the "remnants" of Halsey's supposedly shattered fleet off Formosa. Instead, Shima's fleet had barely escaped the BAITDIV trap set by the Department of Dirty Tricks. For the next week, Shima's ships wandered about receiving conflicting orders until they were told to join forces with Admiral Nishimura's fleet. The two admirals never coordinated their movements. Shima's failure to contact Nishimura may have been partly a matter of face: Shima was senior to Nishimura and did not want to take orders from him. And, by now, Shima was fed up with playing the role of sacrificial fleet. "We were feeling disappointed, angry, indignant," he later recalled.

When Shima saw the wreckage of Nishimura's ships in the predawn hours of October 25, he briefly pondered his options. He was shocked by the sight of two battleships burning. "The fires were terrific," he later recalled. "They looked like steel mill flames." He could hear, through the smoke, "the slow crump of big guns." Soon they would be aiming at him. He gave the order, "Attack! All ships attack!" but his staff had a better idea. The enemy was waiting "with open arms," they argued. It was "foolish to go ahead." Shima was not, like Nishimura, an old sea dog resigned to his fate. He missed those comfortable shore billets. Deciding that his staff's arguments "made good sense," he turned around and fled for home.

In the gray first light of October 25, a day of reckoning for the

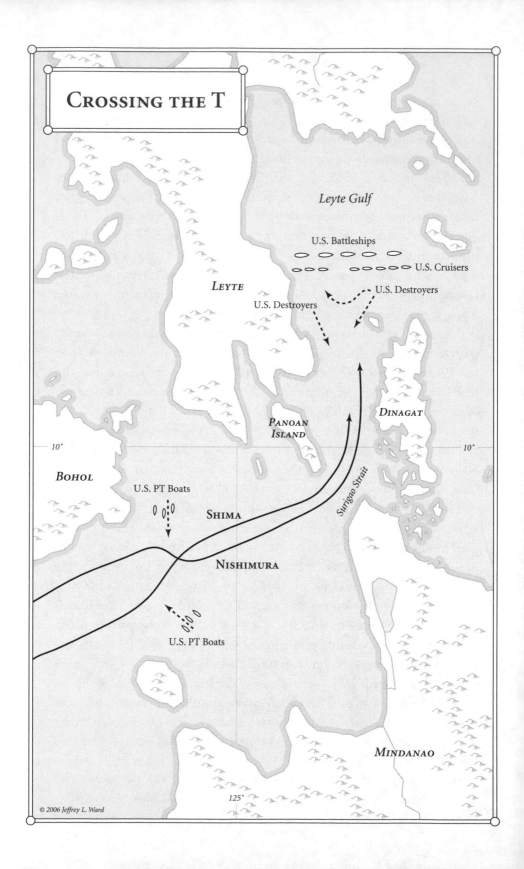

CROSSING THE T

Leyte Gulf

U.S. Battleships

U.S. Cruisers

U.S. Destroyers

LEYTE

U.S. Destroyers

U.S. Destroyers

PANOAN
ISLAND

DINAGAT

10°   10°

BOHOL

U.S. PT Boats

SHIMA

Surigao Strait

NISHIMURA

U.S. PT Boats

MINDANAO

125°

© 2006 Jeffrey L. Ward

Imperial Japanese Navy, thousands of Japanese sailors floated in the oil-slicked waters of Surigao Strait. Most of the men were not waiting to be rescued. When American boats lowered from destroyers and cruisers tried to pick them up, officers could be heard yelling at their men to swim away, to drown rather than be captured. In a whaleboat from the destroyer *Claxton*, a machinist's mate rigged a lasso and roped in a Japanese sailor. One sailor did wish to surrender. As he tried to climb aboard an American destroyer, the USS *Edwards*, he was pulled back by another Japanese swimmer, who unceremoniously slit his craven comrade's throat. Sailors who swam to surrounding islands were greeted by bolo knife—wielding Filipinos with fresh memories of Japanese occupation.

In the early morning hours, Admiral Kinkaid sent a message of congratulations to Admiral Oldendorf for a job well done. Through the night, Kinkaid had listened to reports of the rout from the *Wasatch*, anchored off Red Beach in Leyte Gulf. Kinkaid had been busy attending to myriad details and responsibilities, not the least of which was the care and feeding of his difficult boss, General MacArthur. The commander-in-chief had been quartered aboard the cruiser *Nashville*. When it appeared that the *Nashville* would join Oldendorf's battle line, MacArthur wanted to go along to see the fight. He told Kinkaid that he had read all his life about the "glamour of sea battle"; it excited his "imagination." Kinkaid demurred; the *Nashville* stayed at anchor with Kinkaid's flagship.

Kinkaid had been preoccupied with the battle raging in Surigao Strait. Having intercepted Halsey's Battle Plan to form Task Force 34 earlier that afternoon, he assumed that Halsey would handle the San Bernardino Strait if Kurita's Central Force were to break through and descend on Leyte Gulf from the north.

Shortly after eight on the evening of the 24th, Kinkaid received a message from Halsey, saying that Kurita's Central Force was "heavily damaged." Halsey continued: "Am proceeding north with three groups to attack enemy carrier force at dawn." Kinkaid should have stopped to wonder if Halsey meant, by "Am proceeding," that Halsey, personally, was headed north. Under Halsey's Battle Plan, the Third Fleet commander's flagship, the *New Jersey*, was supposed to be left guarding the San Bernardino Strait with Task Force 34. But Kinkaid does not appear to have pondered Halsey's machinations, perhaps because he was busy with his own.

In hindsight, Kinkaid assumed too much and questioned too little. It is not clear how much warning Halsey gave Kinkaid that Kurita was headed for Leyte. Halsey's message "Am proceeding north" gave Kurita's course direction, 120 degrees southeast—indicating that the Japanese were no longer retiring west. Halsey later claimed that at about 11:00 P.M., the Third Fleet passed on to Kinkaid the report from the *Independence*'s night snoopers that Kurita's fleet had progressed twenty miles closer to the San Bernardino Strait, though there is no record of such a telegram in Seventh Fleet message files. In any case, there can be no doubt that Halsey and Kinkaid— because of separate chains of command, because of personal rivalry or enmity, because of fatigue and the friction of war—made only the most cursory attempts to communicate with each other.

After a warm reception had been arranged for the Japanese in Surigao Strait, Kinkaid asked his staff, as the hour approached 4:00 A.M., if there was anything they had overlooked. Capt. Richard Cruzen, the operations officer, spoke up. "We've never asked Halsey directly if Task Force 34 is guarding the San Bernardino Strait." Kinkaid told him to send a cable to Halsey, just to make sure. The telegram was sent at 0412, 4:12 A.M.

Halsey would not receive it for another two and a half hours, at 0648, 6:48 A.M. It may seem shocking that a telegram of such urgency and time-sensitivity could take so long to be delivered, but instant communication had fallen victim to divided command and the creaky technology of sending encrypted telegrams. Kinkaid's message was sent to Halsey through a radio station 1,500 miles away, where two-hour delays were typical.

The radio station at Manus, a sweatshop of harried operators hunched over telegraphs on a desolate island off the coast of New Guinea, was a notorious bottleneck. Theoretically, messages marked "urgent" had priority, but before long, there were so many messages marked "urgent" that they began to pile up. Messages could take up to four hours to wind their way between Kinkaid and Halsey, and often they arrived out of sequence, further adding to the confusion and delay. It was an atrocious form of communication. At crucial moments, the fleets might as well have been signaling each other with flags.*

Kinkaid took a few steps, inadequate and halfhearted in retrospect, to find out if Kurita's fleet was coming through the strait. Shortly after noon on October 24, he had ordered a squadron of PBYs, slow, fat amphibious planes, based in Leyte Gulf to look for Kurita's fleet. Bothered by mechanical problems, delayed by a Japanese air raid, the squadron managed to send only one Catalina Black Cat up the coast of Samar over the strait. The plane's journey was harrowing. Its radar could not distinguish between islands and ships. Fired on repeatedly by American ships, the PBY's crew began to give every blip on the radar a wide berth, and became lost. The pilot thought he saw the wakes of an enemy fleet, but he could not be sure—and never made a report.

Inattention, flawed assumptions, long and twisted or broken chains of command are the norm, not the exception, throughout the history of warfare. So are fatigue, distraction, emotional and physical overload. So, too, fear, vainglory, error. But the gods of war needed to be particularly fickle, not to mention heartless, to arrange the collision that was about to occur on the morning of October 25, 1944, the last and most destructive day in the long history of fleets fighting at sea.

October 25 was, fittingly, the anniversary day of the Battle of Balaclava (1854) in the Crimean War—the epic blunder memorialized in Tennyson's poem "The Charge of the Light Brigade." But it was

---

*Halsey was aware that communications were poor. On the eve of battle, he had tried to warn Admiral Nimitz in a private letter that "we are still having communications problems, and we will continue to have them until proper communications facilities are installed on Guam. Reception is freakish in this area, and the load is such that a mere 'priority' precedence is frequently several days reaching its destination.... I can assure you that these difficulties are real and can also assure you that the time has come when heroic measures must be taken if fighting communications are to be maintained." But time had run out; Halsey sent the letter on October 22.

also St. Crispin's Day, the anniversary of the Battle of Agincourt (1415), remembered by Shakespeare's Henry V:

> *This day is call'd the feast of Crispian:*
> *He that outlives this day, and comes safe home,*
> *Will stand a tip-toe when this day is nam'd,*
> *And rouse him at the name of Crispian*

October 25, 1944, deserves to be remembered, like the Charge of the Light Brigade, for its errors and foolish waste of life. But it should be remembered, and is remembered by its survivors, for great acts of courage and sacrifice.

Halsey's failure to guard the San Bernardino Strait did not give Kurita clear sailing to Leyte Gulf. MacArthur's navy stood in the way. But it was a much weaker force, and its presence in the path of Kurita's fleet was an accident, an oversight. The commanders of these American ships had not been preparing for heroic battle. On this St. Crispin's Day, there was no King Henry to inspire:

> *We few, we happy few, we band of brothers;*
> *For he to-day that sheds his blood with me*
> *Shall be my brother...*

There were only ordinary men, waiting around in chow lines for breakfast, wondering what the day would bring, and hoping, for the most part, not much.

To support amphibious landings, MacArthur's navy had its own formation of aircraft carriers. The ships were regarded as a bit of a joke, even by the men who manned them. They were called escort carriers or jeep carriers—and sometimes, with greater sarcasm, "Kaiser Coffins," "Tomato Cans," "Woolworth Flattops," and "One-Torpedo Ships." U.S. warships bore official designators—a battleship was a BB, a destroyer a DD, a fleet carrier a CV (heavy) or CVL (light), and so forth. An escort carrier, originally designed to transport planes and escort convoys in the Atlantic, was labeled CVE, which, according to the shipboard wags, stood for "Combustible, Vulnerable, and Expendable." Jeep carriers were about half the size of *Essex*-class fleet carriers, the "fast heavies." The escort carriers were slow, with a maximum speed of about 18 knots, and light. They were built, cheaply and quickly, initially on the hulls of merchantmen. Their steel skins were thin and their armaments weak—a single 5-inch gun. To save money, Kaiser Steel neglected to install the hulls with air blowers, so the men sweltered belowdecks. Jeep carrier sailors had to endure derision as well as discomfort. "Jeep carriers," wrote Adm. Samuel Eliot Morison, "were regarded by many an old sailor as interlopers in the Navy—something like reservists, to be tolerated during the war but not taken too seriously."

Each carrier had about a dozen fighters and a dozen bombers, armed usually with 100-pound antipersonnel bombs, not ship-killing 500- and 2,000-pound bombs or torpedoes. The planes were meant to strafe beaches, not fight fleet actions at sea. The Seventh Fleet's eighteen jeep carriers were divided into three groups with the radio call signs Taffy One, Taffy Two, and Taffy Three. Even the candy name Taffy seemed unwarlike. The Taffy sailors could only envy the "fast heavies" and battle line of the Big Blue Fleet.

All through October 23 and 24, as Halsey's carrier task force maneuvered and sent attack planes in waves against the Japanese, and the Seventh Fleet battle line wreaked havoc in the Surigao Strait, the three Taffys floated off Leyte Gulf. They were not idle—their fighters shot down two dozen Japanese warplanes flying over Red Beach on October 24—but they were not meant to tangle with any Japanese capital ships.

It is clear (again, in hindsight) that Admiral Kinkaid should have moved the Taffys still further from Leyte Gulf during the night of October 24–25, to keep them well clear of any sea battle with Kurita's fleet. Yet Kinkaid did not think it was necessary to warn the Taffys—especially Taffy Three, the northernmost carrier group, less than fifty miles off the coast of Samar. When staff officer Capt. Paulus Powell suggested that the Taffys might be in danger of getting sucked into a fleet action, Kinkaid "rather sarcastically" replied, Powell recalled, "What would you have me do with them, bring them in here?"—meaning bring them into the Seventh Fleet anchorage inside Leyte Gulf. When the staff officer suggested moving Taffy Three out to sea another thirty miles, Kinkaid declined.

There were snide jokes about the Taffy Three commander. Captain Powell remarked that Felix Stump of Taffy Two and Thomas Sprague of Taffy One, would "do the right thing" by sending out scout planes and arming their attack planes with heavy bombs and torpedoes. But the commander of Taffy Three, the group most at risk of being overrun, would need prodding, Powell predicted. Taffy Three's commander, Adm. Clifton Sprague (no relation to Tommy Sprague), was generally known as "Ziggy." Powell referred to him as "Dopey," and suggested he be given an extra nudge to prepare for action in the morning. Again, Kinkaid declined. He said he did not like to give orders to another flag officer and then tell him how to carry them out. It was enough to warn the Taffys to keep an eye out to the north. Kinkaid was a by-the-book man. He was not going to follow the example of his nemesis Halsey, butting in and overriding his subordinates.

As the early morning hours ticked by, the chain of command slowly clanked. At 0115, 1:15 A.M., Kinkaid ordered Sprague, the overall commander of the Taffys, to launch daybreak air searches to the north. At 0330, 3:30 A.M., Sprague ordered Taffy Two to fly those searches. Taffy Two's Adm. Felix Stump received the order at 0430, 4:30 A.M., and ordered one of his jeep carriers, the *Ommaney Bay*, to send out search planes at dawn. The *Ommaney Bay* was slow to get going. Her crew began pushing and pulling planes around a rain-slicked deck before 6:00 A.M., but it would be 0658, 6:58 A.M, before she would launch any planes. Too late.

The Taffys were protected by a screen. Three destroyers and four destroyer escorts steamed in a circle around the half-dozen jeep carriers of Taffy Three, the northernmost of the three groups. One of the destroyers was USS *Johnston*. In the early morning hours of October 25, her captain was awake, but feeling frustrated and a little fretful.

Cdr. Ernest Evans listened to the Battle of Surigao Strait on the radio. The tropics sometimes created freakish atmospheric conditions, allowing short-range Talk Between Ships conversations to be heard many miles away. The reception was unusually good that night, and Evans could hear snatches of excited chatter of warship captains ordering torpedo attacks and broadsides against the enemy. Sitting in the *Johnston's* Combat Information Center, a windowless room crammed with electronic gear down below the bridge, Evans seemed disappointed. If he couldn't be in the thick of the fight to the south in Surigao Strait, the captain of the *Johnston* wished he was heading north with Halsey after the Japanese carriers—not baby-sitting Woolworth Flattops on a calm sea miles and miles from the action.

Lt. (j.g.) Ed Digardi, the communications officer, was on the mid-watch, midnight to 4:00 A.M., and he sat with Evans in the Combat Information Center as they listened to the distant battle crackling through the static. Digardi was struck that Evans did not hide his regret. Though normally taciturn, the Chief had always been open about his desire for action—ever since the day of the *Johnston's* commissioning ceremony, when he had vowed to "sail in harm's way" and challenged the crew to sail with him. The *Johnston* had joined in four shore bombardments during amphibious operations in the Marshalls and Marianas and had sunk a submarine. But Evans had never had the chance to engage an enemy ship in a sea battle.

In three days, it would be the first anniversary of the *Johnston's* commissioning. Evans suggested that the crew be served ice cream to celebrate. He didn't sound very enthusiastic. "Well, Hagen," he said with a sigh. "It's been an uneventful year."

"Yes, sir," Hagen responded, trying to sound gruff. "I wouldn't mind seeing a little action."

A few of the men of the *Johnston* were expressing the same disappointment over missing the battle, or at least pretending to, but more felt relief. They had heard rumors that the Japanese fleet was on the move, and news of the attacks on the Japanese in the Sibuyan Sea and the Surigao Strait quickly spread. A sailor named Harold Beresonsky recalled, "I swore up and down the deck of the *Johnston* that as long as we were not part of the combat force, we would see no units of the Jap fleet."

That was fine with chief boatswain's mate Clyde Burnett. An orphan, Burnett had "learned to adjust at a very young age." Joining the navy at eighteen, he had served aboard an old four-piper destroyer. He was at Pearl Harbor when the Japanese attacked. He had volunteered for submarine duty "as the quickest way to get back at the Japs," but after three years of war he was in no hurry to take on the Japanese fleet. "I thought we were in a pretty safe position being fifty or sixty miles off the shore screening small carriers," he recollected many years later. "I thought surely no one will bother us here."

Most of the men had never been truly scared by the Japanese. Their most intense scrape with danger had come a fortnight earlier, during an early October typhoon in the Philippine Sea. The ship had rolled 70 degrees, almost on her beam ends, and frightened sailors down below cried out in the agonizing seconds before the destroyer righted herself. Digardi recalled the fear that gripped him as he stood on the bridge, looking up at giant waves towering over the ship. The *Johnston* would climb, almost straight up it seemed, vibrating and shaking, then come careening and skidding down the mountainous face of the wave. Digardi could hear and feel the engines racing as the propellers came out of the water when the ship crested. If the *Johnston* lost power and the ability to turn into the waves, she would wallow helplessly and capsize. But Digardi, like most of his fellow officers and men, had confidence in the skipper. As the storm brewed, the *Johnston* had been waiting to refuel. Normally, a ship keeps seawater in empty fuel tanks for ballast, to keep the ship from becoming top-heavy. Ordered to jettison his ballast to prepare to take on fuel, Evans had ignored the command. His weather eye told him he would need a stable ship for the storm ahead.

A little after his watch ended at four, Digardi went to bed. The sea was calm; he was lulled to sleep by the thrum of the ship's two giant steam turbine engines. Commander Evans heard the last radio transmissions from the dying battle in the Surigao Strait and turned into his sea cabin, just off the bridge, for a nap before General Quarters, scheduled every morning at 0530, 5:30 A.M., an hour before dawn.

Less than fifty miles away, and closing, Admiral Kurita's fleet plowed east, then south through the empty sea. On the bridge of the *Yamato*, Kurita's staff was in a state of disbelief. They had received no useful intelligence, as usual, but they had felt sure they would be greeted by American submarines as they exited the San Bernardino Strait. Chief of staff Koyanagi had expected the fleet to fight its way out against American battleships in a night action. But the way was clear. Kurita ordered his twenty-one remaining ships to spread across a thirteen-mile-wide front in a "night search disposition." But there was nothing to see.

Some men began to feel their spirits lift. A kind of giddiness, fueled by relief and sleeplessness, captured at least some of the crew. But Kurita's chief operations officer, Capt. Tonosuke Otani, did not share in the light-headedness. He still expected the fleet to be "completely destroyed" after "doing some damage" inside Leyte Gulf, he would later tell interrogators. Otani was a realist, and he was not eager to commit *hara-kiri* without some good reason. He was one of the officers who had complained about sacrificing a whole fleet to shoot up some transports.

Otani was not encouraged by fragmentary reports from Nishimura's fleet to the south. When Nishimura seemed to be ignoring Kurita's schedule and rushed too quickly into the Surigao Strait, Otani thought he was "taking matters too lightly." Through the early morning hours, as they steamed across the blank sea, Kurita's staff officers anxiously awaited word of the battle that must be raging to the south. At 5:30 they heard the bad news from the *Shigure*, the one destroyer of Nishimura's fleet to escape: it appeared from the brief, fragmentary report that the fleet had been "about wiped out," as Otani recalled the message. There was no word from Admiral Shima's fleet at all. Kurita's fleet was on its own.

Dawn was at 0627, 6:27, but no one saw the sun rise. The morning was misty and gray with a low overcast. The wind was light, about 8 knots, and the sea was slightly choppy with a low swell. On the bridge of the *Yamato*, Admiral Ugaki was mourning—and envying—the death of Nishimura, who had been his Eta Jima classmate and close friend. In his diary, Ugaki recorded the weather, as he always did, commenting that "dark clouds accompanied by squalls hung here and there." Admiral Kurita was about to order his ships into an antiaircraft ring formation, preparing for the onslaught from the air he was sure would come.

*   *   *

Over a hundred miles away and steaming in the opposite direction, Admiral Halsey, with his vast force of sixty-four ships, was in hot pursuit of the Japanese carriers. After three or four hours of badly needed sleep, Halsey had arisen just before 1:00 A.M. He came into Flag Plot and immediately became entangled in a peculiar tug-of-war with Admiral Mitscher's chief of staff—and Halsey's former protégé—Arleigh Burke. Before going to bed, Halsey had left instructions to proceed north at a deliberate pace, 16 knots. Halsey was afraid of sailing past the Japanese carriers in the night. He wanted to engage them at dawn. But while Halsey slept, Captain Burke, acting on behalf of Admiral Mitscher, had resumed "tactical" command of the carriers and ratcheted up the speed to 20 knots. Burke was still worried about the Center Fleet coming through the San Bernardino Strait. He wanted to get up north, finish off the carriers—in the middle of the night if necessary—and be able to head back south to catch the Japanese battleships heading for Leyte Gulf.

Halsey was irked by the insubordination from Mitscher's staff. Asserting his command authority, he slowed the speed back down to 16 knots and ordered a night search. Mitscher had by now arisen from his own nap, and was prowling around his Flag Plot aboard the *Lexington*, dressed in a bathrobe and wearing a duck-billed cap. Mitscher warned Halsey that the night search planes might tip off the Japanese carriers and blow the element of surprise. By now Halsey was testy. "Do you have any information we do not have?" he asked by radio. Mitscher's answer was no. "Launch the search," ordered Halsey.

Shortly after 2:00 A.M., the search planes found the Japanese and reported them at less than a hundred miles away. Halsey gave the order to prepare for battle. In the darkness, the six great battleships of the Third Fleet pulled out and steamed ahead in a battle line, each with more than 2,000 men at their battle stations, hoisting shells into the great guns. Mitscher ordered a first attack wave of 180 planes off the carrier decks before 5:00 A.M.

As dawn broke, Lieutenant Solberg was standing in Flag Plot on the *New Jersey*, filled with a sense of anticipation and excitement about the battle ahead. He had banished, for the moment, the anxieties he shared with his roommate, Harris Cox—the worry that the Third Fleet was being duped by a vast Japanese deception. Solberg stepped out on a wing of the flag bridge to look upon a thrilling sight: the great battleships racing along, line abreast, on a deep blue sea. The *South Dakota* had broken out a battle flag, "an enormous Stars and Stripes that stood gloriously straight out," Solberg recalled.

But where were the Japanese carriers? The search planes had lost them. One snooper had turned back with engine problems, another with faulty radar. Not until 7:10 that morning did a search plane find Ozawa's fleet—one heavy carrier, three light carriers, and the two odd-looking hermaphrodite battleships with flight decks tacked on the stern. They were not fifty or sixty miles away but a good 180 miles away. The night search planes, it appeared, had spooked the Japanese. Ozawa's carriers had turned in the night and run north. No one aboard the *New Jersey* realized that this was precisely what the Japanese had planned for—a wild-goose chase that would lead the American Third Fleet as far north as possible.

In *New Jersey*'s Flag Plot, the atmosphere of high excitement cooled and curdled as the minutes and hours with no enemy contact dragged out. The delays and mixed signals were deflating. Quickly forgotten was a puzzling message that came in at 0648, 6:48 A.M., from Kinkaid of the Seventh Fleet, asking, "Is Task Force 34 guarding San Bernardino Strait?" This was the message, almost an afterthought, that Kinkaid had sent two and a half hours earlier, at 0412, 4:12 A.M.—to wind up on the pile of "urgent" messages stacked up to the elbows of the overworked telegraph operators at Manus. The telegraph operators could not tell which messages were more urgent than others, and this one appears to have drifted toward the bottom of the pile before being sent out on the Fox Schedule distributed throughout the fleet. The message, when it finally arrived and was decoded, was perplexing, but it caused little or no concern among members of Halsey's staff, preoccupied as they were with finding the Japanese carriers. Was Task Force 34 guarding San Bernardino Strait? Why, of course not; hadn't Halsey signaled "Am proceeding north with three groups" before midnight? As Solberg recalled, "With almost a 'why do you ask?' air, Third Fleet shot off this un-

ruffled reply just seven minutes later: 'Negative. Task Force 34 is
with carrier group now engaging enemy carrier forces.'" All of the
attention in Flag Plot was toward the enemy to the north. No one
was thinking about the enemy to the south.

Admiral Koyanagi's leg was throbbing. Kurita's chief of staff had
hurt himself sliding down the sloping deck of the *Atago* as the flagship cruiser heeled over from the American submarine's torpedoes in
the Palawan Passage some forty-eight hours earlier. Koyanagi had
struck his hip on a ringbolt in the rush to abandon ship. His thigh
had turned purple, and he could walk only with a cane. He had been
unable to sleep because of the pain.

His commander had not even tried to rest. Admiral Kurita had not
left the *Yamato*'s bridge since he had transferred his flag on the afternoon of the 23rd, and he had not slept the night before that. He
had hardly budged from his monkey seat in the corner of the bridge.
He ate what the crew ate, an occasional rice ball, and drank water
from a bucket.

Chief of staff Koyanagi worried about Kurita. He had developed a
great affection and respect for his commander-in-chief. The two
men saw each other several times every day, and for the past several
days, they had been inseparable. "We were like one mind, one
body," Koyanagi later recalled. Their thoughts were so close that
they barely needed to speak.

Kurita "practiced silence," Koyanagi would later say, approvingly.
Kurita never grew excited, never argued with his staff. He was never
angry, but rather listened patiently. "He was like a father to me, and
we were like a happy family," Koyanagi recalled. Kurita was not like
other admirals, haughty or flashy and proud, and his men loved him
for it. "Glamour types got no support from the men," recalled Koyanagi. Kurita was "an old salty type," an expert shiphandler, unlike
the political admirals whose skills lay in currying favor with higher-
ranking admirals.

While quiet, Kurita was "warm and human," Koyanagi recalled.
The C-in-C of the First Diversionary Striking Force did not affect an
air of stern remoteness. He was not like Admiral Ugaki, whose cold

mask never dropped. Kurita was a regular fellow who would occa-
sionally say something "sharply humorous" to cheer up his men. He
"loved sake, and became cheerful when he drank," Koyanagi reminisced. Koyanagi knew Kurita to be a good athlete, "quick" and agile.
He no longer played baseball with the men, but he practiced his
archery every day, even at sea, for "spiritual strength." In the opening
minutes of the battle, Kurita's archery set had been sunk with the
Atago. Now the admiral sat on the bridge of the *Yamato,* peering into
the dim gray light of early dawn, seemingly lost in thought.

Koyanagi's own thoughts were bleak. He had expected to die from
enemy bombs the day before in the Sibuyan Sea. Koyanagi was a
gentlemanly, elegant figure, but he had been a farmer's son, at-
tracted to the navy after seeing a relative, an Eta Jima classmate of
the great Yamamoto, return home from the Battle of Tsushima
when Koyanagi was an impressionable twelve-year-old. "I liked the
uniform," Koyanagi recalled.

His war had not been as glorious as he had hoped. His great ambition had been to command a ship in battle, but when he finally did
lead a destroyer flotilla in the evacuation of Guadalcanal, he was sick
with dengue fever. "I commanded from bed," he recalled. Looking
into the faces of the soldiers they had rescued off "Starvation Island" had depressed him. He described the sick, drooping men as
"dogs that had lost their masters."

For Koyanagi, victory was already beyond hope. He had lost heart
after the Battle of the Philippine Sea, when the Japanese air force
had been savaged. He was bitter but resigned about the Sho Plan. "It
had no meaning for me," he said, "except for doing it for the honor of
the Japanese navy." In August, when he had been first told about the
plan by Captain Kami, the low-level staff officer sent down from
Tokyo by Combined Fleet headquarters, Koyanagi had been indignant. "It's *sutebachi* [suicidal]," Koyanagi had told Captain Kami.
"There is no other way," replied the emissary from Tokyo.

When the Kurita fleet sailed out of San Bernardino Strait into an
empty sea after midnight on the morning of October 25, Koyanagi
was sure the Americans were setting a trap. He believed that an
American carrier task force was following them from a distance and
that another task force lay over the horizon ready to destroy the

Japanese with their planes. Silence from Ozawa to the north meant that Ozawa's deception had failed, or so Koyanagi believed.

At 0623, 6:23 A.M., four minutes before dawn, the radar operator aboard the *Yamato* reported blips bearing 150 degrees, to the south-southeast. *Enemy planes*, thought Koyanagi. *Here it comes: the final onslaught from the Americans.* From the bridge, Koyanagi spotted two airplanes circling in the distance.

But eleven minutes later, the *Yamato*'s lookouts, more than 150 feet high in the crow's nest and able to see twenty miles distant even on a misty morning, cried out: Masts on the horizon. Not just masts, but the shapes and silhouettes of aircraft carriers.

Koyanagi was stunned to see actual ships. Planes, yes. But to think that the Americans would be careless enough to allow their carriers to come under his guns was almost too good to believe. If he were to die, he later recounted, he wanted to die "crashing into" an American task force of carriers. He never expected that they would be foolish enough to allow their carriers to come within range of the *Yamato*'s 18-inch guns. Judging from the dim shapes forming on the distant horizon, the Americans had somehow made a critical mistake.

Koyanagi had been at Kurita's side at Brunei when the C-in-C gave his speech urging his captains to believe in divine intervention. Koyanagi had not been particularly moved; he had thought Kurita was going through the motions. But now he wondered if, perhaps, he had been too jaded. Maybe there were such things as miracles.

CHAPTER TWELVE

THEY WERE EXPENDABLE

"That son of a bitch Halsey"

Oh, we're the boys in the CVEs,
A little bit shaky in the knees,
Our engines knock and cough and wheeze
In Doug MacArthur's Navy

While Jeeps are not dependable
Their actions are commendable
But gosh, they are expendable
In Doug MacArthur's Navy

THE DRINKING SONGS were lighthearted but bitter compensation for serving on a jeep carrier. All the glory—as well as most of the creature comforts—went to the pilots in the Big Blue Fleet—the real navy. In the pilot ready rooms of the sweatbox CVEs, temperatures could reach 100 degrees. Returning from their largely uneventful missions on October 24, the pilots aboard the carriers of Taffy Three had heard the reports from the Sibuyan Sea of battleships sunk by the "rich kids," as the Taffy pilots referred to their Third Fleet counterparts. Once again, the Taffys were left to the unglamorous work, flying air cover over tin carriers that were hardly worth trying to sink.

Taking off on a routine patrol before dawn on October 25, Ensign Bill Brooks's Avenger was armed with depth charges for submarines, not bombs or torpedoes for surface ships. Brooks expected to look at an empty ocean through the broken clouds, then head back for a sorry breakfast of powdered eggs. At about 0640, 6:40 A.M., as dawn lightened the sky, he steered around a large squall and looked down to see . . . ships. Many ships, including some very large ones. Destroyers, cruisers, battleships. "Hey look at that," Brooks called out to his gunner and radioman. "Halsey must have come down from the north."

But Brooks paused to wonder where Halsey's carriers were. He did a double take; the ships didn't look American. They had the distinctive pagoda superstructures of the Japanese. He quickly began to count. At 0643, 6:43 A.M., Brooks excitedly radioed Taffy Three: "Enemy surface force of four battleships, four heavy cruisers, two light cruisers and ten to 12 destroyers sighted 20 miles northwest of your task force and closing in on you at 30 knots."

Aboard his flagship, the *Fanshaw Bay*, Adm. Clifton "Ziggy" Sprague was annoyed. Now there, he thought, is some screwy young aviator reporting part of our own forces. "Air plot," he ordered, "tell him to check his identification."

Just then, his radiomen began to pick up a strange gabble of voices—in Japanese, apparently from enemy ships communicating by shortwave radio perhaps twenty miles away.

Confirmation and a little color for emphasis came quickly from Ensign Brooks. "I can see pagoda masts," he said. "I see the biggest red meatball flag I ever saw flying on the biggest battleship I ever saw."

By now the officers and men on the bridge of the *Fanshaw Bay* were looking at each other uneasily. Sprague broke the silence. "It's impossible!" he exclaimed. "It can't be. It can't be!" But now he could see for himself: puffs of antiaircraft fire to the northwest, and just peeking over the horizon, the distinctive pagoda shapes of the ships of the Imperial Japanese Navy. Sprague vented his anger. "That son of a bitch Halsey," the commander of Taffy Three spat out, "has left us bare-assed."

*   *   *

"A sighted enemy is a dead enemy," was an old adage of bravado in the Imperial Japanese Navy. It was extremely rare to sight an American carrier. Indeed, the only Japanese surface ship commander who had set eyes on an American carrier was Admiral Kurita. Flying his flag from the battleship *Kongo*, he had seen, from a distance of several miles at night, the bombed and sinking USS *Hornet* at the Battle of the Santa Cruz Islands in the fall of 1942.

To bring American carriers under the 14-, 16-, and 18-inch guns of the Japanese battleships seemed like the kind of gift from the gods most Japanese officers paid lip service to but had trouble believing in, at least since Guadalcanal. It had been two years since a Japanese fleet enjoyed material superiority over the Americans. Kurita dictated a message to Combined Fleet headquarters:

BY HEAVEN SENT OPPORTUNITY, WE ARE DASHING TO ATTACK THE ENEMY CARRIERS. OUR FIRST OBJECTIVE IS TO DESTROY THE FLIGHT DECKS, THEN THE TASK FORCE.

To see for himself, operations officer Otani scrambled up into the crow's nest to peer over the low mist. He came down sure he had spotted two aircraft carriers. Kurita's staff was convinced they had stumbled upon one of Halsey's carrier groups, and that they were up against four or five fleet carriers, the *Essex*-class fast carriers. They could not tell, from a distance of some twenty miles, that they were looking at smaller jeep flattops, which had the same profile as the larger ships. Japanese ship identification was poor. In any case, Kurita's fleet had no drawings or photographs of the American CVEs.

An American fast carrier could move at over 30 knots. The *Yamato*, down at the bow from getting holed by a bomb the day before, could sail no faster than 26 knots. Another battleship, the *Nagato*, was a knot or two slower. Kurita felt that it was imperative to get a jump on the Americans, to head off the carriers before they could turn into the wind and launch their planes. Kurita had been bombed enough over the last twenty-four hours; he wanted to punch holes in the carriers' launchpads. He ordered the fleet to sail southeast, to try to cross the bows of the carriers as they swung into the northeast wind.

At Eta Jima, the midshipmen played a game called *Go*. It was not so much a game as a melee; the object was to knock down the opposition's pole, and the best way to do it was simply to rush en masse. Kurita used the same tactic against the Americans. He did not form up a line of battle or try to bring his destroyers and cruisers forward to stage torpedo runs. He simply ordered "General Attack," in other words, every ship against any enemy ship, catch-as-catch-can.

Kurita did not act instantly. There was some confusion and hesitation on the bridge of the flagship. The fleet had just begun to shift from a spread-out night search disposition to a circular antiaircraft formation, and there was uncertainty in the fleet as changing and sometimes conflicting signals flew back and forth. It was by now a cliché among American forces that the Japanese, rigid and often stuck on ceremony, did not deal well with surprises and that the Japanese would be unable to improvise if their elaborate plans went awry. Fortunately for the Americans, the cultural stereotype was true.

Sitting in his corner of the *Yamato's* bridge, watching Kurita and his staff fumble as they tried to settle on the right approach, Admiral Ugaki visibly seethed. Finally he spoke out: "Firing should be under my command!" He was the battleship division commander; he felt sidelined and useless and wanted something to do. Kurita was sensitive to his proud subordinate's vexation and told him to take over the flagship's maneuvering and gunfire.

Later writing about the battle, Ugaki somewhat stiffly vented his frustration. Never mentioning Kurita by name (it was poor form for the Japanese to make ad hominem attacks, even in a personal diary), Ugaki wrote: "Each unit seemed very slow in starting actions due to uncertainty about the enemy condition. Actions of the fleet headquarters [i.e., Kurita, standing a few feet away] were also apt to lack promptness. . . . The fleet's attacking directions were also conflicting and I feared the spirit of all-out attack at short range was lacking. I so advised the chief of staff [Koyanagi]."

Several of the Japanese cruisers and battleships had already opened fire on the Americans. At two minutes before 7:00 A.M., Kurita ordered the flagship to open fire with its main battery of 18-inch guns, or "special 16-inch guns," as they were called to keep their true size a secret. In almost three years of war, the guns had never been fired at the enemy. On the wing of the bridge, Petty Officer Koitabashi was told to hang on; the percussion of the great guns could knock a man down. With a thunderous roar the mighty guns belched fire and shot projectiles weighing more than a ton and a half apiece at the thin-skinned American carriers and their thin-skinned destroyer escorts. Koitabashi had snapped out of his grogginess. He felt thrilled watching another battleship, the *Kongo*, steam by at nearly 30 knots, its enormous battle ensign, the Rising Sun, streaming in the wind. *It's just like the movies*, Koitabashi thought to himself.

Aboard USS *Johnston*, one of the three destroyers surrounding Taffy Three, Lt. (j.g.) Ellsworth Welch was the officer of the deck on the 4:00 to 8:00 A.M. watch. As OOD, the twenty-one-year-old Welch, normally the ship's antisubmarine warfare officer, was responsible for the safety of the ship. A little after 0650, 6:50 A.M., he was leaning over the port wing of the bridge, "smelling delightful breakfast odors wafting up from the galley," he recalled, when he suddenly saw "huge geysers of salt water" thrown up near a jeep carrier astern. He instinctively looked up at the sky for enemy planes and saw none. He peered out to sea. The Japanese ships were still "hull down," but their masts could be seen peeking over the horizon. Over the loudspeaker inside the bridge, he heard an anxious voice announce over Talk Between Ships that a "major portion" of the Japanese fleet was fifteen to twenty miles astern.

Commander Evans "came barreling out of his sea cabin ordering all hands to General Quarters," Welch recalled. The captain barked out more orders to light off all boilers for maximum speed and to make smoke. "Why didn't I think of that?" young Welch wondered, relieved to see the captain taking charge.

Bob Hagen, the gunnery officer, was in the Combat Information Center, waiting for a fried egg sandwich ordered from the galley. He had been listening, with growing apprehension, to the exchange picked up on Talk Between Ships between Ensign Brooks, flying his Avenger 4,000 feet above the Japanese fleet, and the Taffy Three flagship, skeptically insisting on better identification. When he heard Brooks recite "four battleships, four heavy cruisers, four light cruisers . . ." his heart sank. As gunnery officer, he knew that his 5-inch guns fired projectiles weighing 54 pounds apiece. They would bounce off the steel plate of a battleship. "I felt like David without a slingshot," Hagen recalled.

At his battle station in a 40-mm gun tub just in front of and below the bridge, eighteen-year-old Bill Mercer heard the captain call for "Flank speed." *Thank God*, Mercer thought, *we're getting out of here*. Then he heard the command, "Left full rudder." The bow of the destroyer began to swing from east to north to northwest—toward the Japanese fleet. Mercer pulled on his life jacket. He wondered how his mother would react to the news of his death.

Clyde Burnett, the chief boatswain's mate, the senior enlisted man on the ship, was lying in his bunk when the insistent, atonal bonging of the General Quarters alarm sounded. As he pulled himself up and out of his rack, he heard someone say over the PA system that the Japanese fleet was approximately fifteen to seventeen miles astern.

Destroyers make smoke in the battle off Samar

Burnett "thought someone was joking" until he reached the deck and looked aft. "The whole horizon seemed to light up from the gunfire of the Jap ships," he recalled. Burnett knew right away, he recalled, that "this was it," that "the captain was going to sacrifice the ship."

The *Johnston* began to zigzag, heeling one way, then the other, shuddering and straining, as she picked up speed and steered back around on a west-northwest course. Evans was interposing his destroyer between the enemy ships and the carriers. He wanted to lay a smoke screen in front of the carriers, but that required exposing his own ship. Men and machines balked at first. In the engine room, the order to "make smoke" was relayed to the fire room, where it was misunderstood. "But we're not making smoke," complained a petty officer, who was tired of being chewed out by the bridge for making too much smoke in day-to-day cruising. Charles Landreth, a sailor manning the phone to the bridge, heard Captain Evans bark, "I want a smoke screen and I want it now." The engine room began adding less air to the fuel, and the ship's two smokestacks' funnels were soon streaming oily black clouds.

In the stern, by the depth charge rack, were four chemical smoke-making machines. The valves on the smoke generators were stuck fast from corrosion. Someone got a wrench, and soon sulfurous white smoke was billowing aft in the ship's foaming wake. It mixed with the sooty black smoke from the funnels and, in the humidity and light breeze, hung in a thick wreath low on the water.

The chief engineering officer was unhappy. Lieutenant Digardi, who had relieved Lieutenant Welch as officer of the deck, had ordered the engine room to mix diesel and fuel oil. At high speeds, the *Johnston* burned 5,000 gallons an hour, and the fuel report showed only 12,000 gallons of fuel oil remaining. Digardi decided to dip into the 10,000-gallon reserve of diesel fuel. Digardi wasn't sure the *Johnston* would last more than three hours, but he didn't want to run out of fuel. "The chief engineer came charging to the bridge and complained to the captain that such a mixture would foul the tubes and require extensive cleanout," Digardi recalled. Evans told him to do as he had been ordered and smiled slightly; the captain seemed amused by the engineer's fussy insistence on keeping his engines clean at a time when the *Johnston* was sailing into the heavy salvos of a dozen Japanese capital ships.

On the bridge, Lt. (j.g.) Joe Pliska was the ship's "recognition officer." He had joined the ship a few weeks earlier to instruct the men of the *Johnston* on spotting different Japanese ships and planes. He had never before actually seen a Japanese ship, just photographs and diagrams. Watching the pagoda superstructures rise out of the sea as the Japanese fleet emerged on the horizon, heavy-caliber guns blinking in the distance, all that young Lieutenant Pliska could splutter was "Jesus Christ!" A few men on the crowded bridge joined in with expletives and oaths. They weren't sure exactly what they were looking at, but it was no secret that the main Japanese battle fleet had two mega-battleships, larger than anything that the Americans had ever seen. Evans normally discouraged profanity on the bridge, but this time he let the cussing pass.

Enemy shells were beginning to hurtle over the *Johnston*. From his gun tub, Mercer watched with appalled fascination as distant guns flowered with orange and yellow blooms and tiny specks rose and grew into black dots racing across the sky. The shells made a "whoosh-whoosh" sound as they flew overhead, he recalled. From his battle station by the depth charge racks on the stern, sailor Robert Deal was startled to see that the Japanese shell splashes were in all colors, red, orange, green, blue. He realized that shells had been tagged with dye markers, to help the Japanese gunners identify where each ship's shells were landing. They were falling pretty close to a nearby carrier, the *White Plains*, which was being repeatedly straddled by giant sheets of colored water. The shells that passed overhead, Deal thought, sounded like a trouser zipper opening and closing.

To Digardi and others on the bridge, the shells thundered past "like freight trains." When a young sailor ducked, Captain Evans told him, "Don't duck, son. The ones you hear have already missed you." Evans went on the PA to give a situation report to the crew. He told them that units of the Japanese navy were fifteen miles away, but that he expected Admiral Halsey's forces to arrive soon. Evans did not know that Halsey was more than six hours' steaming time distant, unaware that the Taffys were under attack.

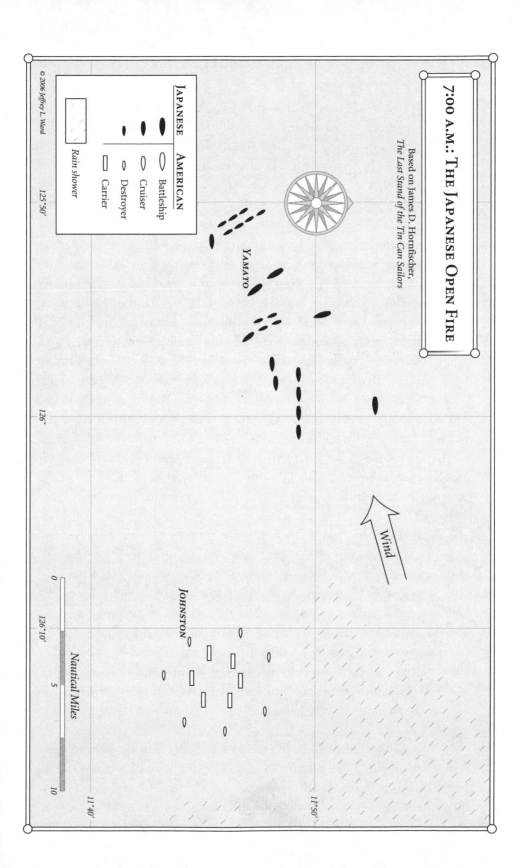

7:00 A.M.: THE JAPANESE OPEN FIRE

Based on James D. Hornfischer,
The Last Stand of the Tin Can Sailors

JAPANESE   AMERICAN
● Battleship ○
● Cruiser ◊
● Destroyer □
Carrier

Rain shower

YAMATO

JOHNSTON

Wind

Nautical Miles
0   5   10

125°50'   126°   126°10'

11°40'   11°50'

© 2006 Jeffrey L. Ward

A few sailors allowed themselves to be reassured. "I thought that our planes from all our carriers would arrive any minute and begin sinking the Jap ships," recalled Jim Correll, a spotter on a 5-inch gun. "I thought that would be interesting to see, the burning and sinking of all the Jap ships." ("I'm still waiting," he wrote in 1990 for a privately printed collection of oral histories, *The Fighting and Sinking of the USS* Johnston *DD 557 as Told by Her Crew*). But fear—real fear, the grim, certain apprehension of death—was gripping most others. The crew was largely populated by teenagers who began the morning believing they were immortal and invincible. By evening, the survivors would be prematurely old men. Years later, many *Johnston* survivors skirted around the question of fear and did not wish to dwell on memories of the natural, profound longing of men under fire to be somewhere, anywhere else. But others acknowledged that most of the brave talk, before the battle, about wanting to "see a little action" was obliterated by the first salvo of 14-inch shells. Seaman Ed Takkunen recalled simply thinking at the time, "I want to be home."

In his recollections included in *The Fighting and Sinking of the USS* Johnston, sailor Bobby Chastain, a "trainer" on the crew of Gun 54, one of the two 5-inch guns facing aft, forthrightly wrote,

> One thing that should be covered right now . . . while on the ship during most of the battle I was very frightened. I, along with all the other crew members, thought we would not survive against these odds and to this day it is very difficult to understand how anyone could make it. We survivors have discussed this many times and cannot understand it. This feeling was not for just a brief moment. It was with us constantly during the three-hour battle, easing slightly when our ship would enter a rain squall or a smoke screen, then return full force when returning to battle.

During the battle, Chastain was sighting the 5-inch gun through a telescopic sight. "The enemy ships . . . looked very close and I could see their gun flashes as they fired at us. This prompted me to close the small open-air sight door (at eye level) so I wouldn't have to watch." Somehow, the ships seemed less real visualized through the telescopic sight than seen with the naked eye. "Psychological reaction," explained Chastain.

The reaction of Gun 54's "captain," Petty Officer Bob Hollenbaugh, was blunter and earthier. Raised by straight-laced Amish in Goshen, Indiana, Hollenbaugh forgot, for a moment, his strict religious upbringing when he stuck his head out of the hatch of Gun 54 and saw the pagoda masts on the horizon. Years later, he recalled that his first thought was: "Holy shit! We don't have much of a chance."

After the *Yamato* fired its second salvo a minute or two after 7:00 A.M., the lookouts cried, "Pillar of fire!" From the bridge, chief of staff Koyanagi thought he saw smoke broiling up from one of the American carriers in the distance. "A very great explosion," he later recalled. The carrier *White Plains* had been straddled, but not hit. Near-misses were falling all around the *Fanshaw Bay* and *Kalinin Bay*. Aboard the *Yamato,* still more than fifteen miles distant, the lookout and the chief of staff were confused by the smoke screen billowing out from the *Johnston* and two or three other destroyers racing to interpose themselves between the jeep carriers and the Japanese. Ten minutes into the battle, the fog of war was already settling in.

"They're shooting at us in Technicolor!" shouted a sailor on the bridge of the *Fanshaw Bay*, Adm. Ziggy Sprague's flagship. Giant splashes of dyed water rained down in yellow and red and green on the decks of the jeep carrier.

The *Fanshaw Bay* had been pronounced "the worst ship ever seen in any navy" by Taffy Three's last task group commander, Gerry Bogan. The *Fanshaw Bay*'s crew was disgruntled and slow-moving, their equipment was poor, and the ship was dirty. The perfectionist, by-the-book Bogan had been only too happy to get off her and take command of a fast carrier group. His successor, Ziggy Sprague, a shambling, wryly ironic New Englander, lacked spit and polish. Senior staff officers (like Paulus Powell, who called him "Dopey") sometimes mistook Sprague's offhand manner to be sloth, even stupidity. But that was a misperception.

It's true that Sprague had little time for formalities. Sprague did not waste time complaining; he did not waste time at all. Playing golf, Sprague did not pause to check the length of a putt; he just walked up and hit the ball. He had been in command of a lowly seaplane tender, the *Tangier*, at Pearl Harbor. His was the first ship to shoot back at the Japanese planes overhead.

Sprague did not dither now. He had turned his fleet east, into the wind, to launch planes at 0650, 6:50 A.M., and he was hoping to slip into a squall he could see forming to the east-northeast. First he wanted to get some planes in the air to bomb the Japanese. Some of his carrier captains complained that their planes were not properly armed with munitions to attack heavily armored ships. Sprague cut them off: "Get the damn things up," he barked.

Sprague thought his fleet could be wiped out in the next fifteen minutes. Jeep carriers could make at most 18 knots. Japanese battleships, he knew, were faster. But he wanted to give the Japanese a merry chase, and he wanted to draw the Japanese away from Leyte Gulf, for a short while, anyway. He was determined, he later wrote, "to give them all we've got before we go down." He began giving orders to Taffy Three ship commanders over the TBS. Amidst the excited radio chatter, his voice was relatively calm, but not everyone else was so cool. Some thirty miles to the south, Adm. Felix Stump, the commander of Taffy Two, could be heard on the TBS trying to reassure Sprague and Taffy Three.

"Don't be alarmed, Ziggy!" said Stump, his squeaky voice rising. "Remember, we're back of you—don't get excited—don't do anything rash!" Stump's voice grew so high that the officers on the bridge of the *Fanshaw Bay* began smiling and chuckling. The comic relief was momentary as the Japanese shells continued to fall all around, ever closer.

The single 5-inch guns on each carrier and the batteries of 5-inch guns on the destroyers were not likely to make much of a dent on the Japanese battleships. But the destroyers in the Taffy Three screen did carry torpedoes, "fish" tipped with several hundred pounds of high explosives. The destroyer escorts in the screen had not practiced torpedo runs, as far as anyone could remember. But there was no time like the present. The destroyers would be vulnerable and the little destroyer escorts even more so, but at 0716, 7:16 A.M., Sprague went on the TBS and gave the order to get ready: "Stand by to form two torpedo groups, big boys [destroyers] in one group and little fellas [destroyer escorts] in another group."

Aboard the *Johnston*, Commander Evans was not waiting. On his own initiative, before he heard Sprague's order to "stand by," he had given the command to commence a torpedo run.

In the defensive screen around Taffy Three, the *Johnston* was the closest destroyer to the advancing Japanese. By 0710, 7:10 A.M., she was less than ten miles away from the nearest Japanese warship. Water spouts were rising all around; shells were straddling her as the Japanese gunners narrowed their aim. Up in the cramped gun director, the claustrophobic chamber just above the bridge that controlled the aiming and firing of the 5-inchers, gunnery officer Hagen had been feeling "sickeningly impotent." He opened fire with his five guns at 7:10 but their total broadside weighed about 275 pounds, and, with a range of under seven miles, the shells were falling short. (Lying in a bunk, recovering from his ordeal a few days later, Hagen did some math in his head: the Japanese broadsides weighed about 80,000 pounds.) The only hope of sinking a Japanese ship was with a torpedo attack.

Standing beside Evans on the bridge, Digardi heard the captain say, "We can't go down with our fish." Evans was the only destroyer captain in Taffy Three who had actually taken a torpedo run against the enemy, aboard the creaky old four-piper *Alden* at the Battle of the Java Sea in the war's early days. He was bent on avenging that fiasco. Evans pointed to the nearest Japanese cruiser, which appeared to be a *Tone*-class 12,000-tonner, and began calling commands. The *Johnston* rattled and vibrated as her 60,000-horsepower twin-steam turbines pushed the long, thin hull along at 35 knots.

The *Johnston* did not head straight for her target. She veered and fishtailed. Evans was following the splashes, steering toward the spots where shells had just landed off the ship's bow. It was the tactic he had studied from the Battle of Jutland and explained to his wide-eyed son, Ernest Jr.: lightning never strikes in the same place twice.

The torpedo run lasted perhaps five minutes and seemed like eternity. No one wanted to get too close to the onrushing phalanx of Japanese capital ships. Inside the turret of Gun 55 on the stern, the gun crew listened as Evans announced on the PA that they were going in on a torpedo run. "We just looked at each other," recalled sailor William Rogers. "No one spoke."

Gunnery officer Hagen recommended firing the torpedoes at 10,000 yards, five nautical miles from the target. Evans wanted to get in closer, to within 8,000 yards. Hagen was "afraid we'd get blown out of the water before we got our torpedoes off," but he aye-ayed the captain. The gunnery officer was desperately trying to appear calmer than he felt. Water dyed red from a shell splash came streaming through an open hatch in the gun director. "Looks like someone's mad at us," Hagen lamely joked. No one laughed.

At last, Evans shouted, "Fire torpedoes!" One by one, at three-second intervals, ten 25-foot-long torpedoes jumped from their tubes amidships. With a whoosh of compressed air they smacked, propellers whirring, into the water. "Hot, straight, and normal," called out Lt. (j.g.) Jack Bechdel, the torpedo officer. The *Johnston* did not wait around to watch for the impact (with the torpedoes set at low speed, about 30 knots, roughly seven minutes) but turned hard to port and disappeared into the relative safety of her own smoke screen. Intently, the officers on the bridge listened. Five minutes . . . six minutes . . . then a sonar man in the Combat Information Center excitedly yelled out: one, then two underwater explosions. As the smoke parted for an instant, Lieutenant Welch thought he saw an enormous column of water rising by a distant cruiser. He was not imagining. A torpedo had ripped into the *Kumano*, flagship of one of Kurita's cruiser divisions. The cruiser's bow was blown off.

Aboard the *Yamato*, lookout Koitabashi saw a lone American destroyer coming out to take on the Japanese fleet. Many years later, he recalled thinking, "My God, these are really courageous guys. We were always told that the Americans were sissies but, all of a sudden, here they are."

The bravery of the American sailors was matched by the bravery of the American pilots, most of them, at any rate. Lt. (j.g.) Henry Pyzdrowski had climbed into his Avenger to take off from the jeep carrier *Gambier Bay.* Ahead of him on the catapult was Lt. (j.g.) William Gallagher. "Wait! Wait! You've got no gas!" cried a crewman. Gallagher just waved him off and gave the signal to launch. He had enough gas to last maybe five minutes in the air—but his was one of the few planes to be armed with a torpedo, and he wanted to use it before his own ship went down. Taking off, he did not even bother to gain altitude. Gallagher simply banked his plane and flew over the wave tops right at the Japanese. He launched his torpedo at a battleship (it missed), ditched his plane, and was never seen again.

As Pyzdrowski was watching this drama play out, he heard someone shouting his name. It was another pilot, his roommate, Lt.

Gambier Bay *under fire*

George Bisbee. Bisbee was standing on the flight deck, yelling at Pyzdrowski to tell him the combination to his locker in the stateroom they shared. "We need a drink!" yelled Bisbee. Pyzdrowski had just received a shipment of scotch from home, and it was safely secured in his locker. Pyzdrowski yelled down the three-number combination and waited his turn to take off. The giant geysers of colored water from enemy shells were marching closer toward the *Gambier Bay.*

Planes from the Taffys were buzzing around Kurita's ships. Interrogated after the war, Kurita's staff officers testified that they were surprised by the skillfulness of the American pilots. With few heavy bombs or torpedoes, they were dropping depth charges, antipersonnel bombs, even flares. When they had nothing to drop, some pilots opened their bomb bays and made dummy runs, firing their machine guns. Even Ugaki was forced to admit, "They strafed courageously and one of our ships got as many as 500 bullets. They assaulted *Yamato* four times too, but," Ugaki wrote loftily, "I didn't pay too much attention to them."

With the big guns of the *Yamato* once again under his command, Ugaki was absorbed with trying to sink American ships. Ugaki claimed to have "destroyed a ship" with the *Yamato*'s first two or three salvos. He, too, had been fooled by the smoke. But at a little after 0730, 7:30 A.M., Japanese salvos finally did connect.

The men and officers of the *Johnston* barely had time to celebrate their successful torpedo run when the Japanese shells struck home. Three 14-inch shells, probably from the battleship *Kongo*, slammed into the aft engine room and fire room. The explosion rolled the ship over so far that William Rogers, loading 5-inch shells onto a hoist under Gun 55 in the stern, thought the *Johnston* had been struck by a giant wave. At the depth charge rack, sailor Robert Deal thought the ship must have run into some huge underwater obstruction. To Hagen, the jolt was like a "puppy smacked by a truck."

Sailor Joseph Check was supposed to be manning a 20-mm gun amidships on the starboard side, but without any airplanes to shoot

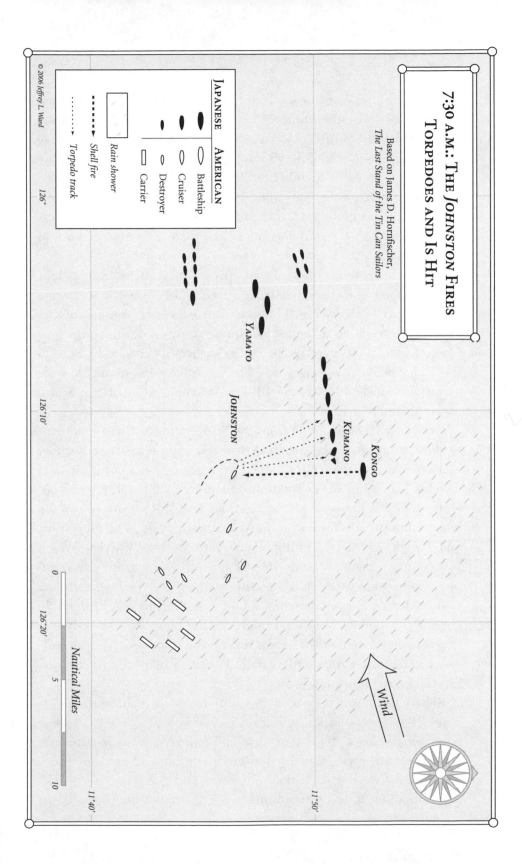

7:30 A.M.: THE JOHNSTON FIRES
TORPEDOES AND IS HIT

Based on James D. Hornfischer,
The Last Stand of the Tin Can Sailors

JAPANESE AMERICAN

Battleship
Cruiser
Destroyer
Carrier

Rain shower
Shell fire
Torpedo track

© 2006 Jeffrey L. Ward

YAMATO

JOHNSTON

KUMANO

KONGO

Wind

Nautical Miles

0   5   10

at, he was taking cover near a first-aid station. The concussion from the Japanese salvo lifted him off his feet. His helmet struck an overhang and he fell to the deck. Woozily rousing himself, he saw three men emerge from a hatchway to the engine room and lie against the bulkhead. The men, members of the engine room "black gang," were turning a ghastly white and swelling; their skin was peeling off in sheets. Steam-broiled, all three men were soon dead. With supercharged 840 degree steam blasting below, no one else made it out of the wrecked engine room.

Within ten seconds of the salvo, three 6-inch shells from a light cruiser ripped into the superstructure behind the *Johnston's* bridge and the port bridge wing. The mast broke in half and one of the radars, wire-coiled like a giant bedspring, toppled down. In the gun director, Hagen's seat collapsed, and he gashed his knee. He looked to the bridge below to see far worse. The pilothouse was so riddled with shrapnel it looked like "a kid's BB-target." Men were lying in heaps, moaning and bleeding.

Ellsworth Welch came in from the bridge wing to find Lieutenant Bechdel propped in the corner. Just a few minutes earlier Bechdel had been exulting over his torpedoes running "hot, straight, and normal." Now he was complaining about his shoulder. He did not seem to notice that one of his legs had been blown off below the knee. The ship's doctor had given Welch some syrettes of morphine, and Welch wordlessly plunged one into Bechdel's wrist. Welch wasn't sure what else to do. He began collecting body parts and pitching them over the side, "to maintain morale," he later recalled.

Bill Mercer had taken cover under the wing of the bridge. He heard someone yell from the bridge, "Stand by below!" A body was slowly lowered to the deck. As its torso came into view, Mercer realized the body was missing its head. The dead man was Lieutenant Pliska, the recognition officer.

Robert Billie was a lookout on the flying bridge above the pilothouse. The explosion knocked him out. When he came to, he was lying by his shoes. A piece of shrapnel had struck his headphones and his mouth was full of broken teeth and blood. "My thoughts," he recalled, "were what in the hell are we doing this for?"

Commander Evans seemed unfazed. His helmet had been blown

off, his shirt ripped off his back, and his face and torso had been cut up by shrapnel. He was missing two fingers. The ship's doctor, Robert Browne, tried to attend to him, but he said, "Don't bother me now. Help some of those guys who are hurt," and wrapped a handkerchief around his bloody hand.

Evans was taking stock of the damage. The gyroscope was knocked out, power was cut to the aft three guns, one of the engine rooms was wiped out. But the other engine was still working, which meant that the *Johnston* could still turn one of its two screws and make half-speed. Steering was a problem; the steering cables had been cut. Warships are built with redundancy, however. It was possible to steer a destroyer by hand-cranking the rudder shaft in the ship's stern. Evans ordered a party of sailors to be sent aft to man the cranks; he would communicate his steering orders by headphone from the bridge.

A very few sailors cracked. A senior petty officer, normally a crew stalwart, crawled inside the signal flag bag, whimpering and gibbering. Others rallied. With the cables running aft severed, it was no longer possible to electronically control the aiming and firing of all five guns from Lieutenant Hagen's gun director. Robert Hollenbaugh, the Amish boy from Indiana, asked permission to fire Gun 54 in "local control." Recalled Hollenbaugh: "Gun 54 declared its own war on the Japs." After the torpedo run, sailor Jim O'Gorek had left his station on the torpedo tubes and moved forward under the wing of the bridge, looking for some kind of cover. He was horrified when Lieutenant Pliska's severed head came rolling over the edge of the bridge and dropped into the sea before his eyes. But he snapped to and joined a repair party putting out a fire. It had begun to rain heavily; the water streaming into the scuppers was, O'Gorek could not help but notice, "solid red," a mix of the dye used to mark the Japanese shells and blood.

The *Johnston* had sailed into a merciful squall. Obscured from the enemy, the crew gained a fifteen-minute respite to make repairs and collect their wits. Hagen reached into his pocket for a cigarette; his pack was soaked. He felt more grateful than frustrated; the downpour was keeping them alive a few minutes longer.

At 0750, 7:50 A.M., the *Johnston* emerged from the squall into a

chaotic scene. Over the TBS, Admiral Sprague was ordering destroyers to form up for a torpedo attack. On the bridge, quartermaster
third class Neil Dethles was manning the log. He had already inflated his life vest. ("I have often wondered if my shipmates thought
I lacked confidence in the outcome of the battle from the start,"
Dethles recalled many years later.) He had been faithfully, if errati-
cally, making log entries as the orders and shells flew. When he
heard the order from the Taffy Three commander for a torpedo attack, he thought, "Thank God, we have already fired our torpedoes
and won't have to go in there again."

Evans had other ideas. Digardi, the officer of the deck, was hoping
to head south after the retreating jeep carriers, but Evans ordered the
ship to come around and follow the other destroyers as they went in
against the Japanese. "We'll provide fire support for the others," he
said. Lieutenant Hagen protested: they were supposed to be guarding
the carriers, not other destroyers. The officers debated for a moment.
Hagen recalled that Digardi joined in on his side of the argument,
and the ship actually went around a full 360 degrees as the three men
talked back and forth (Digardi did not recall this episode).

If there was a moment's indecision by the captain, it was the only
moment, and the *Johnston* was soon following two other destroyers,
the *Hoel* and the *Heerman,* and a destroyer escort, the *Samuel B.
Roberts,* as they made their torpedo runs. The *Johnston* nearly collided with the *Heerman,* as the two destroyers came barreling out of
the smoke. A lookout cried out and Digardi ordered "All engines
back full," forgetting, for a moment, that the *Johnston* had lost one
of its two engines. As the *Johnston's* single working screw bit into the
water, the stern plowed back into its wake. The two ships missed by
no more than twenty feet. A cheer went up from the *Johnston's* crew.

The cheering died quickly. Less than three miles away was the
Japanese battleship *Kongo.* A single 16-inch gun shell detonating in
the *Johnston* would sink her. It was not much consolation that the
heavy armor-piercing shells were more likely to pass right through
the thin metal skin of a tin can than explode. Survivors of the *Johnston* later speculated that the giant battleship could not depress her
guns low enough to sink the low-riding destroyer. More likely, the
Kongo was firing over the *Johnston* at the carriers beyond.

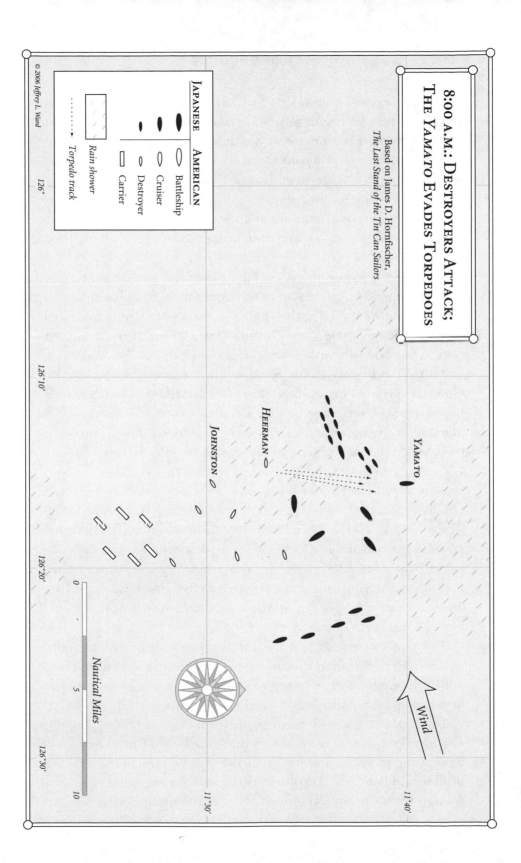

8:00 A.M.: DESTROYERS ATTACK; THE YAMATO EVADES TORPEDOES

Based on James D. Hornfischer,
The Last Stand of the Tin Can Sailors

JAPANESE   AMERICAN

Battleship
Cruiser
Destroyer
Carrier

Rain shower

Torpedo track

YAMATO

HEERMAN

JOHNSTON

Nautical Miles

Wind

© 2006 Jeffrey L. Ward

Idle gun crews, whose guns had been destroyed or were useless against ships, had begun to huddle under the wing of the bridge, hoping they were safer there. It was an illusion. The thin metal over and around them just meant more shrapnel flying about if a shell struck nearby. A few crewmen looked for heavier metal and pitifully hid behind a large winch outside the bakery. Seeing the Japanese battleship and several cruisers and destroyers on both sides of the *Johnston*, a seaman called up to the bridge, "Let's get the hell out of here!"

In the gun director, Hagen was in a "dreamy" state, "wrung out" and "detached." His guns had been peppering battleships and cruisers with 5-inch shells, but he didn't think they were doing much damage. The *Johnston* would fire 800 rounds over three hours, but "it was like bouncing paper wads off a steel helmet," he recalled.

At 0830, 8:30 A.M., Evans could see that one of the carriers, the *Gambier Bay*, was under heavy fire from a cruiser. "Commence firing on that cruiser, Hagen," Evans yelled up at his gunnery officer. "Draw her fire on us and away from the *Gambier Bay*." Hagen responded, "Aye, aye, sir," and said under his breath, "Surely you jest."

From the bridge of the *Johnston*, it seemed that the Japanese were moving in for the kill. Evans spotted a cruiser and four destroyers closing in on the carriers, apparently commencing their torpedo run. The officers of the *Johnston* knew they were all alone. The destroyer *Hoel* had vanished under a deluge of Japanese shells. The destroyer escort *Samuel B. Roberts* was furiously burning a few miles away. Evans began giving orders to head off the five attacking ships. In so doing, historian Samuel Eliot Morison wrote, "the *Johnston* signed her own death warrant."

The Japanese cruiser was the *Yahagi*. The squadron commander aboard, Adm. Susumu Kimura, later wrote in his battle report: "0850. Enemy destroyer plunged out of smokescreen on our port bow and opened gunfire and torpedo attack on us."

The *Johnston* had no torpedoes, only 5-inch guns bravely banging away. In Gun 55, recalled gunner's mate third class Clint Carter, "we were firing so fast and so long that the paint on the gun barrel was blistered and on fire." The gunners couldn't get ammunition up fast enough from the handling room. "I was screaming for ammo," re-

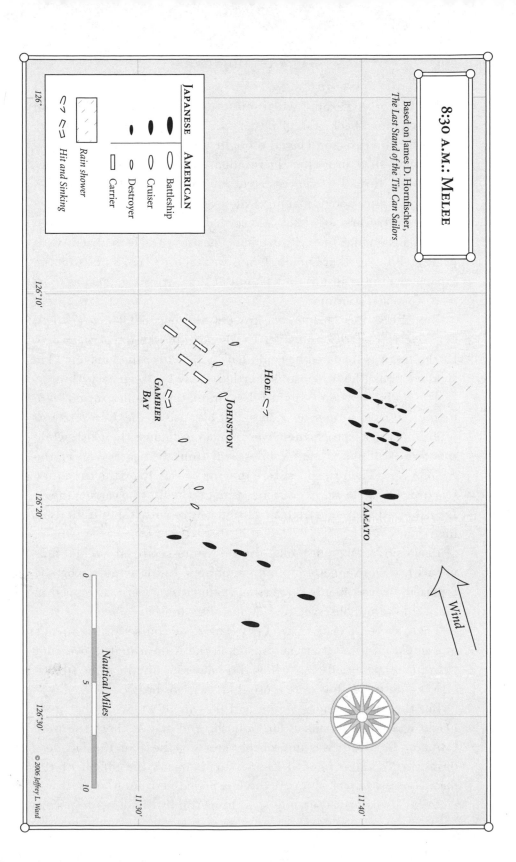

8:30 A.M.: MELEE

Based on James D. Hornfischer,
The Last Stand of the Tin Can Sailors

JAPANESE   AMERICAN

Battleship
Cruiser
Destroyer
Carrier

Rain shower

Hit and Sinking

HOEL

JOHNSTON

GAMBIER
BAY

YAMATO

Wind

Nautical Miles
0   5   10

126°   126°10'   126°20'   126°30'

11°40'   11°30'

© 2006 Jeffrey L. Ward

called Carter, a Texan, "when one of the sailors in the handling room screamed back, 'I'm glad there ain't no Japs from Texas.'"

In the gun director, Hagen thought he could see hits on the *Yahagi*'s superstructure. Then, he recalled, "a most amazing thing happened. She turned 90 degrees right and broke off action." "*Yahagi* executed right rudder, making wide evasive turn, at same time ordering destroyers to attack," recorded Admiral Kimura. Hagen opened up on the line of advancing destroyers. He realized, with pride and horror, that Captain Evans was trying to cross the T on the Japanese column, just as they taught at the war college, just as if he were Togo at Tsushima.

Incredibly, the Japanese destroyers all turned 90 degrees and began to retreat. "Commander Evans, feeling like the skipper of a battleship, was so elated he could hardly talk," recalled Hagen. "He strutted across the bridge and chortled, 'Now I've seen everything.'"

The reality was only slightly less dramatic. The destroyers were turning to launch their torpedoes. But because of the *Johnston*'s improbable attack, the Japanese were forced to launch their fish while they were still more than six miles away from the nearest carrier, the *Kalinin Bay*. The torpedoes were moving so slowly by the time they reached the carriers that evasion was not difficult. One carrier, the *St. Lo*, deflected a torpedo from a collision course with a shot from its 5-inch gun.

In classic Japanese fashion, Admiral Kimura compensated for failure with wild exaggeration to his superiors. In his action report, he reported: "three enemy carriers and one cruiser were enveloped in black smoke and observed to sink one after another."

There were no cruisers in Taffy Three, of course. In the squalls and smoke, Kurita's men had mistaken the American destroyers for "*Baltimore*-class cruisers," which did have roughly the same silhouette as a destroyer, but were more than twice as heavy.

But the men of the *Johnston* had no way of knowing that their David was being mistaken for Goliath. And at just about the time Commander Evans was improbably crossing the T of the Japanese destroyers, a sailor handed Lieutenant Digardi, the officer of the deck, a message picked up off the Fox Schedule from Manus. It was Admiral Kinkaid desperately signaling Admiral Halsey, imploring

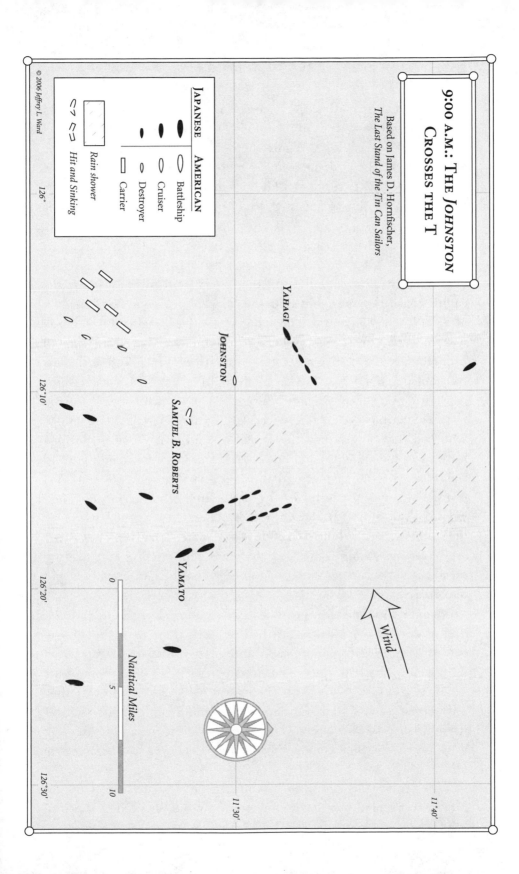

9:00 A.M.: THE *JOHNSTON*
CROSSES THE T

Based on James D. Hornfischer,
The Last Stand of the Tin Can Sailors

JAPANESE AMERICAN

Battleship
Cruiser
Destroyer
Carrier

Rain shower
Hit and Sinking

YAHAGI

JOHNSTON

SAMUEL B. ROBERTS

YAMATO

Wind

Nautical Miles

© 2006 Jeffrey L. Ward

126°   126°10'   126°20'   126°30'

11°40'   11°30'

him to send fast battleships to rescue the embattled Taffys: "Help needed from heavy ships immediately." (Years later, Digardi recalled the message as reading, "Where the hell is Halsey?" But he got the essence right.) Digardi showed the message to Evans. It was at that point, Digardi later recalled, that both men realized that Halsey was not coming to the rescue, and that the fate of the *Johnston* was sealed.

Admiral Kinkaid was following the battle from inside his tiny sea cabin aboard his command ship, the *Wasatch*, in Leyte Gulf. Shortly after 7:00 A.M., Kinkaid had been handed a message that Taffy Three was under attack by major elements of the Japanese fleet. Kinkaid immediately began firing off telegrams to Halsey. He sent an uncoded dispatch at 0707, 7:07 A.M., telling him that enemy battleships were firing on Clifton "Ziggy" Sprague's carrier task force off of the island of Samar. At 7:25 he wired Halsey that Admiral Oldendorf, who had just demolished the Japanese Southern Force in Surigao Strait, was low on ammo and thus could not be counted on to sail to the rescue. At 7:27 he more urgently requested that Halsey send Admiral Lee's fast battleships—the battle line that he had assumed would be guarding San Bernardino Strait—at "top speed," while requesting "an immediate strike" by the planes of Halsey's fast carriers. With increasing franticness, Kinkaid kept writing and sending messages. SITUATION CRITICAL, he cabled when the battle really began to turn dire around 8:30 A.M.

None of these messages reached Halsey for at least an hour and a half after they were sent. They had to make their way through the overwhelmed radio operators at Manus. When Kinkaid began bleating for help, he had not yet received Halsey's negative reply to his 4:12 A.M. message (received by Halsey at 6:48 A.M.) asking whether Task Force 34 was guarding San Bernardino Strait. ("Staff work at its best," sarcastically wrote Ziggy Sprague in the margin of an early work on the battle, C. Vann Woodward's 1947 *The Battle for Leyte Gulf*.)

Capt. Ray Tarbuck, the naval officer assigned to General MacArthur's planning staff—and the only one to predict that the

Japanese fleet would attack Leyte Gulf—had watched the Battle of
Surigao Strait from the bridge of a command ship, the *Blue Ridge*.
"Your prediction is coming true," said Adm. Dan Barbey, one of the
amphibious force commanders, as they watched the big-caliber gun
flashes light up the sky after midnight. Now, in the light of day, with
the news of Halsey's blunder and the sudden attack on Taffy Three,
Barbey and the other commanders were fearful that Japanese battleships would soon be shooting at their ships as they sat moored in
Leyte Gulf. Tarbuck went to see Admiral Kinkaid in the *Wasatch*,
"to see what the situation was," Tarbuck recalled. He found Kinkaid
sitting at his desk with his helmet pulled down. "His helmet was too
big for him," recalled Tarbuck. "He was very worried and all shriv-
eled up." There was nothing Kinkaid could do. Halsey was more
than 300 miles away.

CHAPTER THIRTEEN

THE WORLD WONDERS

"Where is Task Force 34"

Admiral Kurita was winning the battle—but he couldn't tell. He had the speed and power to overwhelm the Taffys—but he didn't know it. After the first few salvos, the American ships had disappeared into squalls and smoke. Admiral Ugaki switched from visually sighting his guns to using radar, a new innovation on Japanese ships. Too late, the Japanese had given up faith in their superior eyesight. The newly installed radars had difficulty tracking the enemy. Even under the best of circumstances, it was difficult for a moving ship to get an accurate "firing solution" on another moving ship. After the battle, Kurita would ruefully admit that the shooting by his great fleet had been poor.

Shortly before 8:00 A.M., a lookout on the *Yamato* warned of torpedo tracks coming out of the smoke. A destroyer, probably the *Heerman*, had fired off all her fish at the Japanese flagship. The basic evasive maneuver for a ship faced with multiple torpedo tracks is to "comb" them—to sail parallel rather than broadside. The *Yamato* swung her mighty bow to comb the tracks—now six torpedo wakes, four on one side, two on the other. But the great ship turned *north*, away from the battle, not south. She was forced to run along with the torpedoes until their alcohol fuel burned out and they sank. The detour took ten minutes, "but it felt like a month," recorded Ugaki. In his diary, he insisted that the turn had been taken at the "direction of the commander-in-chief," i.e., on Kurita's command. Normally, such maneuvers are the preserve of the ship's captain, not the fleet commander. Kurita later blamed the ship's captain, Adm. Nobuei Morishita. Most naval officers preferred to comb torpedoes by turning the bow first toward the torpedo wakes, in part because the bow has more armor than the stern, where the highly vulnerable rudder is located. Turning away, and presenting the ship's stern, was a notably nonaggressive maneuver. By the time the *Yamato* turned around and rejoined the chase, she had fallen seven miles behind the pack.

"A stern chase," in navy lore, "is a long chase," and the constant need to maneuver to avoid attacking planes and the torpedo attacks of the American destroyers slowed and spread the Japanese fleet. Nonetheless, the gap between hunter and hunted closed in the second hour of battle, between the hours of 8:00 and 9:00 A.M. The constant deluge of heavy-caliber shells on the Japanese destroyers and carriers began to tell. The advancing Kurita fleet slowly enveloped the Taffy stragglers. The carrier *Gambier Bay* was listing and on fire when the *Yamato* drew near shortly after 8:30 A.M.

Kurita could have finished off the small carrier with the battleship's great guns, but he chose not to. The *Gambier Bay* was done for; there was no point in pouring more shells into her except to kill more of her men. Instead, Kurita gave the order to the crew of the *Yamato* to line the rails. Men from the engine room were permitted to come on deck to see the sight of the burning American carrier. From his perch on the *Yamato*'s superstructure, lookout Koitabashi could see men with fire hoses vainly spraying down the deck of the stricken American carrier. At the time, Koitabashi wondered about his admiral's choice not to open fire at such close range. He later reflected that Kurita was "not a man to kill unnecessarily."

A couple of miles away, pilot Henry Pyzdrowski was wondering if the Japanese meant to capture the *Gambier Bay* as a prize. He felt the .38 pistol in his holster and survival knife in his belt and wondered: are we going to have to repel boarders? He decided that as a boy he had read too many sea stories from the Age of Fighting Sail.

(Pyzdrowski wasn't the only officer to feel as if he had been dropped back in the age of gunwale-to-gunwale sea battles. *If we get any closer,* thought Lieutenant Hagen aboard his destroyer as they closed within 4,000 yards of an enemy cruiser, *I'm going to have to get my sword.*)

Pyzdrowski had missed his chance to fly off the deck of the *Gambier Bay.* In the opening moments of the battle, he had watched, with awe, as Lieutenant Gallagher took his plane, its fuel tanks nearly empty, and charged right at the Japanese. Pyzdrowski had expected to follow shortly. But before he could launch his Avenger, the ship turned and ran south and southwest, downwind. Carrier planes can only take off into the wind, so Pyzdrowski was left stranded.

Quick-thinking Admiral Sprague was leading the Japanese on a roundabout (but purposeful) chase—first to the east, to launch planes, then veering south and southwest in the direction of hoped-for help. Kurita sailed straight east to try to cut off the Americans to windward, then turned and followed. The superior speed of his ships slowly allowed them to gain on the Americans, despite the twisting and turning to dodge the brave counterattacks of the American destroyers. "Look at the little DE [destroyer escort] committing suicide, Mac," one of Sprague's lieutenants had remarked to a fellow officer as they watched the attack of the "little fellas" from the bridge of the *Fanshaw Bay.*

Without any duty station, Pyzdrowski stood on the flight deck, a spectator to acts of astonishing bravery. A Japanese cruiser, the *Chikuma,* had zeroed in on the *Gambier Bay,* and her 8-inch armor-piercing shells began to cut holes in the Kaiser Coffin's thin deck. Many of them went right through, like a bullet through a shoe box, but others detonated.

Wondering if he could be useful, Pyzdrowski went to the ship's sickbay. It had been gutted by a shell. The beheaded body of the ship's surgeon lay in a corner. Recoiling, Pyzdrowski went to his cabin. His locker, where he kept his liquor, was open and empty. He had shouted the combination to his roommate, Lieutenant Bisbee, as he had waited to take off, and now he found Bisbee and several others, crouched, amidst a litter of empty scotch bottles, beneath a teepee of mattresses.

As the order to "Abandon Ship" squawked over the PA, the pilots stumbled on deck. On the way, Pyzdrowski encountered a pilot who had been badly burned and was near death. The man held up his hand. Pyzdrowski was unsure why, then he realized what the man wanted. As gently as he could, he removed the man's wedding ring and promised to bring it to his wife. Then, as the *Gambier Bay* burned and began to roll over, the pilot jumped into the sea.

Shortly before 9:00 A.M., the American planes, which had been attacking in groups of two and three, began arriving in waves. Some of the Taffy Three pilots were making dummy runs. After he exhausted his bombs and ammo, Lt. Thomas Lupo of New Orleans threw a Coke bottle at a Japanese warship as he flew over. Lt. Earl "Blue" Archer of Hope, Arkansas, took out his .38 caliber service revolver and fired a few shots into the superstructure of a battleship. But other, better-armed planes from Taffy Two were entering the fray, dropping torpedoes and heavier bombs. Two of Kurita's cruisers, the *Chokai* and *Chikuma*, were hit so badly they were dead in the water; *Chokai* began to sink.

Kurita was sure that these air attacks presaged even heavier ones. He and his chief of staff, Admiral Koyanagi, were convinced that they were surrounded—chasing one carrier group to the south, but in turn being shadowed by an American carrier group to the north. Japanese radio operators had intercepted Admiral Kinkaid's call to Admiral Halsey for help—sent in the clear in plain English. The same message that convinced Commander Evans and Lieutenant Hagen aboard the *Johnston* that they were doomed—that Halsey would never make it in time—gave no encouragement to Kurita. The Japanese understood the message to mean that Halsey was within two hours of catching up with Kurita—that by the time Kurita finished battling one carrier group, he would have to turn and fight another.

Perhaps Kurita should have read the desperation in Kinkaid's messages. But he was desperate himself. Far from seeing that he was on the verge of wiping out a group of jeep carriers, he felt surrounded, sure that he was caught in a vise. His fears were not unwarranted. Kurita's ships were running low on fuel and ammunition. He had already lost half his fleet. In the two hours since the battle began, four of his cruisers had been hit so hard by American planes or destroyers that they had to drop out of the battle. When Kurita left Brunei, his fleet included ten heavy cruisers and two light cruisers. Now after two days under assault, only two heavy and two light cruisers remained to fight. He faced the real prospect that if he continued this running battle, none of his ships—none of the thirty-two warships that left Brunei—would return home.

Standing behind his commander-in-chief on the bridge of the *Yamato*, Admiral Koyanagi had shed his brief faith in miracles. The fight seemed chaotic to him. Radio communications were poor, as usual, and after the flagship had turned around to evade the torpedoes, she had lost sight of some of her own fleet. Koyanagi felt uneasy, "in the dark," he later recalled. Still believing that his ships were chasing fleet carriers that could make 30 knots—and not jeep carriers poking along at 18 knots—he didn't know that the Japanese were on the verge of overrunning the Americans. He wasn't sure how the battle was progressing, or what they were truly up against, and he was troubled by the nagging sense that they had been tricked, led into a trap.

The chief of staff whispered into the commander-in-chief's ear: "Let's discontinue this chase," Koyanagi recalled saying. "There's still Leyte to attack." Kurita did not need any persuading. He gave the order: the fleet was to "reassemble" around the *Yamato*—heading north, away from the Americans and away also from Leyte Gulf.

It was about 0915, 9:15 A.M. Lookout Koitabashi was on the wing of the bridge when the word was passed. There was the usual communications breakdown. Koitabashi watched as the cruiser *Tone* continued to forge ahead, seeming to ignore the signal. "The officers on the bridge looked rather puzzled," recalled Koitabashi. Some were quietly grumbling, wondering why Kurita had broken off the chase. "We have to assemble and make a formation to go into Leyte," one of the officers explained.

At 9:30 A.M. the giant battleship swung north. She was relatively unscratched. A single 5-inch shell from a destroyer had landed in a rice locker. The shell was a dud.

*   *   *

The men on the bridge of Ziggy Sprague's flagship, the *Fanshaw Bay*, were giddy with disbelief. "God damn it, boys, they're getting away," yelled a signalman near Admiral Sprague. Sure enough, they could see Japanese warships around them breaking off the engagement and sailing north. The admiral let out a whoop. "I could not believe my eyes," Sprague wrote, "but it looked as if the whole damn Japanese fleet was indeed retiring. At best, I had expected to be swimming by this time, along with all my crews."

It was too late for the *Johnston*. A whole flotilla of Japanese destroyers had prematurely launched their torpedoes when Commander Evans crossed their bows shortly before 9:00 A.M. Now they turned on the wounded American ship with a vengeance. Even after Kurita gave his signal to withdraw and reassemble, the destroyers kept firing into the *Johnston*, circling her like Indians around Custer.

The Japanese destroyers were firing at point-blank range. The trajectory of their shells was so flat that Lieutenant Jesse Cochran, the junior engineering officer, saw holes in the port and starboard sides of the aft engine compartment where shells had entered and exited without exploding. The forward engine and fire compartments were in shambles from shell hits at 7:30 A.M. Incredibly, survivors had hid in the bilge, between the skin of the ship and the engine room filled with scalding steam. After about an hour, they emerged like ghosts. Machinist's mate third class Robert Sochor recalled one of them shaking like a dog, "as if to get the hot, steaming clothes off his skin." Sochor helped the men to the officers' wardroom where the ship's doctor was trying to do what he could. "It was an awful sight to see," recalled Sochor, "all those pathetic men sitting and lying on the crowded deck." The ship's doctor, Robert Browne, was trying to put life jackets on the wounded.

At about 9:10 A.M. a shell hit one of the forward guns, knocking it out and igniting its 40-mm ammunition, which began popping off just below the bridge. Lieutenant Welch, sent aft by the captain to check on a gun that had stopped firing, returned to find the bridge deserted. Welch described the eerie scene: The ship "drove under the spray of a near-hit of dye-loaded shells. Reddish water cascaded over the deck, evaporating instantly from the heat of a magazine on fire from the deck below. Suffocating smoke blew over the bridge. Classified publications were gone."

The bridge had become uninhabitable. Commander Evans had ordered the bridge detail to evacuate. The captain told Lieutenant Digardi, the ship's communications officer, to destroy all the *Johnston's* codebooks and classified information. Digardi took three men into the radio shack, where everyone was dead, and blew up the coding machine with a grenade. He emptied a safe full of classified documents into a mattress cover, put in a 5-inch shell casing for weight, and threw it over the side.

Leaving the abandoned bridge, Lieutenant Welch found the captain standing on the fantail. He was shouting orders down the hatch into the aft steering room, where sailors pulled and pushed, like ancient galley slaves, to manually shift the rudder. Gunner's mate second class Jim Herring had been standing in the spotter's hatch of Gun 55, the aftmost 5-inch gun, when he saw "the skipper" pull open the deck hatch to the aft steering room and start "bellowing orders." Evans's shirt was almost burned off his back. It hung in tatters. He was smeared with blood from his wounds, and his hand was wrapped in a blood-soaked handkerchief. He was standing beneath the barrel of Gun 55, which barked and flashed every few seconds. "This didn't seem to faze him," recalled Herring, who was moved by the sight of his captain, bloodied and defiant, a figure out of a lost age. Evans might as well have been John Paul Jones, personally aiming a 9-pounder cannon at the British from the ravaged quarterdeck of the *Bonhomme Richard* a century-and-a-half before. "His guts and determination to whip the Japs, single-handed, it seemed, kept me from really being scared," Herring recalled. "It just made you want to help him whip the hell out of them, too."

The *Johnston* had impossibly survived for over two hours, but her luck was running out. A Japanese shell smashed into the forward fire room, knocking out the boilers. The starboard screw stopped turning. The *Johnston* lay dead in the water. Flames were shooting up the forward superstructure. Only a single gun was firing, and its ammo was down to star shells. There was nothing more that Evans could do. He gave the order to pass the word: "Abandon Ship."

In the gun director, so smoke filled his men were choking, Lieutenant Hagen said, "What the hell are we doing here? Let's abandon ship." The last word "was hardly out of my mouth" when his men scrambled past him and headed for the rail. Hagen started aft to look for the captain, but his way was blocked: the dead and dying were stacked amidships, a mound of torn and anguished flesh. "Please help me," a man called out. Hagen looked at the man, who was larger than he, and whose legs were horribly mangled. "I can't," replied Hagen. ("I still dream about this," Hagen recalled forty years later.) Hagen walked forward and, "like a man in a dream," carefully took off his shoes and socks and dove over the side.

Men were jumping and clambering off the ship. Digardi stopped to try to help Lieutenant Bechdel, the torpedo officer whose leg had been blown off below the knee. Dr. Browne had dressed the stump, but Bechdel was so weak from shock and morphine that Digardi had to lift him over the side. A shell hit and blew Digardi right out of his socks and shoes into the water thirty feet from the ship.

The scene in the water was at once panicky and surreal. Jim O'Gorek, Hagen's torpedoman, swam over and said to him, Hagen recalled, "as brightly as if he was meeting me on the street corner, 'Mr. Hagen, we got off all ten of them torpedoes, and they ran hot, straight, and normal!'" As they bobbed on the swell, Bill Mercer watched a sailor named Bob Marquard pull his comb from his pocket, neatly part his hair, and throw away the comb saying, "I don't guess I'll ever need that again." Mess room steward Robert Bandy cried, "Someone help me! I can't swim!" Someone yelled that "now is a good time to learn," and Bandy, a large black man, must have, because he was the only steward's mate to survive. Charles Landreth had left his life jacket hanging on his bunk when he ran to his battle station in the engine room. Jumping into the water, he tried to hang on to another sailor who did have his life jacket, but the man fought him off. Landreth told the man that if he made it out alive, he would "get" him. (Landreth survived; the man did not.)

Treading water, Hagen saw Dr. Browne, who was his roommate, carrying wounded men out of the deckhouse and laying them on the

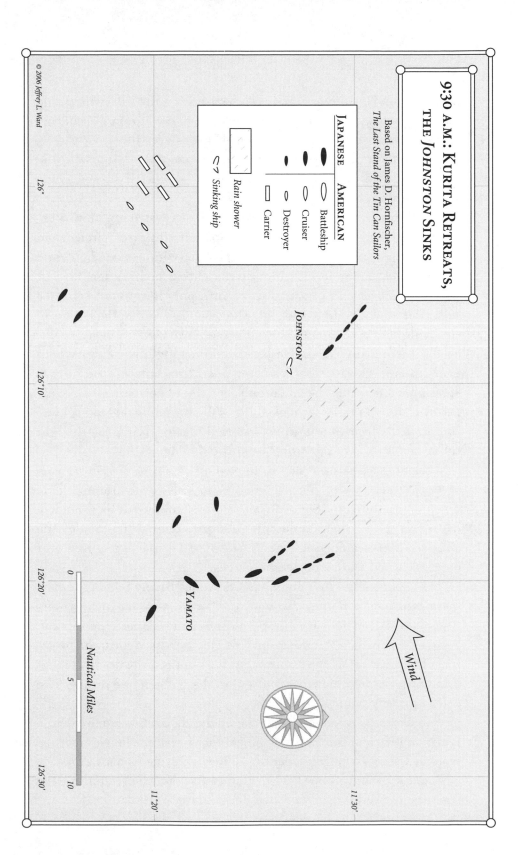

9:30 A.M.: KURITA RETREATS,
THE *JOHNSTON* SINKS

Based on James D. Hornfischer,
The Last Stand of the Tin Can Sailors

JAPANESE   AMERICAN

Battleship
Cruiser
Destroyer
Carrier

Rain shower

Sinking ship

JOHNSTON

YAMATO

Wind

Nautical Miles

0   5   10

© 2006 Jeffrey L. Ward

126°   126°10'   126°20'   126°30'

11°30'   11°20'

deck. Hagen called out to Browne, "Abandon ship!" Browne yelled back something and turned to go back into the wardroom / charnel house when a shell obliterated him. Hagen's eyes filled with tears. He wept for thirty seconds, tried to get control of himself, and started swimming away, worried that he would be sucked down when the ship sank.

The *Johnston*, by now a blackened hulk of twisted metal, was beginning to settle by the bow as a Japanese destroyer circled and pumped shells into her. "There she goes!" a swimmer cried out, and the *Johnston*, home for 330 men living cheek to cheek for the past year, rolled over and began to sink, until only her fantail could be seen. With a last rumble and sigh, she disappeared into the depths of the Philippine Sea. Tom Dixon, a fuse setter in Gun 54, began to cry. So did Lieutenant Welch. He had been ducking underwater whenever he saw the Japanese destroyer open fire, but because he was wearing a life jacket, he could only get the upper part of his body below water. "I must have looked like a duck feeding on food below," he recalled. His eyes brimming, he tried to stop crying. He thought to himself that his body might need the liquid.

A Japanese destroyer slowly moved in amongst the ship's survivors. About sixty of the crew had been killed in battle and gone down with the ship. Some 270 survivors, many badly wounded, drifted in the oil slicks amidst the flotsam. At first, the men of the *Johnston* were convinced that they would be machine-gunned or depth-charged as they floated helplessly.

The Japanese warship, flying an enormous Rising Sun battle flag, drew within a hundred yards of the swimmers. Japanese sailors lined the rail. They were not holding guns. Some clapped and laughed, or made a "number one" sign. One tossed a can of tomatoes. Then several of the *Johnston*'s sailors noticed the destroyer captain, in his white uniform, standing on the wing of the bridge. The officer gravely saluted.

The Japanese steamed away. Hagen recalled the sudden silence. Guns were no longer crashing, machinery was no longer roaring, wounded were no longer screaming. They were alone on a vast sea.

Captain Evans was nowhere to be seen. No one had seen him leave the ship. He had simply vanished beneath the waves.

*　*　*

Some 400 miles to the north, Admiral Halsey was plunging from euphoria to anger and depression.

While the Taffys had been running for their lives from Kurita's opening salvos, Halsey impatiently waited for his planes to strike Ozawa's carriers. At 0803, 8:03 A.M., Halsey's restless staff heard a pilot cry out over the radio frequency broadcast into Flag Plot, "I have the target in sight!" Waves of Third Fleet warplanes dove down through antiaircraft fire at Ozawa's four carriers, desperately zigzagging on the blue sea below. Halsey's climactic battle had finally begun.

But at 0822, 8:22 A.M., an ominous message arrived. It was from Admiral Kinkaid in Leyte Gulf. The Seventh Fleet commander was passing on a report from Admiral Sprague of Taffy Three that Japanese warships were fifteen miles astern and firing on him. This was the first warning that Kinkaid had sent out—at 7:07 A.M. Thanks to the circuitous radio traffic, it was reaching Halsey over an hour later.

Standing by the intelligence staff's stand-up desk in Flag Plot, Lieutenant Solberg understood right away that the dour Mike Cheek and Solberg's roommate, Harris Cox, had been prescient. The battleships of the Japanese Center Force had come right through the unguarded San Bernardino Strait and were now like wolves among the sheep. Solberg noted that the formerly unshakable Doug Moulton, who had been so adamant about going after the carriers with everything they had the night before, was now looking not quite so sure of himself.

In his memoirs, Halsey insisted that—at first—he was not worried by Kinkaid's message. He assumed, he wrote, that the sixteen small carriers of the Taffys could muster enough airpower to hold off Kurita's damaged force until Admiral Oldendorf's battleships of the Seventh Fleet could sail up to relieve them. Halsey gave no thought to turning around. This was not the time to hesitate: here he was, on the verge of a victory that he believed would finish off the Imperial Japanese Navy's carrier force, and hence eliminate Japan's most lethal weapon, hastening an end to the war. Halsey felt his determination rewarded when, at 0850, 8:50 A.M., Admiral Mitscher signaled the first returns from the air strikes: two carriers had been hit and a third, a light carrier, had already exploded and sunk.

But the messages kept coming, much delayed, out of order, but revealing increasing desperation by Kinkaid. REQUEST FAST CARRIERS MAKE IMMEDIATE STRIKE, Kinkaid had radioed at 0727, 7:27 A.M.— and Halsey finally received at 0900, 9:00 A.M. Halsey was sufficiently moved to order Admiral McCain's carrier task force to attack Center Force. But McCain's carriers were still hundreds of miles away, rushing back from their diversion to replenish at Ulithi, and McCain's planes could not arrive before early afternoon. Halsey acknowledged that he became "angrier," and admitted that he was shaken when Kinkaid informed him, at 0922, 9:22 A.M., that Oldendorf's old battleships were low on ammunition. "Low in ammunition! Here was a new factor, so astonishing that I could hardly accept it. Why hadn't Kinkaid let me know before?" Halsey spluttered in his memoirs. He protested too much. Halsey could have guessed that Oldendorf's ships might be depleted after sinking the Japanese Southern Force in Surigao Strait, and in any case, the failure of communication was mutual. Halsey's equivocations and rationalizations in his memoirs, as he described this terrible scene, verge on the pathetic. But denial may have been the only way he could have coped with the shock of his blunder revealed at the precise moment of his greatest triumph.

Observing his commander as the messages flowed in that morning, Solberg noticed that Halsey's "face was ashen." John Marshall, Solberg's fellow air combat intelligence officer, watched Halsey sitting in stubborn silence on the leather bench he often occupied in Flag Plot. Marshall recalled: "Suddenly, to no one in particular, but as if talking to himself, he muttered, 'When I get my teeth into something, I hate to let go.' Then he lapsed into silence, his jaw set like a bulldog's."

At 10:00 A.M., two more messages arrived. The first shocked Halsey. It was from Kinkaid: MY SITUATION IS CRITICAL. FAST BATTLESHIPS AND SUPPORT BY AIR STRIKES MAY BE ABLE TO KEEP ENEMY FROM DESTROYING CVES AND ENTERING LEYTE. The second message was from Admiral Nimitz, and it would make Halsey so upset that he wept.

* * *

Thousands of miles away, in Hawaii and Washington, the top brass of the United States Navy anxiously followed the progress of the battle by wireless telegraph. The senior officers at CINCPAC at Pearl Harbor and COMINCH at the Pentagon had their opinions about what Halsey should do, or should have done. On the night of the 24th, when it appeared that Kurita was coming through the San Bernardino Strait, Adm. Raymond Spruance looked at the chart of the battle area. He placed his hand on a spot just to the east of the strait. "If I were there," he said, as if to himself, "I would keep my force right there." But he was not there. Spruance was back at Pearl, waiting his turn to take control of the Big Blue Fleet after New Year's. He knew enough not to suggest that Halsey be *ordered* to keep the Third Fleet on guard off the strait. Indeed, he knew that he, along with all the admirals in the Pacific Fleet, as well as those gold-braided flat hats back in Washington, would not even *suggest* that Halsey hold back his fleet.

It was the navy way, born of hundreds of years of naval tradition that commanders at sea in the midst of battle must be allowed to decide for themselves what to do, without meddling from the admiralty on land. The tradition was born partly of necessity. In the pre-electronic age, captains had been isolated and controlled only by flag signals from their fleet admirals, if that. (Ordered by the fleet admiral's flag signal to break off his attack on Copenhagen in 1803, Admiral Nelson is said to have clapped his telescope to his blind eye and exclaimed, "I really cannot see the signal." Then he proceeded to destroy the Danish fleet.) Halsey—glorified in the newspapers as America's Nelson—was on his own; he would not be second-guessed.

At CINCPAC, Admiral Nimitz assumed that Halsey had left Task Force 34 guarding San Bernardino Strait. He had interpreted Halsey's Battle Plan sent at 1512, 3:12 P.M., on October 24—the afternoon of the day before—to mean that Halsey was setting up the battle line to guard San Bernardino Strait.

And yet, doubts nagged at Nimitz. He was bothered by Halsey's dispatch at 8:24 the night before—"Am proceeding north with three groups." Nimitz wondered whether Halsey had actually detached the battle line or taken it north with his three carrier groups. Sitting in his office at Pearl Harbor, where it was late morning (six hours ahead of the Philippine Sea), he continued to fret.* He buzzed for Capt. Bernard Austin, his assistant chief of staff. He was concerned, he told Austin. He had seen nothing to indicate that Halsey had blockaded the San Bernardino Strait. Captain Austin responded that the dispatches were unclear, and other officers were beginning to wonder the same thing. Nimitz uneasily told Austin to keep him informed. As morning became afternoon, Nimitz continued to buzz Austin and ask him if there was any news about Halsey guarding the strait. Austin finally mustered the courage to say to the commander-in-chief of the Pacific Fleet, "That's what you want to know. Why don't you ask him?"

Nimitz paused. No, he said, he did not want to send a dispatch that would appear to influence, even indirectly, the decisions of the commander on the scene.

At COMINCH in Washington, where it was early evening, doubts were stirring. Capt. William Sebald, a naval intelligence officer who worked for Admiral King, was increasingly worried about a Japanese trick. He had read the Combined Fleet's Z Plan—the same captured documents that had seized the attention, and excited the anxiety, of Mike Cheek and Harris Cox of Halsey's staff. He understood that the Japanese were considering a decoy plan. At COMINCH's offices at the Navy Yard in Washington, Sebald stared at a large chart showing Halsey's carriers east of the Philippines, a Japanese carrier force somewhere to the north, and Kurita's Center Force just west of the San Bernardino Strait.

It occurred to Sebald that Halsey was being set up. "My God, I hope Halsey doesn't swallow the bait and go north," Sebald said to another intelligence officer. The man answered, "He wouldn't be that foolish."

"We let it go at that. I was a bit uneasy," Sebald recalled, about whether COMINCH should send a message warning Halsey. Instead, he followed "the almost invariable rule that the fellows on the sidelines mind their own business and don't interfere with opera-

---

*Because of the international date line, it was still October 24 in Hawaii and Washington. So 8:30 A.M. on October 25 in the Philippines is 2:30 P.M. on October 24 in Hawaii and 7:30 P.M. on October 24 in Washington, D.C.

tions, particularly as a message like this coming from COMINCH would, in effect, be telling Halsey what COMINCH thought he ought to be doing."

At Pearl Harbor, CINCPAC intelligence officer W. J. Holmes was scanning the radio traffic, "reading victory in every dispatch," until he encountered an "astounding report" that the escort carriers were under fire from Japanese battleships off Samar. He, too, had assumed that Halsey had left Willis Lee's battle line behind to guard the strait, but now he began to wonder. He called fleet intelligence officer Edwin Layton and asked, "Where is Task Force 34?"

Layton, recalled Holmes, was "irate." He had concluded, based on Halsey's cryptic messages, that Halsey had taken the battleships with him when he headed north to chase the carriers. Holmes suggested that perhaps Halsey had given Lee orders by visual signals—by flag or signal lamp—and that maybe the battle line was somewhere off San Bernardino Strait, closing in on the Japanese.

"I doubt it," Layton replied and slammed down the phone.

By mid-afternoon Hawaiian time—mid-morning in the Leyte Gulf—Nimitz was becoming ever more perturbed about the whereabouts of Task Force 34. Handing him the latest dispatches, reporting Kinkaid's desperate pleas, Nimitz's staff aide, Captain Austin, ventured, "Admiral, couldn't you just ask Admiral Halsey the simple question: Where is Task Force 34?"

Nimitz's worried-looking eyes creased a little more. "Go out and write it up," he instructed his aide. "That's a good idea."

Austin dictated the simple question to a yeoman, an enlisted man who thought he heard a little extra emphasis in the voice of the assistant chief of staff. The message to be sent Halsey read: WHERE IS TASK FORCE THIRTY FOUR REPEAT WHERE IS TASK FORCE THIRTY FOUR.

When radio messages were encrypted, they were buffered at either end by nonsense phrases, often nursery rhymes. This padding, intended to confuse enemy code breakers, was to be separated from the text by double consonants, and—importantly—the padding was not supposed to have any connection to the text. But the ensign coding the message may have had an active subconscious and a literary sensibility. For his first bit of nonsense, he wrote, harmlessly enough, "Turkey trots to water." But the rest of the message went on:

WHERE IS TASK FORCE THIRTY FOUR REPEAT WHERE IS TASK FORCE
THIRTY FOUR RR THE WORLD WONDERS

The ensign later explained that the phrase "The world wonders"
was "just something that popped into my head." But the words were
heavy with meaning. In the first half of the twentieth century every
schoolboy had read, if not memorized, Tennyson's words:

> *When can their glory fade?*
> *O the wild charge they made!*
> *All the world wonder'd.*
> *Honour the charge they made!*
> *Honour the Light Brigade,*
> *Noble six hundred!*

The message, sent at 9:44 A.M. (local Philippines time, 2:44 P.M. in
Hawaii) by Nimitz, passed with unusual celerity through the usual
channels to the radio room aboard USS *New Jersey*. A communications officer handed the message to the commander of the Third
Fleet as he sat on his leather bench in Flag Plot.

Halsey might, if he had stopped for a moment, noticed the "RR"
separating WHERE IS TASK FORCE THIRTY FOUR from the acid phrase
THE WORLD WONDERS. He would have realized that the phrase was
just padding. But he did not. It looked to him, in his highly wrought-
up state, that he was not only being second-guessed but mocked by
the commander-in-chief, Pacific Fleet.

"I was stunned as if I had been struck in the face," recalled Halsey.
"The paper rattled in my hands. I snatched off my cap, threw it on
the deck, and shouted something I am ashamed to remember."
Halsey, to the utter astonishment of his staff and the enlisted men
standing around watching this spectacle, let out an anguished sob.
Horrified, Mick Carney "rushed over and grabbed my arm," Halsey
recalled. "Stop it!" yelled Carney, like a mother to a teenage boy.
"What the hell's the matter with you? Pull yourself together!"

Halsey handed him the dispatch and turned his back. He was
speechless. "It was utterly impossible for me to believe that Chester
Nimitz would send me such an insult," he recalled. Halsey was not

done with his tantrum. He grabbed the dispatch from Carney, hurled it to the floor, and stomped on it. "What right does Chester have to send me a God-damn message like that?" he implored no one in particular.

Then he wheeled and went down the steps to his cabin. Carney anxiously followed. It will never be known exactly what was said down there—neither man discussed the conversation in his memoir— but the conversation must have been excruciating. When Halsey emerged an hour later, he gave the order to turn around—to change course from due north to due south. The battle line was less than two hours from Ozawa's carriers and their escorts, or as Halsey put it, "exactly 42 miles from the muzzles of my 16-inch guns." The *New Jersey* could have led the way into an old-fashioned—and extremely one-sided—sea battle, blasting away at the remnants of Ozawa's fleet. But with glory in his grasp, Halsey had no choice but to open his hand and let it slip away. Nimitz's telegram had been intended as a "nudge," but to Halsey it felt like a sledgehammer blow. He felt

Nimitz and Halsey

obliged to turn around and sail toward Leyte Gulf. The chances of his getting there in time to do any good were very low. He did not expect his fleet to arrive at Leyte until 8:00 A.M. the next morning. Halsey would never recover from the bitterness he felt. "I turned my back on the opportunity I had dreamed about since my days as a cadet," he wrote after the war.

October 25, 1944, was the last day of the great fleets. It was also the first day of the suicide bombers.

Lt. Yukio Seki had been trying to die for the past five days. He was the commander of the *Shikishima* unit of the Special Attack or *Shimpu* (Divine Wind) squadron. *Shikishima* is an ancient holy name for Japan—like *Yamato*. Seki was an Eta Jima graduate, recognized as a natural leader. Approached about leading the first kamikaze unit, he had closed his eyes, run his hands through his long hair, looked up and said, in an unfaltering voice, "You absolutely must let me do it."

On October 20, at a remote airfield on the Philippine island of Luzon, he had stood proudly in front of his twenty-four-man squad, listening to Admiral Onishi, the commander of the First Air Force and the creator of the kamikazes. "You are already gods, without earthly desires," Onishi told his men, his voice quaking with emotion. "But one thing you want to know is that your own crash dive is not in vain. Regrettably, we will not be able to tell you the results. But I shall watch your efforts to the end and report your deeds to the Throne."

Young Lieutenant Seki had led his men in song:

> *If I go away to sea*
> *I shall return a corpse awash;*
> *If duty calls me to the mountain,*
> *A verdant sward will be my pall;*
> *Thus for the sake of the Emperor*
> *I will not die peacefully at home.*

Seki's men were all volunteers. One of them had already labeled his bag "Personal effects of the late Lt. Cdr. Naoshi Kanno." They had flown off that day looking for American ships to plunge into, but couldn't find any. For the next four days they had dodged around heavy rainstorms, fruitlessly searching for the Americans. Even Lieutenant Seki, who was suffering from severe diarrhea, was becoming demoralized.

Finally, after 10:00 A.M. on October 25, good tidings arrived: an American carrier group had been spotted fifty miles east of Leyte. Once more, Lieutenant Seki affixed his *hachimaki* bandanna and prepared to meet his fate.

The carrier group was Taffy Three, still celebrating its narrow escape from Kurita's gunships. The men of Taffy Three were wrung out and giddy over their good luck. Aboard one of Taffy Three's six CVEs, the *St. Lo*, the captain had just ordered Condition One Easy, allowing half the crew to stand down from General Quarters and get a cup of coffee. Suddenly, the crew saw a lone Japanese "Zeke" fighter, with bombs hanging under each wing, flying flat and low coming at the stern, almost as if the plane was lining up a landing. The plane was about a half-mile away.

It was Lieutenant Seki. He jerked back on the stick, brought up the nose of his plane—and then plunged straight down. The plane hit the flight deck and exploded in a fireball. The burning fuselage smashed right through the four-inch-thick wooden deck and came to rest amidst a stack of torpedoes and bombs. The ensuing blasts—seven of them—peeled back the flight deck, threw pieces of the carrier as high as a thousand feet into the air, and knocked the *St. Lo* on her beam ends. She was gone in fifteen minutes.

Seki was one of a dozen kamikaze pilots to dive on targets that day, though the only one to actually sink a ship. A new era of warfare had begun. Before it was over, 3,912 Japanese airmen would kill themselves for the emperor.

Seki's eagerness was typical of "special attack" pilots, at least at that early state of the kamikaze campaign. Kamikazes believed that they were honoring the ancient tradition of *bushido*, the way of the warrior. Their instructors had told them that throughout Japan's long history of invincibility, true warriors welcomed the chance to sacrifice themselves for the emperor, whatever the cost. This, then, was the essence of *bushido*: warriors were not merely willing to die for the Chrysanthemum Throne. They wanted to die.

Bushido was a powerful motivator. But it was, as historian Karl Friday has written, "bull." Ancient samurai were no more eager to die than warriors of other civilizations. Japanese soldiers were told that if they were captured, they would be shamed forever. But many ancient Japanese warriors had been prisoners of war. Indeed, the first of the great shoguns, Ieyasu Tokugawa, had been captured and released by his enemies without opprobrium. The notion of absolute loyalty to the emperor was also a fiction. In medieval times, a samurai's loyalty to his lord was largely personal, a contract that could be broken—and often was. Even the term *bushido* was a contrivance. Rarely used in ancient times, it was popularized by military leaders in the early Meiji era—the 1870s—to stiffen the morale and discipline of raw conscripts.

The young men in kamikaze squadrons had no way of knowing they were being cynically manipulated. Even graduates of Eta Jima had been fed a highly idealized history of the warrior tradition. The navy men were not, on the whole, as credulous and fanatical as the officers of the Imperial Japanese Army. But many were like Admiral Ugaki: true believers in the myth of *bushido*.

Admiral Kurita knew better. His early education, at the knee of his father, a scholar of the early Meiji period, had been exceptional—more humanistic, more sophisticated, more realistic. Kurita's own children remembered him urging them to read his grandfather's scholarly texts. Interviewed in 2004, Kurita's daughter, Shigeko Terada, recalled that she resisted—the tomes were written in ancient Chinese characters and very difficult to read. But it was clear to her that her father had been affected by his own family's scholarship.

Kurita's grandfather had been a famous scholar of ancient Japan. He was heavily influenced by the Confucianism of the ancients, borrowed from the Chinese more than a millennium before the Meiji Restoration. Confucianism, not *bushido*, was the real Kurita family ideology. Confucianism stressed loyalty and obedience, as well as decency to others. For Kurita, the obligation of loyalty caused a tremendous conflict. Loyalty to whom? To his emperor, surely. But he could not be sure what the emperor truly wanted, for his will was interpreted—and twisted—by the senior military at Imperial General Headquarters. Kurita felt the pull of obligation to his superiors—but also to the men under his authority and to his own family and lastly, to himself, to his own sense of honor and right and wrong.

It was not uncommon for Japanese of this age or any age to feel a tremendous sense of tension from conflicting obligations. The pressure of reconciling the irreconcilable can be strangely enervating, almost paralyzing. It is the theme of many popular tragedies, and it was almost surely a cause of the tragedy facing Kurita. Did he sacrifice his men to obey his superiors, even if he thought his superiors were sending them on a hopeless, futile mission?

In Japan, there is an expression for feeling overwhelmed by stress, conflict, and fatigue, *atama ga masshiro ni naru*. It means, literally, seeing white in one's head, as if in a fog bank or a whiteout in a snowstorm. As Admiral Kurita sailed the warm tropical waters of the Philippine Sea, his brain was befogged, benumbed by a blizzard of conflicting obligations.

CHAPTER FOURTEEN

THE MYSTERIOUS TELEGRAM

"A symphony of moans"

SLOWLY, KURITA'S FLEET regrouped, heading north, while the exhausted, foggy-brained Kurita deliberated his next move. At about 10:00 A.M., *Yamato* sailed into a sea slick, "strewn," Admiral Ugaki wrote, with American sailors. They were probably survivors of the *Gambier Bay*, sunk just an hour earlier. The sea was stained dark red from the dye in the Japanese shells that had struck the American ship. "What did they think of the magnificent sight of our fleet in pursuit?" wondered Ugaki. Admiral Koyanagi's thoughts, as he later recorded them, were typically more benign. He no longer felt enmity toward the stranded sailors. He hoped, and assumed, that they would be rescued before too long.

Suddenly, a 25-mm machine gun opened up on the sailors in the water. From his permanent post on the bridge, Admiral Kurita immediately gave the order to stop shooting. Lookout Koitabashi was not surprised. It was just not in Kurita's nature, he thought to himself, "to shoot drowning dogs." Koitabashi was taken aback when some of the Americans in the water waved at the passing Japanese ship. "It was very strange to me," he recalled. "We were the enemy. I thought Americans must be people who value life. We would have drowned ourselves or tried to swim away."

At 11:20 A.M., Kurita ordered the fleet to turn and head southwest—toward Leyte Gulf. None of Kurita's staff was eager to continue on the mission; all regarded it as suicide. Enlisted men like Koitabashi—and true believers like Ugaki—might have imbibed the cultural cliché that all Japanese warriors longed to die, but the officers on Kurita's staff were not so ready to embrace death—not as pointless sacrifice. Kurita's men knew from intercepted radio messages that American planes were operating out of Tacloban, the airfield just a few minutes' flying time from the gulf. They were sure that Halsey's carrier groups had surrounded them, and that they would be trapped. In an interview after the war, Koyanagi compared Leyte Gulf to a "pond" and the Kurita fleet to a "bag of mice."

"Our heads were cooling," Koyanagi recalled. A more accurate description might be that their emotions were crashing. They had slept little, if at all, for three days. The euphoria of seeing American carriers on the horizon at dawn had worn off, and after a chaotic two-hour running battle, Kurita's men were coming down, hard. The duration of most gun battles at sea during the Second World War was short—often less than a half-hour in the sharp night clashes off of Guadalcanal. Kurita's fleet had been torpedoed, bombed, and shot at repeatedly over three days. It would be surprising if its officers and men were not in a physical and mental condition approaching shock.

What happened next would be the source of enduring controversy and mystery. Sometime before noon, according to Kurita's battle report, the *Yamato* received a signal: an enemy task force had been spotted "bearing 5 degrees distance 113 miles from Suluan Light at 0945." In plainer language, at 9:45 A.M., one of Halsey's carrier groups had been spotted off the coast of Samar—presumably following in the wake of Kurita's fleet, ready to spring a trap. The wireless telegram was read aloud on the bridge, recalled Cdr. Atsuo Ito, the commander of the battleships' floatplane squadron. Ito recalled that Admiral Kurita asked how far away the enemy's position was from his own fleet's current position. The answer came back: about sixty miles to the north.

In a voice "hardly above a whisper," a fellow officer on the bridge suggested to Commander Ito, "We should go after the main force." By "main force" he meant Halsey's carriers—he was guessing that they had tangled with a group of Halsey's carriers to the south, but that the "main force" was trailing along over the horizon to the north. This junior officer's sentiment, whispered at first, was universally shared among Kurita's staff officers. There was no inclination to complete the mission by attacking the American landing force inside Leyte Gulf. True, those were their orders. But their orders also permitted the Kurita force to attack any American carrier task force encountered along the way. The information in the telegram suggested that not too far to the north was just such a target. If they were to die, Kurita's staffers reasoned, better to have a chance to sink a few carriers in a shoot-out in the open sea than to get trapped in the narrow confines of Leyte Gulf. Kurita's men, just like Halsey's men, were fixated on destroying enemy carriers. In a postwar interview, Kurita's chief of staff Koyanagi echoed Halsey's chief of staff Carney: "Carriers," he said, "were our obsession."

Just as they had for the past three days, Kurita's men were feeling abandoned and alone. There had been no communications from headquarters in Tokyo that morning, and no word from Admiral Ozawa's decoy carrier force to the north. Kurita's men assumed that Ozawa's mission had failed or that he had been destroyed. They knew from messages trickling in from Admiral Shima that Admiral Nishimura's Southern Force had been all but wiped out as it tried to force the Surigao Strait. As Kurita's staff huddled to discuss what to do at noon on October 25, the Americans struck again: about seventy planes off of various Taffy carriers, coming in waves, bore in strafing and bombing Kurita's fleet. Kurita's lieutenants were sure that more and worse punishment awaited them inside Leyte Gulf.

At 12:36 P.M. Admiral Kurita issued new orders. The fleet would turn around and head north. It would "crash" into the American carrier task force. Far better to die making a noble sacrifice against the main enemy force, Kurita and his staff had unanimously agreed, than to die pointlessly shooting at empty transport ships. At his lookout post on the wing of the bridge, Petty Officer Koitabashi at first wondered why the great ship was swinging around to the north, but then he heard, over the PA, the *Yamato*'s captain describe the fleet's new, more glorious mission. He joined his mates in shouting *"Banzai!"*

The change of course, presented in such a way, sounded like a bold stroke, an uncharacteristic improvisation, jettisoning one set of

orders to seek a better opportunity. But the circumstances were sus-
pect. There was no American task force "bearing 5 degrees distance
113 miles from Suluan Light at 0945"—or anywhere close. Halsey's
ships were still another 300 miles away. Even if the sighting had
been real, there was no guarantee that Kurita would be able to find a
force spotted two hours earlier sixty nautical miles distant, some
three hours' steaming time away. After that morning's nasty surprise
encounter between Japanese battleships and American carriers, it
was unlikely that the Americans would allow their carriers to once
again come within gun range of Kurita's fleet.

No mention of that 9:45 A.M. wireless telegram has ever been
found in any official message file. Possibly, it was lost. Possibly, a lone
Japanese scout plane saw the Taffys retreating at 9:45, or saw the
shadow of clouds on the water, and sent in a report that was relayed
to the *Yamato*. The Imperial Japanese Navy's official history, *Kokan
Senshi*, surmises that a scout plane saw the tail end of Kurita's own
fleet, mistaking it for the Americans.

Or more likely, as some Japanese naval scholars and IJN veterans
have long suspected, the telegram never existed. According to this
more plausible theory, Kurita's staff needed a face-saving excuse to
escape certain death and destruction in Leyte Gulf, so they concocted
a bogus telegram offering up a new, more worthy enemy to attack.
No one can know for certain—no member of Kurita's staff ever confessed to the fiction. Suspicions have long centered on Captain Otani,
the chief operations officer, who was evasive on the subject after the
war. The *Yamato*'s chief paymaster, Tsuneo Ishida, recalled seeing
Otani coming down from the antiaircraft observation deck to the
main bridge and leaning in to speak quietly to Admiral Kurita, as
the Americans renewed their bombardment after noon. "Kurita-
san," Otani allegedly said, "maybe it's time to go home."

Not everyone on the bridge of the *Yamato* welcomed Kurita's
turnabout. Over in his corner, Admiral Ugaki was seething. "Why?"
he angrily demanded. He did not address this inquiry to Kurita; that
would have been insubordinate. Rather, he looked at Kurita's chief
of staff, Admiral Koyanagi. "Why are we turning?" Ugaki exclaimed. "The enemy is *that* way!" He gestured to the south with his
thumb. Koyanagi tried to placate Ugaki, but it was useless. Ugaki

was in a high state of agitation. He believed that he was, at last, engaged in true Decisive Battle. He credulously recorded in his diary the thoroughly incredible claim of the Tenth Destroyer Squadron (the T crossed by the *Johnston*) to have "accomplished the great feat of sinking three carriers, one cruiser, and one destroyer." If true, such a toll would have surpassed the achievements of any Japanese fleet in a single battle in three years of war.

Ugaki had not yet begun to fight. He had fired only eighty-one of *Yamato*'s 1,080 giant 18-inch shells. But, because of Kurita's retreat, he believed, he might never again have the chance to fire his big guns at an enemy ship. Once more Ugaki was being robbed of the chance to die honorably. In his diary that night, Ugaki avoided criticizing Kurita by name, as was his custom, but spluttered that "they wavered again and canceled the charge into Leyte Gulf. . . . I felt irritated to be on the same bridge seeing that they lacked fighting spirit and promptitude."

As the *Yamato* swung her water-heavy bow to the north, other officers permitted themselves, for the first time in days, to believe that they might live. Commander Ito, the floatplane squadron commander, had not bothered to wear a helmet. What was the point, since he was sure of dying? But now, Ito put a helmet on his head. The next day, as the fleet ran westward to safety, he would put on an armored flak jacket.

At the spot where the *Johnston* went down, the Pacific Ocean is five miles deep. The waters are warm, about 84 degrees in late October, but cold enough after dark to give a man hypothermia over many hours of floating. By day, the sun is powerful enough to sear and permanently scar the skin. Stinging jellyfish and sharks abound. On an empty sea at noon on October 25, the 270-odd surviving officers and men of the *Johnston* clung to floater nets, a few life rafts, and bits of wreckage. On the rising swell, they could see the mountaintops of Samar, sixty miles away.

The men organized themselves: the wounded were placed on the rafts and inside the nets, webs of nylon rope attached to buoys. "A symphony of moans" had started up, recalled Lieutenant Hagen. A pharmacist's mate asked Hagen, "Who gets the morphine?" Hagen replied, "The ones who cry the loudest." Missing a leg, Lieutenant Bechdel was so doped up on painkillers that he began to sing. Blessed with a mellifluous voice, he sang as if he and his buddies were gathered around a campfire.

Shortly after noon, an Avenger torpedo plane flew low overhead and dipped its wings. *It won't be long now,* thought Clint Carter, the Texan gunner's mate who had screamed so hotly for more ammo during the battle. The men of the *Johnston* were adrift no more than a couple of hundred miles from the greatest naval armada ever assembled on earth, thought Carter. Help was surely on the way.

The officers and petty officers began handing out rations—malted milk balls and Camel cigarettes. There was no way to light the cigarettes, so chief boatswain's mate Burnett used his as chewing tobacco. He did not realize how thirsty he might get. The drinking water in the casks attached to the raft was putrid. Someone had forgotten to change it.

As the sun began to sink in the west, the first doubts began to rise. A large stingray—"the size of a dining room table," recalled Joe Check—kept swimming between the rafts, not really dangerous, but eerie. At 3:00 P.M. came the sight they all dreaded: a shark fin. The men splashed and kicked, and the shark veered away. It would return, the men knew, and not alone.

The Avenger pilot who saw the *Johnston* survivors was under radio silence. As soon as he landed, he reported their location, but he misremembered the coordinates. Two destroyer escorts were dispatched, but they found no one, and broke off the search at 11:30 P.M. About twenty miles to the south, the survivors vainly scanned the empty horizon.

Five more times the Americans bombed Kurita's fleet as it staggered north that afternoon at under 20 knots. Every ship was leaking oil from hits or near-misses that popped rivets and broke seams. Finally, when the last American plane had dropped the last bomb and the shadows were lengthening on the worst day in the history of the Imperial Japanese Navy, a few Japanese airplanes—dive-bombers and Zeros—appeared in the afternoon sky.* In a final indignity, two of the Zeros flew down and strafed their own ships, mistaking them for American.

From time to time during that long afternoon as the fleet steamed north, then west around the island of Samar, Admiral Ugaki would urge that the fleet charge to the northeast. Some of the American air strikes had come from the east or northeast; perhaps, Ugaki suggested, the American task force was just over the horizon. Chief of staff Koyanagi informed him that fuel supplies, especially for the destroyers, were too low to go charging about. Ugaki insisted that after they destroyed the enemy, the battleships could refuel the destroyers at night. A stone-faced Kurita ignored his pleadings.

After 5:00 P.M., with the sun sinking in the west and Kurita on a westerly course for the San Bernardino Strait, a message finally came. It was from the previously incommunicado Admiral Ozawa, apparently still alive, somewhere to the north.

Halsey's 400-plus carrier planes had devastated Ozawa's fleet during the morning of the 25th. Ozawa had started with only thirteen planes to defend the fleet, and all of them had been shot down by 9:30 A.M. One by one, Ozawa's four carriers were hit and sunk. As Ozawa's flagship, the venerable *Zuikaku*, began to settle, Ozawa told his staff that he was going down with his ship. His chief of staff, Adm. Toshikazu Ohmae, had to have Ozawa forcibly removed from the bridge. Transferred to a destroyer then to the cruiser *Oyodo* shortly after 11:00 A.M., Ozawa remained bent on self-sacrifice. He telegraphed that he was launching a night torpedo attack on Halsey's forces with his remaining cruiser and called on Kurita, wherever he was, to join him. None of Ozawa's earlier messages from the *Zuikaku* had reached Kurita, thanks to the broken radio transmitter. But the communications gear aboard the *Oyodo,* which had served at times as a headquarters ship, was still in working order, and Ozawa's message, relayed through a Japanese communications center in Japan, caught up to Kurita about forty miles from the strait.

Kurita heard Ozawa's appeal and ignored it. He was not about to

---

*On October 25, the Japanese lost four carriers, two battleships, four heavy cruisers, one light cruiser, and five destroyers.

turn around yet again and accompany Ozawa in his pursuit of martyr-dom. At 1925, 7:25 P.M., just as he was about to enter the treacherous strait on a darkening sea, Kurita received a message from Combined Fleet headquarters. "If there is an opportunity to do so," headquarters commanded, Kurita was to make a night attack on the enemy and mop up its "remnants." This order would have been laughable, if Kurita's bleary-eyed staff had been capable of any feeling beyond numbly try-ing to stay awake. Their response can only be described as a joke; one wonders if the staffer who wrote it (probably Koyanagi) was smiling bitterly as he thought of the proper doublespeak to send back to Tokyo. At 2130, 9:30 P.M., as it passed through the strait back into the Sibuyan Sea, the Kurita fleet signaled headquarters: "We are of the opinion that the situation may offer excellent opportunity for the shore-based air force units to strike the first blow against the enemy and gain control of the air." In other words, Kurita expected to be bombed in the morning and was asking for air cover that would not be forthcoming.

The messages coming into Flag Plot aboard USS *New Jersey* in the early afternoon of the 25th were painful to read. As Halsey's fleet plunged southward, Halsey received a series of distress signals from Kinkaid in Leyte Gulf. The messages were confusing (as Kurita cir-cled and changed his mind) and, owing to the wretched bottleneck at Manus, delivered one or two hours late and out of order. The Japanese fleet was descending on Leyte Gulf! No it wasn't . . . Yes it was . . . Now it was headed north . . . "Each message tore you apart a little bit more," recalled John Lawrence, the air combat intelligence officer. "There was nothing you could do but suffer. It felt like get-ting stomped on." Lawrence had never had an easy relationship with Mike Cheek, the squirrelly, nearly mute naval intelligence man. But Cheek opened up a little to Lawrence that morning, lamenting Halsey's failure to safeguard the San Bernardino Strait.

Cheek was deeply distraught, possibly blaming himself for not pushing harder to leave the battle line at the strait while sending the carriers north. Lawrence's deputy, John Marshall, found Cheek in his stateroom, slumped over, with his head in his hands, groaning, "And it could have been the greatest victory since Trafalgar." After the giddiness of the morning, when victory had seemed so close at hand, the afternoon was a "brutal letdown," recalled Lawrence. The Department of Dirty Tricks did not realize that they had been tricked; indeed, Halsey would not admit that he had been lured by a Japanese deception, even after the Japanese revealed the plan in postwar interrogations. But Halsey's staff knew that they had been on the verge of sinking Ozawa's cripples with their great guns, only to turn around and head off on a wild-goose chase.

Halsey tried to keep his chin up. He had headed south with four battleships and a carrier task force for air cover, leaving two carrier task forces and two battleships in the north to finish off the Japanese carriers; they, too, turned south at the end of the day and escaped Ozawa's feeble counterattack. Shortly after 3:00 P.M., in a last lunge to reach Kurita before he could escape, Halsey pulled his two fastest battleships, his own flagship and the *Iowa*, out of the fleet and sent them flying—at flank speed, 35 knots—toward the San Bernardino Strait. He informed Kinkaid that they would arrive there at about 1:00 A.M. on the 26th.

Then he repaired to his office to write his own version of history. The first step was to declare victory. As night fell, he radioed CINCPAC, Admiral Nimitz: THE JAPANESE NAVY HAS BEEN BEATEN AND ROUTED AND BROKEN BY THE THIRD AND SEVENTH FLEETS. In Washington, COMINCH, Adm. Ernest King, was a little wary when Nimitz passed on Halsey's message. It didn't seem to square with the desperate cable traffic that had been flowing in all day. But, as naval historian E. B. Potter wrote, "The navy's hand was forced by MacArthur." The army general had issued his own victory communiqué. Not to be outdone by the army, the navy wanted to claim credit first. Navy Secretary James Forrestal was anxious about getting ahead of the facts, but the navy's pride was at stake. When President Roosevelt called reporters into the Oval Office on October 25 (October 26 in the Pacific), he read them a paraphrase of Halsey's victory message to Nimitz. "U.S. DEFEATS JAPANESE NAVY" bannered the *New York Times*. "President Elated. Gives News from Halsey That Foe Is 'Defeated, Damaged, Routed.'"

The headlines were not wrong—the Japanese had been dealt a terrible blow. The Japanese navy was crippled. Luck, heroism, and Japan's exhaustion had saved the day. But the triumphalism obscured the reality of Taffy Three's ordeal and Halsey's misjudgment. Despite his preemptive PR strike on MacArthur, Halsey knew he had some explaining to do with Nimitz. That night of the 25th, as the *New Jersey*'s enormous engines throbbed at maximum power for the run south, Halsey sat in his cabin writing his battle report. Halsey related a fairly straightforward account of bombing the Japanese Center Force in the Sibuyan Sea on the 24th, then came to the tricky part: explaining why he left the San Bernardino Strait unguarded. Halsey's words reveal how defensive he felt. He wrote:

> As it seemed childish to me to guard statically San Bernardino Strait, I concentrated Task Force 38 [the entire Third Fleet, battleships as well as carriers] during the night and steamed north to attack the Northern Force at dawn. I believed the Center Force had been so heavily damaged in the Sibuyan Sea that it could no longer be a serious menace to the Seventh Fleet.

Later naval historians would have a field day with Halsey's use of the words "childish" and "static." As Adm. Samuel Eliot Morison wrote, subtly twisting the knife, "[The] Battle Line might have been detached to guard San Bernardino Strait, not statically, but actively."

Shortly after midnight, a destroyer racing ahead of the *New Jersey* detected a Japanese destroyer crawling along the north coast of Samar, heading for the strait. She was the *Nowaki*, a straggler from Kurita's fleet, left behind to rescue survivors from a sinking cruiser. Halsey sent a pair of cruisers ahead to finish her off. When the *Nowaki* blew up, shortly after 1:00 A.M., Halsey could feel the shock wave fifteen miles away. Halsey watched the *Nowaki* burning on the horizon. In his memoir, he wrote, "It was the first and only surface action I saw during my entire career."

As night fell, and the moon came out, the men of the *Johnston* began to feel the cold. Shivering uncontrollably, sailor Joe Check warmed himself by urinating in his pants. Some men began to sing. Others prayed aloud. Silhouetted against the moon, a ship approached, and the men began to yell and wave. Lieutenant Welch studied the pagoda-shaped superstructure and realized that the ship was a Japanese destroyer (probably the *Nowaki*, heavily laden with men from a sunken Japanese cruiser, steaming toward the San Bernardino Strait). "She's Japanese!" Welch called out, and the men instantly quieted. The ship passed within a hundred yards and vanished in the darkness.

After midnight, the moon set, and the sea and sky plunged into blackness. Clint Carter, the Texan, had belted himself to his shipmate, Chuck Campbell, who had belted himself to a life raft that was overflowing with wounded men. Carter felt a sudden tug; then screamed, "Shark!" and crawled up Campbell's back, dragging him under. Campbell came up spluttering; the shark struck again and down they went. Fortunately, the sea monster had bitten mostly kapok. Carter had lost his life jacket, and he was bleeding badly from teeth marks on both sides of his back. But he was still alive. He was permitted to crawl into the crowded raft with the wounded.

The screams began. There would be a flash of phosphorescence, furious splashing, a cry of shock and pain. Then silence as men vanished, dragged into the depths. The sharks only lightly bit a few men, possibly because the man-eaters were sated by the sudden harvest of corpses, the hundreds of men who had died at sea within a few square miles. A shark tore off Lieutenant Welch's pants and underwear but only grazed his buttocks. For others, the wounds were more severe. The chief gunner's mate was bitten so hard on the thigh that his bones were crushed. A man whose stomach had been torn out lay in the raft begging to be put out of his misery. Someone produced a gun; it misfired. Another sailor took a knife and cut the man's throat.

The wounded were dying. Lieutenant Bechdel, his morphine worn off, was no longer singing but screaming for a painkiller; his agony ended when he perished before dawn. The burn victims, suffering horribly from the saltwater on their raw skin, cried out, then whimpered, then fell silent. Their life jackets were removed and given to the men who needed them. Friends bade farewell. "Bill, you go with Jesus now," Ed Takkunen said to his buddy from the radio shack, Bill Williams. "You go with Christ." Then he gently pushed him off the raft. The resourceful Joe Check undressed Donald Coleman, who had been mortally wounded when Gun 52 took a direct hit. Check took off Coleman's life preserver and his shirt, which could be used as a screen against the brutal sun of the coming day.

Overwhelmed by sadness, Check watched as Coleman's body slowly drifted downward into the deep.

At dawn on October 26, Halsey's ships swept east of Samar, looking for survivors. The "Jap swimmers were as thick as waterbugs," recorded Halsey in his memoir. He was eating breakfast when Bill Kitchell, his personal staff officer, "burst in and cried, 'My God Almighty, Admiral, the little bastards are all over the place! Are we going to stop and pick 'em up?'" Halsey responded, "Not until we've picked up our own boys."

Halsey picked up a few downed American fliers, but he did not find the men of the *Johnston*, or the nearly 1,000 still missing men of the other Taffy Three ships sunk in part because of his misjudgment—the *Hoel*, the *Samuel B. Roberts*, and the *Gambier Bay*. Halsey did plot the position of Japanese survivors, along with wind and tide data, so destroyers could return and pick up some prisoners for interrogation. "I ordered our destroyers, 'Bring in cooperative Nip flotsam for an intelligence sample. Non-cooperators would probably like to join their ancestors and should be accommodated,'" Halsey recalled, adding, parenthetically, "I didn't want to risk their getting ashore, where they could reinforce the [Japanese] garrison." The destroyers picked up six IJN sailors.

On the morning of October 26, the first wave of American planes found Kurita's fleet at 0834, 8:34 A.M. By 9:45, the *Yamato* had been hit twice by bombs on the bow, and the cruiser *Noshiro* was disabled by torpedoes. At 1040, 10:40 A.M., came the second wave—this time, large land-based B-24 bombers. Giant water spouts rose up all around the *Yamato*. Struck three times on the bow, she had to flood her aft compartments with 2,000 tons of water, the weight of a destroyer escort, to keep trim.

As the *Yamato* swung to avoid one stick of bombs, another bomb caught the wing of the bridge. Splinters of steel sliced into Admiral Koyanagi's right buttock. Petty Officer Koitabashi's lookout post was sprayed with shrapnel. The man to the right of him was decapitated. The man on the left was disemboweled. Koitabashi was riddled with more than twenty pieces (sixty years later, several of the pieces of the

*Petty Officer Koitabashi. After the war, a friend
painted Koitabashi (center) getting hit aboard* Yamato.

hard metal could be felt under the skin of his foot and ankle). As Koitabashi was carried off, he heard badly wounded men crying "Kill me! Kill me!" He caught sight of Admiral Kurita looking "quiet and subdued." The commander-in-chief was wearing a short-sleeved white tropical uniform. Across the bridge, Admiral Ugaki was in full dress whites. Kurita's staff wore flak jackets; Ugaki's staff wore none.

"This was the last of their attack against the Main Force. Surely we had had enough!" Ugaki wrote in his diary that night. "The enemy cleaned up the sea thoroughly, leaving nothing, with the feeling of a victor disposing of the remnant of the defeated enemy." He added a wistful note: "We also had times like that some time ago."

The next day, the *Yamato* buried twenty-nine men at sea. "I felt refreshed taking a bath after a long time," wrote Ugaki.

A kapok life jacket remains buoyant for about twenty hours. On the morning of the second day, Bill Mercer took his off and watched it sink. Broiling in the sun, the men of the *Johnston* were beginning to break down and drink saltwater. They would hallucinate, have convulsions, and die. Their visions were vivid and varied: native girls bringing tropical fruit. A case of beer. A bar just down the street. A few men saw Captain Evans. One officer announced that he wanted to join him on the mountaintop, and just swam away.

Exhaustion was taking a toll. Men would fall asleep and drift off. Some snapped to when their faces hit the water. Others stopped caring. "If you slept, you died," recalled James Johnson, a sailor. "If you took morphine, you died." Some men would do anything to live. Johnson had watched a shipmate chew through the tendon that attached his nearly severed hand to his arm. But the man had no way of stopping the bleeding, and he died anyway.

By the second night, it was every man for himself. The conversation and the prayers died away. Men who had helped the wounded onto rafts now waited for the wounded to die so they could replace them. Lieutenant Hagen had become delirious; command, such as it was, fell to Lieutenants Digardi and Welch. They could see Samar Island in the distance to the west, and with an easterly wind, Digardi had the idea of trying to sail there. He erected a tiny sail on one of the life rafts with two paddles and a shirt and asked some sailors to paddle and kick. The sail collapsed; the men gave up.

Digardi coped as best he could. When a sailor went berserk he knocked him out and tied him to the raft. (After the war, the man located Digardi and thanked him.) As they floated along, Digardi looked down and saw a group of sharks drifting in the shadow of the raft. One was huge, about fifteen to twenty feet. Digardi told Welch to look down, but motioned him to keep his mouth shut. There was no point in alerting the others.

The second night passed in a nightmare of hallucination and screams. Almost half the 270 men who had gone into the water after the *Johnston* sank had died or disappeared. As the sun rose on the third day, Bobby Chastain looked around and saw men who barely looked like men anymore. Their faces and shoulders were raw with sunburn, their lips were grotesquely swollen and blistered, and their eyes were bloodshot, dead, or haunted.

Then, as Chastain recalled, "a miracle occurred." He saw, far on the horizon, several small ships approaching. Through his badly sunburned eyes he saw a familiar and glorious sight streaming from the masts of the ships: the stars and stripes of the American flag.

The ships were LCIs, landing ships sent out by the Seventh Fleet. The navy, after initial confusion and delay, had not given up on them after all. For a moment, the men of the *Johnston* thought they were going to be killed by their own men; gunners on the bows of the ships were blazing away with machine guns. But then the men in the water realized that the gunners were shooting at circling sharks.

A voice called out from the lead ship: "Who won the World Series last year?" The answer came back: "To hell with baseball! Get us out of this water!"

Slowly, painfully, 141 survivors were pulled from the water. Most of them lay down on the deck and went to sleep. A couple of Japanese planes strafed the LCIs as they steamed back to Leyte Gulf. The men of the *Johnston* slept through the air raid.

The Battle of Leyte Gulf was over.

It had been confused, tragic, deadly, and heroic, and it is largely forgotten, though not entirely. Herman Wouk's World War II epics, *The Winds of War* and *War and Remembrance*, were inspired by the novelist's fascination with the battle (his original title, before the novel grew into two volumes and expanded to take on the entire war, was "The Gulf"). In *War and Remembrance*, Wouk's hero and main character, Pug Henry, is the captain of the battleship *Iowa* for Halsey's belated, futile dash to the south, bitterly remembered as "Bull's Run." Henry is galled by Halsey's blundering failure to guard the San Bernardino Strait. And yet, when Halsey finally does decide to plunge south at flank speed to try to catch Kurita, Wouk's hero is thrilled by the order. Wouk writes:

> by God, here was *Form Battle Line*, at long last; wrong, rash, tardy, but the thing itself! And Halsey would be right there. Pug could not keep out of his voice a flash of reluctant regard for the crazy old fighting son of a bitch.

Wouk honored, too, the brave men of Taffy Three. He has Pug Henry write in a postbattle analysis:

> The vision of Sprague's three destroyers—the *Johnston*, the *Hoel*, and the *Heerman*—charging out of the smoke and rain straight towards the main batteries of Kurita's battleships and cruisers, can endure as a picture of the way Americans fight when they don't have superiority. Our schoolchildren should know about that incident. Our enemies should ponder it.

In four days, from October 23 to October 26, the Americans had sunk four Japanese aircraft carriers, three battleships, ten cruisers, and nine destroyers. The Japanese had sunk three carriers (one light, two escort), two destroyers, and one destroyer escort. Some 13,000 men had died, most of them Japanese.* The Japanese navy was effectively finished as a fighting force. It was now nothing more than a "weapon of despair." But Japanese spirit had become a Japanese death wish, and there was still a great deal of dying to be done.

---

*There were roughly 2,800 American casualties—473 killed, 1,100 missing, and 1,220 wounded.

CHAPTER FIFTEEN

THE LAST KAMIKAZE

"Leave the Bull alone"

O N NOVEMBER 11, 1944, two weeks after the Battle of Leyte Gulf, Carnes Weeks, Halsey's doctor and wardroom morale officer, wrote his wife a letter. The *New Jersey* was at anchor at Ulithi, the coral atoll in the Pacific where men could have a drink and a breather. Halsey and his staff were finally resting for a few days after two months at sea. "The Admiral asked me to go with him alone to visit the hospital ships and see the wounded," Dr. Weeks wrote his wife, Margaret:

> God, he is something. He hates to see these poor kids and just makes himself do it. You ought to see the faces of these poor kids when he comes in a ward—even the badly burned faces, just the eyes showing. He comes in and jokes, shakes hands, tells stories, and cusses a lot about the Japs.

Halsey had to continue to play the Bull, but it was an effort for him. Heartless about picking up Japanese survivors, he was nonetheless torn up by the suffering of his own men. Visiting the wounded took some moral courage; some commanders could not bring themselves to do it. Halsey apparently revealed himself a little to Weeks—not admitting error, but at least showing his emotional side.

In the same letter home, 'Piggy' Weeks wrote: "He opens his heart to me when he and I are alone—what a wonderfully sweet character he has under his military brusqueness and boy how soft his heart is. It just [word illegible] him to hear of dead, missing, and wounded."

Halsey's confessional was brief and exceptional. He was still the lion of the wardroom. On his sixty-second birthday on October 30, his Filipino steward had made him a cake in the shape of a battleship, and he had raised a glass with his Department of Dirty Tricks. In the aftermath of the battle, Radio Tokyo was still screaming "We dare the American people to ask where Halsey is!" and Halsey declared to his staff, "If CINCPAC would let me, I'd send 'em my latitude and longitude!" But the conviviality and bluster had been forced that day. True, the Japanese had been overwhelmingly defeated. But Halsey had missed his chance for immortality. His men knew that the verdict of history on their actions would be, at best, mixed.

Halsey after the battle

Awarded a Navy Cross by Halsey for his role in the battle, chief of staff Mick Carney did not like to wear the decoration because, he told his daughter, Betty, he felt that he hadn't deserved it. There was no victory celebration in the Third Fleet. In Pearl Harbor, Halsey's carrier commander, Admiral Mitscher, gave a briefing on the battle to Admiral Nimitz at CINCPAC. The briefing lasted all of three minutes. Mitscher apparently had nothing good to say, so he said nothing. Respectful of his line commanders, sensitive to Mitscher's obvious exhaustion, Nimitz did not press. In Washington, the more volatile Ernest King, COMINCH, was feeling less forgiving. On the morning of the battle, Admiral King had paced, "blue with rage," damning Halsey for failing to guard the San Bernardino Strait, according to Adm. Joseph "Jocko" Clark, who was in King's office at the time. In November, King told Nimitz that Halsey was "tired" and should be given a "rest."

General MacArthur responded to the bungled victory with heroic hypocrisy. For the record, on October 29, MacArthur sent a gushing telegram to the commander of the Third Fleet:

WE HAVE COOPERATED WITH YOU SO LONG THAT WE ARE ACCUS-
TOMED AND EXPECT YOUR BRILLIANT SUCCESSES AND YOU HAVE
MORE THAN SUSTAINED OUR FULLEST ANTICIPATIONS X EVERYONE
HERE HAS A FEELING OF COMPLETE CONFIDENCE AND INSPIRATION
WHEN YOU GO INTO ACTION IN OUR SUPPORT.

On a copy of this telegram in MacArthur's records, in a note penciled at the bottom, is the real account of what transpired between Halsey and MacArthur. The note was written and signed by Gen. Richard Sutherland, MacArthur's chief of staff:

This follows verbal castigation of Halsey by Gen. MacArthur who repeatedly charged him with failure to execute his mission of covering the Leyte operations. When Halsey failed to get into the Battle of Leyte Gulf, thus threatening the destruction of our shipping, Gen. MacArthur repeatedly stated that Halsey should be relieved and would welcome his relief as he no longer has confidence in him.

Even so, MacArthur cut off his subordinates when they began to mock Halsey at dinner. "That's enough!" MacArthur bellowed, pounding the table for attention. "Leave the Bull alone. He's still a fighting admiral in my book."

To his credit, Halsey did not shy away from other men who had reason to scorn him. At Ulithi, he came up to Taffy Three's Adm. Clifton "Ziggy" Sprague and said, "Ziggy, I didn't know whether you would speak to me or not." Sprague replied, "Why Admiral Bill, I'm not mad at you." Halsey graciously told Sprague, "I want you to know I think you wrote the most glorious page in American naval history."

Halsey had no one, with the partial exception of Dr. Weeks, to whom he could truly unburden himself. His family ties were weak. Suffering from manic depression, Fan was unreachable, even by letter, and Halsey suffered for it. His son, Bill, was also apparently distant. In December, Dr. Weeks wrote his wife that Halsey "just got pictures of Bill's wedding—imagine! Bill has never written him— what a funny family they are and he feels it so very much."

Halsey sought consolation in other ways. In his role as sea dog, he had a well-deserved reputation for seeking a girl in every port. One of Weeks's jobs was to keep Halsey and his staff entertained off duty. "I am running a little party for the Admiral and getting some nurses from a hospital ship—God help them, the nurses I mean!" Weeks wrote his wife from Ulithi after the difficult visit to see the wounded aboard the hospital ship on November 11. A week later, Weeks wrote his wife, "The nurses were grand, good sports—they had been working very hard with the wounded and were just as ready for a break as we were." The nurses needed to be good sports. An admiral's aide to the chief of nursing aboard a hospital ship described a nurses' party with Admiral Halsey and his staff:

> After the meal, one of the celebrants flipped a live cigarette in the wastebasket, which caught fire, whereupon an officer grabbed a CO_2 bottle, stuck the cone in the basket, and quickly extinguished the flames. Then he pushed the nozzle up the dress of one of the nurses and squirted her between the legs. She let out a scream as the dry ice burned. Other schnockered

officers grabbed CO_2 bottles and started chasing nurses around the wardroom.[*]

Halsey and his men had only a few days to debauch in Ulithi. By Thanksgiving they were dodging kamikazes off the Philippines. "Yesterday we had a very severe attack by Jap planes," Weeks wrote his wife on November 27. "I have never seen anything like it so far this war—planes diving and exploding all around us." Three carriers were damaged, the *Intrepid* severely. "An instant after she was hit, she was wrapped in flames," recalled Halsey in his memoir. "Blazing gasoline cascaded down her sides; explosions rocked her; then oily black smoke, rising thousands of feet, hid everything but her bow." At first, Halsey had dismissed the kamikazes as "a sort of token terror, a tissue paper dragon." He did not believe the Japanese "for all their hari-kari traditions, could muster enough recruits to make such a corps really effective." But his disdain for the Japanese gave way to real concern as he watched his carriers burn.

Halsey's fortunes continued to worsen in mid-December when the Third Fleet sailed into a typhoon. It was a particularly vicious storm, and during the height of it, Admiral Carney had "grave doubts" that the mighty *New Jersey* would survive. "It's difficult to describe the sickening lurch of that ship when she went way over," he recalled. The enormous battleship would hang in the trough and then slowly right. The *New Jersey* was "tossed . . . as if she were a canoe," recalled Halsey. "We . . . were buffeted from one bulkhead to another; we could not hear our own voices above the uproar. What it was like on a destroyer one-twentieth the *New Jersey*'s size I can only imagine."

The typhoon, later fictionalized by Herman Wouk in *The Caine Mutiny,* was deadlier than the Japanese. Top-heavy because they

---

[*]Though Halsey claimed his nickname "Bull" had been bestowed by newspapermen, in fact he had been dubbed "Bull" by fellow officers for his conquests ashore. Carnes Weeks's son, Carnes Jr., a marine corporal, was invited to have drinks with Halsey at the St. Francis Hotel during a home leave in 1944. "When he partied, he really let himself go," Weeks recalled. "He always had a marine guard outside his door, and I was asked to stand guard there that night. Inside, I could hear him down on all fours barking like a dog with this nice lady who was his friend for the evening."

lacked ballast as they were waiting to fuel, three destroyers turned turtle and vanished, taking with them almost 800 men. Because the destroyers could have been temporarily ballasted with seawater, Halsey was later criticized by a Court of Inquiry for poor seamanship in waiting too long to abandon refueling operations. As usual, he was pressing to get after the enemy with an air strike (in support of MacArthur's landings on the island of Luzon).

Halsey was determined to find and sink the battleships that had escaped from the Battle of Leyte Gulf. In January, the Third Fleet roamed the coast of Indochina, launching air attacks, shooting up Japan's dwindling merchant fleet, but finding few significant warships. Halsey's forces sank but a single light cruiser, the *Kashii*, formerly used as a training ship and submarine headquarters.

At the end of January, Halsey was relieved by Admiral Spruance. The change of command was all part of an orderly transition, long scheduled, to rest Halsey and his staff while Spruance took over for the invasions of Iwo Jima and Okinawa. Halsey did not exactly return to headquarters wreathed in laurels; on the other hand, he was not castigated or shunned. He was denied, for the time being, a fifth star for the newly created rank of fleet admiral. Even so, Admiral King had cooled off and decided that Admiral Kinkaid was primarily to blame for the failure to watch San Bernardino Strait. Halsey's welcome-back meeting with King was only slightly awkward. The first words out of Halsey's mouth when he entered King's office were: "I made a mistake in that battle." King held up his hand. "You don't have to tell me any more. You've got a green light on everything you did." But Halsey wasn't referring to his failure to guard the San Bernardino Strait. His only "mistake," he told King, was "to turn south when the Japs [Ozawa's fleet] were right under my guns." King, no doubt recalling Nimitz's pointed "Where is Task Force 34" telegram, replied, "No, it wasn't a mistake. You couldn't have done otherwise."

That same month, when the post-typhoon Court of Inquiry blamed Halsey for "errors in judgment" in the loss of men and ships, King softened the verdict. After "errors in judgment" King inserted the phrase "from insufficient information" and changed "from a commendable desire to meet military requirements" to "firm determination to meet military requirements." Nimitz had already toned down a CINCPAC analysis of the Battle of Leyte Gulf because it was too tough on Halsey. The top brass understood that criticism of Halsey could not be allowed to creep into the public press. Halsey was the navy's hero. He could not be besmirched. The Japanese would have understood; it was all a matter of saving face.

The Japanese government responded to defeat at Leyte Gulf by declaring victory. At the end of October, Radio Tokyo reported that "Japanese forces now have complete air and sea superiority on and around Leyte." There were some inconvenient facts to be covered up. Several hundred of the thousand survivors of the *Musashi* were virtually imprisoned on an island in the Inland Sea, and the rest were formed into a naval infantry brigade to fight to the last man in defense of Manila, besieged by MacArthur's advancing army.

Admiral Kurita was beached, but in a dignified way. Under his dovish friend Adm. Shigeyoshi Inoue, vice minister of the navy, Kurita became commandant of the naval academy. As early as 1942, Inoue had started protecting naval cadets from being sent into the fleet. Inoue wanted them to be leaders in postwar Japan, not martyrs. English language, like jazz music, had been largely driven from Japanese culture, but Inoue made sure that Eta Jima cadets learned English. By installing Kurita as its head, Inoue hoped to keep Eta Jima from becoming an academy for suicide.

Kurita went home to his comfortable house in a "naval suburb" of Tokyo, where he kept an archery target in the garden and a Western sitting room for guests. Kurita's teenage daughter Shigeko was shocked to see how gaunt her father had become. Kurita refused to speak about the war and sat quietly drinking sake. Still, Shigeko was happy to have him home. Her family had been praying for his safety at the Meiji Shrine. In February, Kurita and his family moved from Tokyo to the commandant's quarters at the academy on the island of Eta Jima, in the Inland Sea across from the great naval port of Kure. They left the capital just in time. The American B-29 raids were intensifying.

* * *

Admiral Ugaki celebrated the birthday of the Emperor Meiji on November 3 with a bitter poem:

> Day of chrysanthemum brings
> Devil's cloud with enemy wings

Relieved of command, he drifted "from one farewell party to another," recalling an old adage, "Drinking after a long time dry makes a man with no job tight." Attached to the Navy General Staff without much to do, he tried to be philosophical. "Like a floating weed," he wrote, "I have to leave it to the stream."

Late November found him at the Navy Ministry in Tokyo, "feeling ashamed," he wrote, of the thin results yielded by the sacrifices at Leyte Gulf. That day, November 27, the B-29s hit Tokyo for the second time. Awakened by air raid sirens, Ugaki stood in his garden listening to the drone of bombers high in the clouds overhead. "A bomb dropped on the Togo shrine," wrote Ugaki. "It was really irritating." Experiencing domestic life for the first time in many months, he was shocked by the small rations, "a slice of funny little fish and two leaves of vegetable." He poked about in his flower garden and was "having a few drinks" when his son, Hiromitsu, who had just been commissioned a "surgeon sub-lieutenant" in the naval medical corps, came home. "Father and son at last!" he wrote. "I was very glad to see he had grown up to be a man, getting to be an officer." On December 18, Ugaki was granted, along with six other admirals, an audience with the emperor. "How can I repay such an honor?" he wondered. "My thoughts ran wild seeking ways to save the empire," he wrote on the last day of 1944, "the year of the decisive battle" that had somehow "failed to turn the tide of the war."

On that dreary New Year's Eve, Ugaki wrote, "Average people have now realized the gravity of the situation, but only too late." Indeed, a touch of cynicism was beginning to creep into the public mood. On November 8, Prime Minister Kuniaki Koiso had compared Leyte to "Tennozan" (literally, "imperial mountain"), a mythical Japanese victory. But by New Year's Day 1945, Prime Minister Koiso announced in his national radio address that the Philippine island of Luzon was now "Tennozan." Tokyoites quipped, "Koiso even seems to move mountains." After the failure of the Sho Plan, Emperor Hirohito had inquired of his ministers, "Was not the use of our warships inappropriate at Leyte Gulf?" In the stilted politeness of the throne room, such a question amounted to an imperial rebuke. And yet Hirohito was still chasing the chimera of Decisive Battle. The emperor was a victim of his own stubbornness and the deceit of the military, which continued to swallow its own propaganda; at Leyte, instruments of surrender had been prepared for General MacArthur, along with a Japanese victory communiqué to be read on the beach. Hirohito still believed, after three years of increasingly disastrous war, that one great military victory would drive the Americans to the negotiating table and force them to sue for peace. He could not see that the United States was headed in precisely the opposite direction, increasingly determined to exact an unconditional surrender.

The proper course, the emperor's advisers believed, was to bleed the Americans, without regard to Japan's sacrifice. Admiral Ugaki was a natural choice for such a mission. In February, he was summoned by "police telephone" to the home of the navy minister and given his new duties: commander of the Fifth Air Fleet, guarding Japan's southern flank. The Fifth Air Fleet was to be a suicide air force. Without a fleet, the navy was committed to human sacrifice. Production lines were devoted to turning out planes, *Kaiten* (manned torpedoes), and *Ohka* bombs (manned rocket bombs). Ugaki was thrilled with his assignment. It offered "the key to the gate of the imperial fortunes," he wrote. He would be headquartered in Japan's southern island of Kyushu, warmed by tropical currents. Ugaki was glad to get out of war-torn Tokyo. Without hot water, he recorded, his piles had become worse.

Ugaki's first mission was to mount a suicide attack on the American warships anchored at Ulithi. Some two dozen long-range, twin-engine bombers were mustered to plunge into carriers and battleships anchored at the atoll, where they were readying for the upcoming invasion of Okinawa. The night before the raid, Ugaki served an elaborate banquet for the pilots, offering blowfish, a rare delicacy, and many bottles of sake. Speeches were made, toasts were drunk, tears were shed.

But after the mission was launched in the morning, it was aborted

and the planes turned around and came home. Intelligence was reporting that the American carriers and battleships had departed
from Ulithi. It was all a mistake; the American fleet was still at its
moorings in Ulithi. But Tokyo headquarters was distracted and in an
uproar. B-29s had firebombed Tokyo that night, March 9–10, using
high winds and incendiaries to create an inferno that destroyed
261,000 homes and killed more than 100,000 people. (Japanese
cities, made of paper and wood, were eventually evacuated, but at
first the attitude was "fight, don't run." Human bucket brigades
were formed to fight firestorms.)

Ugaki dutifully sent out his bombers once again the next day.
Eleven of twenty-four planes reported engine problems (a reluctance to die was the more likely explanation) and only six reached
Ulithi. They caused mild damage to one carrier. The raid was a
"complete failure," Ugaki gloomily recorded.

But he kept sending more young men to die. The plan to thwart
the invasion of Okinawa in late March and early April was to overwhelm American defenses with waves of *Kikusuis* ("floating cherry
blossoms"), suicide planes by the hundreds. Novice pilots—all volunteer, at this stage—were "herded" by more experienced pilots toward
their targets. The assault was called *Ten-Go*—Operation Heaven.
The attacks did do great damage, battering hundreds of ships, including Admiral Spruance's flagship, the *Indianapolis* (Spruance
himself manned a fire hose). But the toll was not nearly as great as
Ugaki wished for or feverishly imagined.* If one were to believe
Ugaki's diary entries, his *Kikusuis* sank every American carrier and
battleship many times over. Again and again, Ugaki would deliriously report wildly exaggerated numbers ("confirmed" on March
21: five carriers, two battleships, one heavy cruiser, two cruisers, and
one unidentified ship sunk). Yet he would lament, "each day we try
to finish the enemy task force, and yet they can't be finished."

One senses, reading Ugaki's diary, a man becoming unhinged. He
explains to himself that he can send young men off to die "with a

---

*At Okinawa, the Japanese sunk thirty-four warships, the largest a destroyer. Another 368
ships were damaged, including eight carriers, four escort carriers, ten battleships, five
cruisers, and sixty-three destroyers.

smile" because "I had made up my mind to follow the example of those young boys some day." He went on, "I was glad to see that my weak mind, apt to be moved to tears, had reached this stage."

Ugaki's demented bloody-mindedness was shared, not universally, but widely at the upper levels of command. In April, the navy decided that the battleship *Yamato* should become a suicide ship. With its crew of over 3,000 men, the *Yamato* was to sail to Okinawa and beach there—to become a giant gun platform until her doom. Long before she reached Okinawa, American planes found the *Yamato* and her escorts. Lanced by scores of torpedoes and bombs, the mighty superbattleship began to founder. As the *Yamato* heeled over, the fleet commander, Adm. Seiichi Ito (who had studied at Yale and had opposed the war), announced, "Stop the operation," and went into his sea cabin to shoot himself. Young officers had been issued lengths of rope ("line," in maritime lingo), which they hung from their belts, so that when the time came they would resist the urge to escape and instead lash themselves to the sinking ship. In a memoir, *Requiem for Battleship Yamato*, a young ensign, Mitsuru Yoshida, described the last minutes on the bridge:

> I see the navigation officer (a commander, responsible for the operation of the ship) and the assistant navigation officer (a lieutenant junior grade, his assistant) face each other and bind themselves together.
> Knees rubbing and shoulders touching, they attempt to bind each other's legs and hips to the binnacle. . . .
> Seeing them, I naturally reach for my side, touching the line readied some time ago. That such might be the end of a special attack was something we fully foresaw.
> "What are you doing? You young ones, swim!" Chief of staff [Nobuei] Morishita strikes an angry pose, lacing his angry words with blows of his fist. He hits me from the side. I have no choice but to follow his orders and, changing my mind, throw away the line; still, my resentment does not go away.[*]

---

[*]Yoshida lived, one of 269 survivors out of 3,063 men aboard *Yamato*. A Tokyo University graduate, he worked for the Bank of Japan and died in 1979.

Yamato *under attack*

The popular slogan of the time, Yoshida recalled, was "one hundred million deaths rather than surrender." But as time went on, some young Japanese men had to be persuaded to volunteer for the special attack forces.

By late April, even the obtuse Ugaki observed that his special attack squadrons were becoming less effective. In Tokyo, Ugaki's family dependents wanted to flee the burning city. Ugaki at first told them to do their patriotic duty and stay, then relented and let them leave. His family's chief concern, at least as Ugaki expressed it in his diary, was for the protection of his military uniforms and decorations, stored at his home for safekeeping.

Ugaki himself had taken to living in a cave on Kyushu in order to avoid the American bombers. He was becoming increasingly delusional, claiming in his diary on April 13 that the *Ten* ("Heaven") Operation No. 1 "killed Roosevelt." (FDR died of a cerebral hemorrhage in Warm Springs, Georgia.) In early May, he mourned the suicide of Adolf Hitler but hoped that the Nazi leader's spirit would live on in the German people. His one relaxation was hunting and horseback riding, though he complained that the bomb craters now pitting Japan were "dangerous to the horse's legs."

At the end of May, Admiral Halsey took back command of the Big Blue Fleet from Admiral Spruance. He promptly, and unbelievably, sailed back into a typhoon. No ships were sunk, but the flight decks of two carriers buckled and the bow of a cruiser ripped off. This time, the Court of Inquiry squarely blamed Halsey. The secretary of the navy, James Forrestal, wanted to retire the commander of the Third Fleet, but he was blocked by Admirals King and Nimitz. The Bull, they argued once again, was too much of a symbol to the troops. In July, the cover of *Time* magazine showed Halsey, eyes glinting, jaw jutting, before a portrait of a giant tidal wave about to crush an ancient, bearded emperor in a silk robe with a quiver of arrows on his back. "Kill Japs," read the words below Halsey's portrait. "Kill Japs, and then kill more Japs."

Some of the troops—the fliers and sailors aboard the carriers—were beginning to ridicule Halsey. Adm. Jocko Clark, task group commander aboard the *Yorktown,* and his staff wrote a parody screenplay of a dialogue between a publicity-hound Halsey, bellowing about his plans to "rub out these yeller-bellied little monkeymen bastards," and his weary, exasperated boss Chester Nimitz. *Yorktown* poets also wrote a long epic, "Ode to the Big Wind," which included verses such as these:

> *Bull his name and bull his nature*
> *Bull his talk will always be*
> *But for me and many like me*
> *He's a perfect S.O.B.*

> *Typhoons never worry this guy*
> *Though they come from north or south*
> *Typhoons, Bah, he has one every*
> *Time he opens his mouth*

In June and July, the Third Fleet roamed up and down the coast of Japan, looking for ships to sink, but good naval targets were far and few between. The heavy work—bombing Japan's cities—was being done by Army Air Force B-29s from Guam and now Okinawa, the last bastion in Japan's chain of island defenses. The next invasion would be of Japan itself.

Admiral Nimitz intended to let Spruance command the invasion of the southernmost island, Kyushu, scheduled in November, with Halsey's fleet further offshore flying cover. King and Nimitz did not trust Halsey to handle complex amphibious operations. Halsey's fellow admirals were quietly questioning Halsey's competence. Adm. Ted Sherman, a task group commander, agreed with a fellow admiral that "Halsey has not been thinking straight lately." After the war, Admiral Clark would tell naval historian Clark Reynolds that the war had become too complicated for Bull Halsey.

"Does the enemy intend to destroy all of the cities in this country?" Admiral Ugaki wondered in his diary on June 18. The answer was yes, unless Japan surrendered unconditionally. "We could bomb and burn them until they quit," Gen. Curtis LeMay told the Joint Chiefs of Staff in Washington. The only hitch was that by October he would "run out of cities to burn." By mid-August, LeMay's XXI Bomber Command was scheduling "burn jobs" on no fewer than sixteen urban-industrial areas per "operational" day (usually every three or four days).

Ugaki was preparing himself for the apocalypse by becoming a "nihilist," he wrote in his diary, in order to "clear the mind." In July, he proudly read in the *Naval Gazette* that he had been awarded the First Order of the Sacred Treasure for his achievements, and he inspected secret underground hangars where the navy was building thousands of suicide boats for the American invasion. He was informed that he was now commander of all kamikaze planes—but ordered not to fly them. The empire was holding back its *tokko* forces for the final battle, *Ketsu-Go,* the "Decisive Operation."

Japan was, in effect, preparing for mass suicide. The scale of the carnage is appalling to contemplate. The battle for Okinawa had cost

12,000 American lives and 200,000 Japanese soldiers and civilians. The death toll for the Battle of Kyushu alone would be many times that. The Japanese had more than 7,000 planes hidden in caves and tree groves. According to historian Richard Frank, the Japanese planned to "saturate the invasion fleet with as many kamikazes in three hours as they had sent against Okinawa in three months." Schoolgirls, organized into the "Patriotic Citizens Fighting Corps," were given bamboo spears and practiced bayoneting posters of Franklin Roosevelt and Winston Churchill.

Japan had lost close to three million people. The country was facing mass famine; as many as 10 million people were suffering from serious malnutrition. The emperor and Japan's war leaders knew that the war was lost, but they did not know how to end it. One faction wanted to secretly negotiate a peace through the Soviet Union, but another group clung to the hope that Operation *Ketsu* would be so deadly that the Americans would agree not to occupy Japan or end the imperial system. American code breakers watched the Japanese heading down both tracks, trying to enlist the Soviets with peace feelers while at the same time preparing for Armageddon. Armed with their ULTRA intelligence, it is no wonder that the Americans saw a potential trap, another Pearl Harbor—that the Japanese would try to lull them with diplomacy while girding for a violent surprise.

As ever in this war between uncomprehending nations, mistrust led to escalation. President Harry Truman ended the war—and launched a new and fearful age—by dropping two atomic bombs, on Hiroshima (August 6) and Nagasaki (August 9). Both cities were flattened in blinding flashes. In the meantime, on August 8, the Soviet Union entered the war against Japan. Finally, Hirohito stopped his bitter hand-wringing. The emperor was worried about his jewels, literally. If the Americans invaded Japan, they might capture the imperial regalia—a sword, jewel, and mirror that were symbols of 2,600 years of *kokutai*, the Japanese polity of divine imperial family and loyal subjects. Hirohito determined to surrender unconditionally, if the Americans would allow the emperor to carry on as divine ruler.

It was a close thing. The Americans rejected an initial secret peace offering that would have preserved considerable imperial authority during the occupation. The Americans demanded complete subordi-

nation of the emperor. During these delicate negotiations, Admiral
Onishi, the creator of the kamikaze units, burst into a meeting of
Japan's war rulers on August 13 to deliriously cry, "If we are prepared to sacrifice 20,000,000 Japanese lives in a special attack effort,
victory will be ours!" When a Japanese diplomat explained to the
emperor that he risked losing his throne, the emperor reluctantly accepted the American terms. Meanwhile, hotheaded army officers
were plotting a coup to kill all the emperor's advisers. The last gasps
of madness fizzled, in part because the army officers searching the
palace could not find and destroy the recording of Hirohito's surrender speech. On August 15, Japanese listening to their radios at noon
heard a voice they had never before heard, the sacred Crane, the
Showa Emperor—the reedy, thin voice of Hirohito.

His speech was beautiful, if, in parts, a little mind-boggling. He
never used the word surrender. He acknowledged, with breathtaking
understatement, that "the war situation has developed not necessarily
to Japan's advantage." But he told his people they would have to "bear
the unbearable" and "endure the unendurable" and lay down their
arms to avert not just the "ultimate collapse and obliteration of the
Japanese nation" but also "the total extinction of human civilization."

Hirohito's subjects listened, and almost all obeyed. There was very
little armed resistance against the Americans after Hirohito's speech.
In Tokyo, commanders disarmed and took the propellers off aircraft
to prevent fanatics from seizing them. Many military men tried to
cover up their complicity in Japan's defeat or destroy evidence of
atrocities that might be used in war crimes trials. For many days after
the emperor's speech, it was sardonically said, the sky over Tokyo was
black with the smoke of burning documents. Some officers turned
their shame and anger on themselves. Hundreds committed suicide,
some in the painful, traditional way of *hara-kiri* (literally, belly-
cutting). Admiral Onishi, the kamikaze creator, wrote a haiku:

> *Refreshed,*
> *I feel like the clear moon*
> *After a storm*

Then he slit his abdomen and stabbed himself in the chest and throat.

* * *

Admiral Ugaki listened to the emperor's speech at an airbase on Kyushu, where he was preparing for *Ketsu-Go*. Because of static, he had trouble hearing the emperor's words, "but I could guess at most of it," he wrote in his August 15, 1945, diary entry, his last. "I've never been so ashamed of myself," he wrote.

Ugaki had already decided that he would lead the last kamikaze mission. His plan was to "ram enemy vessels at Okinawa." He decided he was not guilty of insubordination, not exactly ("we haven't yet received the cease-fire order," he rationalized). At 1600, 4:00 P.M., he drank a last toast with his staff, stripped his dark green uniform of badges of rank, and picked up the short samurai sword given him by Admiral Yamamoto. At the airfield, eleven *Suisei* ("Comet") dive-bombers had been lined up. Their two-man crews, with Rising Sun headbands affixed, were standing at attention. Ugaki protested that he only wanted five planes to go with him, but the commander of the unit insisted on accompanying Ugaki "at full strength."

Ugaki turned to the pilots. "Will you all go with me?" he asked.

Ugaki's last flight

The flight crews did not hesitate. "Yes, sir!" they shouted, raising their right hands.

A small crowd had gathered. Among the curious was Hiroshi Yasunaga, the floatplane pilot with Kurita's fleet who had survived Leyte Gulf and was now a reconnaissance pilot, temporarily but fortuitously grounded because of tuberculosis. Yasunaga watched as Ugaki tried to climb up on the wing of a plane. The kamikaze commander seemed a little plump, Yasunaga thought. He stifled a snicker when a noncommissioned officer was summoned to give Ugaki a shove from the rear to boost him into the rear seat.

Ugaki saluted his officers and turned to salute the crowd. Yasunaga and three of his fellow pilots refused to return the salute. They believed that Ugaki should have chosen to die alone and not take twenty-two young men with him.

The planes roared off against a setting sun. Three later returned with "engine trouble." At 1924, 7:24 P.M., as darkness was settling over Japan, Ugaki's last message was received. He was going to "ram into the arrogant American ships," he vowed, "displaying the real spirit of a Japanese warrior. . . . The emperor Banzai!"

Less than fifteen minutes later, at about 7:40 P.M., the crew of *LST 296* was "unloading foodstuffs" but mostly drinking beer at the island of Iheyajima off Okinawa when they heard aircraft engines. Some seven or eight planes came around the small island. As jazz music blared over the PA aboard *LST 296*, a few men waved and threw beer cans. Then the planes opened fire with machine guns and someone yelled, "They're Japs! Kamikazes!" Lights were doused and men ran to their antiaircraft guns.

All of the kamikazes were shot down or crashed into the sea. In the morning, the men of *LST 296* found the smoldering cockpit of one of the Japanese planes, crumpled upside down on the beach. It held three men, not the usual two. The third man was dressed in a dark green uniform. His head was crushed and his right arm was missing. A small sword lay by his side. Soldiers came and tied ropes around the feet of the dead men and dragged them out of the cockpit using a jeep. Without ceremony, the corpses were buried in the sand.

*   *   *

It is likely that Admiral Kurita heard and felt the atomic blast, and he may have seen the mushroom cloud rising over Hiroshima, some twenty miles north of the island of Eta Jima. The naval academy was partly sheltered by a small mountain, and the prevailing winds blew the radiation away. Kurita had long ago turned his back on the war. He was training his academy graduates to rebuild Japan. Some fifty Eta Jima cadets had been aboard the *Yamato* before her suicide mission in April; Kurita had ordered the youngsters removed (over their protests) from the battleship.

As commandant of Eta Jima, Kurita stressed "moral education." With his scholarly hand, Kurita took his brush and wrote, with elegant calligraphy in the ancient style, these five reflections for each cadet to ponder every night:

> *Hast thou not acted against sincerity?*
> *Hast thou not felt ashamed of thy words and deeds?*
> *Hast thou not lacked vigour?*
> *Hast thou exerted all possible efforts?*
> *Hast thou not been slothful?*

On September 23, 1945, Kurita gave the last address to the cadets as Eta Jima was formally closed. "He told us, 'You will be the light of rebuilding the empire,'" recalled Manabu Yoshida, who graduated in the Imperial Naval Academy's last class that day.

In his memoirs, Halsey wrote that Commander Moulton interrupted his breakfast on the morning of August 15 to show him the transcript of President Truman's proclamation of victory. "Yippee!" Halsey yelled and pounded on the shoulders of his staff. His chief of staff, Admiral Carney, recalled that he and Halsey actually learned of Japan's surrender the night before, as they were on deck watching a film starring swimming champion Esther Williams. A messenger whispered in Halsey's ear that U.S. Army radio in Europe had picked up word of the Japanese surrender. Halsey made a "derogatory and unprintable" remark, remembered Carney, and said, "Let's just watch the picture."

Halsey disapproved of the atom bomb. He thought it was unnecessary; he had predicted in midsummer that Japan was a house of cards that would collapse by October. Halsey was disappointed that the surrender allowed Hirohito to retain his throne. The Third Fleet had been forbidden to bomb the emperor's palace in Tokyo "because somebody had some pantywaist idea about not knocking off the emperor," recalled Carney.

On August 27, for the second time since he had been an ensign nearly forty years before, Halsey steamed into Tokyo Harbor. Back in 1908, the Great White Fleet had been greeted by the legendary Admiral Togo. This time Halsey, at the head of the mightiest fleet in history, was greeted by a shabby Japanese destroyer, her gun muzzles pointed down, breeches open, torpedo tubes empty. Two Japanese officials came aboard. One was Captain Otani—Kurita's old operations officer, now assigned to the Navy General Staff. Carney recalled that Otani looked like "a caricature of a treacherous Japanese brute." (The other official, the port commander of Yokosuka, looked like "Bugs Bunny," according to Carney.) Before deigning to meet his Japanese supplicants, Halsey required them to take a shower and relieved them of their ceremonial swords. When MacArthur later agreed to allow the Japanese officers to keep their sidearms—just as Grant had done for Lee's army at Appomattox—Halsey was appalled. He told MacArthur that the Japanese, unlike the Confederates, had not been "an honorable foe." MacArthur, who rarely modified his stances to suit anyone, backed down and changed the order.

Halsey mistrusted the Japanese to the end. After the formal cessation of hostilities on August 15, he ordered his air patrols to keep watch for suicide planes and "shoot them down," as he put it, "in a friendly way." He arranged to have American submarines meet Japanese submarines at sea to disarm them and bring them into port.*

When Halsey went ashore at the Japanese base at Yokohama, he was revolted, he recalled, by the filth and the size of the rats. But Carney recalled that he was surprised by the deference of the Japanese they

---

*According to a story passed on to Sen. John McCain by his father, a World War II sub captain, the crew of one American sub was shocked to board a Japanese sub and find all of the men dead by their own hands.

met—old men bowing and young boys giving them the "V" sign. Halsey and his men could not resist a sophomoric celebration. They ordered the best meal they could find at one of the only Tokyo hotels still standing and, when the check came, Halsey signed "Hirohito."

The formal surrender ceremony on September 2, aboard the "veranda deck" of the battleship *Missouri*, was carefully rehearsed. Halsey signaled the destroyer fetching the Japanese delegation not to offer coffee or cigarettes or any other courtesy. Nimitz, who had earlier issued a directive banning all racial slurs (with Halsey clearly in mind), countermanded Halsey's order.

A table had been set up by the turret of a 16-inch gun. Senior American and Allied officers, standing erect, some in dress uniforms, some in workaday khakis, crowded around. The Japanese foreign minister, Mamoru Shigemitsu, who was to sign for the emperor, seemed to procrastinate. He fiddled with his hat, dropped his cane, shuffled papers, fumbled for his pen. Standing a few feet away, Halsey seethed.

Nimitz accepts Japan's surrender

He later told MacArthur, "I wanted to slap him and tell him, 'Sign, damn you, sign!'" ("Why didn't you?" asked MacArthur.)

But at last the deed was done, and MacArthur nudged Halsey and whispered, "Start 'em now." "Aye, aye sir!" said Halsey and gave the prearranged signal. Before long, waves of B-29s and assorted navy bombers and fighters by the hundreds were roaring overhead, lest the Japanese forget what they had been up against. According to Carney, Halsey's staff expected one of the Japanese generals to commit *hara-kiri* right there. ("We brought Kodachrome film just in case," recalled Carney.)

There was one more mission remaining for Halsey. In Washington over the spring, Halsey had been asked by a reporter if the emperor's palace was a target. "No," replied Halsey, though he allowed a B-29 might hit it "by mistake." He hoped not; he added, "I'd hate to have them kill Hirohito's white horse because I want to ride it."

In response to his flippancy, Halsey had been sent bridles, blankets, saddles, lariats, even spurs by various chambers of commerce and sheriff's offices around the United States. "My cabin in the *Missouri* began to look like a tack room," Halsey recalled.

Sure enough, when Halsey arrived to inspect the American occupation troops in Tokyo, there was a white horse—not *the* white horse, Halsey recorded, but a reasonable facsimile, if a little swayback. Halsey gamely climbed aboard and grinned for the photographers. In the photograph, he is trying to look jaunty, but he looks oddly sepulchral. He had been wasted by the war he won.

WHY THEY FOUGHT

O N OCTOBER 15, 1945, Halsey returned home to a hero's welcome. He stood "rigid, silent, alone" on the veranda deck of his last flagship, the battleship USS *South Dakota*, as she passed beneath the Golden Gate Bridge. According to a newspaper account, Halsey raised a gold-striped arm to wave, and cheers erupted along the span, jammed with spectators. "To hell with standing at attention!" yelled a sailor, lined up with his mates on the bow. The homeward-bound swabbies began wildly cheering and waving. On deck, the band played "There'll Be a Hot Time in the Old Town Tonight."

Halsey's victory tour took him to San Francisco, Los Angeles, Indianapolis, St. Louis, Boston, and Philadelphia (but not New York, Chicago, or Washington—the more senior, if less celebrated, Admiral Nimitz had already paraded through those cities). Halsey was showered in praise and ticker tape and presented with a silver tea service in his hometown of Elizabeth, New Jersey. In December, Halsey was given his typhoon-delayed fifth stripe and made a fleet admiral. It was mostly a gesture by the top brass; Halsey had already announced his retirement. "My only fear," Halsey wrote a friend, "is that the extra stripe is going to interfere with my drinking arm."

Halsey suffered from postwar letdown. It was a malady common to victorious generals and admirals. The tightly controlled Admiral Nimitz "at length came to terms with the problem, but it killed Admiral King," wrote naval historian E. B. Potter. Halsey's great friend and carrier task force commander Adm. John "Slew" McCain had been the first victim. The day of the cease-fire, August 15, McCain's chief of staff, Capt. John Thach, found McCain lying in his bunk in his sea cabin. "I feel lost," McCain confessed. "I don't know what to do. I know how to fight, but now I don't know whether I know how to relax or not. I am in an awful let down. I do feel bad." McCain had wanted to go home and skip the surrender ceremony, but Halsey persuaded him to stay. The day afterward McCain flew home to California, and the next day he died of a heart attack.*

Halsey drank too much. As a fleet admiral, he was attended to by a yeoman whose chief duty appeared to be refilling his glass with scotch. Remembering happy days at St. Anthony Hall, he took a job raising money for the University of Virginia, but he was remarkably unsuccessful at it, considering his hale-fellow gifts. He was bored. Life at home with Fan was not easy. Suffering from mania, she talked constantly and often put him down. He, in turn, was abrupt with her. In Charlottesville, a visiting naval commander, A. K. Murray, who had been sent to paint Halsey's portrait, recalled an awkward scene. "Did I ever tell you," Fanny said, "about how you should never discount the power of women in the navy?" Halsey cut in, "Oh for God's sake, don't tell him that one." Mrs. Halsey ignored her husband and launched into a long story about wearing a low-cut dress and going for a walk at night in the garden with Admiral King, in order to manipulate him to advance the career of another officer.

In the summer of 1948, Halsey published his memoirs, *Admiral Halsey's Story* as an eight-part series in *The Saturday Evening Post*. His version of the Battle of Leyte Gulf, self-serving and defensive, was sure to cause trouble. Admiral King rebuked him for his criticism of other officers, particularly his implicit criticism of King for allowing a divided command. Halsey's treatment of Kinkaid was shabby. In an offhand way, he blamed the Seventh Fleet commander for Taffy Three's rude surprise by Kurita's fleet. "I wondered how Kinkaid had let 'Ziggy' Sprague get caught like this," Halsey wrote.

Kinkaid was incensed. Having finished with Halsey's portrait, Commander Murray went to paint Kinkaid's picture and mentioned

---

*In 1954, Halsey dedicated a ship named after McCain, but broke down giving a speech and couldn't continue. Afterward, he encountered McCain's sixteen-year-old grandson (now Senator) John McCain. "Boy, do you drink?" asked Halsey. "Er, no," said McCain, eyeing his mother. "Bring this young man a glass of bourbon!" Halsey commanded the waiter.

Halsey's *Saturday Evening Post* article. Kinkaid became so angry that he refused to leave his office for lunch or answer the telephone. An aide found him lighting one cigarette from the last as he furiously paced about. Kinkaid's ire festered until he finally wrote a lucid and fairly persuasive rebuttal to Halsey that appeared in a book by the *New York Times*'s military correspondent, Hanson Baldwin, in 1955.

The Battle of Leyte Gulf haunted Halsey. In late 1947, *Life* magazine, then in its heyday, ran an unflattering article, read by millions, entitled "Bull's Run" ("Did a Japanese Blunder Save an American Army from a Halsey Mistake?"). Halsey could not escape second-guessing even in private settings. At a wedding in Honolulu, Halsey ran into his old staff officer, Harris Cox, who was still stewing over the failure to guard San Bernardino Strait. "Admiral, you made a big mistake," said Cox, who may have been emboldened by a cocktail or two. Halsey was so shocked by Cox's blunt accusation that he dropped his cigarette and started a small fire in the couch where he was sitting.

Only once, and then somewhat elliptically, did Halsey concede that he should have guarded the strait. In 1953, he confessed to Admiral Mitscher's biographer, Theodore Taylor, "I wish that Spruance had been with Mitscher at Leyte Gulf and I had been with Mitscher at the Battle of the Philippine Sea." In other words, Halsey acknowledged, he had been bold where caution was called for, and Spruance had been cautious where boldness was called for.

He kept a running battle going with the greatest of naval historians, Samuel Eliot Morison. During the war, Morison had moved from ship to ship while writing the navy's official wartime history, and after Leyte Gulf, the historian (who had been given the rank of captain) showed up aboard the *New Jersey*. Morison was a haughty Harvard Brahmin, and Halsey found him tiresome. "He went to your college," Halsey told John Lawrence. "You take care of him." Morison may have felt snubbed; in any case, Halsey always suspected that Morison harbored a "personal animosity" toward him. In 1951, Morison irked Halsey by declaring in a lecture that Halsey had "blundered" at Leyte Gulf. Then in 1958, Halsey was apoplectic when Morison's volume on Leyte verged on snideness. "Ham Dow came in to see me last Friday and we discussed a son-of-a-bitch named Morison," Halsey wrote Mick Carney. "From his book, 'Leyte,' it is apparent to me that it had got to be answered in some way, or I and my staff are down in history as dubs. I'm not willing to do this without showing my claws." To Rollo Wilson, Halsey wrote, "My idea is to get the son-of-a-bitch's cajones in a vise."

Carney restrained him. "My dear Admiral Bill," he wrote back, any attempt to hit back at Morison, a "widely acclaimed" historian, was likely to "boomerang." After many more such letters back and forth, Halsey finally cooled off.*

With little to do, in declining health, Halsey was living in New York in a grand Park Avenue apartment, summering on Fishers Island, and being chauffered in a Cadillac with a five-star admiral's flag flying from the bumper. But he was no longer living with Fan, who had moved to the West Coast and was increasingly under supervisory medical care.

His consolation was nostalgia. He visited the set of *The Gallant Hours*, originally named "Admiral Halsey's Story," depicting Halsey's heroic turnaround of the battle at Guadalcanal in 1942. By now the star, Jimmy Cagney, looked more like Halsey than the old admiral, who limped with a cane and wore thick eyeglasses for his cataracts. Halsey's happiest moment came in May 1957 when he joined all of the surviving top U.S. naval commanders from World War II at Annapolis for a celebration called Operation Remember. Halsey straightened when the Brigade of Midshipmen passed in review, on the parade ground where "Pudge" Halsey had braced almost six decades earlier.

Halsey's navy had vanished into the mists. It is revealing that after Halsey returned to the United States in 1945, he had denounced the atomic bomb as a cruel and unnecessary tool of war, blaming not only the politicians who decided to use it, but the scientists who made

---

*Halsey won a measure of redemption after he died from the release of a series of working papers from a U.S. War College analysis of the Battle of Leyte Gulf. The study, commissioned after the war and never completed, faulted Halsey for not guarding the San Bernardino Strait. But underlying documents suggested that Admiral Oldendorf's fleet, returning from Surigao Strait, did have the firepower to defeat Kurita within the narrow confines of Leyte Gulf, though the battle would have been closely fought.

it. Halsey was railing against inhumanity, but also against modernity, against a world in which there would be no place for a sea dog like Bill Halsey.

When the Federation of American Scientists protested Halsey's remarks and demanded a disavowal, Admiral Nimitz had to soothingly step in and say, "I hope that Admiral Halsey's clarifying press statement will inform the public of his real intentions in this matter, and that the scientists will continue to accept him as the heroic, indomitable naval leader he is."

After Halsey died, at the age of seventy-six, on August 16, 1959, in his sleep while he was vacationing at Fishers Island, it was Admiral Nimitz who stood at the head of his casket as he was buried at Arlington National Cemetery. Nimitz had not forgotten that when the Japanese were riding high after Pearl Harbor, it had been Halsey who damned defeatism and demanded to sail in harm's way.

Halsey was buried with full military honors, lying in state in Bethlehem Chapel at the National Cathedral. His flag-draped casket was placed on a caisson drawn by six white horses. Halsey's son, William III, had wondered if maybe his father wouldn't have preferred a more modest ceremony. No, replied Mick Carney, only a state funeral would do. He was not being grandiose. Halsey had become the nation's admiral, the embodiment of American energy and can-do-ism, a bit reckless and crude, to be sure, but dominating and lionhearted.

In the impoverished, antimilitarist world of postwar Japan, there was not much work for former admirals of the defunct Imperial Japanese Navy. One former flag officer eked out a living as a laborer on a railroad. Some turned to religion: Yasugi Watanabe, Yamamoto's "Staff Officer for Chess" who had mournfully walked behind the C-in-C's caisson, became a Buddhist priest. Mitsuo Fuchida, who led the first wave of planes against Pearl Harbor, became a Christian missionary.

Takeo Kurita became a scrivener. With his cultivated, perfect brush-strokes, he was able to get work copying documents in Japanese. His strong, supple hands were also put to use as a masseur for paying clients. He grew vegetables. He scrounged for wood. "He never complained," recalled his daughter Shigeko Terada. As a naval officer on home leave, he had worn kimonos. Now the family kimonos were sold for a few yen and Kurita wore working clothes.

He did not miss the sea, his daughter said. He watched baseball and sumo wrestling on TV and practiced archery in the garden and still, from time to time, engaged in ancient sword-fighting with *kendo* sticks. He played mah-jongg with his grandchildren and indulged them when they jumped on the sofa. "He taught us games. He was very gentle and very precise," said his granddaughter, Kazuko Naoe. He had no interest in politics, and "never talked about the war. He had a rule," said Shigeko. He told her he wished to leave no war records and no diary.

Kurita liked to drink: hot water in his whiskey before dinner, and more whiskey after dinner. He liked small hors d'oeuvres, bamboo shoots and soy sauce. He had a sweet tooth (his favorite was sweet bean cake), which his family tried to indulge when there was enough money. But mostly he liked to sip whiskey and sake—he preferred a brand of sake called Eta Jima, after the island home of the naval academy. He always sat stiff, straight-backed when he imbibed.

Over time, books and articles began appearing speculating on his actions at Leyte Gulf, the "mysterious retreat," as some called it. "Father never mentioned them," recalled Shigeko. "But we knew he suffered." Once, she heard him mutter, "I want to go somewhere else." For years, as he silently drank his scotch or sake, Kurita tried to work through in his mind what he had done and not done during those sleepless nights and days on the bridge of the *Yamato*. From time to time, he broke his silence. His remarks, which evolved over time, suggest that he slowly, painfully, came to acknowledge and accept his true motivations.

In 1954, Kurita granted a brief interview to the journalist Masanori Ito, later the author of a widely read book *The End of the Imperial Japanese Navy*. "His attitude seems to have been, 'A defeated general should not talk about his battles,'" wrote Ito. Kurita was "taciturn" but apologetic. He told Ito that he had made a mistake by turning around and not continuing with his attack on Leyte

Gulf. "At that time, I believed it was the best thing to do," Kurita told Ito. "In thinking about it since that time, I have concluded that my decision may have been wrong. I had been given orders and, as a military man, I should have carried them out."

He blamed the stress of staying awake for three days under frequent attack. "My mind was extremely fatigued," he said. "It probably should be called a 'judgment of exhaustion.'" The telegram locating Halsey's task force was "unconfirmed," as Kurita gingerly put it, and in any case, "his carriers were 100 miles away. No matter how much we pursued we could not engage his force. It was a mistake on my part to think that we could. The destruction of enemy aircraft carriers was a kind of obsession to me, and I fell victim to it." The journalist Ito ventured that thousands of lives had been spared because Kurita had not entered Leyte Gulf. From that perspective, wasn't his decision "fortunate"? The admiral, Ito wrote, "replied simply, 'Yes, I suppose that could be a point.'"

Ito asked Kurita's opinion of the decision by the C-in-C, Adm. Soemu Toyoda, to stay at headquarters in Tokyo and not come down to join in the last-ditch fight. "To these questions," Ito wrote, "Admiral Kurita remained silent and merely smiled a wry smile."

Kurita did volunteer one remark: "I was, so to speak, the pitcher of the losing team." To Ito, he said, "You appear to be fond of statistics. Well, my fleet holds the world's record for number of air attacks sustained. *Yamato* alone was the target of nineteen such attacks during the Leyte operation."

Kurita soon regretted the interview and retreated back into silence. Twice a year, he would make a pilgrimage to Yasukuni Shrine to pay homage to his dead comrades. In 1966, when Admiral Ozawa lay dying, Kurita went to his bedside and held his hand. Ozawa gripped Kurita's hand and wouldn't let go. Ozawa said nothing, Kurita later recalled, but tears streamed down his face.

Kurita befriended a younger former naval officer, Jiro Ooka, who had been in the last graduating class at Eta Jima in 1945. Ooka, along with two other classmates from Eta Jima, visited Kurita every two months. "He used to open a new bottle of Johnnie Walker Black and enjoyed drinking it straight," recalled Ooka. "He looks so severe in his photo, but he broke into a smile when he was with us."

One autumn day in 1970, Kurita said, "all of a sudden, 'Ooka, you should write my biography. I do not trust magazine reporters and writers, but I will tell you everything.'" Kurita began to retract the story he had told journalist Ito sixteen years before. It was not true, he said, that he had misjudged at Leyte Gulf because of fatigue. "Ah, that," he said, when Ooka raised the subject. "Ito made me say it in that way." Kurita "smiled a bitter smile," Ooka recorded. "In a war," said Kurita, "you don't get tired. If you make a mistake in decision-making because you did not sleep three or four days, then you are not qualified to be the commander of a fleet. I did not make mistakes."

Kurita was all injured warrior pride with his former student. He insisted that his decisions during the battle were his alone. He related the story of the mysterious (and phony) wireless telegram. "A telegram arrived," Kurita told Ooka. "There was a task force in the north. . . . We could catch them if we were within thirty nautical miles northeast. I thought it was only natural to go fight against the stronger forces. The ones in the south were small fries." Ooka interjected that "there have been theories that the telegram did not exist or was a telegram sent by the U.S. side." Kurita bridled. The telegram, he said, was from Adm. Gunichi Mikawa, the commander of the Southwest Area Fleet in Manila, who had been his classmate at Eta Jima. Mikawa was giving him the chance to "die honorably," said Kurita.

Kurita was entering his ninth decade. It was time for him to face up to reality, that the telegram was a fiction. He couldn't bring himself to admit the truth to his former students. But at least once, he opened up in a more honest way. Sometime before he died (in 1977, at age eighty-seven), Kurita spent an afternoon with Seiichiro Tokoi, who hailed from Kurita's hometown of Mito and had attended the same middle school. Tokoi had been an Eta Jima graduate and for many years a city assemblyman. In 2004, Tokoi recalled a visit with Kurita:

> I wanted to know what happened at Leyte Gulf because he never really talked about it. He liked sake, so I visited him bringing two bottles with me each time. The first two times,

Kurita-san kept silent and did not answer my question. He was a quiet man and of very strict manners. He would drink a lot, but in the same position with his back always straight.

On the third visit, Tokoi brought some Eta Jima sake. He said to Kurita that General MacArthur had already landed when Kurita was descending on Leyte Gulf, so what good would it have done to sink some empty transport ships? And if Admiral Halsey's carriers had turned around and "caught your fleet, that could have been a real disaster," added Tokoi. That was the reality, said Tokoi. "Wasn't it?"

Kurita replied, "Tokoi-kun," using the informal diminutive "kun," "I could not bear losing 80,000 lives by having the joint fleet completely destroyed."

Finally, it seems, the real story had come out. Kurita exaggerated the potential loss of life—20,000 to 30,000 fatalities are probably closer to the death toll if all his remaining ships had been sunk. But the point was the same. In the end, Kurita had not been willing to sacrifice his men in a futile gesture of nobility. The motto of Kurita's fleet, Masanori Ito wrote, was "fight bravely, but die not in vain." That is a good credo for any navy, and Kurita had been faithful to it.

Kurita's comrades could never admit the actual reason for the "mysterious retreat," even after Kurita died. At his memorial service at the shrine to Admiral Togo in Tokyo on March 11, 1978, officer after officer rose and praised Kurita as a "seaman of seamen." But none honored him for his humaneness, as a commander who chose not to foolishly waste the lives of his men in a grand but empty act of *bushido*.

In the final volume of his history of the Second World War, Winston Churchill tried to make sense of Kurita's decision to turn around at Leyte Gulf. "It may well be that [his] mind had become confused by the pressure of events," wrote Churchill, who was never one to turn away from a fight. But then, with the knowingness of someone who had faced enemy fire and known defeat, Churchill added, "Those who have endured a similar ordeal may judge him."

Churchill's question can be fairly asked about Evans, Ugaki, and

Halsey as well. Who can know what it is really like to stand, bone-weary, on the bridge of a ship in action, responsible for hundreds if not thousands of lives, unsure of the enemy's strength and where-abouts, yet forced to make fatal decisions?

In any culture, there are warriors who meet timeless and univer-sal standards of courage and resolve, who do not seem to need to think or ponder or question—who know, instinctively, when to lay their lives, and those of their men, on the line. That is not to say their judgment is always correct, just that their bravery cannot be denied.

Ernest Evans did not hesitate. His posthumous Medal of Honor citation begins:

> For conspicuous gallantry and intrepidity at the risk of his life above and beyond the call of duty as Commanding Officer of the USS JOHNSTON, in action against major units of the enemy Japanese Fleet during the Battle off Samar on October 25, 1944 . . .

The citation goes on to describe how Evans was the first to lay smoke, to attack the heavier Japanese ships, to fire his torpedoes. It uses words like "undaunted" and "unhesitating," "gallant," and "in-domitable courage" and "brilliant professional skill." The medal ci-tation concludes, "His valiant fighting spirit throughout this historic battle will endure as an inspiration to all who served with him."

That was true; sixty years later, most of the twenty-five or so sur-vivors of the *Johnston* spoke reverently of their captain as a brave and great hero. And yet a few asked, with some discomfort and usu-ally not for the record: Did he really have to turn back again and again to attack the Japanese fleet? Wasn't there some way he could have escaped with honor to live to fight again another day? In the battle off Samar, one of the three destroyers (the *Heerman*) and three of the four destroyer escorts survived the action. Some of the fellows, recalled Ed Takkunen, a member of the hard-fighting crew of Gun 55, thought that Evans went "beyond the call of duty." Evans "pushed way too much," said Robert Sochor, who was one of the last men to see Evans as the *Johnston* was sinking. The two men passed as the ship was heeling over; Sochor was scrambling to abandon ship and Evans, bloodied and his uniform in tatters, had left his post on the fantail and seemed to be heading back to the abandoned bridge. According to Sochor, Evans's face was "blank—he was just staring with a bewildered look." Possibly, Evans was in shock from loss of blood and three hours of unrelenting stress. Perhaps he was not sure how to die.

Matome Ugaki was too sure. Among aging veterans of the Imperial Japanese Navy, Ugaki was not revered. It might have been perfectly honorable for him to take his own life at the end of the war (estimates vary, but at least 500 officers committed *hara-kiri*). But in the opinion of most veterans, Ugaki should not have taken twenty-two others with him on a futile last kamikaze mission after the emperor had called on his subjects to lay down their arms. "This is a delicate question," said Adm. Manabu Yoshida, the head of the IJN alumni association. "In my personal opinion, he shouldn't have taken the youngsters with him. He defied an order from the emperor."

Ugaki was willful. Yet even Ugaki's decision was born of deep shame, disillusionment, and possibly, by the end, a touch of madness. Ugaki was a kind of apotheosis of the sickened, suicidal militarism that ruined Japan. It is hard to exaggerate how deeply the psychosis penetrated Japanese society. In October 1943, 130,000 university students were inducted into the military en masse at a rally at the Meiji Stadium in Tokyo. As they stood in the drizzle, shouldering rifles for the first time, each school group chanted, "Naturally, we don't expect to return alive."

Takeo Kurita is harder to judge. Defying an order and possibly embracing a bogus excuse to justify his actions are grave acts in any military. Kurita could not admit until the end of his life, and then only privately and to an old hometown crony, that he had acted to save lives. But given Japanese wartime culture, Kurita's decision to turn around, to sail away from Leyte Gulf, was brave. The expected step would have been to die, pointlessly, but gloriously. In truth, Kurita represented a better Japan, before (and fortunately after) the insane militarists tried to turn a nation of 70 million people into a "shattered gem."

Bill Halsey was in a more benign way a product, or at least a tool, of cultural hysteria. Rattled by the Japanese surprise attack at Pearl Harbor, Americans needed to have a damn-the-torpedoes hero in the early years of the war. "Bull" Halsey perfectly fit the part. But he became his own caricature, and his superiors didn't seem to know how gracefully to remove him from high command. The irony is that Halsey was not really a plastic man, a prop, but an intensely human figure who cared deeply about his men and suffered with them. He was, like Kurita, required to maintain a pretense that really did not describe him.

Human nature can transcend national culture. On battlefields, men of all countries and races usually fight for their buddies more than they do for a flag or some abstract notion of country. And when they die, battlefield witnesses say, they cry out for their mothers (and not *Banzai!*). Character—the courage, decency, and compassion that men sometimes show in the midst of horrific battles—can inspire and redeem. But it is a mistake, and a particularly western one, to romanticize individual will in the face of crushing cultural imperatives. There has never been, and may never again be, a war at sea on the scale of the one that climaxed at Leyte Gulf in October 1944. It should be remembered for its individual acts of heroism and defiance, but more so for the blunders and misunderstandings that are inherent in war.

ACKNOWLEDGMENTS

I was extremely lucky to have two great companions on my researches into the lives and times of the men portrayed in this book. In Japan, Hideko Takayama helped me find surviving officers and sailors of the Imperial Japanese Navy, naval scholars and experts, and family members and friends of my subjects. She translated books and articles, corrected my mistakes, and, with patience and some bemusement, helped me to grapple with the culture of wartime Japan. Together with my wife, Oscie, we took a fascinating tour of Eta Jima, the Japanese naval academy near Hiroshima, and visited the Yasukuni Shrine and its war museum, the Yushukan, in Tokyo. She was able to persuade veterans to open up in a way that I never could have. (I knew we were getting somewhere when Kosaku Koitabashi, a petty officer and lookout aboard the *Yamato*, took off his shoe and sock so we could feel the pieces of shrapnel still inside him.) Oscie and I treasure our friendship with Hideko.

My friend Mike Hill has now worked with me on three books. I do not know what I would do without him. He is unfailingly resourceful, good-natured, fun, reliable, and intelligent in his judgments. Together we "walked the battlefield," standing on the bridge of the USS *New Jersey*, where Admiral Halsey hurled down his cap, and exploring the nooks and crannies of the USS *Cassin Young*, a *Fletcher*-class destroyer like the USS *Johnston*, which rests a mile deep off the coast of Samar.

John Lawrence, Admiral Halsey's air combat intelligence officer, was a warm host to Oscie and me at his house in Hamilton, Mass. With humility and self-reflection, he helped me sort through the mysteries of the battle he witnessed at first hand. Ed Digardi, the officer of the deck on the *Johnston* on the day of the battle, gave me a feel for what it is like to stand on the deck of a destroyer being bom-

barded by battleships, as did his fellow officers Robert Hagen and
Ellsworth Welch. I am awed by their courage—and the courage of
all the men of the *Johnston* interviewed by either Mike or me—Ed
Bloch, Lloyd Campbell, Jesse Cochran, Robert Hollenbaugh, James
Allen Johnson, William Mercer, Harold Rhodes, Robert Sochor, Ed-
ward Takkunen, Clarence Trader, and Beverly Sterling (wife of the
Johnston's executive office, Elton Sterling). On a trip to Muskogee,
Okla., I received a warm welcome and much help in trying to under-
stand Ernest Evans's Cherokee roots from Richard Allen, Ed Moore,
Jamie Noble, Marian Hagerstrand, Robert Conley, Chad Smith,
Mark Miller, Joyce Bear, and Jennifer Kilgore. A special thanks to
Ernest Evans Jr., and to John Clement Evans.

On my tour of the USS *New Jersey* in Camden, N.J., Mike and I
were well cared for by Scott Kodger and Doug Buchanan, and on the
USS *Cassin Young* at the Boston Navy Yard by Ethan Beeler and
Emily Prigot. Tom NeSmith gave me an illuminating tour of the
USS *Kidd,* a perfectly preserved World War II–era *Fletcher*-class destroyer docked in Baton Rouge, La. We received great assistance
from Capt. Todd Creekman, Dr. David Winkler, Robert Cressman,
Michael Crawford, Ed Marolda, and Bob Schneller at the Naval His-
torical Center and Foundation and from Dr. Jeffrey Barlow, historian
of the Contemporary History Branch. Many thanks, too, to James
Zobel, archivist at the MacArthur Museum and Archives, Norfolk,
Va.; Robert Clark of the Franklin D. Roosevelt Presidential Library
in Hyde Park, N.Y.; Jeffrey Flannery of the Library of Congress in
Washington, D.C.; Helen McDonald of the Nimitz Museum in Fredericksburg, Texas; James Cheever and my friend Steve Wrage of the
U.S. Naval Academy, Annapolis, Md.; and Paul Stilwell and Tom
Cutler of the U.S. Naval Institute in Annapolis. Adm. James Holloway offered me a deck-eye view of the Battle of Surigao Strait,
and Dr. Carnes Weeks shared with me his father's letters home, with
their fresh insights into the health of Halsey and his staff at the critical moment. Thanks to Betty Taussig for her permission to see the
wide-ranging oral history of her father, Halsey's chief of staff,
Adm. Robert "Mick" Carney, and to Steve Moulton and R. K. Lickle
for talking to me about their fathers' experiences on Halsey's staff.

I benefited enormously from the knowledge and care of Rich

Frank, a superb World War II scholar who carefully read, corrected, and annotated my manuscript. And I received useful advice and counsel from Don Goldstein at the University of Pittsburgh and Mark Peattie at Stanford, experts both on the Imperial Japanese Navy. Edward Drea of the historian's office of the Secretary of Defense generously shared his knowledge of Japanese wartime culture, and Clark Reynolds, a great naval historian, shared important correspondence and insight. My fellow authors John Wukovits and Jim Hornfischer were very gracious about offering information and insights, as was my friend Ted Barreaux. (The detail maps of the Battle off Samar are adapted from Hornfischer's excellent *The Last Stand of the Tin Can Sailors*.) Thanks as well to Steve Ossad, a military historian who first had the idea of writing about Ernest Evans and kindly turned over his research leads.

In Japan, I was extremely fortunate in my guides and mentors. Naoyuki Agawa, a model of understanding and diplomacy, led me to his father, Hiroyuki Agawa, who wrote a splendid biography of Admiral Yamamoto. Kosaku Koitabashi kindly spent four hours reliving the battle over a many-course meal with Hideko, Oscie, and me at a restaurant outside Tokyo. At his home in Fukuoka, Hiroshi Yasunaga described how he did not salute Admiral Ugaki as he departed on the last kamikaze mission. Over tea with me (and in several conversations with Hideko), Shigeko Terada and Kazuko Naoe described their father and grandfather, respectively, Admiral Kurita. Kenzo Ebina and Masatake Okumiya told Hideko of their experiences with Admiral Ugaki, and Seiichiro Tokoi told us of Kurita's remarkable confession, shared over a bottle of sake toward the end of Kurita's life, that he had been motivated to turn around the fleet to save lives. I received expert knowledge and advice as well from naval scholars Haruo Tohmatsu, Kazutoshi Hando, Kazushige Todaka, Yoichi Hirama, and Manabu Yoshida, former president of the Suikokai, the IJN's old-boy society. At Eta Jima, thanks to a tour set up by Toshiyuki Ito of the Japanese Maritime Self-Defense Force, I learned much from the former deputy superintendent, Capt. Taisei Tamai. Hideko offers her deepest thanks to Seiji Sakanashi of Kojinsha Publishing, who was invaluable in helping her find naval journals and tracking down IJN veterans.

This is my sixth book with the great Alice Mayhew of Simon & Schuster. In one lunch, she managed to help me figure out what my book was about—after I had been stumbling for months. As always, I want to thank many pros at S&S, including Roger Labrie, Serena Jones, Jackie Seow, Dana Sloan, Fred Chase (my excellent copy editor), Gypsy da Silva, Jeffrey Ward, Tracey Guest, and Victoria Meyer. At ICM, Amanda Urban continues to represent me with her unique combination of affection, savvy, and toughness. At *Newsweek*, thanks to Mark Whitaker and Rick Smith for giving me time to write my books, and to Steve Tuttle and Ann McDaniel, whose judgment and care I value.

I am blessed to have great friends as editors. Stephen Smith, Jon Meacham, and Richard Darman all made important suggestions—which I took in a heartbeat. My daughter Louisa is becoming a formidable, discerning editor and her sister Mary is, in her own beguiling way, an inspiration. My true love—and best editor in all ways—is my wife, Oscie.

NOTES

PROLOGUE: CULTURE, CHARACTER, AND THE LONELINESS OF COMMAND

1 *"Kill Japs"*. Paul Fussell, *Wartime: Understanding and Behavior in the Second World War* (New York: Oxford University Press, 1989), 118.

1 "We are drowning": Dwight Macdonald, *Memoirs of a Revolutionist: Essays in Political Criticism* (New York: Farrar, Straus, 1957), 93.

1 racial stereotypes: John W. Dower, *War Without Mercy: Race and Power in the Pacific War* (New York: Pantheon, 1986), 81, 241.

2 roots of mutual contempt: Ibid., 142, 157, 164, 178, 232.

3 cultural misunderstanding: Ibid., 105, 203, 261.

3 "the entire population": Richard B. Frank, *Downfall: The End of the Imperial Japanese Empire* (New York: Penguin, 1999), 188. It is important to note that in the spring of 1945, the government of Japan legally and practically made the entire adult civilian population of Japan into combatants by creating a national militia of all males ages fifteen to sixty and females seventeen to forty.

3 Japanese neglect antisubmarine warfare: Ronald H. Spector, *Eagle Against the Sun: The American War with Japan* (New York: Macmillan, 1985), 48, 186; but see John Prados, *Combined Fleet Decoded: The Secret History of American Intelligence and the Japanese Navy in World War II* (Annapolis: Naval Institute Press, 1995), 627. The Japanese preferred "offensive" military. Subs were dismissed as "defensive." Japanese assumed that since they could not build a sub that would dive deeper than 300 feet, the Americans couldn't either. Late-war U.S. subs routinely dove 400 feet. Richard Frank interview.

3 Japanese lax about codes: Dower, *War Without Mercy*, 261. The Japanese did change code books twice, but that was not enough.

3 scale of the battle: James A. Field, Jr., *The Japanese at Leyte Gulf: The Sho Operation* (Princeton: Princeton University Press, 1947), vii; Thomas J. Cutler, *The Battle of Leyte Gulf, 23–26 October 1944* (New York: HarperCollins, 1994), xii; H. P. Willmott, *Battle of Leyte Gulf: The Last Fleet Action* (Bloomington: Indiana University Press, 2005), 6.

4 "mysterious retreat": Evan Thomas, "'Kurita Was a Coward!' Or Was He?" *Naval History*, October 2004.

5 history of sea battles: Ronald H. Spector, *At War at Sea: Sailors and Naval Combat in the Twentieth Century* (New York: Viking, 2001), 1–223.

5 Johnny comes marching home: H. P. Willmott, *The Barrier and the Javelin:*

Japanese and Allied Pacific Strategies, February to June 1942. (Annapolis: Naval Institute Press, 1983), quoting Russell Spurr, *A Glorious Way to Die: The Kamikaze Mission of the Battleship Yamato, April 1945* (New York: Bantam, 1983), 295.

I. DOUBTING SUPERMEN

7 "It may be": Capt. Tameichi Hara, *Japanese Destroyer Captain* (New York: Ballantine, 1961), 46.

7 Japanese training: Prados, *Combined Fleet Decoded,* 62.

8 *seishin*: Admiral Matome Ugaki, *Fading Victory: The Diary of Admiral Matome Ugaki* (Pittsburgh: University of Pittsburgh Press, 1991), 7; David C. Evans and Mark R. Peattie, *Kaigun* (Annapolis: Naval Institute Press, 1997), 500.

8 *Senso Roku*: Ugaki, *Diary,* xv, 8.

8 officers' social status: Arthur J. Marder, *Old Friends, New Enemies: The Royal Navy and the Imperial Japanese Navy* (Oxford: Clarendon Press, 1981), 256–57.

9 samurai impunity: James A. Bradley, *Flags of Our Fathers* (New York: Bantam, 2000), 17.

9 failure to salute: Mitsuru Yoshida, *Requiem for Battleship Yamato* (London: Constable, 1999), 21.

9 "the Golden Mask": Hiroshi Yasunaga interview.

10 "Did the persons": Ugaki, *Diary,* 5.

10 Ugaki's guilt: See Edwin P. Hoyt, *The Last Kamikaze: The Story of Admiral Matome Ugaki* (Westport, Connecticut: Praeger, 1993), 1–5.

10 "whether this will": Ugaki, *Diary,* 5.

10 Ugaki and Buddhist philosophy: Kenzo Ebina interview.

11 web of obligations: Ruth Benedict, *The Chrysanthemum and the Sword: Patterns of Japanese Culture* (Rutland, Vermont: Charles Tuttle, 1976), 99.

11 *arigato*: Ibid., 105, also translates as, "Oh, this difficult thing."

11 *47 Ronin*: Ibid., 183, 192, 199, 205.

11 Ugaki raised modestly: Kenzo Ebina interview.

11 meals on *Nagato*: Hiroyuki Agawa, *The Reluctant Admiral: Yamamoto and the Imperial Navy* (Tokyo: Kodansha International, 1979), 14.

11 Zeros in ox carts: Evans and Peattie, *Kaigun,* 506.

11 "for 2,600 years": Haruko Taya Cook and Theodore F. Cook, *Japan at War: An Oral History* (New York: New Press, 1992), 69.

12 Zero's flaws: Richard B. Frank, *Guadalcanal: The Definitive Account of the Landmark Battle* (New York: Penguin, 1990), 66. In the 1930s, when the Zero was designed, American planes also lacked armor or self-sealing tanks. But combat experience in the Battle of Britain in 1940 taught the British and Germans to refine their planes, and the British taught the Americans. The Japanese, who saw limited air combat over China, did not get the word. Richard Frank interview.

12 Inoue and Ozawa: Marder, *Old Friends,* 445.

12 Eta Jima: Cecil Bullock, *Etajima: The Dartmouth of Japan* (London: Sampson Low, Marston, 1942), *passim*.

12 Hirohito's expression: Herbert P. Bix, *Hirohito and the Making of Modern Japan* (New York: Perennial, 2001), 88.

12 emperor worship: Bernard Millot, *Divine Thunder: The Life and Death of the Kamikazes* (New York: Pinnacle, 1971), 11.

12 High school principals: Benedict, *Chrysanthemum*, 151.

12 captains and portrait: Marder, *Old Friends*, 273.

12 emperor's attitude: Bix, *Hirohito*, 441.

13 "Across the sea": Marder, *Old Friends*, 272.

13 "extraordinary grand festival": Ugaki, *Diary*, 11.

13 Yasukuni: Author's tour; Denis Warner and Peggy Warner, *The Sacred Warriors: Japan's Suicide Legions* (New York: Avon, 1982), 39–40.

13 "You and I": Martin Cruz Smith, *December 6: A Novel* (New York: Simon & Schuster, 2002), 319.

14 Ugaki's soul: Ugaki, *Diary*, 11.

14 Passengers on streetcars: Saburo Ienaga, *The Pacific War, 1931–1945: A Critical Perspective on Japan's Role in World War II* (New York: Pantheon, 1978), 109.

14 Samurai's toothpick: Benedict, *Chrysanthemum*, 148, 182–83.

14 *bushido*: Ibid., 175.

14 not to be taken prisoner: Cook and Cook, *Japan at War*, 264; see Paul Varley, *Warriors of Japan: As Portrayed in the War Tales* (Honolulu: University of Hawaii Press, 1994), 18–19, for history.

14 General Nogi: Bix, *Hirohito*, 42–43; Warner and Warner, *Sacred Warriors*, 42; Varley, *Warriors of Japan*, 65 (for origins).

15 drinking acceptable: Marder, *Old Friends*, 347.

15 Sake parties: Benedict, *Chrysanthemum*, 189.

15 Yamamoto on Ugaki: Hiroyuki Agawa interview.

15 "the commander in chief bantered": Ugaki, *Diary*, 11.

16 Yamamoto's gambling: Agawa, *Reluctant Admiral*, 8, 148.

16 "S [for sex] Play": Kenzo Ebina interview.

16 Yamamoto's geisha: Hoyt, *Last Kamikaze*, 7.

16 "80 Sen": Agawa, *Reluctant Admiral*, 2.

17 Yamamoto physical description: Ibid.

17 performed handstands: Prados, *Combined Fleet Decoded*, 125.

17 Ugaki not Yamamoto's choice: Hoyt, *Last Kamikaze*, 3.

17 Ugaki and Yamamoto do not understand each other: Hiroyuki Agawa interview.

17 Ugaki and Germany: Haruo Tohmatsu interview; Yoichi Hirama interview; Kazutoshi Hando interview.

17 Yamamoto and the British: Hiroyuki Agawa interview.

17 Eta Jima: Bullock, *Etajima;* and author's tour.

18 automatons: Hiroyuki Agawa interview.

18 paper-pushers rise in ranks: Hara, *Japanese Destroyer Captain*, 23; Marder, *Old Friends*, 348.

18 Japan's cities fire traps: Agawa, *Reluctant Admiral*, 127.

18 *Life* magazine: Ibid., 233; Marder, *Old Friends*, 378.

18 night battle: Evans and Peattie, *Kaigun*, 273–80; Masanori Ito, *The End of the Imperial Japanese Navy* (New York: Jove, 1986), 17.

18 army generals: Agawa, *Reluctant Admiral*, 128; Ienaga, *Pacific War*, 39; Marder, *Old Friends*, 289.

19 "They talk of": Agawa, *Reluctant Admiral*, 158.

19 Yamamoto threatened: Ibid., 158–62.

19 spy fever: Prados, *Combined Fleet Decoded*, 31.

19 anti-Western mood: Ienaga, *Pacific War*, 105; Hiroyuki Agawa interview.

19 Thought police: Thomas R. H. Havens, *Valley of Darkness: The Japanese People and World War Two* (Lanham, Maryland: University Press of America, 1978), 22.

19 government lied: Ienaga, *Pacific War*, 100, 102.

19 children chant: Ibid., 6.

19 lop off heads: Bix, *Hirohito*, 335.

20 more equal than others: Ienaga, *Pacific War*, 12, 154.

20 September 29 letter: Prados, *Combined Fleet Decoded*, 114.

20 Yamamoto fatalism: Agawa, *Reluctant Admiral*, 231.

20 In a single blow: John Toland, *The Rising Sun: The Decline and Fall of the Japanese Empire, 1936–1945* (New York: Bantam, 1970), 211.

20 Yamamoto fascinated with General Mitchell: Marder, *Old Friends*, 304.

21 "My plan is": Agawa, *Reluctant Admiral*, 235.

21 Kuroshima described: Ibid., 272.

21 navy cultlike: Evans and Peattie, *Kaigun*, 141.

21 "Magnificent indeed!": Ugaki, *Diary*, 12.

21 *Yamato* described: Capt. Kitaro Matsumoto, "Design and Construction of the *Yamato* and *Musashi*," *U.S. Naval Institute Proceedings*, October 1953.

22 *Yamato* secret: Prados, *Combined Fleet Decoded*, 26; Evans and Peattie, *Kaigun*, 373.

22 ship names: John W. Dower, *Embracing Defeat: Japan in the Wake of World War II* (New York: Norton, 1999), 213.

22 "Let's go!": Ienaga, *Pacific War*, 27.

22 "a consummate expression": Spector, *War at Sea*, 24.

23 Mahan's influence: Ibid., 25.

23 Mahan translated: Evans and Peattie, *Kaigun*, 24.

23 *Der Tag*: Spector, *War at Sea*, 120.

23 War Plan Orange: See Edward S. Miller, *War Plan Orange: The U.S. Strategy to Defeat Japan, 1897–1945* (Annapolis: Naval Institute Press, 1991), *passim*.

24 *Yogeki Sakusen*: Evans and Peattie, *Kaigun*, 186.

24 "A battleship had": Marder, *Old Friends*, 324.

25 Yamamoto free of cant: Agawa, *Reluctant Admiral*, 91–93; Marder, *Old Friends*, 313; Prados, *Combined Fleet Decoded*, 126–27.

25 Yoshida and flying: Clark Reynolds, *The Fast Carriers: The Forging of an Air Navy* (Annapolis: Naval Institute Press, 1968), 5.

25 "the great follies": Agawa, *Reluctant Admiral*, 92.

25 Yamamoto persuades admirals: Prados, *Combined Fleet Decoded*, 131–35.

25 "evading others' notice": Ugaki, *Diary*, 18.

25 "The autumn sky": Ibid., 19.

26 "You die": Ibid.

26 family photograph: Ibid., 380.

26 "All my family": Ibid., 21.

27 fishermen go back to oars and sails: Smith, *December 6,* 51.

27 "queer-shaped submarine": Ugaki, *Diary,* 25, 26.

27 Yamamoto's concerns: Ito, *Imperial Japanese Navy,* 33.

27 Submarine *No. 6*: Marder, *Old Friends,* 274.

28 Eta Jima social customs: Ibid., 266–67, 275, 283.

28 Hara punched: Hara, *Japanese Destroyer Captain,* 15–16.

29 Imperial Rescript: Allied Translator and Interpreter Section, South West Pacific Area, "The Emperor Cult As a Present Factor in Japanese Military Psychology. Research Report, No. 76, Part II, APO 500, 21 June, 1944," General Douglas MacArthur Foundation Archives, Norfolk, Virginia, passim.

29 "War is a serious": Ugaki, *Diary,* 29.

29 Ugaki composes message: Ibid., 33; Ito, *Imperial Japanese Navy,* 2.

30 *Nagato* described: Prados, *Combined Fleet Decoded,* 190.

30 "I was having a smoke": Ugaki, *Diary,* 43.

30 "Did you get": Agawa, *Reluctant Admiral,* 266.

31 "sneak thievery": Ugaki, *Diary,* 47–48.

31 popular joy: Ienaga, *Pacific War,* 142.

31 "The Emperor wore": Bix, *Hirohito,* 437.

31 Yamamoto depressed: Agawa, *Reluctant Admiral,* 283, 285–86, 288; Cook and Cook, *Japan at War,* 82–83.

31 Ugaki and submarine crews: Ugaki, *Diary,* 44, 51.

34 "The whole world": Ibid., 52.

34 "zeal": Ibid., 54.

CHAPTER 2: DAMN THE TORPEDOES

35 Halsey described: William F. Halsey and J. Bryan III, *Admiral Halsey's Story* (New York: McGraw-Hill, 1947), Introduction, ix–xvii; *Lucky Bag, 1904,* U.S. Naval Academy Archives, Annapolis, Maryland; E. B. Potter, *Bull Halsey* (Annapolis: Naval Institute Press, 1985), 1–7.

37 morning of December 7, 1941: Halsey, *Halsey's Story,* 75–77; Potter, *Halsey,* 9; Draft of Halsey's memoirs, 312, courtesy John Wukovits.

37 "That joke's": Interview with Douglas Moulton, Jr.

38 "Battle Order No. 1": Halsey, *Halsey's Story,* 75–76.

38 "burned in my brain": Ibid., 128.

38 "Get there first": Potter, *Halsey,* 37.

39 "I have the consolation": Ibid., 12.

39 "Look! She's sinking!": Halsey, *Halsey's Story,* 83.

39 Halsey sailing into Pearl Harbor: Potter, *Halsey,* 13.

40 "Before we're through": Halsey, *Halsey's Story,* 81.

40 Kimmel and Halsey: Potter, *Halsey,* 14.

41 "Those Japs had better": Ibid., 15.

41 Halsey family background: Ibid., 19; Halsey, *Halsey's Story,* 2.

42 Halsey at University of Virginia: Potter, *Halsey*, 26.

42 Naval Academy described: Jack Sweetman, *The U.S. Naval Academy: An Illustrated History*, revised by Thomas J. Cutler (Annapolis: Naval Institute Press, 1995), 141–59.

43 English is "Bull": Spector, *War at Sea*, 136–37.

43 "everybody's friend": *Lucky Bag, 1904.*

43 Halsey on *Mikasa*: Halsey, *Halsey's Story*, 8.

44 "You could tell a destroyer man": Ibid., 42.

45 Halsey a bad flier: Potter, *Halsey*, 130.

45 "Big Bill": Ibid., 90.

45 "the Flying Jackass": Draft of Halsey's memoirs, 269.

45 Nimitz described: Edwin P. Hoyt, *How They Won the War in the Pacific: Nimitz and His Admirals* (Guilford, Connecticut: Lyons, 2000), 28, 70.

45 America after Pearl Harbor: Winston Groom, *1942: The Year That Tried Men's Souls* (New York: Atlantic Monthly Press, 2005), 51–55, 86–97, 214–15.

47 Nimitz needed an aggressive fleet commander: E. B. Potter, *Nimitz* (Annapolis: Naval Institute Press, 1976), 35–36. But in his own memoir, Halsey says he was not really enthusiastic about the carrier raids. He may have been playacting at the CINCPAC meeting. Halsey, *Halsey's Story*, 85.

48 "Get away from that cruiser": Halsey, *Halsey's Story*, 92.

48 actual score: Potter, *Halsey*, 47.

48 Halsey under fire: Halsey, *Halsey's Story*, 93.

48 "the Americans fought to live": Halsey to Hanson Baldwin, Richard Bates Papers, Naval War College, Newport, Rhode Island.

49 "Nice going!": Potter, *Halsey*, 50.

49 swinging from the trees: William Manchester, *Goodbye, Darkness: A Memoir of the Pacific War* (Boston: Little, Brown, 1980), 234.

49 "daze": Ibid., 206.

50 Japanese invasion of the Philippines: Groom, *1942*, 130–46; Manchester, *Goodbye, Darkness*, 171–213.

50 "There are times": Groom, *1942*, 139.

50 "Rain, later cloudy": Ugaki, *Diary*, 81–84.

51 cliché about American women: Frank, *Guadalcanal*, 21.

52 Teddy Roosevelt sought Cherokees: Theodore Roosevelt, *The Rough Riders* (New York: Scribner's, 1899), 232.

52 Evans's aptitude test: Otis Aptitude Test taken by Evans, August 24, 1927, Personnel File, Nimitz Library, Special Collections and Archives Division, U.S. Naval Academy, Annapolis, Maryland.

52 Evans at Central High: 1926 Muskogee Central High School yearbook, *The Chieftain*; Evans records at Central High School, courtesy Barbara Kilgore, Librarian, Muskogee High School.

52 Muskogee, Native Americans, and Evans's childhood: Interviews with Dr. Richard Allen, Historian of the Cherokee Nation; Edwin Moore, Creek elder and World War I veteran; Marian Hagerstrand, Cherokee Nation; Robert Conley, author; Maxine Glory, Director of Indian Education, Muskogee school system; Dr. George Leeds, Cherokee scholar; Harry Long, World War II veteran; Ellen Johnson, Native American scholar, Cherokee Nation; John Ketcher, Vice

Chief, Cherokee Nation; C. W. "Bob" West, *Muskogee: From Statehood to Pearl Harbor* (Muskogee, Oklahoma: Muskogee Publishing Company, 1976); Angie Debo, *And Still the Waters Run Deep* (Princeton: Princeton University Press, 1940).

53 Evans's family background: Monograph on George Washington Evans, Dawes Rolls records of Pinkney Evans, courtesy of Joyce Bear, Librarian, Muskogee (Creek) Nation; Evans family tree: Courtesy John Clement Evans (cousin).

55 American Indians enlist: Duane Hale, "Uncle Sam's Warriors: American Indians in World War II," *Chronicles of Oklahoma*, Winter 1991–92.

55 Evans at Annapolis: *Lucky Bag, 1931*, Evans Personnel File, Nimitz Library, Special Collections and Archives Division, U.S. Naval Academy, Annapolis, Maryland; John Colwell interview; author's tour of U.S. Naval Academy, courtesy James Cheever.

57 "Doesn't that guy": Ed Digardi interview.

57 *Alden* off Singapore: Report of Commander H. E. Eccles of "The Java Sea Battle," August 30, 1942, Bates Papers.

58 "elderly and decrepit": Marder, *Old Friends*, 53.

58 "possibility" of fighter protection: Ibid., 59.

58 "Poor American boys": Theodore Roscoe, *United States Destroyer Operations in World War II* (Annapolis: Naval Institute Press, 1966), 102.

58 Battle of the Java Sea: Ibid., 103–6; *Alden* action report, "Information Concerning Naval Campaign in Orient, 1941–1942, Southwest Pacific Area; Asiatic Defense." Office of Naval Records, Naval Historical Center, Washington, D.C.

60 "from harm's way": Ed Digardi interview; Robert Hagen interview.

CHAPTER 3: LONG JOHN SILVER AND CONFUCIUS

61 *hakko ichiu*: Ienaga, *Pacific War*, 154.

61 "For the Americans": Ugaki, *Diary*, 98.

62 Doolittle Raid: Groom, *1942*, 186–93.

63 "Our homeland has": Ugaki, *Diary*, 114–15.

64 Yamamoto in cabin: Prados, *Combined Fleet Decoded*, 289.

64 "The children's hour": Agawa, *Reluctant Admiral*, 299.

64 Halsey sick: Potter, *Halsey*, 57; Halsey, *Halsey's Story*, 107 ("What brought it on, I don't know. Possibly a combination of nervous tension and tropical sun was to blame.").

64 "Haul Ass Halsey": Halsey, *Halsey's Story*, 95.

64 Halsey and Fan: Ibid., 16, 65; Potter, *Halsey*, 5, 131, 139.

66 Halsey in hospital: Halsey, *Halsey's Story*, 69–82.

66 "his face greasy": Agawa, *Reluctant Admiral*, 299.

66 "Make sure the first test": Potter, *Halsey*, 82.

67 "Missing the Battle of Midway": Ibid., 150.

67 "Boys, I've got": Halsey, *Halsey's Story*, 108.

67 on shooting range: Potter, *Halsey*, 156.

68 "Jesus Christ": Halsey, *Halsey's Story*, 109.

68 "The name will not": Frank, *Guadalcanal*, 333.

68 "Babe Ruth eat shit!": Toland, *Rising Sun,* 460.

69 "had to kick them": Halsey, *Halsey's Story,* 116.

69 "Then we got the news": Ibid.

69 "to his command": Frank, *Guadalcanal,* 335–36.

69 "KILL JAPS": Hoyt, *How They Won,* 166.

69 "we sat on our necks": Halsey, *Halsey's Story,* 137–38.

70 "I can hold": Potter, *Halsey,* 162.

70 Battle of the Santa Cruz Islands: Reynolds, *Fast Carriers,* 33; Spector, *War at Sea,* 211–16; Toland, *Rising Sun,* 462.

70 As you may well imagine: Hoyt, *How They Won,* 172.

70 "like a wonderful breath": Frank, *Guadalcanal,* 422.

70 "It smells of exhibitionism": Halsey, *Halsey's Story,* 123.

71 "We've got the bastards licked!": Ibid., 130–31.

71 three-star collar bars: Ibid., 132.

71 censured destroyer captain: Ken Jones, *Destroyer Squadron 23: Combat Exploits of Arleigh Burke's Gallant Forces* (Annapolis: Naval Institute Press, 1997), 14.

71 Burke and Halsey: Ibid., 22, 33, 35, 40, 103, 172.

72 Halsey publicity: Halsey, *Halsey's Story,* 141–42.

73 "emasculation for the males": James M. Merrill, *A Sailor's Admiral: A Biography of William F. Halsey* (New York: Thomas Y. Crowell, 1976), 66.

73 "We're Gonna Have to Slap": James Bradley, *Fly Boys: A True Story of Courage* (New York: Little, Brown, 2003), 137.

73 historians question Halsey: Frank, *Guadalcanal,* 605.

73 "I remember thinking": Hoyt, *How They Won,* 169.

74 Kurita naval background: Marder, *Old Friends,* 446.

75 naval strategy described: Yoichi Hirama interview.

75 Kurita's attitude described: Ibid.; Kazutoshi Hando interview; Haruo Tohmatsu interview; Hiroyuki Agawa interview.

76 Kurita's family background: Shigeko Terada interview.

76 Confucian scholars: Edwin O. Reischauer, *Japan: The Story of a Nation* (New York: Knopf, 1970), 90–91, 109–10.

77 "Those who appreciate": Allied Translator and Interpreter Section, South West Pacific Area, "The Emperor Cult As a Present Factor in Japanese Military Psychology. Research Report, No. 76, Part II, APO 500, 21 June, 1944," General Douglas MacArthur Foundation Archives, Norfolk, Virginia, 10.

77 Confucianism described: T. R. Reid, *Confucius Lives Next Door: What Living in the East Teaches Us About Living in the West* (New York: Random House, 1999), 111.

77 Kurita and Mito: Haruo Tohmatsu interview; Reischauer, *Japan,* 106–121.

78 "lacked Yamato spirit": Shigeko Terada interview.

78 Kurita smiled and looked pleased: Marder, *Old Friends,* 510.

78 "There certainly appears": H. P. Willmott, *The Barrier and the Javelin: Japanese and Allied Pacific Strategies, February to June 1942* (Annapolis: Naval Institute Press, 1983), 100.

79 Ugaki wanted *Hornet* and *Haruna*: Prados, *Combined Fleet Decoded,* 385.

79 bombardment of Henderson Field: Frank, *Guadalcanal,* 316; Ito, *Imperial Japanese Navy,* 174.

"A man comes close": Groom, *1942,* 322.

CHAPTER 4: POP GOES THE WEASEL

81 Truk described: Potter, *Halsey*, 208.

81 "I regret": Ugaki, *Diary*, 299.

82 "The enemy builds": Ibid., 253.

82 "the Galloping Ghost": Halsey, *Halsey's Story*, 133.

82 "The imperial headquarters announced": Ugaki, *Diary*, 75.

82 "as funds for moral training": Ibid., 291.

82 "the place of bitter struggles": Ibid., 255.

82 "it seems to be": Ibid., 286.

82 "We shall all die calmly": Ibid., 184.

83 "We can't believe": Ibid., 259.

83 attack on Henderson Field: Ibid., 245; Toland, *Rising Sun*, 467.

83 "heaven-sent": Ugaki, *Diary*, 245.

83 "the shortage of": Ibid.

83 Japanese invented light bulb: Ben-Ami Shillony, *Politics and Culture in Wartime Japan* (Oxford: Clarendon Press, 1981), 138.

84 "starving the enemy": Ugaki, *Diary*, 72.

84 death of Yamaguchi: Toland, *Rising Sun*, 389.

84 "Those who can die": Ugaki, *Diary*, 280.

84 Yamamoto on suicide: Ibid., 266; Agawa, *Reluctant Admiral*, 332.

85 "I was firmly determined": Ugaki, *Diary*, 164.

85 Nagumo dragged off: Ibid., 162.

85 Cover-up of Midway: Agawa, *Reluctant Admiral*, 322; Hoyt, *Last Kamikaze*, 65.

85 Ugaki learns of code break: Ugaki, *Diary*, 174.

85 Yamamoto and Ugaki closer: Hoyt, *Last Kamikaze*, 81, 100.

86 Ugaki misses his dead wife: Ugaki, *Diary*, 105.

86 life on *Yamato*: Agawa, *Reluctant Admiral*, 329–31.

86 sugar for children: Ugaki, *Diary*, 87.

86 fish heads: Agawa, *Reluctant Admiral*, 334.

87 "Looking back over the year": Ibid.

87 holiday ration: Hoyt, *Last Kamikaze*, 107.

87 "Starvation Island": Agawa, *Reluctant Admiral*, 338.

87 "Our rice is gone": Ienaga, *Pacific War*, 144.

87 mortality chart: Potter, *Halsey*, 202.

87 evacuation of Guadalcanal: Prados, *Combined Fleet Decoded*, 395.

88 "advancing by turning": Ito, *Imperial Japanese Navy*, 83.

88 emperor demands: Bix, *Hirohito*, 457, 461.

88 running out of planes: Frank, *Guadalcanal*, 615.

88 only sixteen had ever flown: Hoyt, *Last Kamikaze*, 106.

88 Rabaul described: Potter, *Halsey*, 208.

89 "Her beautiful face": Hoyt, *Last Kamikaze*, 112.

89 Yamamoto's "minute" handwriting: Ugaki, *Diary*, 326.

89 "Quite tasty": Ibid., 325.

89 "first day of fever": Ibid., 326.

89 JFK witnessed *Aaron Ward* sinking: Prados, *Combined Fleet Decoded*, 458.

89 Ugaki shouting match: Ugaki, *Diary*, 329.

90 Yamamoto ignores warning: Toland: *Rising Sun*, 499–500.

90 Yamamoto itinerary: Ibid., 500.

90 "We've hit the jackpot!": Ibid.

90 "Our old friend Yamamoto": Potter, *Nimitz*, 233.

91 no record of approval: Prados, *Combined Fleet Decoded*, 460.

91 shoot-down of Yamamoto and Ugaki: Ugaki, *Diary*, 352–59; R. Cargill Hall, ed., *Lightning Over Bougainville* (Washington, D.C.: Smithsonian Institution Press, 1991), 144–57; Agawa, *Reluctant Admiral*, 348–51.

93 Ugaki jokes with Watanabe: Agawa, *Reluctant Admiral*, 355.

94 "You get to use": Ibid., 349.

94 POP GOES THE WEASEL: Halsey, *Halsey's Story*, 157.

94 "met a gallant death": Agawa, *Reluctant Admiral*, 384.

94 state funeral: Ibid., 390; Toland, *Rising Sun*, 444.

94 "superhuman": Ugaki, *Diary*, 359.

96 "God must have": Ibid., 360.

96 Ugaki dictates to Ebina: Kenzo Ebina interview.

97 tradition of vengeance: Varley, *Warriors of Japan*, 35.

CHAPTER 5: THE DEPARTMENT OF DIRTY TRICKS

100 "I shall return!" on matchbooks: Groom, *1942*, 152.

100 Halsey and MacArthur: Potter, *Halsey*, 212–13.

100 "taken the field": William Manchester, *American Caesar: Douglas MacArthur, 1880–1964* (Boston: Little, Brown, 1978), 217.

100 "I refuse": Potter, *Halsey*, 213.

101 "I have seldom": Halsey, *Halsey's Story*, 155.

101 "My God, Bull": Potter, *Halsey*, 266; Betty Carney Taussig, *A Warrior for Freedom* (Manhattan, Kansas: Sunflower University Press, 1995), 89–90.

102 "How about *you*, Bill?": Halsey, *Halsey's Story*, 186.

102 attack on Rabaul: Ibid., 181; Taussig, *Warrior*, 92–93.

103 grumbling about Halsey's staff work: Halsey, *Halsey's Story*, 149, 152; Thomas B. Buell, *Master of Sea Power: A Biography of Fleet Admiral Ernest J. King* (Boston: Little, Brown, 1980), 452.

104 "You ought to be very suspicious": Frank, *Guadalcanal*, 4.

104 King described: Buell, *Master*, 95, 103.

104 disagreement over uniforms: Ibid., 357.

104 Browning described: Clark Reynolds, *On the Warpath in the Pacific: Admiral Jocko Clark and the Fast Carriers* (Annapolis: Naval Institute Press, 2005), 322.

104 new Halsey staff: Potter, *Halsey*, 245.

104 Carney described: Betty Taussig interview; Taussig, *Warrior*, xvii, 33, 37.

105 Carney nicknames: Taussig, *Warrior*, 35.

105 "the Oriental mindset" and Cheek: Ibid., 85.

106 Halsey and Ivy Leaguers: John Lawrence interview; Carl Solberg, *Decision and Dissent* (Annapolis: Naval Institute Press, 1995), 4.

107 "by-passing strategy": Halsey, *Halsey's Story*, 171; Reynolds, *Fast Carriers*, 116; Hoyt, *How They Won*, 260–61.

108 "it would seem": Spector, *Eagle Against the Sun*, 410.

108 Japanese shot in water: Bradley, *Fly Boys*, 140.

108 "It was rich": Halsey, *Halsey's Story*, 172.

108 KEEP 'EM DYING: Ibid., 165.

108 "Shut up!": Ibid., 187; Dr. Carnes Weeks, Jr., interview.

109 reservists in navy: Spector, *War at Sea*, 261–64.

109 *Fletcher*-class described: James D. Hornfischer, *The Last Stand of the Tin Can Sailors* (New York: Bantam, 2004), 44.

110 Evans's speech and Commissioning Ball: Interviews with USS *Johnston* crew members: Ed Takkunen, Robert Hollenbaugh, Lloyd Campbell, Ed Digardi, Robert Hagen, Ellsworth Welch, James Johnson.

112 captains isolated: Adm. Stansfield Turner interview.

113 "I think it": Robert Hagen interview.

113 Evans, the executive officer, and Digardi: Ed Digardi interview.

113 "follow the splashes": Col. E. E. Evans, Jr., interview.

114 *Johnston* described: Author's tour of *Fletcher*-class destroyers: USS *Cassin Young* at Boston Navy Yard and USS *Kidd* in Baton Rouge, Louisiana. Also, War Diary of USS *Johnston*, National Archives, Washington, D.C.

115 Evans's relations with sailors: Bill Mercer interview and Ed Digardi interview.

116 "Relax, Hagen": Bill Mercer interview.

116 "Now, Hagen": Robert Hagen interview.

116 Evans recruits Burnett: Robert Hagen interview; *The Fighting and Sinking of the USS Johnston DD 557: As Told by Her Crew*, written and coordinated by Bill Mercer (Privately printed, Johnston-Hoel Association, September 1991), 26.

116 Evans's relations with officers: Interviews with Ed Digardi, Robert Hagen, and Ellsworth Welch.

117 USS *Johnston* early war record: Robert Hagen interview; War Diary of USS *Johnston*, National Archives, Washington, D.C.

118 *Johnston* probably sinks Japanese sub: Ellsworth Welch interview.

118 Bloch cries: *Fighting and Sinking*, 17.

118 "we were just dumb-assed": Bill Mercer interview.

120 "a shy young thing": Sweetman, *U.S. Naval Academy*, 154.

120 "about the size": Taussig, *Warrior*, 103.

120 Halsey and Spruance close: Halsey, *Halsey's Story*, 42, 57.

121 Halsey gets Third Fleet: Potter, *Nimitz*, 294.

122 Spruance's choice: Thomas B. Buell, *The Quiet Warrior: A Biography of Admiral Raymond A. Spruance* (Annapolis: Naval Institute Press, 1987), 286, 294–95.

122 Plan Z documents captured: Toland, *Rising Sun*, 544–46.

122 "Z Operation Orders": Reynolds, *Fast Carriers*, 180, 185; W. J. Holmes, *Double-Edged Secrets: U.S. Naval Intelligence Operations in the Pacific During World War II* (Annapolis: Naval Institute Press, 1979), 180, 182; Z Plan documents, MacArthur Memorial Foundation Archives, Norfolk, Virginia.

122 Spruance described: Reynolds, *Fast Carriers*, 161–69, 187.

123 Mitscher described: Theodore Taylor, *The Magnificent Mitscher* (Annapolis: Naval Institute Press, 1991), 97–98, 120, 157, 161–62, 199, 242.

123 Mitscher and Burke: Ibid., 10–14.

123 "It might be a hell": Reynolds, *Fast Carriers*, 187.

124 "Hell, this is just": Ibid., 193–94.

124 night of June 20: Ibid., 199–204; Potter, *Halsey*, 240–41.

124 "The enemy had escaped": Reynolds, *Fast Carriers*, 205.

125 "crown prince": Clark Reynolds, *Admiral John H. Towers: The Struggle for Naval Air Supremacy* (Annapolis: Naval Institute Press, 1991), 223.

125 "buffalo hunters": Ibid., 411.

125 "I told them not": Hoyt, *How They Won*, 295.

125 Halsey sides with Towers: Potter, *Halsey*, 272.

125 Towers described: Reynolds, *Towers*, 337, 380, 419.

126 "penny whistle": Ibid., 263.

126 hush and get back to fighting: Taylor, *Mitscher*, 240.

126 Fan's breakdown: Potter, *Halsey*, 273.

127 "based on the assumption": Robert Bostwick Carney, *Reminiscences*, Naval History Project, Columbia University, 1964.

CHAPTER 6: THE SHATTERED GEM

129 Ugaki's hopes: Ugaki, *Diary*, 332–33.

129 "Luxury is the enemy": Cook and Cook, *Japan at War*, 174.

129 Tokyo shabby: Thomas R. H. Havens, *Valley of Darkness: The Japanese People and World War Two* (Lanham, Maryland: University Press of America, 1978), 118–19.

129 "My inside doesn't feel well": Ugaki, *Diary*, 335, 340.

130 "with developments too favorable": Ibid., 365.

130 learned by experience: Willmott, *Barrier*, 111.

130 "I wonder why": Ibid.

130 "I owe her soul": Ibid., 364–65.

130 poor pilots: Ibid., 374, 385; Prados, *Combined Fleet Decoded*, 568; David C. Evans, ed., *The Japanese Navy in World War II: In the Words of Former Japanese Naval Officers* (Annapolis: Naval Institute Press, 1986), 300, 302.

131 "Isn't there someplace": Bix, *Hirohito*, 466.

131 shuttle bombing: Ito, *Imperial Japanese Navy*, 195.

131 "Why can't we": Ugaki, *Diary*, 391.

131 "In the land of the south": Ibid., 390.

132 "Can it be": Ibid., 406–7.

132 June 19 described: Prados, *Combined Fleet Decoded*, 576.

132 "Not only did we fail": Ugaki, *Diary*, 411.

132 June 20 described: William T. Y'blood, *Red Sun Setting: The Battle of the Philippine Sea* (Annapolis: Naval Institute Press, 1981), 153, 171, 176.

133 "Utterly awakened": Ugaki, *Diary*, 415.

133 "The result of the decisive battle": Ibid., 416.

134 "needed his butt kicked"; Edward J. Drea, *In the Service of the Emperor: Essays on the Imperial Japanese Army* (Lincoln: University of Nebraska Press, 1998), 135.

135 Kurita commands Second Fleet: Y'blood, *Red Sun Setting*, 224.

135 "Rear Admiral Kurita, who": Ugaki, *Diary*, 26.

135 Ugaki's views of Kurita: Kenzo Ebina interview.

135 Kurita at Philippine Sea: Ito, *Imperial Japanese Navy*, 110; Y'Blood, *Red Sun Setting*, 177; Kazutoshi Hando interview.

135 Kurita interrogated after the war: *Interrogations of Japanese Officials*, Vols. 1–2, United States Strategic Bombing Survey (Pacific), Naval Analysis Division, Washington, D.C., 1:32, 52; 2:557.

136 Inoue described: Hiroyuki Agawa interview.

137 "strengthened his feeling": Ito, *Imperial Japanese Navy*, 176.

137 Kurita's disgust: Kosaku Koitabashi interview.

137 privations described: Toland, *Rising Sun*, 592.

137 prostitutes work: Havens, *Valley of Darkness*, 150.

137 Hanazono Service Corps: Ugaki, *Diary*, 426.

138 "new ideas": Ibid., 432, 436.

138 Captain Jo described: Bix, *Hirohito*, 450–52.

139 *gyokusai* policy: Bradley, *Fly Boys*, 145.

140 emperor a pawn?: Bix, *Hirohito*, 456, 468; Frank, *Downfall*, 89.

140 balloon bombs: Cook and Cook, *Japan at War*, 175, 188.

140 "No longer can we": Warner and Warner, *Sacred Warriors*, 57–65.

141 Suicide assembly line: Millot, *Divine Thunder*, 139–43, 152–71.

141 "I am going to charge": Ugaki, *Diary*, 428.

141 SUBLIMELY WOMEN TOO: Bradley, *Fly Boys*, 146.

141 "moved to tears": Ugaki, *Diary*, 437.

142 Ugaki's health, no hunting: Ibid., 439, 445, 452.

142 emperor demands a decisive battle: Bix, *Hirohito*, 476–81.

142 "Please give the Combined Fleet": Hornfischer, *Last Stand*, 101.

143 Toyoda's gamble: *Interrogations of Japanese Officials*, vol. 2, 317.

143 Toyoda described: Warner and Warner, *Sacred Warriors*, 12–13.

144 Toyoda and Ozawa: Kazutoshi Hando interview; Kazutoshi Hando, *Leyte-Oki-Kaisen (The Sea Battle Off Leyte)* (Tokyo: PHP, 1999), see chapter on three admirals; Toyoda interrogation and Fuchida interrogation, *Interrogations of Japanese Officials*, 1:130 and 2:316; Prados, *Combined Fleet Decoded*, 588–90.

146 Koyanagi goes to Manila: Tomiji Koyanagi, *Kurita Kantai—Leyte Oki Kaisen-hiroku (The Kurita Fleet—Secret Records of the Sea Battle Off Leyte)* (Tokyo: Kojinsha, 1995).

146 Koyanagi described: Yoichi Hirama interview; Kazutoshi Hando interview; *Interrogations of Japanese Officials*, 2:556.

146 Koyanagi's postwar writings: Frank, *Guadalcanal*, 588; Ito, *Imperial Japanese Navy*, 116, 180.

147 machine guns: Koyanagi interrogation, *Interrogations of Japanese Officials*, 1:147.

147 "soup with nothing": Koyanagi, *Kurita Kantai*, 55.

147 "rush forward": Ibid.

148 "According to this order": Tomiji Koyanagi, "The Battle of Leyte Gulf," Evans, ed., *Japanese Navy*, 358–59.

148 "rarely states his opinion": Koyanagi, *Kurita Kantai*, 53.

148 "On the following day": Ibid.

149 "Outwardly I rejected": Koyanagi, "The Battle of Leyte Gulf," Evans, ed., *Japanese Navy*, 358–61.

149 "Now we have something": Ugaki, *Diary*, 442.

149 "Gone is the sun": Ibid., 446.

149 "little chance of winning a victory": Ibid., 460.

150 "Though I got all wet": Ibid., 459.

150 "Who can guarantee": Ibid., 462.

150 radar in warships: Ito, *Imperial Japanese Navy*, 117–18.

150 "Halsey's forces": Ugaki, *Diary*, 456.

CHAPTER 7: BIG BLUE FLEET

151 "His eyebrows": Solberg, *Decision*, 39.

151 forty miles long: C. Vann Woodward, *The Battle for Leyte Gulf* (New York: Macmillan, 1947), 27.

151 size of Third Fleet: Hoyt, *How They Won*, 431.

151 At Sea Logistics Service Group: Reynolds, *Fast Carriers*, 251.

152 delivering oil: Rear Admiral Worrall Reed Carter, *Beans, Bullets and Black Oil* (Newport, Rhode Island: Naval War College Press, 1998), 251.

152 USS *New Jersey* described: Author's tour of USS *New Jersey*.

152 "spiritual bars": Spector, *War at Sea*, 157.

152 ice cream makers: Ibid., 131.

152 "as if written": Solberg, *Decision*, 23.

152 "rather like being hit": Ibid., 26.

153 surrey fringe on top: Halsey, *Halsey's Story*, 197.

154 Mitscher aware of Halsey's unfamiliarity with carriers: Reynolds, *Fast Carriers*, 257.

154 "I'm going to stick my neck out": Halsey, *Halsey's Story*, 199; Reynolds, *Fast Carriers*, 276–77.

154 Halsey recommends new date: Potter, *Halsey*, 278.

155 Flag Plot described: John Lawrence interview; author's tour of USS *New Jersey*.

155 Halsey "ostentatiously" reading: Solberg, *Decision*, 27.

155 "typical cavalry tactics": Rollo Wilson speech, Bates Papers, Naval War College, Newport, Rhode Island.

156 J. E. B. Stuart at Gettysburg: Stephen Sears, *Gettysburg* (Boston: Houghton Mifflin, 2003), 347–48, 391–92, 459–62.

156 IN CASE OPPORTUNITY: Potter, *Halsey*, 279.

156 "tail that wagged": Morison, *Leyte*, 58.

156 "Thank Heavens Halsey": Reynolds, *Towers*, 490.

157 Halsey writes Nimitz: Potter, *Halsey*, 279.

157 problems of divided command: Richard W. Bates, *The Battle for Leyte Gulf, October, 1944. Strategical and Tactical Analysis* (Naval War College: Prepared for the Bureau of Naval Personnel), Vol. 1, 17–18.

157 board for war games: Notes by Halsey in Hanson W. Baldwin, *Sea Fights and Shipwrecks: True Tales of the Seven Seas* (Garden City, New York: Hanover House, 1955), 175.

158 "We felt it was": Carney, *Reminiscences*, 394–95.

158 "Complete with a black tie": Halsey, *Halsey's Story*, 139.

158 "Things were hammered out": Carney, *Reminiscences*, 401–2.

158 "You, a reserve officer": John Lawrence interview.

159 Weeks described: Dr. Carnes Weeks, Jr., interview.

159 Halsey and drinking: Ibid.; John Lawrence interview; liquor supply records in William Halsey Papers, Library of Congress, Washington, D.C.

159 "We all were": John Lawrence interview.

160 Cheek described: Ibid.; Solberg, *Decision*, 125.

160 Dow discussed: Carney, *Reminiscences*, 394.

161 "Task Force Zero": Halsey, *Halsey's Story*, 204.

161 Raid on Formosa: Potter, *Halsey*, 279.

161 "Chase them!": Kazutoshi Hando, *Nihon Kaigun No Kobo (The Rise and Fall of the Japanese Navy)* (Tokyo: PHP, Kenkyujo, 1999).

161 "Well done!": Toland, *Rising Sun*, 507.

162 training by watching movie: Ibid., 508.

162 one-third shot down: Potter, *Halsey*, 282.

162 red folder: John Lawrence interview; Solberg, *Decision*, 58.

162 battle described: Solberg, *Decision*, 58.

163 Japanese scraping bottom: Carney, *Reminiscences*, 398.

163 *Canberra* and *Houston*: Samuel Eliot Morison, 95–104.

163 "throwing good ships after bad?": Halsey, *Halsey's Story*, 207.

163 Tokyo Rose described: Toland, *Rising Sun*, 555.

163 Japanese fleet sailing: Halsey, *Halsey's Story*, 206.

163 ULTRA intercept: Solberg, *Decision*, 62.

164 "thinking tired": Taussig, *Warrior*, 107.

164 BAITDIV 1: Halsey, *Halsey's Story*, 207; Morison, *Leyte*, 103.

164 a third as many as the Luftwaffe: *The Campaigns of the Pacific War* (New York: Greenwood Press, 1969), 283.

164 THE THIRD FLEET'S SUNKEN: Potter, *Halsey*, 285.

165 Japanese claims: Woodward, *Leyte*, 19–20.

165 monkey cage: Halsey, *Halsey's Story*, 206.

165 "At first": Ibid.

165 Japanese pilots' debriefing: Yasuaki Tsuji, *Maboroshi no Daisenka (The Illusive War Results)* (Tokyo: NHK, 2002), 102–6.

166 "In those days": Kosaku Koitabashi interview.

166 *tenshin*: Kenzo Ebina interview.

167 "I've been thinking": James Holloway interview.

167 Battle of Tassafaronga: Ken Jones, *Destroyer Squadron 23: Combat Exploits of Arleigh Burke's Gallant Forces.* (Annapolis: Naval Institute Press, 1997), 15.

167 bombing *Grayling*: Ibid., 162.

167 Spruance refused to believe: Hoyt, *How They Won*, 377.

167 "We had to think": John Lawrence interview.

168 Spam and beans: Morison, *Leyte*, 77.

168 "a sad picture": Solberg, *Decision*, 66.

168 "We don't hypnotize them": Taylor, *Mitscher*, 243.

168 Mitscher described: Ibid., 252.

168 staff sick: Dr. Carnes Weeks, Jr., interview.

169 "Some of us could see": Solberg, *Decision*, 66.

169 radio intercepts picked up: Radio intercepts, Radio Intelligence Division, Fleet Radio Unit, Pacific Ocean Areas, Traffic Intelligence Summaries, October 1944. National Archives; Prados, *Combined Fleet Decoded*, 629; Morison, *Leyte*, 72–3; but see Holmes, *Double-Edged Secrets*, 189.

169 Halsey chafed: Potter, *Halsey*, 287; Rollo Wilson interview, Bates Papers.

170 Halsey predicted: Morison, *Leyte*, 72.

170 Halsey "obsessed" about carriers: Taussig, *Warrior*, 111.

170 Halsey misread Japanese: Halsey to Baldwin, Bates Papers.

170 "Jap naval air": Halsey to Nimitz, October 22, 1944, Halsey Papers, Library of Congress.

170 Tarbuck: Rear Admiral Raymond D. Tarbuck, *Reminiscences*, September 4, 1971, Douglas MacArthur Memorial Foundation, Norfolk, Virginia.

170 Though the capability: Ibid.

CHAPTER 8: *SHO-GO*

173 Kurita's archery: Prados, *Combined Fleet Decoded*, 637.

173 Kurita has doubts: Ooka, "The Truth of the Turning Around by Kurita's Fleet at the Leyte Gulf." *Maru Magazines*, March 1990.

173 Koitabashi watches Kurita: Kosaku Koitabashi interview.

175 "spirited, diligent": Marder, *Old Friends*, 288.

176 Kurita divided claims in half: *Interrogations of Japanese Officials*, 1:34, 52.

177 Kurita as fall guy: Kazutoshi Hando interview; Haruo Tohmatsu interview.

177 spotty air cover: *Interrogations of Japanese Officials*, 1:51.

177 "sureness of touch": Ibid., 52.

177 Kurita's attitude: Ooka, "The Truth of the Turning Around by Kurita's Fleet at the Leyte Gulf."

178 Kurita prepares on October 16: *Campaigns of the Pacific War*, 297.

178 lacked oil: Field, *Sho Operation*, 5.

179 at 8:55: *Campaigns of the Pacific War*, 297.

179 stripping for action: Kosaku Koitabashi interview.

179 "We sailed quietly east": Ugaki, *Diary*, 479.

180 "a faintly illuminated": Ibid., 481.

180 "We are not afraid": Ibid., 472–81; Cutler, *Leyte*, 73.

180 "We knew": Hiroshi Yasunaga interview.

180 "We heard all kinds": Kosaku Koitabashi interview.

181 Kurita delays: Morison, *Leyte*, 167.

181 floatplanes: Ito, *Imperial Japanese Navy*, 123; *Campaigns of the Pacific War*, 298; Prados, *Combined Fleet Decoded*, 635, puts numbers at 41 to 45 floatplanes, of which nine remained.

181 "I'd hate to be": Ito, *Imperial Japanese Navy*, 123.

181 MacArthur lands: Manchester, *American Caesar*, 385–87.

182 "break through": *Campaigns of the Pacific War*, 297.

183 "Well, if you dare": Ugaki, *Diary*, 483.

184 "such desperate measures": *Interrogations of Japanese Officials*, 2:318.

184 vulnerable to American submarines: Prados, *Combined Fleet Decoded*, 628, 636.

184 battle plan: Field, *Sho Operation*, 31–32.

185 "Some shed tears": Arthur Herman, *To Rule the Waves: How the British Navy Shaped the Modern World* (New York: HarperCollins, 2004), 384.

185 "too complex": *Interrogations of Japanese Officials*, 1:175.

186 captains in revolt: Ito, *Imperial Japanese Navy*, 125.

186 *Atago* described: Stephen Howarth, *The Fighting Ships of the Rising Sun: The Drama of the Imperial Japanese Navy, 1895–1945* (New York: Atheneum, 1983), 163.

186 Kurita's speech: Ito, *Imperial Japanese Navy*, 125–26; Kosaku Koitabashi, *Kashikan Tachi No Taiheiyo Senso (Petty Officer's Pacific War)* (Tokyo: Kojinsha, 1986), 47.

187 "On the last": Ibid.

188 Kurita wished to be aboard *Yamato*: Ooka, "The Truth of the Turning Around by Kurita's Fleet at the Leyte Gulf"; *Interrogations of Japanese Officials*, 1:171.

188 *Darter*: Remarks of Cdr. David McClintock at Pacific War Conference, Nimitz Museum, Fredericksburg, Texas, October 8–10, 1994.

188 *Rain cloud, hell*: Toland, *Rising Sun*, 619.

190 *Dong! Dong!*: Ooka, "The Truth of the Turning Around by Kurita's Fleet at the Leyte Gulf."

191 "What's going on?": Koitabashi interview; Koitabashi, *Kashikan Tachi No Taiheiyo Senso (Petty Officers Pacific War)*, 122.

191 Koyanagi rescued: Koyanagi, *Kurita Kantai*.

192 "Do you have whiskey?": Kosaku Koitabashi interview.

192 *Atago* sinks in nineteen minutes: *Campaigns of the Pacific War*, 298.

192 ships zigzagging: Prados, *Combined Fleet Decoded*, 637.

192 "all of a sudden": Ugaki, *Diary*, 487.

193 "It looks like the Fourth of July": Cutler, *Leyte*, 101.

193 "Ugaki-kun, we were": Koyanagi, *Kurita Kantai*.

193 Kurita and Ugaki staffs: Kosaku Koitabashi interview; Field, *Sho Operation*, 50–51.

194 communications staff: *Interrogations of Japanese Officials*, 1.48, 147, 171.

194 "This may be fate": Ugaki, *Diary*, 489.

194 "it is very probable": *Campaigns of the Pacific War*, 299–300.

194 "A bad day": Ugaki, *Diary*, 489.

CHAPTER 9: A FATAL MISUNDERSTANDING

195 Halsey ill: Dr. Carnes Weeks to wife, October 26, 1944, Weeks Papers.

195 "SECRET URGENT": Solberg, *Decision*, 71–77.

196 "magnified Tokyo Express": Morison, *Leyte*, 72.

197 American superiority: Willmott, *Leyte*, 34–45.

197 staff debate: Solberg, *Decision*, 71–84, 118.

198 Halsey detaches carrier groups: Porter, *Halsey*, 27; Willmott, *Leyte*, 93.

199 "noisy, crowded": Solberg, *Decision*, 98–99.

200 "greeted with cheers": Ibid., 104.

200 McCain's carrier group ordered to reverse course: Halsey, *Halsey's Story*, 213–14.

200 "tension rose": Koyanagi, *Kurita Kantai.*

200 periscopes everywhere: Field, *Sho Operation*, 66.

200 interrupted breakfast: Ito, *Imperial Japanese Navy*, 131.

201 shells like a tropical storm: Kosaku Koitabashi interview.

201 "We had been educated": Ibid.

201 "It's too bad": Ito, *Imperial Japanese Navy*, 132.

201 "Battleship March": Ienaga, *Reluctant Admiral*, 27.

201 "The *Musashi* is unsinkable": Akira Yoshimura, *Battleship Musashi: The Making and Sinking of the World's Biggest Battleship* (New York: Kodansha International, 1992), 144.

202 Koitabashi frightened but thrilled: Kosaku Koitabashi interview.

202 "At 1040": Ugaki, *Diary*, 489.

202 weakness of the superbattleships: Evans and Peattie, *Kaigun*, 380.

203 *sanshiki dan*: Toland, *Rising Sun*, 623–24.

203 little useful intelligence: Field, *Sho Operation*, 61–62; *Interrogations of Japanese Officials*, 1:172.

203 Kurita bitter over no air cover: Field, *Sho Operation*, 67; *Interrogations of Japanese Officials*, 1:147

204 WE ARE BEING SUBJECTED: Field, *Sho Operation*, 67; *Interrogations of Japanese Officials*, 1:38; Ito, *Imperial Japanese Navy*, 133.

204 "turned a deaf ear": *Interrogations of Japanese Officials*, 2:504.

204 "A rainbow rain": Nick Fellner interview.

204 "artist renderings": Prados, *Combined Fleet Decoded*, 640.

205 phosphorus on wings: Raymond T. Stone, *"My Ship"—The USS Intrepid* (South Salem, New York: GP Books, 2003), 151.

205 Iwasa recoils: Jiro Iwasa, *Senkan Yamato Leyte-Oki No Nanokakan (Seven Days Off Leyte on the Battleship* Yamato*)* (Tokyo: Kojinsha, 1998).

206 *Musashi* retired: Ito, *Imperial Japanese Navy*, 134; Ugaki, *Diary*, 490.

206 *hachimaki* headbands: Yoshimura, *Musashi*, 155.

206 "like steel popcorn": Toland, *Rising Sun*, 623.

206 "It was regrettable": Ugaki, *Diary*, 490.

206 sickbay filled with carbon monoxide: Prados, *Combined Fleet Decoded*, 641.

207 rumor starts: Toland, *Rising Sun*, 625.

207 Otani badgers Kurita: Prados, *Combined Fleet Decoded*, 641; Ooka, "The Truth of the Turning Around by Kurita's Fleet at the Leyte Gulf."

208 UNDER THESE CIRCUMSTANCES: *Campaigns of the Pacific War*, 250–52.

208 air cover: *Interrogations of Japanese Officials*, 1:178–79.

208 Haruki flies away: Howarth, *Fighting Ships*, 348–49.

209 "Hey Rube!": Solberg, *Decision*, 101.

209 *Princeton* bombed: Adm. Frederick C. Sherman, *Combat Command: The American Aircraft Carriers in the Pacific War* (New York: Bantam, 1982), 250–52.

209 Halsey guesses wrongly: Morison, *Leyte*, 194.

209 "Where in the hell": Halsey, *Halsey's Story*, 216.

209 ULTRA material: Solberg, *Decision*, 111.

210 "I shall disregard": Ito, *Imperial Japanese Navy*, 156.

210 radio antenna broken: *Interrogations of Japanese Officials*, 1:155–57; Field, *Sho Operation*, 63.

211 "remnants": Morison, *Leyte*, 191–92.

211 Ozawa looks away: Ito, *Imperial Japanese Navy*, 156.

211 Sherman first spots attackers: Solberg, *Decision*, 112.

211 "Battle Plan": Ibid., 115; Potter, *Halsey*, 293.

212 Kinkaid intercepts message: Cutler, *Leyte*, 160.

213 Kinkaid misinterprets message: Ibid., 161. For Carney's defense of his message, see Carney's review of *Leyte* in Bates Papers. He says he used "standard terminology and formulation of orders."

214 staff work in navy weak: Adm. Stansfield Turner interview.

214 Kinkaid and Halsey opposites: Woodward, *Leyte*, 29.

214 Halsey relieves Kinkaid: Admiral Frederick C. Sherman, *Wartime Diary*, Naval Historical Center, Washington, D.C.

CHAPTER 10: SHIPS IN THE NIGHT

217 "We've stopped 'em!": Solberg, *Decision*, 108.

218 "good look": Morison, *Leyte*, 192.

218 meeting of Department of Dirty Tricks: Solberg, *Decision*, 117–18; Halsey, *Halsey's Story*, 215–16; Halsey, draft of memoirs, 504–8; Cutler, *Leyte*, 162–63; Potter, *Halsey*, 284–85; Willmott, *Leyte*, 120–30; John Lawrence interview; review of Samuel Eliot Morison's *Leyte* by Admiral Carney and Halsey to Baldwin in Bates Papers; interview with Clark Reynolds, who provided me with his correspondence with Halsey's staff about the deliberations of October 24, 1944: Ralph Wilson to Reynolds, August 15, 1967; M. C. Cheek to Reynolds, June 16, 1966; Harold Stassen to Reynolds, June 25, 1964, August 12, 1964, in Clark Reynolds Papers. Thanks to Rich Frank for his excellent analysis, "Halsey's 'Great Decision' at Leyte Gulf," September 2004 (for a paper delivered to Battle of Leyte Gulf Conference, September 28–29, 2005, Nimitz Museum, Fredericksburg, Texas).

222 "mea culpa": John Lawrence interview.

222 "miserable position": Ugaki, *Diary*, 491.

223 "a strange anxiety": Kosaku Koitabashi interview.

223 Iwasa on bridge: Iwasa, *Senkan Yamato Leyte-Oki No Nanokakan (Seven Days Off Leyte on the Battleship* Yamato).

223 "heart ached": Ooka, "The Truth of the Turning Around by Kurita's Fleet at the Leyte Gulf."

223 Kurita's decision to turn around: Koyanagi, *Kurita Kantai.* Ooka, "The Truth of the Turning Around by Kurita's Fleet at the Leyte Gulf"; Koitabashi interview; Ito, *Imperial Japanese Navy*, 140.

224 PROBABILITY IS GREAT: Ito, *Imperial Japanese Navy*, 136.

224 TRUSTING IN DIVINE: *Campaigns of the Pacific War*, 301.

224 Toyoda explains: *Interrogations of Japanese Officials*, 2:317.

224 "Leave the fighting": Ito, *Imperial Japanese Navy*, 140.

224 Inoguchi letter: Toland, *Rising Sun*, 627. His apology is not reproduced in a fragment of the letter quoted by Yoshimura, *Musashi*, 175.

224 "The Emperor's portrait!": Spector, *War at Sea*, 295.

225 "Shanghai Gal": Toland, *Rising Sun*, 629.

225 "had sacrificed herself": Ugaki, *Diary*, 491–92.

226 "Here's where I'm going": Halsey, *Halsey's Story*, 217; Third Fleet War Diary, 33–34, National Archives, Washington, D.C.

226 Halsey tells Lee: Paul Stilwell interview.

227 Halsey believes headlines: Potter, *Nimitz*, 335.

227 "We were obsessed": John Lawrence interview.

227 "It was unbelievable": Ibid.

227 Halsey and drinking: Dr. Carnes Weeks, Jr., interview.

228 "Adm. Bill, Mick": Dr. Carnes Weeks to Margaret Weeks, October 26, 1944.

229 "Halsey's favorite": Cheek to Clark Reynolds, June 16, 1955.

229 "They're coming through": Solberg, *Decision*, 125.

229 "finished": Cheek to Clark Reynolds, June 16, 1955.

229 Harris Cox and Solberg: Solberg, *Decision*, 120–24.

229 Z Orders: "Z Orders," Douglas MacArthur Memorial Foundation, Norfolk, Virginia, 14–15.

230 "He kept the document": Solberg, *Decision*, 122.

231 "Since you feel so strongly": Cheek to Clark Reynolds, June 16, 1955. Carney, *Reminiscences*, is silent on the matter.

231 "I silently agreed": Ibid.

233 "Roger": Aerston to Morison, March 6, 1950, Bates Papers.

233 Lee did not press his opinion: Paul Stilwell interview.

233 Bogan and Halsey: Vice Admiral Gerald F. Bogan, *Reminiscences*, 1970, 1986, U.S. Naval Institute, Annapolis, Maryland; Bogan to Morison, July 2, 1957, Morison Papers, Naval Historical Center, Washington, D.C.; Bogan to Clark Reynolds, May 11, 1964, courtesy Clark Reynolds.

233 Mitscher and Halsey: Taylor, *Mitscher*, 260–62; Potter, *Halsey*, 297.

235 "didn't look a day": Cutler, *Leyte*, 212.

235 "Well, I think": Potter, *Halsey*, 297.

236 "Admiral, we better": Taylor, *Mitscher*, 262.

236 Lt. Bill Phelps: Solberg, *Decision*, 126.

CHAPTER 11: SURPRISE AT DAWN

237 "It was": Kosaku Koitabashi interview.

238 "Chancing annihilation": *Campaigns of the Pacific War*, 301.

238 Nishimura speeds up: Prados, *Combined Fleet Decoded*, 658–59.

239 Kurita pep talk: Tomiji Koyanagi interview in John Toland Papers, Franklin Delano Roosevelt Presidential Library, Hyde Park, New York.

239 "We were told": Field, *Sho Operation*, 53.

239 Battle of Surigao Strait: Morison, *Leyte*, 217–34, 240–41.

240 "We have received": Field, *Sho Operation*, 87.

241 "Sorry!": Cutler, *Leyte*, 203.

241 Shima described: Field, *Sho Operation*, 32–33, 89–94; Morison, *Leyte*, 233.

241 Shima at Surigao Strait: Kiyohide Shima interview in John Toland Papers.

241 rigged a lasso: Morison, *Leyte*, 234–35.

243 slit comrade's throat: Bob Chandler remarks, Battle of Leyte Gulf Conference,

Nimitz Museum; Fredericksurg, Texas, Sept. 18–19, 2003.

243 "glamour of sea battle": Manchester, *American Caesar*, 392.

243 Kinkaid's assumption: Kinkaid notes, Bates Papers.

243 "Am proceeding north": Third Fleet Diary, 35, William Halsey Papers, Library of Congress.

244 report of night snoopers: H. P. Willmott, *Leyte*, 244, says Halsey did not notify Kinkaid, but Gerald E. Wheeler, *Kinkaid of the Seventh Fleet: A Biography of Admiral Thomas C. Kinkaid, U.S. Navy* (Washington, D.C.: Naval Historical Center, 1995), 400, and Halsey letter to Baldwin say he did. I could find no record of such a telegram in the Seventh Fleet Message file at the National Archives.

244 "We've never asked Halsey": Wheeler, *Kinkaid*, 400.

244 communications difficulties: Potter, *Halsey*, 290.

245 "we are still having": Halsey to Nimitz, October 22, 1944, Library of Congress.

245 Black Cat: Bandy to Kinkaid, April 21, 1953, Bates Papers.

246 jeep carriers described: John F. Wukovits, *Devotion to Duty: A Biography of Admiral Clifton A. F. Sprague* (Annapolis: Naval Institute Press, 1995), 124; Hornfischer, *Last Stand*, 67.

247 "Jeep carriers": Morison, *Leyte*, 242.

247 Kinkaid should have moved: Rich Frank analysis at Battle of Leyte Gulf Conference at Nimitz Museum, Fredericksburg, Texas, Sept. 18–19, 2003.

247 Powell warns: Paulus Powell to Morison, April 2, 1959, Morison Papers, Nimitz Collection, Naval Historical Center, Washington, D.C.

248 Taffy air searches: Morison, *Leyte*, 244–45.

248 Evans misses action: Ed Digardi interview.

249 "Well, Hagen": Robert C. Hagen, "We Asked for the Jap Fleet—And Got It," *Saturday Evening Post*, May 28, 1945.

249 "I swore up": *Fighting and Sinking*, 6.

249 "learned to adjust": Ibid., 27.

250 *Johnston* in typhoon: Ed Digardi interview.

250 "night search disposition": Field, *Sho Operation*, 98.

251 "completely destroyed": *Interrogations of Japanese Officials*, 1:173.

251 "taking matters too lightly": Ibid., 172.

251 "about wiped out": Ibid., 174; Field, *Sho Operation*, 98.

251 weather at dawn: Field, *Sho Operation*, 99.

251 "dark clouds": Ugaki, *Diary*, 492.

252 "Do you have any": Taylor, *Mitscher*, 263; Potter, *Halsey*, 298–99.

252 "an enormous Stars and Stripes": Solberg, *Decision*, 150–51.

253 "With almost": Ibid., 151.

253 Koyanagi in pain: Tomiji Koyanagi interview in John Toland Papers.

254 "practiced silence': Ibid.

255 Koyanagi spots planes: *Interrogations of Japanese Officials*, 1:150; Kosaku Koitabashi, *Senkan 'Yamato' Imada Shizumazu (Battleship* Yamato *Hasn't Gone Under Yet)* (Tokyo: Kojinsha, 1984), 183.

256 Masts on the horizon: Field, *Sho Operation*, 100; *Campaigns of the Pacific War*, 302, gives time as 0644.

256 Maybe there were miracles: Tomiji Koyanagi interview in John Toland Papers.

CHAPTER 12: THEY WERE EXPENDABLE

257 "Oh, we're the boys": William T. Y'Blood, *The Little Giants: U.S. Escort Carriers Against Japan* (Annapolis: Naval Institute Press, 1987), xiii.

257 "rich kids": Ibid., 166.

257 Bill Brooks: Hornfischer, *Last Stand*, 135–37.

258 "Air plot, tell him": Wukovits, *Devotion*, 142–43.

258 "I can see": Hornfischer, *Last Stand*, 136.

258 "It's impossible!": Ibid.

259 "A sighted enemy": Woodward, *Leyte*, 173.

259 Kurita witnessed *Hornet: Interrogations of Japanese Officials*, 1:52.

259 BY HEAVEN SENT: *Campaigns of the Pacific War*, 303.

260 Kurita battle plan: *Interrogations of Japanese Officials*, 1:150–51; *Campaigns of the Pacific War*, 302–3.

260 Japan weak at improvising: See Carney, *Reminiscences*.

260 "Firing should be": Kosaku Koitabashi interview.

260 "each unit seemed": Ugaki, *Diary*, 492–93.

261 just like the movies: Kosaku Koitabashi interview.

261 "smelling delightful": *Fighting and Sinking*, 181.

261 "major portion": Ibid., b-3.

262 "I felt like David": Ibid., 99.

262 Mercer thinks of mother: Bill Mercer interview.

263 "thought someone was joking": *Fighting and Sinking*, 27.

263 "make smoke": Ibid., 120.

263 valves stuck: Ibid., 69.

263 Digardi and fuel oil: Ed Digardi interview.

264 "Jesus Christ!": Ibid.

264 "whoosh-whoosh": Bill Mercer interview.

264 trouser zipper: *Fighting and Sinking*, 69.

264 "like freight trains": Ed Digardi interview.

264 Evans expected Halsey: *Fighting and Sinking*, 85.

266 "I thought that": Ibid, 67.

266 "I want to be home": Ed Takkunen interview.

266 "One thing": *Fighting and Sinking*, 48–49.

267 "Holy shit": Bob Hollenbaugh interview.

267 "Pillar of fire!": Ito, *Imperial Japanese Navy*, 162.

267 "A very great explosion": *Interrogations of Japanese Officials*, 1:43.

267 smoke confuses: Hornfischer, *Last Stand*, 176–77.

267 "They're shooting": Wukovits, *Devotion*, 149.

267 Bogan happy to get off: Ibid., 113.

267 Sprague described: Ibid., 41, 54–55.

268 "Get the damn things": Ibid., 146.

268 "to give them": Ibid.

268 "Don't be alarmed": Ibid., 148.

269 "Stand by to form": Hornfischer, *Last Stand*, 177.

269 weight of broadsides: *Fighting and Sinking*, 99.

269 "We can't go down": Ibid., 86.

270 "We just looked": Ibid., 158.
270 "afraid we'd get": Robert Hagen interview.
270 "Looks like someone's mad": *Fighting and Sinking*, 99.
270 torpedo run: Hornfischer, *Last Stand*, 184–85; *Fighting and Sinking*, 182.
270 "My God": Kosaku Koitabashi interview.
271 "Wait! Wait!": Pyzdrowski speech at Pacific War conference, Nimitz Museum, Fredericksburg, Texas, October 8–10, 1994.
272 Kurita's officers surprised: Field, *Sho Operation*, 102.
272 "They strafed courageously": Ugaki, *Diary*, 492–94.
272 *Johnston* hit: *Fighting and Sinking*, 54, 70, 99, 158.
274 "to maintain morale": Ellsworth Welch interview.
274 "Stand by below!": Bill Mercer interview.
274 "My thoughts": *Fighting and Sinking*, 13.
275 "Don't bother me now": Ibid., 99.
275 damage to *Johnston:* Ibid., 70.
275 a few sailors cracked: Jesse Cochran interview; Ed Digardi interview.
275 "Gun 54 declared": *Fighting and Sinking*, 105.
275 "solid red": Ibid., 143.
275 Hagen reached for cigarette: Ibid., 99.
276 "I have often": Ibid., 75.
276 "We'll provide": Ed Digardi interview; Robert Hagen interview; Robert Hagen to Ed Digardi, May 9, 1997, courtesy Robert Hagen.
276 near collision: *Fighting and Sinking*, 99; Ed Digardi interview.
278 "Let's get": *Fighting and Sinking*, 137.
278 "dreamy" state: Ibid., 100.
278 "Commence firing": Ibid.
278 "the *Johnston* signed": Morison, *Leyte*, 272.
278 Kimura battle report: Ibid.
278 "we were firing": *Fighting and Sinking*, 41.
280 "a most amazing thing": Ibid., b-5.
280 "Commander Evans, feeling": Ibid., 100.
280 *St. Lo* deflects torpedo: Morison, *Leyte*, 272.
280 "three enemy carriers": Ibid.
282 "Help needed": Ibid.
282 "Where the hell": Ed Digardi interview.
282 Kinkaid messages: Morison, *Leyte*, 293.
282 "Staff work": Sprague notes on C. Vann Woodward book, courtesy John Wukovits.
283 "Your prediction": Tarbuck, *Reminiscences*.

CHAPTER 13: THE WORLD WONDERS

285 Japanese shooting poor. *Interrogations of Japanese Officials*, 1:43.
285 "combing" torpedoes: Ibid., 44, 151.
285 "but it felt like": Ugaki, *Diary*, 493.
286 Kurita blames Morishita: Ooka, "The Truth of the Turning Around by Kurita's Fleet at the Leyte Gulf."

286 *Yamato* falls behind: Field, *Sho Operation*, 103.

286 "not a man": Kosaku Koitabashi interview.

286 Pyzdrowski on *Gambier Bay*: Edwin P. Hoyt, *The Men of the Gambier Bay: The Amazing True Story of the Battle of Leyte Gulf* (Guilford, Connecticut: Lyons Press, 2002), 206–7; Pyzdrowski speech at Pacific War conference, Nimitz Museum, Fredericksburg, Texas, October 8–10, 1994.

287 *If we get any closer: Fighting and Sinking*, 99.

287 "Look at the little": Wukovits, *Devotion*, 171.

288 coke bottle, pistol: Hornfischer, *Last Stand*, 242, 246.

288 *Chokai* and *Chikuma* hit: Willmott, *Leyte*, 180–82.

288 Kurita's assumptions: *Interrogations of Japanese Officials*, 1:42, 44.

288 how Japanese understood the message: Ugaki, *Diary*, 494.

289 Kurita's fuel shortage: *Interrogations of Japanese Officials*, 1:173; Willmott, *Leyte*, 185.

289 Kurita's losses: *Interrogations of Japanese Officials*, 1:186.

289 "in the dark": Tomiji Koyanagi interview in John Toland Papers.

289 "The officers on the bridge": Koitabashi, *Kashikan Tachi No Taiheiyo Senso (Petty Officers Pacific War)*, 193.

289 shell a dud: *Interrogations of Japanese Officials*, 1:174.

290 "God damn it, boys": Wukovits, *Devotion*, 178.

290 trajectory of shells: *Fighting and Sinking*, 65.

290 "as if to get the hot": Ibid., 164.

291 "drove under the spray": Ibid., 183.

291 "bellowing orders": Ibid., 103.

292 "What the hell": Ibid., 100; Robert Hagen interview.

292 Digardi leaves ship: Ed Digardi interview.

292 "as brightly as if": *Fighting and Sinking*, 100.

292 "I don't guess": Ibid., 130.

292 "Someone help me!": Ibid., 34.

292 Landreth would "get" him: Ibid., 120.

294 "Abandon ship!": Robert Hagen interview.

294 "There she goes!": *Fighting and Sinking*, 91.

294 Dixon cries: Ibid.

294 "I must have looked": Ibid., 184.

294 Japanese ship, salute: Ibid., 77, 88, 110, 131, 138, 159.

294 sudden silence: Robert Hagen interview.

295 "I have the target": Solberg, *Decision*, 151.

295 message arrives: Ibid., 152.

295 Halsey not worried: Halsey, *Halsey's Story*, 219–20; Potter, *Halsey*, 302–3.

296 Halsey "angrier": Halsey, *Halsey's Story*, 221.

296 Halsey protested too much: Potter, *Halsey*, 303.

296 "face was ashen": Solberg, *Decision*, 152–53.

296 "Suddenly": Ibid.

296 MY SITUATION: Ibid.

297 "If I were there": Potter, *Nimitz*, 336.

297 "I really cannot see": Herman, *To Rule the Waves*, 367.

297 Nimitz's doubts: Potter, *Nimitz*, 337.

298 "My God, I hope": Ambassador William J. Sebald, *Reminiscences*, Vol. 1, U.S. Naval Institute, Annapolis, Maryland.

299 Holmes and Layton: Holmes, *Double-Edged Secrets*, 192.

300 "just something that popped": John R. Redman to Adm. Chester Nimitz, May 11, 1953, Bates Papers.

300 Halsey sobs: Potter, *Nimitz*, 340–41; Potter, *Halsey*, 303, 403; Halsey, draft of memoirs, 514.

301 "What right does": Solberg, *Decision*, 154.

301 "exactly 42 miles": Halsey, *Halsey's Story*, 220–22.

302 Seki and Onishi: Capt. Rikihei Inoguchi and Cdr. Tadashi Kakjima, *The Divine Wind: Japan's Kamikaze Force in World War II* (Annapolis: Naval Institute Press, 1958), 12, 19, 50.

302 "Personal effects": Ibid., 34.

303 attack on *St. Lo*: Hornfischer, *Last Stand*, 352.

303 3,912 Japanese airmen kill themselves: Frank, *Downfall*, 180.

304 "bull": Karl F. Friday, "Bushido or Bull? A Medieval Historian's Perspective on the Imperial Army and the Japanese Warrior Tradition." *Journal of Alternative Perspectives*, March 2001.

304 Kurita knew better: Shigeko Terada interview.

305 seeing white in one's head: Hiroyuki Agawa interview; Haruo Tohmatsu interview.

CHAPTER 14: THE MYSTERIOUS TELEGRAM

307 "What did they think": Ugaki, *Diary*, 495.

307 Koyanagi's thoughts: Koyanagi, *Kurita Kantai*.

307 "to shoot drowning dogs": Kosaku Koitabashi interview.

307 Kurita orders fleet to head southwest: *Campaigns of the Pacific War*, 305.

308 "pond": Tomiji Koyanagi interview in John Toland Papers.

308 "Our heads were cooling": Ibid.; Willmott, *Leyte*, 187; Rich Frank interview.

308 "bearing 5 degrees": *Campaigns of the Pacific War*, 304.

308 "hardly above a whisper": Yukihiro Fukuda, *Rengokantai: Saipan Reiteoki Kaisen (The Combined Fleet: Battles of the Philippine Sea and Leyte)* (Tokyo: Jiji-tsushinsha, 1981), 353.

309 "Carriers were our obsession": Tomiji Koyanagi interview in John Toland Papers; Rear Admiral Tomika Koyanagi, "With Kurita in the Battle for Leyte Gulf," *U.S. Naval Institute Proceedings*, February 1953, 126–28, 131–32.

309 Kurita issues new orders: *Campaigns of the Pacific War*, 305.

309 *"Banzai!"*: Kosaku Koitabashi interview; Ito, *Imperial Japanese Navy*, 167.

310 controversy over telegram: Fukuda, *Rengokantai*, 348–56. Fukuda credits the existence of the telegram but offers strong evidence to contradict it; interviews with Haruo Tomahtsu, Kazushige Todaka, Kazutoshi Hando—Japanese naval scholars who doubt the existence of the telegram.

310 "Kurita-san": Kazushige Todaka interview.

310 "Why are we turning?": Ooka, "The Truth of the Turning Around by Kurita's Fleet at the Leyte Gulf"; Kazushige Todaka interview.

311 "accomplished the great feat": Ugaki, *Diary*, 495.

311 fired only eighty-one shells: Ito, *Imperial Japanese Navy*, 172.

311 "they wavered again": Ugaki, *Diary*, 496–97.

311 Ito puts on helmet: Fukuda, *Rengokantai*, 354.

311 "A symphony of moans": Robert Hagen interview.

312 Bechdel sings: Hornfischer, *Last Stand*, 375.

312 Carter's thoughts: *Fighting and Sinking*, 42.

312 handing out rations: Ibid., 28, 56, 88.

312 "the size": Ibid., 56.

312 wrong coordinates: Hornfischer, *Last Stand*, 375.

313 Zeros strafe own ships: Tomiji Koyanagi interview in John Toland Papers.

313 Ugaki insists: Ugaki, *Diary*, 496.

313 Ozawa's actions: Ito, *Imperial Japanese Navy*, 159.

314 "If there is an opportunity": Field, *Sho Operation*, 128; *Campaigns of the Pacific War*, 306.

314 messages to *New Jersey*: Third Fleet Diary, 37–38, William F. Halsey Papers.

314 "Each message": John Lawrence interview.

314 "And it could have been": Solberg, *Decision*, 156.

315 Halsey heads south: Third Fleet Diary, 39, William F. Halsey Papers.

315 THE JAPANESE NAVY: Halsey, *Halsey's Story*, 226.

315 Roosevelt calls in reporters: Potter, *Halsey*, 306.

315 "U.S. DEFEATS": *New York Times*, October 26, 1944.

316 "As it seemed childish": Morison, *Leyte*, 194.

316 "It was the first": Halsey, *Halsey's Story*, 224.

316 Check warms himself: *Fighting and Sinking*, 57.

316 singing, praying: Ibid., 49, 66.

316 Japanese ship passes: Ibid., 22, 49, 89.

317 shark attacks: Ibid., 37, 45.

317 Welch attacked: Ibid., 184.

317 cut the man's throat: Ed Digardi interview.

317 Bechdel dies: *Fighting and Sinking*, 93.

317 Life jackets removed: Ibid., 49.

317 "Bill, you go": Ed Takkunen interview.

317 Check and Coleman: *Fighting and Sinking*, 57.

318 "Jap swimmers were": Halsey, *Halsey's Story*, 225.

318 *Yamato* hit twice: Ito, *Imperial Japanese Navy*, 181.

318 *Yamato* floods aft compartments: Ugaki, *Diary*, 500.

318 Koyanagi wounded: Tomiji Koyanagi interview, John Toland Papers.

318 Koitabashi wounded: Kosaku Koitabashi interview.

320 "This was the last": Ugaki, *Diary*, 500–501.

320 Mercer watches life jacket sink: *Fighting and Sinking*, 132.

320 hallucinations: Ibid., 29, 44, 50, 77.

320 "If you slept": James Johnson interview.

320 Second night, third day, rescue: *Fighting and Sinking*, 89, 51, 154, 168.

322 Wouk inspired: Herman Wouk interview.

322 "by God": Wouk, *War and Remembrance*, 961.

322 "The vision": Ibid., 971.

322 total sunk: Cutler, *Leyte*, 285.

322 American casualties: Willmott, *Leyte*, 250.

322 "weapon of despair": Ibid., 240.

CHAPTER 15: THE LAST KAMIKAZE

323 "The Admiral asked": Dr. Carnes Weeks to Margaret Weeks, November 11, 1944, Weeks Papers.

324 "We dare": Halsey, *Halsey's Story*, 203.

325 Carney and Navy Cross: Taussig, *Warrior*, 145.

325 Mitscher briefing: Taylor, *Mitscher*, 298.

325 "blue with rage": Reynolds, *Fast Carriers*, 275, 280.

325 WE HAVE COOPERATED: Lt. Gen. Richard Sutherland Papers, Douglas MacArthur Memorial Foundation, Norfolk, Virginia.

326 "That's enough!": D. Clayton James, *The Years of MacArthur* (Boston: Houghton Mifflin, 1975), vol. 2, 564–65.

326 "Ziggy I didn't": Wukovits, *Devotion*, 206.

326 "just got pictures": Dr. Carnes Weeks to Margaret Weeks, December 14, 1944, Weeks Papers.

326 "I am running": Dr. Carnes Weeks to Margaret Weeks, November 11 and November 18, 1944, Weeks Papers.

326 "After the meal": Reynolds, *Fighting Lady*, 301.

327 "When he partied": Dr. Carnes Weeks, Jr., interview.

327 "Yesterday we had": Dr. Carnes Weeks to Margaret Weeks, November 27, 1944, Weeks Papers.

327 "An instant after": Halsey, *Halsey's Story*, 229–32.

327 "It's difficult to describe": Taussig, *Warrior*, 114.

327 "tossed . . . as if": Halsey, *Halsey's Story*, 239

328 Court of Inquiry: Reynolds, *Fast Carriers*, 293–95; Hans Christian Adamson and George Francis Kosco, *Halsey's Typhoon* (New York: Crown, 1967), *passim*.

328 Sinks *Kashii*: Prados, *Combined Fleet Decoded*, 702.

328 Halsey denied fifth star: Reynolds, *Fast Carriers*, 327.

328 "I made a mistake": Halsey, *Halsey's Story*, 226.

328 "errors in judgment": Adamson, *Halsey's Typhoon*, 144.

329 "Japanese forces now have": Prados, *Combined Fleet Decoded*, 687–90.

329 Kurita and Inoue: Hiroyuki Agawa interview.

329 Kurita at home: Shigeko Terada interview.

330 "Day of Chrysanthemum": Ugaki, *Diary*, 506, 517–18, 522, 528.

330 "Tennozan": Drea, *In the Service*, 196–98.

331 "Was not the use": Ito, *Imperial Japanese Navy*, 191.

331 MacArthur surrender planned: Drea, *In the Service*, 196.

331 Ugaki summoned: Ugaki, *Diary*, 536; Hoyt, *Last Kamikaze*, 155.

331 attack on Ulithi: Hoyt, *Last Kamikaze*, 169; Ugaki, *Diary*, 539.

332 Tokyo bombed: Frank, *Downfall*, 9, 17–18; Havens, *Valley of Darkness*, 122.

332 pilots "herded": Millott, *Divine Thunder*, 15–17.

332 Japanese sink thirty-four warships: Prados, *Combined Fleet Decoded*, 718.

332 Ugaki's diary entries: Ugaki, *Diary*, 559, 580.

332 "with a smile": Ibid., 550.

333 *Yamato* sunk: Prados, *Combined Fleet Decoded*, 711–14; Russell Spurr, *A Glorious Way to Die: The Kamikaze Mission of the Battleship Yamato, April, 1945* (New York: Bantam, 1983), *passim*.

333 Yoshida on bridge: Yoshida, *Requiem*, 106–8.

334 "special attack" squadrons less effective: Ugaki, *Diary*, 599.

334 Ugaki's family: Ibid., 587, 598.

334 Ugaki lives in cave: Ibid., 610.

334 "killed Roosevelt": Ibid., 584, 603.

335 "dangerous to the horse's legs": Ibid., 619.

335 Halsey in typhoon: Potter, *Halsey*, 340; Reynolds, *Fast Carriers*, 347–49.

335 Halsey on *Time* cover: *Time*, July 23, 1945.

335 Halsey ridiculed: Reynolds, *Fighting Lady*, 300, 302.

336 "Halsey has not been": Ibid., 234.

336 war too complicated: Clark Reynolds interview.

336 "Does the enemy intend": Ugaki, *Diary*, 634.

336 "We could bomb": Bradley, *Fly Boys*, 290.

336 "burn jobs": Frank, *Downfall*, 150.

336 Ugaki a "nihilist": Ugaki, *Diary*, 639.

336 Ugaki inspects hangars: Hoyt, *Last Kamikaze*, 201.

336 *Ketsu-Go*: Frank, *Downfall*, 184, 359.

337 "Patriotic Citizens Fighting Corps": Ibid., 189; Bradley, *Fly Boys*, 290–91.

337 Japan lost three million people: Frank, *Downfall*, 350–51.

337 Americans see trap: Drea, *In the Service*, 210.

337 emperor's jewels: Ibid., 211.

338 "If we are prepared": Frank, *Downfall*, 311.

338 Hirohito surrenders: Ibid., 311–22.

338 smoke of burning documents: Dower, *Embracing Defeat*, 39.

338 Onishi suicide: Toland, *Rising Sun*, 965.

339 Ugaki's kamikaze mission: Ugaki, *Diary*, 663–66.

340 Yasunaga watches Ugaki: Hiroshi Yasunaga interview.

340 "ram into": Ugaki, *Diary*, 666.

340 *LST 296*: Hiroshi Ozawa, "The True Account of the Last Moments of Admiral Ugaki," *Maru Magazine*, March 1999.

341 Eta Jima cadets from *Yamato*: Yoshida, *Requiem*, 18–19.

341 "He told us": Manabu Yoshida interview.

341 "Five Reflections": Author's tour of Eta Jima.

EPILOGUE: WHY THEY FOUGHT

345 "To hell with": *New York Herald Tribune*, October 16, 1945.

345 Halsey's victory tour: Potter, *Halsey*, 364–65.

345 "My only fear": Halsey, *Halsey's Story*, 292.

345 "at length came": Potter, *Halsey*, 372.

346 "I feel lost": John Thach, *Reminiscences*, U.S. Naval Institute, Annapolis, Maryland.

346 "Boy, do you drink?": John McCain interview.

346 Halsey drinks too much: Dr. Carnes Weeks, Jr., interview.

346 "Did I ever tell": Cdr. Albert K. Murray, *Reminiscences*, U.S. Naval Institute, Annapolis, Maryland, 1994.

346 *Admiral Halsey's Story*: *Saturday Evening Post* articles appeared in the June 14, June 21, June 28, July 5, July 19, July 26, August 2, 1947, issues.

346 "I wondered": Halsey, *Halsey's Story*, 371.

347 Kinkaid angry: Cdr. Albert K. Murray, *Reminiscences*, U.S. Naval Institute, Annapolis, Maryland, 1983.

347 In Baldwin's book: See Hanson W. Baldwin, *Sea Fights and Shipwrecks: True Tales of the Seven Seas* (Garden City, New York: Hanover House, 1955).

347 "Bull's Run": Gilbert Cant, "Bull's Run: Was Halsey Right at Leyte Gulf?" *Life*, November 24, 1947.

347 "Admiral, you made": Solberg, *Decision*, 176.

347 "I wish that": Taylor, *Mitscher*, 265.

347 "He went to your college": John Lawrence interview.

347 "personal animosity": Halsey to Gil Slonim, May 5, 1959, Halsey Papers, Library of Congress.

347 "Ham Dow came in": Halsey to Carney, November 10, 1958, Halsey Papers, Library of Congress.

348 "My idea is": Halsey to Rollo Wilson, November 10, 1958, Halsey Papers, Library of Congress.

348 "My dear Admiral Bill": Carney to Halsey, November 14, 1958, Halsey Papers, Library of Congress.

348 U.S. Naval War College study: During the years 1953–1958, Admiral Richard Bates conducted an extensive strategic and tactical analysis of the Battle of Leyte Gulf. Only four out of five volumes were actually completed. A copy of the study is available at the Naval Historical Center in Washington, D.C., and the Bates Papers are located at the Naval War College at Newport, Rhode Island.

348 Halsey's consolations: Potter, *Halsey*, 375–76.

348 Halsey and A-bomb: Hoyt, *How They Won*, 496.

349 Halsey's burial: *New York Times* and *Washington Post*, August 17, 21, 1959; Potter, *Halsey*, 381.

349 not much work for IJN admirals: Prados, *Combined Fleet Decoded*, 732.

349 Kurita at home: Shigeko Terada interview and Kazuko Naoe interview.

350 Kurita interview with Ito: Ito, *Imperial Japanese Navy*, 177–79.

351 Kurita and Ooka: Ooka, "The Truth of the Turning Around by Kurita's Fleet at the Leyte Gulf"; Yukihiro Fukuda, *Rengokantai: Saipan Reiteoki Kaisen* (*The Combined Fleet: Battles of the Philippine Sea and Leyte*), 17.

352 Kurita and Tokoi: Seiichiro Tokoi interview.

353 "fight bravely": Ito, *Imperial Japanese Navy*, 200.

353 Kurita funeral: Manabu Yoshida interview.

353 "It may well be": Winston S. Churchill, *The Second World War: Triumph and Tragedy* (Boston: Houghton Mifflin, 1953), 184–85.

354 Evans's Medal of Honor citation: *Fighting and Sinking*, 3.
354 "beyond the call of duty": Ed Takkunen interview.
355 "blank—he was just staring": Robert Sochor interview.
355 "This is a delicate question": Manabu Yoshida interview.
355 "Naturally, we don't": Havens, *Valley of Darkness*, 140–41.

BIBLIOGRAPHY

ORAL HISTORIES, DIARIES, AND REMINISCENCES

Bak, Michael, Jr. *Reminiscences,* 1988. U.S. Naval Institute, Annapolis, Maryland.

Bogan, Vice Admiral Gerald F. *Reminiscences,* 1970, 1986. U.S. Naval Institute, Annapolis, Maryland.

Carney, Robert Bostwick. *Reminiscences.* Naval History Project, Columbia University, 1964.

The Fighting and Sinking of the USS Johnston *DD 557 as Told by Her Crew.* Written and coordinated by Bill Mercer. Privately printed, Johnston-Hoel Association, September 1991.

Hagen, Lt. Robert C. "Narrative of Second Battle of Philippines." December 20, 1944. Film No. 317. National Archives, College Park, Maryland.

Halsey, William F., Jr. Draft of memoirs. Courtesy John Wukovitz.

Hedding, Vice Admiral Truman J. *Reminiscences.* U.S. Naval Institute, Annapolis, Maryland.

Holloway, Adm. James L. Oral History. U.S. Naval Institute, Annapolis, Maryland.

Huffman, Ernest Glenn. *Recollections of the USS* Samuel B. Roberts. September 24, 2003. Author's Collection.

Interview notes of conversation with Fleet Admiral Ernest King by Walter Whitehill. Courtesy Clark Reynolds.

Kenney, Gen. George C. *Diary.* General Douglas MacArthur Foundation, Norfolk, Virginia.

Lamar, Cdr. Hal. Oral History, October 9, 1994. University of North Texas, Oral History Collection, No. 1059.

Murray, Cdr. Albert K. *Reminiscences,* 1994. U.S. Naval Institute, Annapolis, Maryland.

Rochefort, Capt. Joseph. *Reminiscences,* 1983. U.S. Naval Institute, Annapolis, Maryland.

Sebald, Ambassador William J. *Reminiscences,* 1979. Vol. 1. U.S. Naval Institute, Annapolis, Maryland.

Sherman, Adm. Frederick C. *Wartime Diary, World War II.* U.S. Naval Historical Center, Washington, D.C.

Tarbuck, Rear Admiral Raymond D. *Reminiscences.* Interviewer: D. Clayton James. Coronado, California, September 4, 1971. General Douglas MacArthur Foundation, Norfolk, Virginia

————. *Reminiscences,* 1973. U.S. Naval Institute, Annapolis, Maryland.

Thach, Adm. John Smith. *Reminiscences,* November 1977. Vols. 1 and 2. U.S. Naval Institute, Annapolis, Maryland.

Tolley, Rear Admiral Kemp. *Reminiscences,* 1984. Vol. 2. U.S. Naval Institute, Annapolis, Maryland.

Van Deurs, Rear Admiral George. *Reminiscences,* 1974. Vol. 2. U.S. Naval Institute, Annapolis, Maryland.

ARCHIVAL AND MANUSCRIPT COLLECTIONS

Cadet Records of Capt. Ernest Evans. Nimitz Library, Special Collections and Archives Division, U.S. Naval Academy, Annapolis, Maryland.

Papers of Adm. Richard Bates. Naval War College, Newport, Rhode Island.

Papers of Adm. William F. Halsey. Library of Congress, Washington, D.C.

Papers of Gen. Douglas MacArthur. General Douglas MacArthur Foundation Archives, Norfolk, Virginia.

Papers of Samuel Eliot Morison. U.S. Naval Historical Center, Washington, D.C.

Papers of Adm. Chester W. Nimitz. U.S. Naval Historical Center, Washington, D.C.

Papers of Lt. Gen. Richard Sutherland. General Douglas MacArthur Foundation Archives, Norfolk, Virginia.

Papers of John Toland. Franklin D. Roosevelt Presidential Library, Hyde Park, New York.

Papers of Adm. John H. Towers. Naval Historical Foundation Collection, Library of Congress, Washington, D.C.

Papers of Dr. Carnes Weeks. Courtesy Carnes Weeks, Jr.

OFFICIAL SOURCES

Allied Translator and Interpreter Section, South West Pacific Area, #1–5, 1 April–26 May, 1944 ("Z" Operation Plans). General Douglas MacArthur Foundation Archives, Norfolk, Virginia.

————. "The Emperor Cult as a Present Factor in Japanese Military Psychology. Research Report, No. 76, Part II, APO 500, 21 June, 1944." General Douglas MacArthur Foundation Archives, Norfolk, Virginia.

————. "Prominent Factors in Japanese Military Psychology, Research Report, No. 76, Part IV, APO 500, 7 February, 1945." General Douglas MacArthur Foundation Archives, Norfolk, Virginia.

————. "Self-Immolation as a Factor in Japanese Military Psychology, Research Report, No. 76, Part I, APO 500, 4 April, 1944." General Douglas MacArthur Foundation Archives, Norfolk, Virginia.

————. "Superstitions as a Present Factor in Japanese Military Psychology, Research Report, No. 76, Part V, APO 500, 24 February, 1945." General Douglas MacArthur Foundation Archives, Norfolk, Virginia.

————. "Warrior Tradition as a Present Factor in Japanese Military Psychology, Research Report No. 76, Part III, APO 500, 30 October, 1944." General Douglas

MacArthur Foundation Archives, Norfolk, Virginia.

Annual Register of the United States Naval Academy, 1927–1929. Washington, D.C.: U.S. Government Printing Office.

Bates, Richard W. *The Battle for Leyte Gulf, October, 1944. Strategical and Tactical Analysis.* Vols. 1–3, 5, including diagrams and correspondence files. Naval War College. Prepared for Bureau of Naval Personnel, 1953–1957.

Campaigns of the Pacific War, The. United States Strategic Bombing Survey (Pacific), Naval Analysis Division. (Reprint). New York: Greenwood Press, 1969.

History of the USS Johnston *(DD557).* Office of Naval Records and History, Ship's Histories Section, Navy Department, National Archives, College Park, Maryland.

Interrogations of Japanese Officials. Vols. 1–2. United States Strategic Bombing Survey (Pacific), Naval Analysis Division, Washington, D.C.

Naval Communication Service Cable Traffic, CINCPAC and CINCPOA. National Archives, College Park, Maryland.

Report of Operation for the Capture of Leyte Island, Including Action Report of Engagements in Surigao Strait and Off Samar Island on 25 October 1944. Commander, Seventh Fleet, January 31, 1945. National Archives, College Park, Maryland.

ULTRA Documents. Radio Intelligence Division, Fleet Radio Unit, Pacific Ocean Areas, Traffic Intelligence Summaries. National Archives, College Park, Maryland.

BOOKS

Adams, Henry H. *Witness to Power: The Life of Fleet Admiral William D. Leahy.* Annapolis: Naval Institute Press, 1985.

Adamson, Hans Christian, and George Francis Kosco. *Halsey's Typhoon.* New York: Crown, 1967.

Agawa, Hiroyuki. *The Reluctant Admiral: Yamamoto and the Imperial Navy.* Tokyo: Kodansha International, 1979.

Andrew, Christopher, and Jeremy Noakes, eds. *Intelligence and International Relations, 1900–1945.* University of Exeter: Exeter Studies in History, No. 15, 1987.

Astor, Gerald. *Wings of Gold: The U.S. Naval Air Campaign in World War II.* New York: Ballantine, 2004.

At Rest: 4,000 Fathoms Under the Waves—USS Hoel: *The Story of the Valiant Ship's Last Hours and the Survivors Who Manned Her to the End.* Privately printed.

Baldwin, Hanson W. *Sea Fights and Shipwrecks: True Tales of the Seven Seas.* Garden City, New York: Hanover House, 1955.

Beach, Edward L., Sr., and Edward L. Beach, Jr. *From Annapolis to Scapa Flow: The Autobiography of Edward L. Beach, Sr.* Annapolis: Naval Institute Press, 2003.

Behr, Edward. *Hirohito: Behind the Myth.* New York: Vintage, 1990.

Belote, James H., and William M. Belote. *Titans of the Seas: The Development and Operations of Japanese and American Carrier Task Forces During World War II.* New York: Harper & Row, 1975.

Benedict, Ruth. *The Chrysanthemum and the Sword: Patterns of Japanese Culture.* Rutland, Vermont: Charles Tuttle, 1976.

Bix, Herbert P. *Hirohito and the Making of Modern Japan.* New York: Perennial, 2001.

Bradley, James A., and Ron Powers. *Flags of Our Fathers.* New York: Bantam, 2000.

————. *Flyboys: A True Story of Courage.* New York: Little, Brown, 2003.

Brodie, Bernard. *A Layman's Guide to Naval Strategy.* Princeton: Princeton University Press, 1943.

Buell, Thomas B. *Master of Sea Power: A Biography of Fleet Admiral Ernest J. King.* Boston: Little, Brown, 1980.

————. *The Quiet Warrior: A Biography of Admiral Raymond A. Spruance.* Annapolis: Naval Institute Press, 1987.

Bulkley, Capt. Robert J., Jr. *Close Quarters: PT Boats in the United States Navy.* Washington, D.C.: Naval History Division, 1962.

Bullock, Cecil. *Etajima: The Dartmouth of Japan.* London: Sampson Low, Marston, 1942.

Buruma, Ian. *The Missionary and the Libertine.* New York: Vintage, 2000.

Carter, Rear Admiral Worrall Reed. *Beans, Bullets and Black Oil.* Newport, Rhode Island: Naval War College Press, 1998.

Churchill, Winston S. *The Second World War: Triumph and Tragedy.* Boston: Houghton Mifflin, 1953.

Clagett, John. *Typhoon 1944.* New York: Julian Messner, 1970.

Cook, Haruko Taya, and Theodore F. Cook. *Japan at War: An Oral History.* New York: New Press, 1992.

Copeland, Robert W. *The Spirit of the "Sammy B."* USS Samuel B. Roberts Survivors' Association, 2000.

Crenshaw, Russell Sydnor, Jr. *South Pacific Destroyer: The Battle for the Solomons from Savo Island to Vella Gulf.* Annapolis: Naval Institute Press, 1998.

Cutler, Thomas J. *The Battle of Leyte Gulf, 23–26 October 1944.* New York: HarperCollins, 1994.

————. *A Sailor's History of the U.S. Navy.* Annapolis: Naval Institute Press, 2005.

Davis, Donald. *Lightning Strike: The Secret Mission to Kill Admiral Yamamoto and Avenge Pearl Harbor.* New York: St. Martin's Press, 2005.

Debo, Angie. *And Still the Waters Run Deep.* Princeton: Princeton University Press, 1940.

Dictionary of American Naval Fighting Ships. Vol. 2. Washington, D.C.: Navy Department, 1963.

Doscher, J. Henry, Jr. *Little Wolf at Leyte: The Story of the Heroic USS Samuel B. Roberts in the Battle of Leyte Gulf in World War II.* Austin, Texas: Eakin Press, 1996.

Dower, John W. *Embracing Defeat: Japan in the Wake of World War II.* New York: Norton, 1999.

————. *War Without Mercy: Race and Power in the Pacific War.* New York: Pantheon, 1986.

Drea, Edward J. *In the Service of the Emperor: Essays on the Imperial Japanese Army.* Lincoln: University of Nebraska Press, 1998.

————. *MacArthur's Ultra: Codebreaking and the War Against Japan, 1942–1945.* Lawrence: University Press of Kansas, 1992.

Dull, Paul S. *A Battle History of the Imperial Japanese Navy, 1941–1945.* Annapolis: Naval Institute Press, 1978.

Ebina, Kenzo. *Saigo No Tokkoki: Fuhumen No Soshikikan (The Last Kamikaze Plane: Masked Commander, Matome Ugaki).* Tokyo: Chuokoron-Shinsha, 2000.

————. *Shi Ni Iku Chokan (Dying Commanders: Isoroku Yamamoto and Matome*

Ugaki). Vols. 1 and 2. Tokyo: Nishida Shoten, 1989.

Evans, David C., ed. *The Japanese Navy in World War II: In the Words of Former Japanese Naval Officers.* Annapolis: Naval Institute Press, 1986.

Evans, David C., and Mark R. Peattie. *Kaigun: Strategy, Tactics and Technology in the Imperial Japanese Navy, 1887–1941.* Annapolis: Naval Institute Press, 1997.

Fahey, James J. *Pacific War Diary.* Seattle: University of Washington Press, 1993.

Field, James A., Jr. *The Japanese at Leyte Gulf: The Sho Operation.* Princeton: Princeton University Press, 1947.

First Service School, Japan Maritime Self-Defense Force: Etajima. Etajima, Aki-Gun, Hiroshima: JMSDF, 1st Service School.

Fleming, Thomas. *Time and Tide.* New York: Bantam, 1989.

Ford, Lt. Cdr. Christopher. *The Admiral's Advantage: U.S. Navy Operational Intelligence in World War II and the Cold War.* Annapolis: Naval Institute Press, 2005.

Forrestel, E. P. *Admiral Raymond A. Spruance, USN.* Washington, D.C.: U.S. Government Printing Office, 1966.

Frank, Richard B. *Downfall: The End of the Imperial Japanese Empire.* New York: Penguin, 1999.

———. *Guadalcanal: The Definitive Account of the Landmark Battle.* New York: Penguin, 1990.

Friedman, Norman. *U.S. Battleships: An Illustrated Design History.* Annapolis: Naval Institute Press, 1985.

Fukuda, Yukihiro. *Rengokantai: Saipan Reiteoki Kaisen (The Combined Fleet: Battles of the Philippine Sea and Leyte).* Tokyo: Jiji-tsushinsha, 1981.

Fussell, Paul. *Wartime: Understanding and Behavior in the Second World War.* New York: Oxford University Press, 1989.

Gibney, Frank, ed. *Senso: The Japanese Remember the Pacific War.* Armonk, New York. M. E. Sharpe, 1995.

Gluck, Carol. *Japan's Modern Myths: Ideology in the Late Meiji Period.* Princeton: Princeton University Press, 1985.

Goldstein, Donald M., and Katherine V. Dillon, eds. *The Pearl Harbor Papers: Inside the Japanese Plans.* Dulles, Virginia: Brassey's, 2000.

Groom, Winston. *1942: The Year That Tried Men's Souls.* New York: Atlantic Monthly Press, 2005.

Hall, R. Cargill, ed. *Lightning Over Bougainville.* Washington, D.C.: Smithsonian Institution Press, 1991.

Halsey, William F., and J. Bryan III. *Admiral Halsey's Story.* New York: McGraw-Hill, 1947.

Handel, Michael I., ed. *Strategic and Operational Deception in the Second World War.* Totowa, New Jersey: Frank Cass, 1987.

Hando, Kazutoshi. *Leyte-Oki-Kaisen (The Sea Battle Off Leyte).* Tokyo: PHP, 1999.

———. *Nihon Kaigun No Kobo (The Rise and Fall of the Japanese Navy).* Tokyo: PHP Kenkyujo, 1999.

Hanson, Victor Davis. *Ripples of Battle: How Wars of the Past Still Determine How We Fight, How We Live, and How We Think.* New York: Doubleday, 2003.

Hara, Capt. Tameichi. *Japanese Destroyer Captain.* New York: Ballantine, 1961.

Hattendorf, John B., ed. *The Influence of History on Mahan: The Proceedings of a Conference Marking the Centenary of Alfred Thayer Mahan's, "The Influence of Sea Power*

Upon History, 1660–1783." Newport, Rhode Island: Naval War College Press, 1991.

Havens, Thomas R. H. *Valley of Darkness: The Japanese People and World War Two.* Lanham, Maryland: University Press of America, 1978.

Herman, Arthur. *To Rule the Waves: How the British Navy Shaped the Modern World.* New York: HarperCollins, 2004.

Hirama, Yoichi. *Senkan Yamato (Battleship* Yamato*).* Tokyo: Kodansha, 2003.

Holmes, W. J. *Double-Edged Secrets: U.S. Naval Intelligence Operations in the Pacific During World War II.* Annapolis: Naval Institute Press, 1979.

Hornfischer, James D. *The Last Stand of the Tin Can Sailors.* New York: Bantam, 2004.

Howarth, Stephen. *The Fighting Ships of the Rising Sun: The Drama of the Imperial Japanese Navy, 1895–1945.* New York: Atheneum, 1983.

Hoyt, Edwin P. *How They Won the War in the Pacific: Nimitz and His Admirals.* Guilford, Connecticut: Lyons Press, 2000.

———. *The Last Kamikaze: The Story of Admiral Matome Ugaki.* Westport, Connecticut: Praeger, 1993.

———. *The Men of the* Gambier Bay: *The Amazing True Story of the Battle of Leyte Gulf.* Guilford, Connecticut: Lyons Press, 2002.

Ienaga, Saburo. *The Pacific War, 1931–1945: A Critical Perspective on Japan's Role in World War II.* New York: Pantheon, 1978.

Inoguchi, Capt. Rikihei, and Cdr. Tadashi Kakajima. *The Divine Wind: Japan's Kamikaze Force in World War II.* Annapolis: Naval Institute Press, 1958.

Iritani, Toshio. *Group Psychology of the Japanese in Wartime.* London: Kegan Paul International, 1991.

Ito, Masanori. *The End of the Imperial Japanese Navy.* New York: Jove, 1986.

Iwasa, Jiro. *Senkan Yamato Leyte-Oki No Nanokakan (Seven Days Off Leyte on the Battleship* Yamato*).* Tokyo: Kojinsha, 1998.

James, D. Clayton. *The Years of MacArthur,* vol. 2. Boston: Houghton Mifflin, 1975.

Jernigan, Emory J. *Tin Can Man.* Arlington, Virginia: Vandamere Press, 1993.

Jones, Ken. *Destroyer Squadron 23: Combat Exploits of Arleigh Burke's Gallant Forces.* Annapolis: Naval Institute Press, 1997.

Jones, Ken, and Hubert Kelley, Jr. *Admiral Arleigh (31-Knot) Burke: The Story of a Fighting Sailor.* Annapolis: Naval Institute Press, 2001.

Jordan, Ralph B. *Born to Fight: The Life of Admiral Halsey.* Philadelphia: David McKay, 1946.

Karig, Capt. Walter, Lt. Cdr. Russell L. Harris, and Lt. Cdr. Frank A. Manson. *Battle Report: The End of an Empire.* New York: Rinehart, 1948.

Ketchum, Richard M. *The Borrowed Years, 1938–1941: America on the Way to War.* New York: Random House, 1989.

King, Ernest J., and Walter Muir Whitehill. *Fleet Admiral King: A Naval Record.* New York: Norton, 1952.

Koitabashi, Kosaku. *Kashikan Tachi No Taiheiyo Senso (Petty Officer's Pacific War).* Tokyo: Kojinsha, 1986.

———. *Senkan 'Yamato' Imada Shizumazu (Battleship* Yamato *Hasn't Gone Under Yet).* Tokyo: Kojinsha, 1984.

Koyama, Michiyo. *Saigo No Tokko Ugaki Matome (The Last Kamikaze Matome Ugaki).* Tokyo: Kojinsha, 2002.

Koyanagi, Tomiji. *Kurita Kantai—Leyte Oki Kaisenhiroku (The Kurita Fleet—Secret*

Records of the Sea Battle Off Leyte). Tokyo: Kojinsha, 1995.

Lamar, H. Arthur. *I Saw Stars.* Fredericksburg, Texas: Admiral Nimitz Foundation, 1985.

Layton, Rear Admiral Edwin T. *"And I Was There": Pearl Harbor and Midway—Breaking the Secrets.* New York: Quill/Morrow, 1985.

Leach, Douglas Edward. *Now Hear This: The Memoir of a Junior Naval Officer in the Great Pacific War.* Kent, Ohio: Kent State University Press, 1987.

Leahy, Fleet Admiral William D. *I Was There.* New York: Whittlesey House, 1950.

Leary, William M., ed. *We Shall Return!: MacArthur's Commanders and the Defeat of Japan, 1942–1945.* Lexington: University of Kentucky Press, 1988.

Lehman, John. *On Seas of Glory.* New York: Free Press, 2001.

Lewin, Ronald. *The American Magic: Codes, Ciphers and the Defeat of Japan.* New York: Penguin, 1982.

Lord, Walter. *Incredible Victory.* New York: Harper and Row, 1967.

Lucky Bag, 1904, Vol. II. U.S. Naval Academy, Annapolis, Maryland.

Lundstrom, John B. *The First Team: Pacific Naval Air Combat from Pearl Harbor to Midway.* Annapolis: Naval Institute Press, 1984.

Macdonald, Dwight. *Memoirs of a Revolutionist: Essays in Political Criticism.* New York: Farrar, Straus, 1957.

MacIntyre, Donald. *Leyte Gulf: Armada in the Pacific.* New York: Ballantine, 1970.

Manchester, William. *American Caesar: Douglas MacArthur, 1880–1964.* Boston: Little, Brown, 1978.

———. *Goodbye, Darkness: A Memoir of the Pacific War.* Boston: Little, Brown, 1980.

Marder, Arthur J. *Old Friends, New Enemies: The Royal Navy and the Imperial Japanese Navy.* Oxford: Clarendon Press, 1981.

Mears, Lt. Frederick. *Carrier Combat: A Young Pilot's Story of Action Aboard 'The Hornet' in World War II.* New York: Ballantine, 1944

Merrill, James M. *A Sailor's Admiral: A Biography of William F. Halsey.* New York: Thomas Y. Crowell, 1976.

Miller, Edward S. *War Plan Orange: The U.S. Strategy to Defeat Japan, 1897–1945.* Annapolis: Naval Institute Press, 1991.

Miller, Nathan. *War at Sea: A Naval History of World War II.* New York: Oxford University Press, 1997.

Millot, Bernard. *Divine Thunder: The Life and Death of the Kamikazes.* New York: Pinnacle, 1971.

Monsarrat, Nicholas. *The Cruel Sea.* New York: Knopf, 1951.

Morison, Samuel Eliot. *Leyte, June 1944–January 1945.* Edison, New Jersey: Castle, 2001.

———. *The Liberation of the Philippines: Luzon, Mindanao, the Visayas, 1944–1945.* Edison, New Jersey: Castle, 1959.

———. *The Struggle for Guadalcanal: August, 1942–February, 1943.* Boston: Little, Brown, 1969.

———. *The Two-Ocean War: A Short History of the United States Navy in the Second World War.* Boston: Little, Brown, 1963.

———. *Victory in the Pacific, 1945.* Boston: Little, Brown, 1968.

Muir, Malcolm. *The Iowa Class Battleships.* New York: Sterling, 1988.

Myrer, Anton. *Once an Eagle: A Novel.* New York: HarperTorch, 2001.

Nagatsuka, Ryuji. *I Was a Kamikaze.* New York: Macmillan, 1972.

Naylor, Roger C. *The Rangefinder: Tarawa to Tokyo.* Privately printed, San Marcos, Texas, 2002.

Nish, Ian, ed. *Anglo-Japanese Alienation, 1919–1952: Papers of the Anglo-Japanese Conference on the History of the Second World War.* Cambridge: Cambridge University Press, 1982.

O'Connor, Raymond, ed. *The Japanese Navy in World War II.* Annapolis: Naval Institute Press, 1971.

Okumiya, Masatake. *Teitoku to Sanbo: The Admirals and Staff Officers.* Tokyo: PHP, 2000.

Parshall, Jonathan, and Anthony Tully. *Shattered Sword: The Untold Story of the Battle of Midway.* Dulles, Virginia.: Potomac Books, 2005.

Peattie, Mark R. *Sunburst: The Rise of Japanese Naval Air Power, 1909–1941.* Annapolis: Naval Institute Press, 2001.

Potter, E. B. *Bull Halsey.* Annapolis: Naval Institute Press, 1985.

———. *Nimitz.* Annapolis: Naval Institute Press, 1976.

———. *Sea Power: A Naval History.* Annapolis: Naval Institute Press, 1981.

Potter, E. B., ed. *The Great Sea War: The Story of Naval Action in World War II.* New York: Random House, 1960.

Prados, John. *Combined Fleet Decoded: The Secret History of American Intelligence and the Japanese Navy in World War II.* Annapolis: Naval Institute Press, 1995.

Pratt, Fletcher. *Fleet Against Japan.* New York: Harper & Row, 1946.

Raines, James Orvill. *Good Night Officially: The Pacific War Letters of a Destroyer Sailor.* Boulder, Colorado: Westview, 1994.

Reid, T. R. *Confucius Lives Next Door: What Living in the East Teaches Us About Living in the West.* New York: Random House, 1999.

Reischauer, Edwin O. *Japan: The Story of a Nation.* New York: Knopf, 1970.

Reynolds, Clark. *Admiral John H. Towers: The Struggle for Naval Air Supremacy.* Annapolis: Naval Institute Press, 1991.

———. *The Fast Carriers: The Forging of an Air Navy.* Annapolis: Naval Institute Press, 1968.

———. *The Fighting Lady: The New "Yorktown" in the Pacific War.* Missoula, Montana: Pictorial Histories, 1986.

———. *On the Warpath in the Pacific: Admiral Jocko Clark and the Fast Carriers.* Annapolis: Naval Institute Press, 2005.

Roosevelt, Theodore. *The Rough Riders.* New York: Scribner's, 1899.

Roscoe, Theodore. *United States Destroyer Operations in World War II.* Annapolis: Naval Institute Press, 1966.

Sears, Stephen. *Carrier War in the Pacific.* New York: American Heritage, 1966.

Sherman, Adm. Frederick C. *Combat Command: The American Aircraft Carriers in the Pacific War.* New York: Bantam, 1982.

Shillony, Ben-Ami. *Politics and Culture in Wartime Japan.* Oxford: Clarendon Press, 1981.

Shiroyama, Saburo. *Skikikan-Tachi No Tokko (Kamikaze Attacks by Commanding Officers).* Tokyo: Shinchosha, 2001.

Smith, Martin Cruz. *December 6: A Novel.* New York: Simon & Schuster, 2002.

Solberg, Carl. *Decision and Dissent.* Annapolis: Naval Institute Press, 1995.

Spector, Ronald H. *At War at Sea: Sailors and Naval Combat in the Twentieth Century.* New York: Viking, 2001.

———. *Eagle Against the Sun: The American War with Japan.* New York: Macmillan, 1985.

Spurr, Russell. *A Glorious Way to Die: The Kamikaze Mission of the Battleship Yamato, April, 1945.* New York: Bantam, 1983.

Stafford, Cdr. Edward P. *Little Ship, Big War: The Saga of DE343.* New York: Jove, 1984.

Stillwell, Paul. *Battleship New Jersey: An Illustrated History.* Annapolis: Naval Institute Press, 1986.

Stone, Raymond T. *"My Ship"—The USS Intrepid.* South Salem, New York: GP Books, 2003.

Sweetman, Jack. *The U.S. Naval Academy: An Illustrated History.* Revised by Thomas J. Cutler. Annapolis: Naval Institute Press, 1995.

Sweetman, Jack, ed. *The Great Admirals: Command at Sea, 1587–1945.* Annapolis: Naval Institute Press, 1997.

Taussig, Betty Carney. *A Warrior for Freedom.* Manhattan, Kansas: Sunflower University Press, 1995.

Taylor, Theodore. *The Magnificent Mitscher.* Annapolis: Naval Institute Press, 1991.

Terkel, Studs. *"The Good War": An Oral History of World War Two.* New York: New Press, 1984.

Thomas, David. *The Battle of the Java Sea.* New York: Stein & Day, 1969.

Tohmatsu, Haruo, and H. P. Willmott. *A Gathering Darkness: The Coming of War to the Far East and the Pacific, 1921–1942.* Lanham, Maryland: SR Books, 2004.

Toland, John. *The Rising Sun: The Decline and Fall of the Japanese Empire, 1936–1945.* New York: Bantam, 1970.

Tsuji, Yasuaki. *Maboroshi no Daisenka (The Illusive War Results).* Tokyo: NHK, 2002.

Tsurumi, Kazuko. *Social Change and the Individual: Japan Before and After Defeat in World War II.* Princeton: Princeton University Press, 1970.

Ugaki, Admiral Matome. *Fading Victory: The Diary of Admiral Matome Ugaki.* Pittsburgh: University of Pittsburgh Press, 1991.

Van der Vat, Dan. *The Pacific Campaign: World War II—The U.S-Japanese Naval War, 1941–1945.* New York: Simon & Schuster, 1991.

Varley, Paul. *Warriors of Japan: As Portrayed in the War Tales.* Honolulu: University of Hawaii Press, 1994.

Vego, Dr. Milan. *The Battle for Leyte, 1944.* Annapolis: Naval Institute Press, 2005.

Warner, Denis, and Peggy Warner. *The Sacred Warriors: Japan's Suicide Legions.* New York: Avon, 1982.

West, C. W. "Bob." *Muskogee: From Statehood to Pearl Harbor.* Muskogee, Oklahoma: Muskogee Publishing Company, 1976.

Wheeler, Gerald E. *Kinkaid of the Seventh Fleet: A Biography of Admiral Thomas C. Kinkaid, U.S. Navy.* Washington, D.C.: Naval Historical Center, 1995.

Willmott, H. P. *The Barrier and the Javelin: Japanese and Allied Pacific Strategies, February to June 1942.* Annapolis: Naval Institute Press, 1983.

———. *Battle of Leyte Gulf: The Last Fleet Action.* Bloomington: Indiana University

Press, 2005.

Winton, John. *Ultra in the Pacific: How Breaking the Japanese Codes and Cyphers Affected Naval Operations Against Japan, 1941–1945*. Annapolis: Naval Institute Press, 1993.

Woodward, C. Vann. *The Battle for Leyte Gulf.* New York: Macmillan, 1947.

Wouk, Herman, *War and Remembrance*. Boston: Back Bay Books, 2002.

Wukovits, John F. *Devotion to Duty: A Biography of Admiral Clifton A. F. Sprague*. Annapolis: Naval Institute Press, 1995.

Yasunaga, Hiroshi. *Samurai Sakutekiki Tekikubo Miyu.* Tokyo: Kojinsha, 2002.

Y'Blood, William T. *The Little Giants: U.S. Escort Carriers Against Japan*. Annapolis: Naval Institute Press, 1987.

———. *Red Sun Setting: The Battle of the Philippine Sea.* Annapolis: Naval Institute Press, 1981.

Yoshida, Mitsuru. *Requiem for Battleship Yamato*. London: Constable, 1999.

Yoshimura, Akira. *Battleship Musashi: The Making and Sinking of the World's Biggest Battleship*. New York: Kodansha International, 1992.

ARTICLES

Ahlstrom, Captain John. "Leyte Gulf Remembered." *U.S. Naval Institute Proceedings,* August 1984.

Ash, Leonard D., and Martin Hill. "In Harm's Way." *Retired Officer Magazine,* October 1994.

Brodie, Bernard. "Battle for Leyte Gulf." *Virginia Quarterly Review,* Vol. 23, No. 3 (Summer 1947).

———. "Our Ships Strike Back." *Virginia Quarterly Review.* Vol. 21, No. 2 (Spring 1945).

Burke, Arleigh. "Admiral Marc Mitscher: A Naval Aviator." *U.S. Naval Institute Proceedings,* April 1975.

Cant, Gilbert. "Bull's Run: Was Halsey Right at Leyte Gulf?" *Life,* November 24, 1947.

Condon, Maj. Gen. John P. "Bringing Down Yamamoto." *U.S. Naval Institute Proceedings,* November 1990.

Davis, Spencer. "Jap Admiral Recalls Leyte Fight." Associated Press, 1969. General Douglas MacArthur Foundation, Norfolk, Virginia.

Deac, Wilfred P. "The Battle Off Samar." *American Heritage,* December 1966.

Dean, Lt. Ralph J. "Eta Jima: Hallowed Halls." *U.S. Naval Institute Proceedings,* March 1983.

Field, James A. "Leyte Gulf: The First Uncensored Japanese Account." *U.S. Naval Institute Proceedings,* March 1951.

Friday, Karl F. "Bushido or Bull? A Medieval Historian's Perspective on the Imperial Army and the Japanese Warrior Tradition." *Journal of Alternative Perspectives,* March 2001.

Fukudome, Vice Admiral Shigeru. "Strategic Aspects of the Battle Off Formosa." *U.S. Naval Institute Proceedings,* December 1952.

Hagen, Robert C. "We Asked for the Jap Fleet—And We Got It," *Saturday Evening*

Post, May 28, 1945.

Hale, Duane. "Uncle Sam's Warriors: American Indians in World War II." *Chronicles of Oklahoma.* Oklahoma City, Oklahoma, Winter 1991–92.

Halsey, Admiral William F. "Admiral Halsey Tells His Story." *Saturday Evening Post,* June 14, June 21, June 28, July 5, July 12, July 19, July 26, August 2, August 9, 1947.

———. "The Battle for Leyte Gulf." *U.S. Naval Institute Proceedings,* May 1952.

Hamilton, Capt. Andrew. "Where Is Task Force Thirty-Four?" *U.S. Naval Institute Proceedings,* October 1960.

Holloway, Adm. James L. "The Battle of Surigao Straits." *Naval Engineers Journal,* September 1994.

Howard, Warren S. "The *Kongos* in World War II." *U.S. Naval Institute Proceedings,* November 1948.

Jones, George E. "Brain Center of the Pacific War." *New York Times Magazine,* April 8, 1945.

Karig, Capt. Walter. "Jeeps Versus Giants." *U.S. Naval Institute Proceedings,* December 1947.

Kinkaid, Adm. Thomas C. "A Naval Career." *U.S. Naval Institute Proceedings,* May 1959.

Koyanagi, Rear Admiral Tomika. "With Kurita in the Battle for Leyte Gulf." *U.S. Naval Institute Proceedings,* February 1953.

Kurita, Takeo. "The 20th Century—People from Ibaraki: Unsolved Mystery of the Sea Battle History—A Sea Warrior Makes No Excuse." *Asahi Shimbun,* October 31, 1998.

"Leahy Feared Loss of Pacific at Leyte." *New York Times,* October 31, 1953.

"Leyte Gulf: An Eternal Question." *Military History,* October 1995.

MacDonald, Scot. "Saga of the 'Sammy B.'" *Surface Warfare,* February 1980.

———. "Small Boys Off Samar . . . Survival Could Not Be Expected." *Surface Warfare,* February 1980.

Matsumoto, Capt. Kitaro. "Design and Construction of the *Yamato* and *Musashi.*" *U.S. Naval Institute Proceedings,* October 1953.

Neumann, William L. "Franklin Delano Roosevelt: A Disciple of Admiral Mahan." *U.S. Naval Institute Proceedings,* July 1952.

Ooka, Jiro. "The Truth of the Turning Around by Kurita's Fleet at the Leyte Gulf." *Maru Magazine,* March 1999.

Ozawa, Hiroshi. "The True Account of the Last Moments of Admiral Ugaki," *Maru Magazine,* March 1999.

Potter, E. B. "Arleigh Burke Buries the Hatchet." *U.S. Naval Institute Proceedings,* April 1990.

———. "The Command Personality." *U.S. Naval Institute Proceedings,* January 1969.

———. "The Japanese Navy Tells Its Story." *U.S. Naval Institute Proceedings,* February 1947.

Preston, Anthony, ed. *Warships in Profile.* Vol. 3. "IJN Yamato and Musashi." Essay by Masataka Chihaya. Garden City: Doubleday, 1973.

Reynolds, Clark G. "The Maritime Strategy of World War II: Some Implications." *Naval War College Review,* Vol. 39, No. 3 (May–June 1986).

Sweetman, Jack. "Great Sea Battles of World War II." *Naval History,* May–June

1995.

————. "Leyte Gulf." *U.S. Naval Institute Proceedings*, October 1994.

Thomas, Evan. "'Kurita Was a Coward!' Or Was He?" *Naval History*, October 2004.

Tully, Anthony P. "Solving Some Mysteries of Leyte Gulf: Fate of the *Chikuma* and *Chokai.*" *Warship International*, No. 3, 2000.

Vego, Milan N. "The SHO-1 Plan." *U.S. Naval Institute Proceedings*, October 1994.

Yokoi, Rear Admiral Tioshiyuki. "Thoughts on Japan's Defeat." *U.S. Naval Institute Proceedings*, October 1960.

INDEX

ILLUSTRATION CREDITS

Numbers refer to book pages.

U.S. Naval Historical Center, Washington, D. C.: xii (top and bottom), xiii (bottom), 2, 16, 103,
     111 (top and bottom), 115, 144, 153, 166, 178-179, 207, 215, 234 (bottom), 343.

Courtesy Donald Goldstein Collection, University of Pittsburgh Archives, Pittsburgh, Pennsyl-
     vania: xiii (top), 9, 26, 339.

National Archives, Washington, D.C.: 22-23, 262, 271, 301, 324, 334.

Courtesy Toby Solberg and Solberg Family: 36, 234 (top).

U.S. Naval Academy, Annapolis, Maryland: 41, 44, 56, 183.

Library of Congress, Washington, D.C.: 62.

Author's collection, Courtesy of Kosaku Koitabashi: 319 (top and bottom)

ABOUT THE AUTHOR

EVAN THOMAS is assistant managing editor of *Newsweek*. He has written more than a hundred cover stories on national and international news. He has won a National Magazine Award and taught writing at Harvard and Princeton. He has written five other books, one of which, *John Paul Jones*, was a *New York Times* bestseller. He is a fellow of the Society of American Historians. He is married and has two children and lives in Washington, D.C.

Sea of Thunder

Thomas, Evan